"I am Jugoslovenka!"

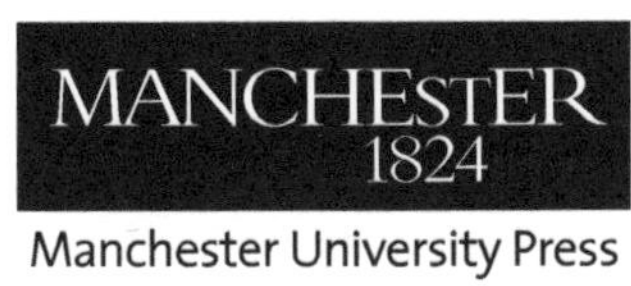

Manchester University Press

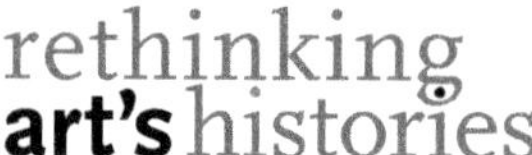

SERIES EDITORS
Amelia G. Jones, Marsha Meskimmon

Rethinking Art's Histories aims to open out art history from its most basic structures by foregrounding work that challenges the conventional periodisation and geographical subfields of traditional art history, and addressing a wide range of visual cultural forms from the early modern period to the present.

These books will acknowledge the impact of recent scholarship on our understanding of the complex temporalities and cartographies that have emerged through centuries of world-wide trade, political colonisation and the diasporic movement of people and ideas across national and continental borders.

To buy or to find out more about the books currently available in this series, please go to: https://manchesteruniversitypress.co.uk/series/rethinking-arts-histories/

"I am Jugoslovenka!"

Feminist performance politics during and after
Yugoslav socialism

Jasmina Tumbas

Manchester University Press

Published by Manchester University Press
Oxford Road, Manchester M13 9PL
www.manchesteruniversitypress.co.uk

British Library Cataloguing-in-Publication Data
A catalogue record for this book is available from the British Library

ISBN   978 1 5261 5647 1   hardback
ISBN   978 1 5261 6904 4   paperback

First published 2022

The publisher has no responsibility for the persistence or accuracy of URLs for external or any third-party internet websites referred to in this book, and does not guarantee that any content on such websites is, or will remain, accurate or appropriate.

Typeset
by New Best-set Typesetters Ltd

To Eržebet and Petar Tumbas

Contents

List of figures

Every effort has been made to obtain permission to reproduce copyright material, and the publisher will be pleased to be informed of any errors and omissions for correction in future editions.

Acknowledgments

This book was conceptualized and drafted during the midst of my father, Petar Tumbas's eighteen-month struggle with cancer, the most difficult time of unimaginable heartbreak for my family and me. I am indebted to his civil courage, ethics, unrelenting commitment to others in need, and supreme love of life, especially for his wife, Eržebet Tumbas, my mother, and his two daughters, Svetlana and myself. Confronting his death and the memory of our struggles as a family fleeing the political conflicts in Yugoslavia forced me to look closely at the region from a new perspective. My parents' dedication to their two daughters' paths to education and emancipation, and their unbroken trust in the good of the people, has been a solid foundation beneath my feet since we first arrived in the Nürnberg refugee camp, when I was seven years old. I could not have written this book without their commitment to what I now understand as the antifascist, pro-feminist, and pro-multiculturalist legacy of Yugoslavia. In addition, my parents also helped support my research in former Yugoslavia since I began my PhD studies at Duke University in 2007. My mother's hard work as a seamstress paid for many books, train tickets, airplane flights, meals, clothes, rent, and anything else that I could not cover with institutional funding during my research trips. My father, on the other hand, was my constant support on the ground: he introduced me to the city of Belgrade, helped me find books locally, searched endlessly for books online (and usually found them!), and challenged me to work even harder and believe in my work. When, in 2011, I received the first invitation to attend the preview of the Venice Biennale, my father took time off work to drive me to Venice, an unforgettable trip that changed my life and research, and which ultimately led to the writing of this book. During his last months in hospitals and at home in Palić, my father also allowed me to interview him about his experiences of living in Yugoslavia. My academic training and insights often conflicted with his and my mother's memories, which led to heated debates between the three of us—frequently, and to my delight, interrupted by my parents playing songs from Yugoslavia to make their points—a memory I now treasure most deeply. I am the feminist Jugoslovenka I am because of them.

I am astonished when I consider how many extraordinary people have supported my work for this book. My dearest friend Zach Blas, who, since we met as graduate students at Duke University, has been the most vitalizing force in my thinking through what I wanted to do with this book: Zach's fierce energy, bold vision, and unwavering commitment to pushing beyond imposed limits is a constant source of motivation and inspiration for me. I also want to thank my dear friend and colleague Ana Grujić, whose feminist and queer politics remain a well of encouragement, solidarity, and knowledge. She was the first person with whom I discussed my book idea, and she was also the most enthusiastic and supportive in the very beginning when it is hardest to trust one's own insights and directions. In addition, her critical eye as an editor and reader of all my chapters, several of them numerous times and at different stages, also forced me to go back to my text many more times than I anticipated; I am grateful for her insight and for pushing me to consider multiple and often divergent perspectives. As a queer scholar and activist who came of age in Yugoslavia, but who also lived through the country's disintegration, Grujić's constructive feedback was critical for forming and substantiating my argument throughout the entire manuscript.

Many thanks also to my dear friend and colleague Judith Goldman, who read and provided feedback on several of my chapters and listened to me talk about my book endlessly, cooked countless meals for me, and who, with Damien Keane, shared many dinners with me in the hard times after my father passed away. This friendship was the comfort and warmth I needed during that time, and their passion and rigor for their respective academic fields was a huge inspiration for me to continue my work on the book. Special thanks to Andrew Barron, who frequently read random excerpts from my book and gave brilliant comments during my most intense year of writing, and with whom I had many conversations about Lepa Brena, contemporary art, popular culture, gay and lesbian history, and feminism, all of which helped me formulate my position in this book. Notably, Barron frequently sent me music—thank you especially for Mariah Carey's "Runway"—a gift that kept my tired mind and typing hands going. I also want to thank Charla Fisher, who proofread my manuscript and helped me with various aspects of the research for this book during its last stages, including inquiry into the enigmatic world of female Bosnian snipers. Fisher also took me on many hikes during my writing breaks, from the very onset of the COVID-19 pandemic, which made it possible for me to retain the calm and focus necessary to finish this manuscript. I am deeply grateful for that support.

Thank you, Amelia G. Jones, for helping me articulate the stakes of my project in our early conversations about the book. I am deeply grateful to Jones and Marsha Meskimmon for accepting my book in their excellent series, Rethinking Art's Histories. Special thanks to Emma Brennan, who worked with me on all the details of the publication from the very beginning to the end. Thanks to Andrew Hibbard for editing all of my chapters numerous times, and for the persistent brilliant and provocative comments and questions, which helped strengthen my arguments and research tremendously; to Adam Drury, for the most speedy and careful editing of several of my chapters; Nicola King for creating the index; and Sara Appel and Lin Gibson, for providing edits and feedback during the early stages of my manuscript.

A big hug and a huge thanks to Elizabeth Otto, my colleague and mentor at the University at Buffalo (UB), who read and provided feedback on many versions of my book proposal and who believed in my book from the very beginning. Her mentorship in navigating the world of university presses was fundamental, as were late-night phone calls offering encouragement and constructive advice for my book project. I am indebted to her for her generosity and kindness, and inspiration to pursue unconventional paths in my research. Other faculty whose support was pivotal at UB (though many have left since) include Carrie Bremen, Susan Cahn, David Castillo, James Currie, Amy Graves-Monroe, Lindsay Brandon Hunter, John Jennings, Jonathan Katz, Carl Lee, Chris Lee, Arabella Lyon, Carla Mazzio, Theresa McCarthy, Alyssa Mt. Pleasant, Miriam Paeslack, Marla Segol, LaKisha Simmons, Gwynn Thomas, Christine Varnado, Kari Winter, and Hershini Young. I am deeply grateful to Caitlyn Strong, who not only helped me secure funds to pay for multiple aspects of the production costs, but who also assisted me every step of the way in navigating the complicated processes of reimbursement.

The book would not have been possible without the generosity of many institutions, fellowships, and grants, such as the Dr. Nuala McGann Drescher Leave Program—thank you, Jonathan Katz, Elizabeth Otto, and Becky Koenig for supporting my application and nominating me during a difficult time of transition at the department; the Humanities Institute at UB, which assisted my research with OVPRED/HI Seed Money in the Arts and Humanities fund early on, and also with a Humanities Institute Faculty Fellowship—special thanks to fellow awardees Amy Graves-Monroe and Katja Praznik for their engagement with my work; deep gratitude to the Graduate School for East and Southeast European Studies at Ludwig Maximilian University of Munich for inviting me to become a fellow in 2018/2019, especially Burcu Doğramacı and Caroline Fricke; the Dean's Travel Fund at UB, which allowed me to participate at many conferences, including the Association for Slavic, East European, and Eurasian Studies conference in Zagreb in 2019, where I chaired a panel discussing Zsófia Lóránd's book, *The Feminist Challenge to the Socialist State in Yugoslavia* (2018), which was extremely generative and inspiring; the Individual Development Award through the Union of University Professionals; the Gender Institute for providing last-minute funds to support paying for the rights of war-era photographs in the Getty Images collection; the Julian

Park Publication Fund at UB, which provided a large subvention for the production of the book; the Harter Foundation Fund, which provided a second subvention to cover additional publication costs; and last but not least, the Department of Global Gender and Sexuality Studies at UB, which provided funds for this book, as well as for travel and research, and offered mentorship and guidance throughout many stages of the book.

I also would like to thank my early mentors and teachers in the academy, including, first and foremost, Kristine Stiles at Duke University, whose belief in my work from when we first met in 2006 became a decisive moment in my career as a young scholar. Her guidance, dedication, and insight as my mentor and the chair of my dissertation were invaluable, as was her exceptional generosity in connecting me with archives, institutions, and artists for my research. I also want to thank the other dissertation committee members at Duke University, Patricia Leighten, Pamela Kachurin, and Steven Mansbach, who believed in my work and provided crucial insights. Thanks to Adrian Parr, for pushing political questions in contemporary art to the forefront of my mind during my MA studies; special thanks also to Carl Gombert, Autumn and Mark Hall, Neil McWilliam, Edward A. Shanken, and Lori Schmied.

One of the things that kept me going throughout the entire process was reading my colleagues' work and having discussions. I want to thank my two North American Yugoslav diaspora *drugarice* (female comrades) Katja Praznik and Bojana Videkanić, with whom I have shared many hours talking about Yugoslavia at conference panels, and many more hours in private, especially in the early stages of the book. I read Bojana Videkanić's discussion of Antun Augustinčić's *Peace* monument in her book, *Nonaligned Modernism: Socialist Postcolonial Aesthetics in Yugoslavia, 1945–1985* (2019), at a difficult moment of grief and writer's block. Her dedication to Yugoslavia's antifascist legacy has always inspired me, but particularly her careful analysis of Augustinčić's *Peace* sculpture at the United Nations Headquarters in New York, highlighting a female Yugoslav equestrian as a symbol of world peace. Days later, Videkanić's words reminded me that my father had left a red Yugoslav 100 Dinar banknote for me, which features Augustinčić's sculpture, and which ultimately led me to consider the importance of the circulation of that banknote in the Introduction. I want to thank my dear friend and feminist comrade Ivana Bago for early conversations about my interest in gender and sexuality in the region when I was leaving graduate school, for her encouragement and support, and for her great suggestions and feedback. Other friends, colleagues, and interlocutors who work in or on the region, whose work I admire and from whom I have learned tremendously during the course of researching and writing this book, are as follows: Irina Aristarkhova, Maria Alina Asavei, Zdenka Badovinac, Jon Blackwood, Chiara Bonfiglioli, Amy Bryzgel, Katalin Cseh-Varga, Eda Čufer, Branka Ćurčić, Adam Czirak, Olga Dimitrijević, Adnan Džumhur, Zoran Erić,

Dušan Grlja, Beáta Hock, Renata Jambrešić, Dijana Jelača, Vladan Jeremić, Klara Kemp-Welch, Katja Kobolt, Vladimir Kulić, Tevž Logar, Zsófia Lóránd, Suzana Milevska, Jelena Petrović, Melissa Potter, Rena Rädle, Adair Rounthwaite, Carol Silverman, Jelena Vesić, Tamara Vukov, Shannon Woodcock, and Mechtild Widrich.

An art historical study always relies on archives, collections, and the generosity of those who maintain and make them accessible to scholars like me. I am grateful to the following archives, collections, libraries, and individuals for granting me access to the majority of the material that makes up this book: Una Popović at the archive of the Museum of Contemporary Art in Belgrade; Jasna Jakšić and Jadranka Vinterhalter at the archive of the Museum of Contemporary Art in Zagreb; Janka Vukmir at the Institute for Contemporary Art in Zagreb; Darko Šimičić and Zora Gotovac at the Tomislav Gotovac Archive; Karla Železnik at the International Center of Graphic Arts in Ljubljana; Dragica Vukadinović and Ljubinka Gavran at the Student Cultural Center Archive in Belgrade; Nataša Velikonja at the Lesbian Library and Archive at ŠKUC-LL in Ljubljana; Gordana Nikolić and Jovan Jakšić at the Museum of Contemporary Art of Vojvodina in Novi Sad; Marinko Sudac from the Marinko Sudac Collection; Catherine Koutsavlis at Abramović LLC; Timea Junghaus at Gallery8 in Budapest; Frane Tomašić at Croatia Records; Zdravko Mihočinec for the Josip Kovačić collection; Branko Franceschi at Moderna Galerija in Zagreb; and Sanja Iveković, Dušan Mandić, and Zoran Popović for granting me access to their private archives.

I couldn't have written Jugoslovenka's diverse stories without the indispensable voices of many protagonists, who spoke to me in person, on the phone, or provided feedback through lengthy e-mail correspondences. A comprehensive list with dates of cited exchanges is included at the end of this book, but here I want to thank everybody who offered their time, advice, insights, and expertise, especially Jiryis Murkus Ballan, Barbara Borčič, Jasmina Cibic, Eda Čufer, Vlasta Delimar, Olga Dimitrijević, Mojca Dobnikar, Dubravka Đurić and Miško Šuvaković, Joshua S. Goldstein, Marina Gržinić, Mirko Ilić, Sanja Iveković, Jasna Jakšić, Helena Janečić, Dijana Jelača, Šejla Kamerić, Saša Kesić, Katja Kobolt, Leonida Kovač, Marinela Koželj and Raša Todosijević, Katalin Ladik, Suzana Milevska, Boris Miljković, Lepa Mlađenović, Miran Mohar, Amal Murkus, Ivan Novak, Tanja Ostojić, Vesna Pavlović, Bojana Pejić, Una Popović, Zoran Popović, Lala Raščić, Berislav Sabolić, Selma Selman, Darko Šimičić, Jasna Tijardović, Biljana Tomić, Suzana Tratnik, Zoran Trbović, Bojana Videkanić, Borut Vogelnik, Dragica Vukadinović, Staša Zajović, and Želimir Žilnik. Here, I also want to also thank every artist who granted me permission to reproduce their artwork in this book. I am deeply grateful to all of you. Additionally, so much gratitude to all who hold rights to images, as well as those who helped me navigating the complicated world of image permissions, who shared email addresses and phone numbers with me, and who made it possible to include such a large number of artworks in this book. It is a dream come true to have these images reproduced here, and it would not have been possible without your help. Huge thanks to Šejla Kamerić for the honor of featuring her work on the cover.

I also must single out queer icons Suzana Tratnik, Lepa Mlađenović, and Susanne Sachsse. Tratnik was not only a wealth of knowledge, she was exceedingly generous and connected me with more institutions and individuals than I can list here. Sachsse's magnificent piece with her art collective CHEAP, "A Woman Walks Through Socialism," inspired me to trust my own instincts and passions for this book project. Mlađenović's enthusiastic and supportive welcome in Belgrade was pivotal for pursuing the book's focus on queer and activist Yugoslav women. Many more have inspired me and/or have supported my path, including Željko Z. Blaće, Micha Cardenas, Cassils, Kency Cornejo, Heather Davis, Heather Dewey-Hagborg, Sinan Goknur, Karen Gonzalez Rice, Natalie Houston, Yelena Kalinsky, Olga Kopenkina, Ana Paulina Lee, Tanya Loughead, China Medel, Chris McCormack, Samantha Noël, Jennifer Rhee, Jam Rostron, Girish Shambu, Marc Siegel, Julia Steinmetz, Eliza Steinbock, and Pinar Yoldas.

I want to conclude by thanking my allies, companions, and dear friends, who have supported me during the journey of writing this book: Borislava and Mirko Aladžić, Corina Apostol, David Alexander and Sofia Jasmina Bauer, André Berger, Nitasha Dhillon, Rebecca Hardtke, Teresa Hörter, Stefanie Klute, Paula Paradise, Anna Pesavento, Zlata Poturović, Marika Schmiedt, Mary Sullivan, Darnell Witt and Tom and Louise Yots. It does take a village; I am grateful that those living in my "village" are from all over the world, a solid army of feminist, queer, and/or antifascist lovers of culture, art, and collective resistance.

Introduction
Jugoslovenka: the unique position of Yugoslav women during and after socialism

The Socialist Federal Republic of Yugoslavia (1945–1992) represents one of the most intriguing and paradoxical examples of women's emancipatory power during twentieth-century socialism.[1] The most politically West-leaning of all the socialist countries during the Cold War, Yugoslavia became a place where new trends in avant-garde art and film flourished while Marxist maxims held sway, antifascist ideology reigned in tandem with sex and rock and roll, and women enjoyed more legal rights and social mobility, including access to education and labor mobility, than in any other East European and some Western countries. In August 1945, women were legally declared equal to men; as early as 1951, lesbian sex was decriminalized (and by 1977, homosexuality);[2] abortion was legalized in 1952, and paid maternity leave and the right to divorce were socially and legally accepted by the 1950s.[3] In fact, as early as 1928, some seventeen years before the founding of Yugoslavia, a leaflet distributed by the communist and partisan leader Josip Broz Tito—who would become the president of Yugoslavia in 1945—declared that women were essential to fighting the bourgeoisie's "imperialist war" and invited them to join the Communist Party in large numbers to "fight till the end for the liberation of the working class."[4] In 1936, the magazine *Žena Danas* (*Woman Today*) was founded, and its first issue, titled "Novi feminizam" (New Feminism), emphasized that "the fight for women's rights is the fight against fascism."[5] The Anti-Fascist Front of Women of Yugoslavia (AFW) was founded in the midst of World War II (1942) and had over two million members by the end of the war.

By 1953, all this extraordinary advancement for women led the male-dominated Yugoslav communist elite to declare that it had reached its goal of the liberation of women and that feminism was thus obsolete—not just obsolete, but as a political movement, ran counter to the larger goal of the liberation of the people, and was therefore self-interested and divisive. The AFW was abolished in 1953, and many women were asked to retreat back into the sphere of the home. Historian Jelena Batinić's research has shown that partisan women, who were an indispensable force during World War II, were suddenly

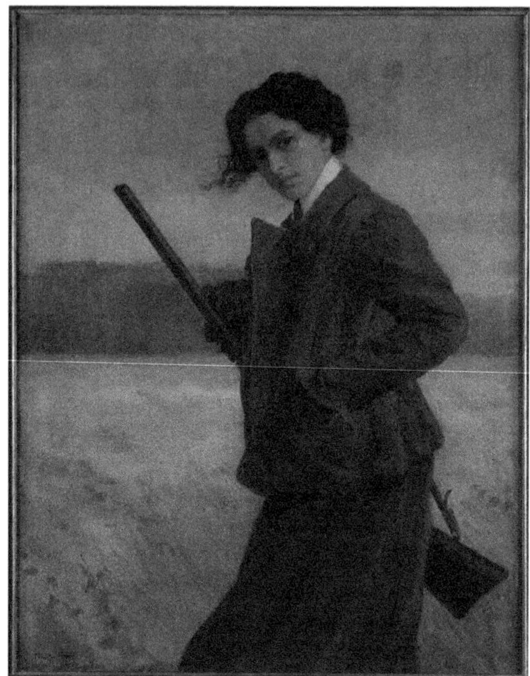

left off of "the conscription lists for the Yugoslav army" and out of the history books.[6] The arts, too, in the immediate postwar period, became dominated by men. Ljubo Babić, who had cooperated with the Ustaša, the Croatian fascist movement, but who was close friends with elite communists such as Miroslav Krleža during the socialist era, became one of the most influential figures in the cultural sectors of socialist Yugoslavia. What many overlook, or do not know, is that he often repressed the work of women artists, including that of Nasta Rojc, a lesbian artist who actively supported the antifascist struggle (Figure 0.1).[7] In *Autoportret u Lovačkom Odijelu* (*Self Portrait: Hunter*) (1912), Rojc is standing in an impressive profile pose with a large gun slung over her right shoulder. Her serious and self-assured gaze instantly embodies Yugoslav women's emancipatory strength and swagger. Because Babić, as the teacher of many Yugoslav artists who went through the academy after World War II, did not support her work, she has been missing from many history books from the period.[8] Only recently, such as in the curatorial work of queer art historian Leonida Kovač, has the work of Nasta Rojc been reintroduced in art historical discourses; for example, being featured at the Art Pavilion in Zagreb in 2014.

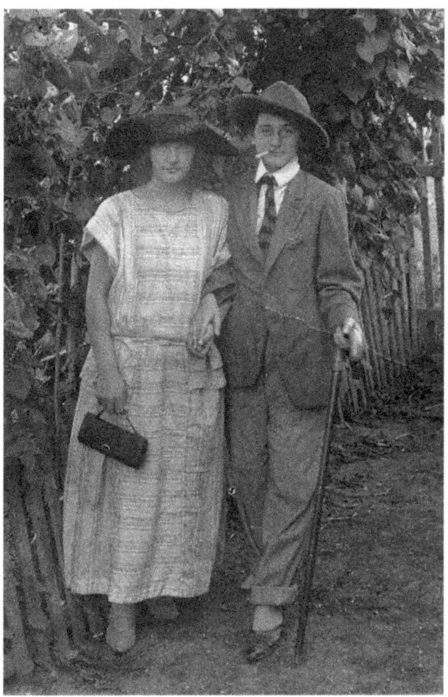

Two Belgrade feminists, *c.*1930.   **0.2**

An image of two Belgrade feminists from circa 1930, crowning the introduction to Dubravka Đurić and Miško Šuvaković's edited volume *Impossible
Histories: Historical Avant-Gardes, Neo-Avant-Gardes, and Post-Avant-Gardes
in Yugoslavia, 1818–1991* (2003), signifies just how important feminism was in
the region for the arts even before the advent of Tito's Yugoslavia (Figure 0.2).
Dressed in what easily could be perceived as femme and butch lesbian fashions, and holding hands, the two women in this photograph not only prefigure
a robust generation of straight and lesbian feminists essential to the antifascist
socialist cause in Yugoslavia, but they invite a more urgent look at the many
unnamed or unacknowledged feminists in Yugoslavia's art history. The closeness of their bodies, the tender way in which they hold hands, and the confidence and bravado with which they look at the camera, activate feminist and
queer emancipatory readings often overlooked in the "impossible histories"
of Yugoslav art. Prominently placed at the beginning of one of the most
important books on the region, they remain unnamed, but are far from irrelevant: further research reveals that the butch woman is Šuvaković's mother's
aunt, Ljuba Petković, "who was a graphic worker and died young."[9] As one of
the most prolific writers on the region, Šuvaković's own history is deeply

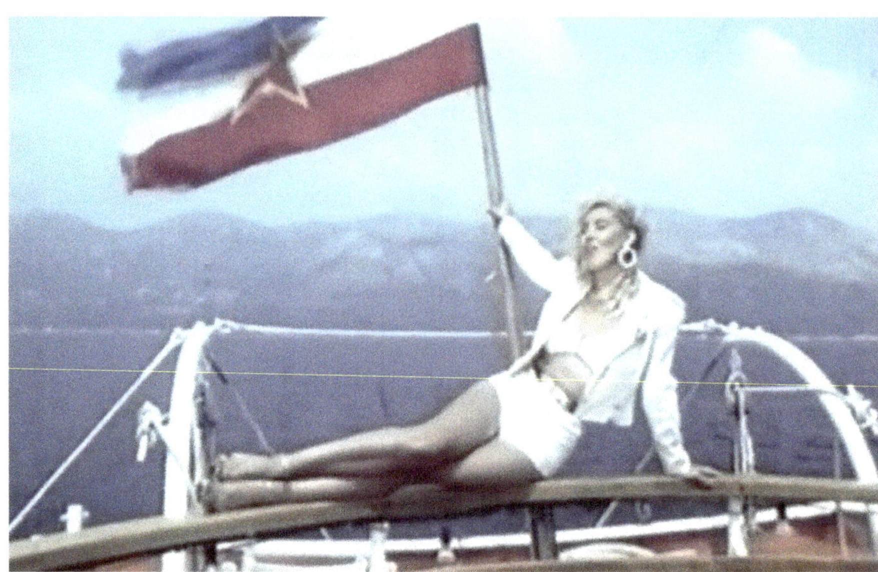

0.3   Lepa Brena, "Jugoslovenka," 1989. Video still.

entwined with the history of feminism, here tied to a mysterious photograph which manifests the underrecognized but powerful emancipatory legacy of women in the Yugoslav region.

A visual history of women's emancipation and the feminist movement evident in art and culture during Yugoslav socialism provides an essential narrative about a nation that has since perished, but which remains the foundation for the work of feminist artists, theorists, and historians from the region. The title of this book is inspired by—and indebted to—the legendary folk pop music performer Lepa Brena's 1989 song and music video "Jugoslovenka" (Figure 0.3). This hit delivered an epic celebration of Yugoslavia's socialist multiculturalism in a music video that put to shame the state-sponsored Socialist Realist paintings of prior decades: it featured a gorgeous smiling blonde in a flowing white dress, running in fields of green grass and golden grain, flowers in her hands, like a young bride of the land. Brena is shown followed by a marching group of male and female athletic flag bearers, all dressed identically in white, swinging their Yugoslav flags to the spellbinding chorus: "Ja sam Jugoslovenka" (I am Jugoslovenka). Her eyes are the "Adriatic Sea," she sings in Serbo-Croatian; she likens her hair to "Pannonian wheat"; and her soul is "Slavic."[10] In the most iconic image from the video, Brena is shown on the deck of a ship, lounging on her side and holding the Yugoslav flag. Her blonde hair moves with the wind, as does the Yugoslav flag, while she is singing. She is like a figurehead of a ship; behind her, on the shore, mountains rise to the skies. A pop-culture legend by the mid-1980s, Brena was a proponent of multiculturalism and pro-Western inclusiveness, but also an avid champion of what were considered to be the more "primitive" forces in Yugoslav culture, such as local folk music shot through with Middle Eastern influences. A self-made woman, she was no stranger to stigmatization, as she was often called "Tito's Barbie" because of her beauty and popularity. While, four decades into her career, she has begun to articulate explicitly feminist ideas, this book embraces a more open-minded look at feminism that includes multiple, divergent, and sometimes even conflicting forms of emancipatory resistance in Yugoslav women's performances. Brena's charm, wit, and ambition were feminist strategies that helped her to successfully evade marginalization by men. She managed her own career and changed the face of Yugoslav music; she even became the first and most successful female pop star throughout all Eastern Europe, selling out stadiums in Romania, Bulgaria, and Poland. While Brena is perhaps the best-known Jugoslovenka, she was not the first or the last of these female types: emancipated women who challenged and altered the status quo in Yugoslavia and beyond.

"I am Jugoslovenka!" Feminist Performance Politics during and after Yugoslav Socialism probes the ways in which performative representations of women's emancipation in the Socialist Federal Republic of Yugoslavia were crucial for the rise of gender equality in the socialist project and examines the complex changes in women's agency from the republic's birth to demise, and to the present day. Central to my study is the concept of the Jugoslovenka, or Yugoslav woman, a term that encompasses multiple generations of women who lived under or were born during Yugoslav socialism, a multinational and multiethnic state based on the promotion of the unification of South Slav people. In the 1990s, this mythic pan-Slavic identity was broken up into regional identities that became the basis of the independent nations of Slovenia, Croatia, Bosnia and Herzegovina, Serbia, North Macedonia, Montenegro, and Kosovo. Bridging over a half century of violent rupture and nation-building, my case studies include an array of Jugoslovenkas with multiple and often conflicting artistic motivations and political investments. Ranging from self-declared feminists, lesbians, and activists who were sharp critics of the socialist system and of patriarchal state policies and propaganda within the arts and culture, to women who rejected or were unaware of feminism as a movement, this book investigates the possibility of discerning feminist performance politics evident in women's emancipatory positions in Yugoslav art and culture even when, or especially when, they were not labeled as such.

If an atmosphere of freedom and experimentation dominated art and culture in Tito's Yugoslavia, how might we then reassess what "totalitarianism" meant then and the way we understand it now through the work of artists from former Yugoslavia? And how did the ideology of this more open type of socialism inform the art of the region? What inspired the rise of nationalist, misogynist, racist, and homophobic rhetoric after 1989? Why was the end of socialism linked to increased violence for women and minorities in that region? What might we learn about fascism and its constitutive interrelation to patriarchal violence in twentieth-century Europe and beyond? After the breakup of the republic, key Jugoslovenkas were deeply critical of the emergent neoliberal capitalist systems that replaced the Yugoslav socialist system within the rising independent nations. What connects all these diverse Yugoslav women, I argue, is the prominence of their emancipatory performance politics within visual culture and avant-garde art, specifically 1980s pop music and underground lesbian, gay, bisexual, transgender, and queer (LGBTQ) artistic practices and film, performance, and activist artworks from the 1990s to today.

By reorienting these inquiries toward the body and the state as sites of desire, experimentation, and politics, I argue for a new historical understanding of how Yugoslavia's brand of socialism fostered a climate in which visually expressed and performed emancipatory feminist strategies could expose, celebrate, and interrogate the political ideology of the socialist state and its aftermath. As a point of departure and an analytical thread throughout the entire manuscript, *"I am Jugoslovenka!"* hones in on the work of the most famous and prominent Jugoslovenka in the art world, then and now—Marina Abramović—whose oeuvre is deeply linked to her socialist upbringing and her mother's antifascist partisan background. While Abramović cannot be called a feminist in the Western sense, and indeed has refused to call herself that in the past, my book introduces this new analytical framework of Jugoslovenka to examine the emancipatory performance politics in her work and how such work is deeply bound up with Yugoslavia's history of women's antifascist resistance during World War II and the 1990s.

In its broader consideration of feminist art and visual culture in the region, this project confronts the notable but unspoken absence on the map of transnational feminist scholarship, especially Western feminist discourse, which, after a brief moment of engagement in the late 1990s through the early 2000s, has shown little contextual awareness of the outstanding and unique feminist practices and projects cultivated in the former Yugoslavia. *"I am Jugoslovenka!"* attempts to provide a nuanced insight into this feminist legacy, which was deeply influenced by modern socialist ideals and their destruction during the nationalist wars in former Yugoslavia. The critical subjects of this study involve feminist performance and embodiment as evident in visual cultural production, the extraordinary roles played by Yugoslav women during the periods of socialism, war, and nationalism, along with the centrality of feminist emancipatory visual and performative cultures of the region.

Employing overlapping chronological and thematic approaches, I use the lens of performance politics to consider the emancipated politicization of gender and sexuality in myriad aspects of Yugoslav visual culture. My analysis shows that feminist performance in art and popular culture was a pivotal component of Yugoslavia's unique brand of socialism, which was more porous to Western influence than in any other socialist country. In this light, this book provides an unconventional perspective on European socialism and nationalism, wherein debates around gender and sexuality cultivated a robust new generation of resilient feminists and anti-patriarchal movements that flourished into the 1980s in Yugoslavia, but which were subsequently vulnerable due to the collapse of communism in 1989 around the world, and the nationalist and ethnic wars in the 1990s. In these contexts, visible Jugoslovenkas served both as key feminists in the socialist and post-socialist Yugoslav region, and as popular cultural icons of women's and LGBTQ empowerment in the 1990s.

By grounding my analysis in an emphasis on visual rather than written culture, along with a focus on emancipatory performance and feminist embodiment, my book engages in a novel way with scholars whose works have addressed questions of gender in Yugoslavia. Zsófia Lóránd's 2018 book, *The Feminist Challenge to the Socialist State in Yugoslavia*, provides a long overdue and in-depth overview of the history of feminism in Yugoslavia, including a detailed discussion of feminist organizing within the arts, an indispensable source for my own understanding of the region. Similarly, the 2017 anthology, *The Cultural Life of Capitalism in Yugoslavia: (Post)Socialism and Its Other*, edited by Dijana Jelača, Maša Kolanović, and Danijela Lugarić, addresses a range of topics that include feminist organizing in the arts during the 1970s, 1980s, and beyond. Branislav Jakovljević's theorization of performance in Yugoslavia in *Alienation Effects: Performance and Self-Management in Yugoslavia, 1945–1991* provides the essential basis upon which I build a discussion of performance politics and nationalism, especially with an expanded lens on the question of gender. Bojana Pejić's 2009 exhibition and catalogue *Gender Check: Femininity and Masculinity in the Art of Eastern Europe* has also been an invaluable resource for my own book, particularly pertaining to debates around socialism and gender; due to its vast geographical scope, its discussion of Yugoslavia is limited, but its critical approach to the visual intersections of gender and politics in the realm of fine art is invaluable. While my book, which shares these works' historical framework, necessarily addresses many of the same events, exhibitions, and artists, my focus on the feminist emancipatory content and performative aspects within these expressions of visual production—avant-garde art, magazines, underground queer music, pop music, and performance art—seeks to add a new perspective to these histories of Yugoslavia. I do so by conjoining the impact of works indispensable to art history with remarkable elements of popular visual culture to reveal how gender and sexuality wove the political paradigm of socialism into the emancipatory politics of Yugoslav women. Consequently, my book foregrounds the significance of feminist performance by privileging Yugoslav women as central interlocutors between socialist (Eastern) and democratic (Western) emancipatory politics.

Since the 2000s, new generations of historians, sociologists, theorists, literary scholars, and art historians, among others, have fused the interrelated fields of Yugoslav studies, Yugoslav histories, and Yugoslav revivals with feminist and gender studies. Many of these young scholars, including myself, lived through the nationalist wars of the early 1990s as teenagers or were scattered across the diaspora, and have faint though meaningful memories of what Yugoslavia was before the beginning of the wars. Others witnessed the disintegration of the republic through ethnic wars with horror. Tanya Renne's edited collection of essays in *Ana's Land: Sisterhood in Eastern Europe* (1997) has served as an invaluable resource for my understanding of the immediate war and postwar era, as well as the foundation of feminist work in Yugoslavia preceding its disintegration. Celebrating socialist Yugoslavia was taboo for most of the 1990s, because individual nations (such as Slovenia and Croatia) had forcefully declared independence from the former republic and its ideas, culture, and mythology, and many leaders of those new nations resented the idea of Tito's imposed "brotherhood and unity." Subsequently, much has been written out of Yugoslav history in the name of nationalist agendas of erasure. Renne's feminist historiography of Yugoslavia ran counter to such erasures and remains an extraordinary document of what Ann Cvetkovich has termed "an archive of feeling," privileging the intersection of traumatic encounters, emotional experiences, and personal insight with feminist and queer perspectives to preserve minoritarian histories.[11]

"I am Jugoslovenka!" offers a feminist critique of socialism that responds to the lack of accounting for questions of gender in research centered on Yugoslavia by highlighting the generative elements that made Yugoslav socialism exceptional: women's emancipatory interventions in art and culture. In a 2018 interview titled "I am Jugoslovenka," Yugoslavia's celebrated actress, Mirjana Karanović, proclaimed:

> I was born in Yugoslavia. I am a Yugoslavian. Many times, after the disintegration of that country, I wondered what that meant for who I am now, especially since the formation of those new [nationalist] states [in the 1990s] came with an obligatory denunciation of any connection to that "communist prison." Being a Yugoslavian then, or a Yugonostalgic today, has negative and almost derogatory implications. Today, I am called a Serb. But Yugoslavia played an important role in forming my personality, my relationship with people, towards the world around me. It is an inseparable part of my identity. … For me,

Yugoslavia was the most beautiful and most exciting country in the world ...
I was endlessly proud of the fact that I lived in Yugoslavia. ... I know that
country is dead forever and I've cried over it and have moved on. I know where
I live, I've accepted unfriendly border guards and new stamps in my passport.
And yet what I know to be true, without any doubt, is that I will continue to
be a Jugoslovenka at the core of my being.[12]

Karanović is but one example of women from the Yugoslav generation who
have remained committed to the idea of Yugoslavia, and whose lives took a
dramatic turn during and after the disintegration of Yugoslavia. To them, as
to many others of their generation, the emergence of nationalist and religious
conservatism in the region contrasts with the much more open Yugoslav
socialism, an aspect that is often ignored in sweeping narratives about so-
called "backwards" socialism in the twentieth century. Perhaps even more
surprisingly, the end of socialism and rise of liberalism resulted in an increase
of homophobia, sexism, and violence against LGBTQ people in the early
1990s. This book is written in response to such cultural developments, and
seeks to reveal a more complex historical and analytical context for feminist
performance in Eastern Europe. At a time when dramatic confrontations
between far left and far right ideologies are taking place across Europe and
the USA, this book seeks to function as a tool for better understanding the
political projects of socialism and nationalism through the lens of performance and visual art.

Contending the male body politic: a feminist history of Yugoslav socialism

Every year from 1945 until 1988, socialist Yugoslavia celebrated Marshal Tito's
birthday on May 25 with a national holiday,[13] Youth Day, honoring their leader
with extravagant ceremonies and dances, including a performative handing
of the *štafeta* (relay baton) to the Yugoslav leader during a relay race.[14] These
ceremonies grew in scale over time, but were crucial to mapping out a celebration of the nation centered on the father of the people, Tito, who through his
heroic antifascist leadership had united the country during World War II. The
various routes of the *štafetas* signified a unity that transcended the geographical lines drawn on a map by politicians or suggested by ethnic divisions;
instead, young athletes would carry the *štafetas* and chart what performance
studies scholar Branislav Jakovljević has called "a capillary system that joined
the entire country into an interconnected organism."[15] Jakovljević elaborates
on the changes in routes as well as the number of participants over time:

Some 12,500 runners participated in the first relay race in liberated Yugoslavia.
The countrywide trail ended in a mass meeting in Slavija, one of the main
Belgrade city squares, from which Tito himself was absent. He was in Zagreb,

so the final leg of the baton's journey was made in an airplane. By the following year, there was a protocol in place, according to which the arrival of Tito's Baton (*Titova štafeta*) in the capital of Yugoslavia was celebrated in one of the main city squares, usually the Square of the Republic, after which it was handed to the president in a special ceremony arranged at his residence in the White Palace (*Beli dvor*). From the inception of this tradition, which was by far the largest mass celebration in post-World War II Yugoslavia, devotion to Tito was measured by the number of bodies and the distance traveled: in 1950, 93,000 km and over a million runners; in 1951, 128,000 km and 1.5 million runners. The largest relay run was organized in 1952, when some 1,555,000 runners covered over 130,000 km. In the early 1960s, the format of the relay was changed, and the multitude of small local batons was replaced by the single Youth Baton.[16]

Mass demonstrations of people's love for and loyalty to Tito's unified Yugoslavia were expressed in the celebration of the tremendous athleticism of his country's people; this body politic dominated public performances of devotion to socialist ideology and became the oxygen nourishing the organs of the state.

Jakovljević discusses these types of mass celebrations in Yugoslavia as a baroque model "according to which the state abandons the simple principle of ruling by presence in order to adopt the dynamic model of ruling through participation."[17] Tito was not an autocratic leader who ruled by inducing fear or using overtly punitive measures. Instead, Jakovljević argues, the loyalty of the followers was "accomplished through a delicate balance of violence and pleasure."[18] This violence, Jakovljević explains, "is manifested in the emergence of standing armies and the pleasure in the equally emergent concept of culture."[19] Elaborate creations of a new Yugoslav culture evident in mass ceremonial spectacles mounted the power of this young state—a state that had succeeded in defeating the National Socialists during World War II—which Jakovljević characterizes as showing "uniquely baroque dynamics of conservatism and progressivism."[20] The dynamism between these two forces would play out most vividly in state-sponsored mass spectacles.

Jakovljević's characterization of Yugoslavia as a state that negotiated conservatism and progressivism in its dogmatic cultural production offers a valuable starting point from which to understand the complicated position of women's emancipatory strength in the Yugoslav project. Tito's Yugoslavia was instrumental in building a society that prided itself on egalitarian gender roles, freedom of expression, and liberation through collective action. But women's egalitarian roles were enmeshed in a patriarchal logic of emancipation: according to the ruling male establishment, women had "earned" the right to be granted equality. In 1942, Tito gave a speech at the first national conference organized by the AFW,[21] in which he stressed that women had *"passed the maturity test"* and had *"proven it by their lives, by their blood on the battlefield* against German, Italian, and Hungarian fascists."[22] He added that these women had demonstrated their value to the Yugoslav project both by following and executing their duties at home while simultaneously going to battle "*with rifles in their hands*," proving, "that they can rule and hold power in their hands."[23] The staunch paternalism and condescension toward women, coupled with approbation, echo Jakovljević's notion of "a delicate balance of violence and pleasure," a balancing act that was a recurring challenge for women in the Yugoslav socialist state.

Championing the equality of women was a key part of male Yugoslav leaders' narrative on gender emancipation, but feminist historian Chiara Bonfiglioli suggests that it was not socialism that brought about women's emancipation; instead, she argues, rather women's emancipation brought socialism to Yugoslavia.[24] However, women's push against gender inequalities was soon to be abandoned. Already on August 7, 1945, the Program of the People's Front of Yugoslavia pledged that "The People's Front has always actively promoted the equality of women. Today, when that equality has been achieved, the further consolidation [of that equality] and the complete participation of women in all areas of political and social life must be one of the assignments of every adherent of the Front."[25] In 1946, the first postwar constitution included an even more confident statement about the equal status of women:

> Women enjoy equal rights with men in all spheres of state economic and social life. Women are entitled to a salary equal to that of men for the same work, and enjoy special protection in the labor relationship. The state particularly protects the welfare of mother and child by the establishment of maternity hospitals, children's homes and day nurseries, and by ensuring the right to paid leave before and after confinement.[26]

Feminist historian Sabrina P. Ramet has noted that, while all these advances for women were extremely important and beneficial, they were mostly confined to "paper," with the communist leadership failing to implement ideas around gender equality in education.[27] Other feminists would object to the emphasis on women as mothers and servants for the Yugoslav state. Prominent Yugoslav feminist theorist Rada Iveković blamed the "patriarchal mentality" of the Yugoslav system for "fostering confusion" by legally announcing women's equality, while asking women to "perform household duties" and keeping them from advancing in the self-management system.[28] This was disappointing, considering the fact that in the first two decades of the Yugoslav project, the idea of the partisan Jugoslovenka, *partizanka*, had "emerged as an eminent source of legitimacy for Tito's Yugoslavia and a symbol of supranational Yugoslavism."[29] But by the 1960s and into the 1970s, Batinić has noted, the image of *partizanka* "was shaped by an ever-growing dose of misogyny and sexism."[30]

This intricate and paradoxical combination of emancipatory politics at the heart of socialism and the imposition of an ever-expanding specter of patriarchal political leadership would drive what I call the feminist performance politics of the women artists discussed in this book. My focus on feminist performance politics allows me to combine five points of inquiry: (1) a look at the complicated and conflicting history of women's emancipation within the specific context of Yugoslav socialism beginning in the late 1960s through the 1980s and 1990s, to 2021; (2) a rethinking of performance art and various forms of related experimental art forms through the lens of gender and sexuality in the region; (3) a mobilization of performance art and its emphasis on the body as a site of political resistance in this unique socialist context and its aftermath; (4) the establishment of the Yugoslav woman, Jugoslovenka, as a crucial, albeit complicated, voice in the history of feminist performance art and culture in the post-1945 era; and (5) a theorization of Jugoslovenka as the radical embodiment of Yugoslavia's antifascist, transnational, and feminist legacies, evident in the post-Yugoslav era of neoliberalism and the rise of conservative values of gender and sexuality.

Although the stakes for women in Yugoslavia were unique in their political and social context, women globally shared the common burden of pervasive patriarchal attitudes. In this regard, it is important to elucidate how and why I use the term "feminist performance politics" in the Yugoslav context, when many of the women performance artists discussed in this book explicitly rejected any association with the feminist movement or were indifferent to the actual movements of feminism in Yugoslavia. Why even bother looking at these works through a feminist lens? What is to be gained from such a reading? In her 1998 book, *Cunt: A Declaration of Independence*, (American) feminist writer Inga Muscio offers an astute insight about the scope of feminism:

> The only dimly representational, identifying term that advocates truly authentic recognition for the actual realities of women in this world is "feminism." This is a relatively youthful word. Our actual realities, on the other hand, are rooted deep. We are born with them in our hearts.
>
> Inherited them from our mothers.
>
> Grandmothers.[31]

Muscio suggests that feminism is merely a word that encapsulates generational struggles of female experience. One need not explicitly act as a feminist to be one. Rather, simply acknowledging the complexities of womanhood and the struggles imposed by patriarchy across generations positions one within the broad scope of feminism. This decidedly broad definition of feminism resonates deeply with my own positionality toward the question of feminism and Yugoslav nationhood. As a young immigrant woman, part of the Yugoslav diaspora during the breakup of the republic in the early 1990s, I came of age in Germany with a working-class Yugoslav mother who spent most of my youth and adolescence working illegally as a seamstress. My grandmother, too, was a working-class woman from Yugoslavia who had spent decades in Germany as a *Gastarbeiter* (guest worker/labor migrant), working in industrial laundries and later as a seamstress. Both of these women were matriarchs in our family, role models in their perseverance and independence from men.[32] Neither one considered herself a feminist, nor did they participate in feminist organizing. My grandmother never went to grade school, and while my mother graduated from high school, she never attended college. Yet both of them taught me more about emancipatory resistance than much of my higher education, or many of the feminist texts that I have since read. Most importantly, their teachings did not come from the academy, but from lived experiences under Yugoslav socialism, which, despite its patriarchal foundation, still, at its core, empowered women.

In these lived experiences, resistance is more deeply tied to action, to my knowledge, than any written doctrine. Even on the most nominal or private scale, action can have political dimensions. The site of the female body (cis or trans) is a site of resistance, because female-identified bodies are burdened with having to negotiate the political weight of patriarchal power despite (and sometimes because of) advances in gender equality. Feminist art historian and curator Jelena Petrović has argued that the figure of Jugoslovenka was "double burdened (inside and outside the home)," regardless of "the modernist and new socialist image of an independent, working woman who had all rights to decide about herself and to choose her way of life."[33] Jugoslovenkas had to confront the "survival of patriarchy in socialism."[34] I highlight the figure of Jugoslovenka in feminist performance to move beyond US and Western European contexts to a regionally specific discussion of feminist strategies—not feminist movements—in Yugoslavia. In my use of the term, the idea of Jugoslovenka is politically charged with an emphasis on feminist body-centered work, which summons bodily resistance to a set of political issues that concern women and the implications of structural patriarchal violence in Yugoslavia. This, of course, evokes historical connotations of the term feminism, including consciousness-raising efforts and activist organizing, particularly in Western countries. My evocation of the term is certainly inflected by these ideas, but it rejects the implied coherence of such an ideology and instead focuses more on a shared impulse by these artists to confront systems of power and the ways they affected women in Yugoslavia.

Branislava Anđelković and Branislav Dimitrijević have argued that performance art in the 1990s had changed dramatically since the 1970s and lost its radicalness as a "weapon against conventions of established art."[35] While this might be true, feminist performance in the 1970s was never solely dealing with unfolding or challenging established art conventions. As T. J. Clark has asserted, art is always embedded in the society in which it is made. Performance art was one way in which women's otherwise marginalized experiences found a language and point of entry into the sphere of art. As such, performance was deeply tied to shifting ideas about the body that came out of emancipatory theories and histories of women's liberation.

But geopolitical context in this history also matters, as so much of what we in the early twenty-first century consider performance art theory emerged during the Cold War. For artists, especially those coming from communist/socialist countries or from non-white contexts, body art was already burdened with gender, racism, erasure, and marginalization in the history of performance. Bojana Pejić, for example, has demonstrated how Thomas McEvilley's 1989 analysis of Marina Abramović's training in the gym in preparation for her *Great Wall Walk* (1988) performance revealed his preference for a "marvelously slim" Abramović, who he claimed had managed to "shake off the thickness of the communist body" for that performance.[36] Abramović, who is Serbian, had left Yugoslavia more than a decade earlier at this point and was practicing in the West, but was still clearly subject to the West's gaze as an outsider. In McEvilley's description of Abramović's "fat-hipped body-style," he equated her body to Yugoslavia's "dismal bleakness," from which the artist "free[d] herself" through physical exercise.[37] This type of Western male gaze, a phantasmagorical projection in which "the gym could facilitate a new (Western) body,"[38] was deeply tied to the erasure of Abramović's own context.

I want to approach Yugoslav women's body art from a feminist angle that privileges analyzing how different forms of resistance to patriarchal oppression play out in the Yugoslav context. Yugoslav women artists' emphases on their bodies as sites of resistance and emancipation come with their own complicated, and sometimes paradoxical, emancipatory politics. For example, Leonida Kovač has noted how much homophobia and anti-feminism were part of avant-garde circles, mostly because association with those social and cultural movements was not profitable for artists and museums in the 1980s and 1990s:

> [D]uring the 1990s, when there was no funding for feminist projects, and of course no international funding [because of the wars], no Croatian women artists wanted to be labeled as feminist. And after feminism became something that was internationally funded, when as an artist you could get a resident's card, everyone became feminists, just like how everyone tried to be queer later.[39]

Notably, Kovač's description here already takes on the national denominator of "Croatian" in the 1990s, which for many artists was a new way of identifying within the context of former Yugoslavia and its emerging nations. In this book,

I avoid such national descriptions and instead turn to Jugoslovenka, or Yugoslav woman, as an umbrella term to hold together both multiple generations of self-declared feminists and non-feminists from all the former republics of Yugoslavia. I do so because those generations working in the 1990s came out of the Yugoslav project and were forced into a new national identity that was divisive and, for many, a traumatic break from the collective unity they had experienced under Yugoslav socialism. Moreover, I limit my analysis to artists who produced feminist or queer content, even if their identities or statements might contradict such political readings, whether because of "funding," as argued by Kovač, or due to a lack of solidarity with women's and queer movements as a result of adopting homophobic and patriarchal attitudes. How, for example, can we reconcile the fact that someone like Vlasta Delimar remains one of the most radically sex-positive and transgressive artists of the 1980s, putting her own pleasures—no matter what—at the center of her work, while at the same time being a notorious woman artist charged with making homophobic and anti-feminist statements? How can an artist, who has been said to have proclaimed, "I despise feminists because all of them are lesbians," still produce feminist content in her art?[40] How can we include such a complicated case in feminist and queer art histories? Why should we?

In order to meet these questions with varied approaches, it may be useful to call on one case from 1991 to elucidate just how complicated and contradictory narratives of feminist resistance can be in the Yugoslav and post-Yugoslav context: the iconic photo of Dragana Milojević at the March 9 demonstration against Slobodan Milošević in Belgrade (Figure 0.4). The deeper one looks into this (or any) iconic image, the more complicated its meaning becomes, with the inevitable realization that icons remain abstract and absolute for a reason: to create simple narratives with clear villains and heroes. The 1991 image of Milojević has become one such iconic image, which has circulated widely in the local and international media since the day it was taken.

The breathtaking show of defiance concentrated in Milojević's raised arm as she stands in front of the crowd of protesters and the police, soaking wet from water cannons spraying at her, is frequently shown as a symbol of disobedience against the violent establishment. Milojević here emerges as a figure echoing Eugène Delacroix's *Liberty Leading the People* during the July Revolution of 1830 in France. She was celebrated as "a symbol of courage and freedom" in the press, and in 2010, the newspaper *Novosti* declared:

She is a woman whose courage hurt the regime of Slobodan Milošević more than all the stones, assaults and strong words. It is a woman who, in front of the "Russian Tsar" with three fingers raised, completely alone, with a bag nonchalantly hanging on her shoulder, with her head raised, was waiting for a police cannon from which ice water was gushing.[41]

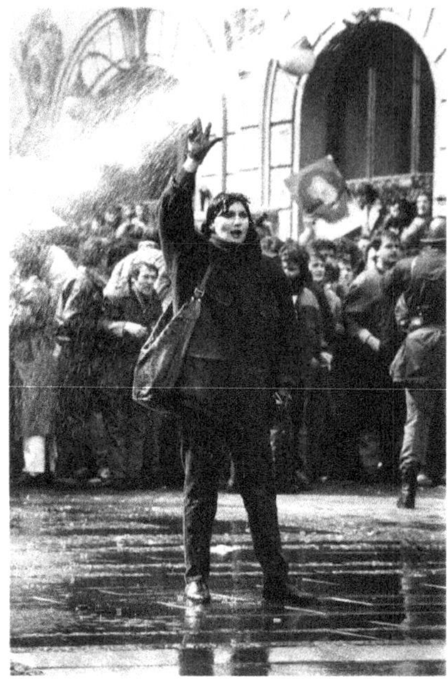

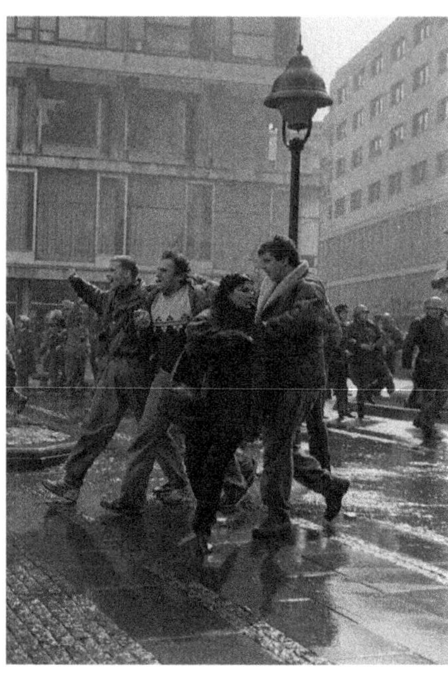

0.4   Predrag Mitić, *Dragana Milojević, March 9,* Belgrade, 1991.   Goranka Matić, *Dragana Milojević, March 9*, Belgrade, 1991.

Such a heroic narrative is quickly complicated by another photograph of Milojević at the same demonstration, probably shot just minutes apart, which illustrates a different story (Figure 0.5); not an unstoppable female leader anymore, Milojević is overtaken by taller demonstrating men who are shouting and walking by without even looking at her, apparently shoving her out of the way as if she didn't exist. In the background, we see police with their helmets. Milojević pivots out of the men's way, with a look on her face that is stern and pensive. The feminist photographer Goranka Matić here captured just how challenging and dangerous it was for women to negotiate their right to a political voice, with little to no solidarity from men who marched onward with disregard for women's struggles or existence. Of course, being shoved out of the way like that is nothing new for many women who go to demonstrations, concerts, or any large public events, be they in Berlin, New York, or Belgrade. But at this moment, in 1991, the demonstration of masculine dominance acutely signaled the coming women's struggles of the 1990s, fueled by men's ignorance of and contempt for women's political movements.

Protests and marches in Belgrade were more than once hijacked by proudly chauvinist, misogynist, and violent sports fans, who, through the leadership of criminal figures like Arkan,[42] became increasingly emboldened and ended up playing a significant role during the wars in Bosnia (1992–1995) and Kosovo (1998–1999). Furthermore, women had to negotiate their positions within a rapidly changing landscape of political parties, groups, and their leaders, many of whom wanted to distance themselves from Tito's socialist regime and were aligned with more liberal bourgeois ideas (such as the Democrats led by Dragoljub Mićunović and Zoran Đinđić). Others, like Slobodan Milošević, pandered to the working class and exploited the Yugoslav name, political connections, and, most importantly, the power of the Yugoslav People's Army (Jugoslovenska Narodna Armija; JNA) to push for a "Greater Serbia."

Some women who rose to influence in this political landscape, such as Mirjana Marković, Milošević's wife, supported the patriarchal legacy of communist party politics. Marković led the Yugoslav United Left Party (Jugoslovenska Udružena Levica; JUL), which was primarily made up of Tito's old generals and their opportunistic associates working closely with the JNA. Marković self-identified as a feminist and decreed her Marxist principles were derived from Tito's legacy of equality. To augment her legitimacy as an antifascist communist, she frequently referenced in elaborate and often disputed details a personal narrative of being birthed in the forest during combat by her Yugoslav partisan mother. But a third of her JUL party consisted of nouveaux rich Serbs with companies that had profited from the wars in the early 1990s while international sanctions were in place.[43] Marković's feminism and socialism instrumentalized the ideas of Tito and his old regime as a façade behind which JUL's profiteering and clandestine power flourished. At the same time, her husband pushed policies, laws, and rhetoric justifying and facilitating ethnic cleansing. Consequently, both Marković's feminism and her socialism ran counter to the Yugoslav principles of equality, pan-ethnic solidarity, and liberation I associate with Jugoslovenka. For many from the region, it was extremely disconcerting to be labeled a Yugoslav sympathizer or Yugonostalgic in the 1990s, as it connoted an association with the old regime and figures like Milošević and Marković who represented little of the socialist political legacy of unity, but all of its patriarchal state power, corruption, and nepotism, to support their Serbian version of Yugoslavia.

In that regard, I want to return once more to Milojević, who was an "ordinary" brave woman without ambitions in politics. Her story complicates what first appears as a simple narrative of women's strength and resistance against patriarchy and oppression in the 1990s. At around the age of forty, when photographed during the Belgrade demonstration, she was a supporter of the Serbian Renewal Movement (Srpski Pokret Obnove, led by Vuk Drašković), an anti-regime royalist, but also anti-Yugoslav, opposition party steeped in nationalist values and rhetoric. Like many who unwittingly became heroes of resistance years later, she remained disappointed by the stark contrast between her status as an exploited revolutionary icon and a woman whom the movement and its leaders quickly forgot about: "I didn't know then that my photo would travel the world and I would become a nameless symbol on March 9th."[44] When she died twenty years later, one of her obituaries noted that she had regretted ever going to the protest, and that she had told her grandchild: "Make sure you never stand alone in front of a crowd, especially not when there are water cannons used."[45]

The opposing narratives of Milojević's agency within the two photographs of the same event bring to the foreground incongruities that help us gauge just how difficult it is to have one narrative of feminist resistance in Yugoslavia and its aftermath: on the one hand, the tension of representing an emancipated heroine versus a random, overpowered woman getting pushed out of the way by men; on the other, the idea of her as an opposition leader against nationalism when in reality she was affiliated with a conservative and nationalist party at the time. The tensions of meaning within these contrary representations of the same woman in the same political moment contest any definitive understanding of emancipation and point to the tenuousness of unfolding the political hostilities of the early 1990s in a coherent manner.

Jugoslovenka, as a figure, is precisely so fascinating because she doesn't allow for simple narratives. The complicated and traumatic history of Yugoslav socialism is intertwined with an equally complicated story of feminism, all of which is legible in the figure of Jugoslovenka.

Socialism and its virulent paternalism: Jugoslovenka and her discontents

While 1968 was a pivotal year for student uprisings globally, in Yugoslavia it marked a moment that divided the "old left" feminists, who were seen "as complicit with … the Soviet military interventions in Budapest (1956) and Prague (1968),"[46] from new feminist organizers who often didn't use that label at all, but who were frequently derogatorily called feminists by their male colleagues. Moreover, "the generation of antifascist women was skeptical towards the emergence of [new] feminism, which they saw as an extremist, bourgeois, overtly intellectual phenomenon, which risked alienating the majority of female public opinion."[47] While I do not seek to unpack the differences between these generations of feminists, 1968 is an important marker for Yugoslav feminism because it accelerated discourses around liberation that included more intense calls for gender equality by women intellectuals and artists, not all of whom identified as feminists at the time for diverse reasons. However, they still belong to the history of Yugoslav feminism as a whole.

Reminiscing about the 1968 student revolts in her city, Belgrade-based feminist literary critic Svetlana Slapšak recalled that, while a student there, she and others at the University of Belgrade fantasized about stealing Marshal Tito's relay baton on the Day of Youth.[48] In this imagined performative action, they would have stolen the *Titova štafeta* and left it at the university's department of philosophy.[49] As a quintessentially phallic and Olympian object, the relay baton was elemental to the ceremonial renewal of Yugoslav nationalism under Tito; to steal it was one way of undermining the sensational crowd psychology mimicking Greco-Roman traditions of venerating male leaders and their young followers. Art historian and performance artist Bojana Videkanić has theorized the importance of the relay baton to the conceptualization of the Yugoslav national body as both mimetic of Tito himself and as a symbol carried forth by Yugoslavia's youth (male and female):

> The Day of Youth provided a ritual, symbolic network through which Yugoslavian society renewed its commitments to shared ideological mechanisms. … While carrying the youth batons, citizens symbolically outlined an image of Tito, carved into the land itself, and into the geography of each region. The landscape of the country became the landscape of Tito's body, transforming the entire nation into his physical presence. … Through translation of the leader's aging body into the bodies of young people Tito's symbolic transformation from a mere mortal to an immortal was complete.[50]

This symbolic transformation of a country into the omnipotent figure of Tito was extremely effective in developing a coherent sense of Yugoslavian identity, but one that was suspect among the contemporary generation of feminists. In an essay titled "How We Hated Tito," Slapšak described how she and her colleagues continually ridiculed the leader, especially by mimicking his "clumsy" behavior and accent.[51] One must recognize that the inscription of Tito's body onto the land meant the inscription of the male body as the outline of the Yugoslav nation; and that this multiethnic conglomeration required the propaganda of paternalistic nationalism to maintain its power.

Batinić's research has demonstrated that Yugoslavia as a unified and socialist country was an extremely masculine project from the outset, one oriented toward Tito's male leadership. While women partisan soldiers in the AFW were recognized as "indispensable to the party's war effort,"[52] they had tremendous problems with their bodies still being put in the service of men, rather than themselves or their country. Sometimes high-ranking AFW members had to abandon their positions because their husbands intervened.[53] At the same time, women contested these gendered pressures, marking moments of resistance that, by way of gossip, would frequently become anecdotes for the amusement of the male party elite, most famously in the case of a woman in Bukovača whose husband was sentenced to twenty-five lashes for beating his wife.[54] Tito was "greatly entertained" by this story, but told AFW president Kata Pejnović he was skeptical of the AFW's teachings "if they nearly killed the man for such a trifle—for beating 'his own' wife?"[55]

Tito's tacit approval of domestic abuse foregrounds how much women and women's emancipation (and degradation) were in the hands of men, not women, as was the power over women's bodies. One of the major burdens of women's emancipation during World War II was that their new roles were still confined to deep-rooted gender hierarchies.[56] Even on the battlefield, women soldiers were asked to wash their male comrade's clothes, as "the traditional markers of their womanhood" persisted.[57] Batinić recounts one story when, "at a conference in Srem, among the speeches about female Partisans' courage and strength, the peasants could also hear how 'it is touching to watch them as they, in their free time, take the clothes of male comrades to mend and wash.'"[58] So this emphasis on women's strength in the household was also projected onto women who were thought to have ascended to the masculine sphere by being partisan soldiers and who now benefitted from "the freedom, higher status, and respect reserved for military men."[59] This parallels a rhetoric well documented in same-sex relationships among women, in which heteronormative hierarchies of male and female are replicated: the femme lesbian takes care of her more masculine-presenting (butch) lesbian partner.[60] Batinić writes about one moment in 1943 when a peasant woman rose up during an AFW conference and exclaimed, "our comrade female-fighters will not do the laundry, neither for themselves nor for other comrades."[61]

Such compliance with traditional gender roles relates to Petrović's argument that women in Yugoslavia had "failed in liberating themselves from the patriarchal position of 'powerlessness'"[62] because they eclipsed their own needs in favor of appealing to "the universal programme and strategy in the struggle for equal rights and freedom [for men and women]" advocated by the Communist Party of Yugoslavia (CPY). While women had won some autonomy with the AFW, they still submitted to the CPY's "paternalistic position in the new state," which sidelined "the importance of the role of women in the interwar and wartime periods, ascribing the majority of their achievements to the universal historical process of general social emancipation."[63] But it is also important to remember that from the inception of the AFW in 1942, "most men saw the front of women [AFW] in derisive terms" and suspected the women of dividing the common cause for liberation.[64] Batinić illustrates that even though peasant women, for example, "became politically active in a manner unthinkable before the war [World War II]," the male party leadership did little to help facilitate such political work, thus leaving women "to their own devices."[65] Men still received more votes from men and women alike, and those women "who managed to get into the councils tended to accept passively instructions from their male peers."[66] In the end, the AFW "(self)abolished" in 1953,[67] as the male-dominated communist leadership claimed that the so-called woman question had now been solved by socialism. In short, the acceleration of socialism enabled the peaceful merging of the multiethnic Yugoslav republics, but sexism, patriarchy, and the ideology of nationalism nevertheless remained at the core of Yugoslav society.

This was especially evident to women in the academy and culture, many of whom began to write about their disenchantment with Tito's paternalism. Following the 1968 protests, when Slapšak fantasized about stealing Tito's phallic relay baton and thereby ridiculing his patriarchal leadership, her student magazine *Frontisterion*, which used satire and Greek mythology to implicitly critique the Yugoslav government, was censored and eventually banned by the Yugoslav state in 1970.[68] The government ended up confiscating her passport,[69] she remembers, and she was beaten severely.[70] Slapšak's harassment was part of a larger climate of contentious resistance, which Jakovljević has described as "internecine struggles within the League of Communists of Yugoslavia that raged in the late 1960s and early 1970s."[71] Interestingly, the idea of the relay baton historically has some feminist underpinnings and is, as such, even more symbolically charged when considering Slapšak's fantasy of stealing Tito's baton along with her actual experience of censorship. Bonfiglioli's research shows that the word and idea of the *štafeta* (štaffette, in Italian) was used to describe Italian women antifascist couriers at the front during World War II.[72] Italian antifascist partisans were very close to those fighting in Yugoslavia. Most importantly, being a "štaffette" involved dangerous underground activities at the front. With this history in mind, Slapšak's fictional account of stealing the relay baton and bringing it to the university can be read as a powerful allusion to taking women back to the "front" of the struggle, being couriers who tread in some of the most dangerous territories, and who should be housed at the most inquisitive intellectual front: philosophy. As literary feminist historian Zsófia Lóránd has noted, "it was this environment [of censorship], entangled with the academic-activist scene at the universities, where feminist art and art theory emerged."[73]

During the 1968 strikes at the university, Slapšak recalled that Neda Nikolić took the stage during the speeches at the inner courtyard of the philosophy department, but once she began to talk about feminism, she was booed.[74] Dramaturge and activist Borka Pavićević, who graduated in 1971 from the Department of Dramaturgy at the Academy for Theater, Film, Radio and Television in Belgrade, summarized the male intelligentsia's negative arguments against feminism in 1968 in the following way: "It's not the right time [for feminism], we [men] are dealing with important things, the theoretical weight of our movement is different in comparison to feminist theory, which is theoretically light and insignificant; thirdly, why do you women push yourselves into the first row when you already have all your rights?"[75] These explanations were not only dismissive, but also at times rather hostile. Feminist theorist

Vesna Kesić remembers, for example, how in the 1970s the music newspaper *Polet* published an article stating that "[f]eminists should be kicked in *pička*,"[76] meaning in their "cunts," for *being* "cunts."[77] The blatantly misogynist implication of this statement was emblematic of the attitudes toward women in Yugoslavia in the 1960s and 1970s. Women were told that they had achieved their freedoms and that their issues were not important. As Jelena Vesić has noted:

> Despite social state investments in women's liberation through different supports such as education, equal right to work, organized support for reproductive and family care (free medical service, kindergartens, and education), the Yugoslav socialist culture remained essentially patriarchal—the "bourgeois morality," with all its taboos and constraints remained to loom on the path of "universal emancipation."[78]

Socialism was treated as if it could absorb feminism and dissolve gender difference for the purpose of higher political goals. Among other things, this fraught ideology of universal emancipation also failed to account for the marginalized positions of ethnic Roma, Non-Aligned Movement students from what was then called "Third World" countries who came to live in Yugoslavia and encountered racism as dark-skinned outsiders, or Kosovo Albanians in Yugoslavia, all of which would have disastrous consequences in the 1980s and 1990s.

Feminist theorist Adriana Zaharijević has argued that Yugoslav women coming out of this post-World War II generation "insisted on what had not been asserted strongly enough: that there were patriarchal remnants which formal policies did not or could not reach."[79] Zaharijević described these women as "embittered with socialism," an embitterment they channeled toward feminist resistance. "By introducing feminism, they criticized the socialism which had allowed itself the deception that, where women were concerned, it differed fundamentally from bourgeois capitalist societies."[80] The introduction of this feminist lens was considered suspect by the party leadership, which found many ways to discredit feminist thought and movements. According to art historian and curator Bojana Pejić, "feminism was officially rejected as an 'import' from the capitalist West."[81] Kesić characterized this dishonest sense of moral superiority over the "West" by the male elite as a self-serving ploy to dismiss women and any dissenting voices as morally corrupt intruders: "The party had been the highest criteria for good and bad, justice and injustice, as well as the creator of public morale." "The party had been the inexhaustible source of patriarchal male power, as well as sexist and ideological domination over women," Kesić added.[82]

Lóránd groups feminist resistance during the 1970s and 1980s under the category of New Yugoslav Feminism (*neofeminizam*),[83] which had its own specific influences, challenges, and, ultimately, motivations to address the "unfulfilled equality of women in Yugoslavia." She expands:

> They argued from a feminist base, inspired and infused by critical Marxism, post-structuralist French feminism, new theories in psychology, anthropology and sociology, but also referring to the Yugoslav partisan tradition as an emancipatory ideology for women. … It was a generation born after the war, from mothers who had a first-hand war experience and very often were themselves active participants of the partisan movement. Unlike their mothers, these women were puzzled by the contradiction between the promise of the regime and their own experience of their "emancipation," the lives of their mothers who were supposedly equal to their fathers and the women around them, who on the level of discourse were equal to men.[84]

These feminist ideas manifested in varying ways, including writing, art, literature, theory, activism, and popular culture.[85] I want to push beyond the historically specific notion of New Yugoslav Feminism and use the idea of Jugoslovenka as a way to speak about womanhood and an embodied subject under a set of varying political conditions and times rather than as a present political idea of gender. It is also important to remember that from the time of its foundation in 1942, the AFW was "by no means homogenous; all nationalities, ages, and classes were represented, and women joined for very different reasons, contributing to it in different ways."[86] Batinić has written extensively on the diversity of Yugoslav women's mass political mobilization during World War II and their important contributions to the Yugoslav project.[87] She elucidates how women's roles were gradually diminished during the war and after the establishment of Tito's Yugoslavia, which furthermore complicated women's self-identification as feminists. Being feminist was often seen as an affront to collectivism, as a selfish endeavor. In that regard, we must also recognize that the label of feminism has shifted for individuals over time; for example, Slapšak considered herself more of a dissident than a feminist in 1968, then later reversed her position to identify as a feminist in the 1980s during a period she called the "golden age for feminism" in Yugoslavia.[88] Conceptualizing feminist performance politics within the figure of Jugoslovenka helps me to bridge temporalities tied to various stages and terminologies in the history of women's resistance in Yugoslavia.

Performance works from the 1970s and early 1980s are fascinating because women's emphases on their bodies offered a different idea of the Yugoslav national body. This aesthetically and culturally unapologetic experimentation by women pushed the body and sexuality of women to the center of the art scenes, such as at the student cultural centers in Belgrade and Zagreb in the 1970s and Ljubljana in the 1980s. This was unprecedented in Yugoslavia. One might speculate that if it had been up to the government, the socialist body would have remained merely an implicitly male laborer's muscular, hard-working machine, building railways and bridges and happily working in factories, as was typical of the early phase of Yugoslav nationalist imaginaries of the new man, *homo Yugoslavikus*. Franko Dota's research has shown that the figure of *homo Yugoslavikus* changed within Yugoslavia itself over time, with the early phase of Yugoslav socialism connoting a more Stalinist idea of "an ultra-modernist neo-traditionalist sexual ideology that professed sexual purity and socialist orthodox morality in intimate relations." In the 1950s, following Tito's break from Stalin in 1948, this was replaced with a new idea of *homo Yugoslavikus* that was "no longer a Soviet duplicate, but neither too Americanized, suspended between the East and the West, destined to self-manage not only the factories, but also his intimate and sexual relations."[89] Jakovljević describes Yugoslavia's model of self-management as "a form of industrial democracy modeled after the examples of the worker's councils that emerged at the peak moments of revolutionary ferment, from the Paris Commune, to Petrograd's soviets, to the uprising in Budapest and the strikes of Turin of the 1920s."[90] The break with Stalin in 1948 motivated "the Yugoslav authorities" to move in a new direction, "to establish an alternative model of state socialism."[91] Jakovljević notes the effect such a political shift had on the art scene at Belgrade's Student Cultural Center (SKC), which although funded by the state, nevertheless granted "full artistic autonomy" to those "artists and art historians associated with the gallery."[92] In addition, many of those active at the SKC gallery were women, most prominently, among others, curators and art historians Bojana Pejić, Jasna Tijardović, Biljana Tomić, Marinela Koželj, and Dunja Blazević, and artists Marina Abramović and Katalin Ladik (who was a frequent guest from Novi Sad).

Discourses around *homo Yugoslavikus* are gendered even in 2021, and *homo Yugoslavikus* is usually assumed to be a male subject. How might our understanding of socialist embodiment change with a new look at women's contributions? Considering how feminist embodiment varied and shifted over time allows us to establish a more female-centered Yugoslav subjectivity. Of course, the title of Jugoslovenka was not categorically assigned to those women back then, whether they were partisans or New Yugoslav Feminists. Instead, I am using the term to find new ways of thinking through and acknowledging women's contributions and gauging what it might have meant to identify as female and be emancipated within the cultural milieu of Yugoslav socialism.

Gender and sexuality in the Yugoslav art scene: Jugoslovenka's subtle rise

Jugoslovenkas were important players in the avant-garde art scene of the 1970s and established the context and foundation of the many case studies in this book. Although images documenting art exhibitions and art groups often show one or two women in a sea of men, women curators, artists, and theorists were often doing the groundwork to include more representations and discussions of women's emancipation in the Yugoslav avant-garde art centers. A rare photograph by Goranka Matić from 1988 offers a tour de force array of Yugoslav women—including Žarana Papić, Ljubica Seka Stanivuk, Dunja Blažević, Goranka Matić, Marija Dragojlović, Dragica Vukadinović, Biljana Tomić, Bojana Pejić, Jasna Tijardović, and Nadica Seferović—whose work was influential in the 1970s and 1980s (Figure 0.6).[93] Many of these and other women brought the Yugoslav avant-garde art scenes to international recognition, especially in the spheres of performance, conceptual, and mail art practiced at various student cultural centers. The most thriving of these student cultural centers in the 1970s were in Belgrade (SKC), Zagreb (SC), and by the end of the 1970s, Ljubljana (ŠKUC). Feminist art historian and curator Suzana Milevska has noted how these histories differed significantly in relation to their locations. Belgrade was relevant for feminist history a decade before Ljubljana, with self-declared feminists such as Žarana Papić, Rada Iveković, Dunja Blažević, and Bojan Pejić gaining attention. The field of art and culture "was under the influence of feminist theory" with a woman president at the SKC in Belgrade, Dunja Blažević, who was the main protagonist of that feminist charge.[94] There, Blažević organized "Drug-ca" in 1978, the first feminist

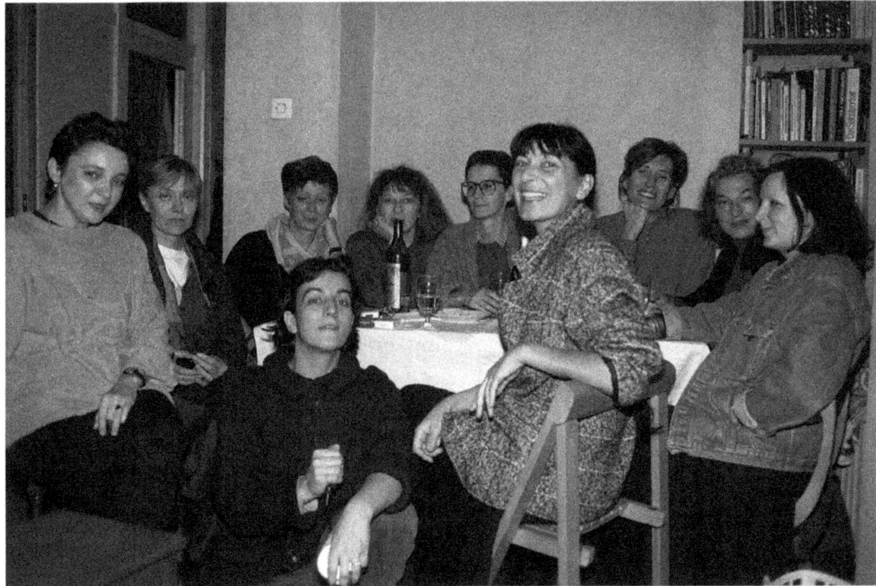

Goranka Matić, *Women's Party*, 1988.   **0.6**

conference in Eastern Europe that brought together local and international feminists to discuss the relationship of women's emancipation to socialism.[95] That same year, the SKC mounted *Comrade Woman*, the first exhibition devoted to women in Yugoslavia.

Whereas Belgrade is the focal point for most studies of Yugoslav feminism in culture, I want to begin with a different point of departure by emphasizing an exhibition in Zagreb that has thus far not been examined within the history of gender and sexuality in Eastern Europe: Želimir Koščević's *Exhibition of Women and Men* at the Galerija Studentskog Centra (Students' Center Gallery, SC) in 1969. *Exhibition of Women and Men* should be considered one of the first exhibitions probing questions of gender in the region. At the heels of the 1968 student protests in Yugoslavia, this exhibition was part of an emphasis that touched on the real lives of people living in cities and discarded the "out-of-touchness" of state-sponsored art. Confined to the plastic arts, state-sponsored art was regarded as a dogmatic extension of the country's political project. In contrast, contemporary artists embraced various modes of experimentation with their bodies to break from artistic traditionalism. In the discourse surrounding this embrace of the corporeal body, feminism has mostly been left out of the equation, which is not surprising, as we have already seen how feminist voices were often disparaged in the intellectual circles of the left in Yugoslavia at the time. But Yugoslav women still participated in the 1968 protests out of disenchantment with the promises of socialism and vigorously pushed their colleagues to recognize and address the role of gender-based inequality within Yugoslav socialism. It is within this context of a feminist investment in gender equality that I approach Koščević's *Exhibition of Women and Men*.

Koščević left the walls of the gallery empty and transformed the unsuspecting viewers into the living and breathing artworks of the exhibition. He stated: "Be the exhibition itself."[96] Drawing on the political ideology of socialist realism associated with the Eastern Bloc, Koščević enlivened the concept of art about life with the actual people that comprised socialism in Yugoslavia, provoking viewers to think beyond traditional art objects. The openly gay curator and art historian Davor Matičević wrote in 1978 that Koščević's exhibition was part of a new interest in a "shifting of the accent from the exhibit to the audience."[97] These new aesthetic directions, turning away from plastic arts and toward the context and specificity of reception, institution, and the artist's body, were indicative of the new directions in Yugoslav experimental, conceptual, and performance art that would thrive in the 1970s and which would influence feminist and queer art in the 1980s.[98] This specific New Art Practice under socialism, according to curator Marijan Susovski, was symptomatic of the fact "that the development of a progressive socialist system also required a new artistic language which was already being practiced in the world."[99]

Indeed, this type of provocative gesture in Koščević's *Exhibition of Women and Men* was typical of the conceptual art of the 1960s, such as Yves Klein's *The Void* (1958) at the Iris Clert Gallery in Paris, an installation that featured a space painted white and emptied of everything but the artist's aura. Moreover, art historian Katherine Ann Carl commented on how, for Koščević, *Exhibition of Women and Men* at SC was an important platform that invited "viewers to reflect on the space itself and the experimental programming for which it [SC] was becoming known."[100]

This line of thinking about Koščević's exhibition highlights his contribution to New Art Practice's emphasis on experimental intervention in the art/life barrier in the region.[101] I diverge in reading it for its implications for gender, even though Koščević was not motivated by feminism. The exhibition was one important marker of the burgeoning debates and conversations about gender happening at universities in Yugoslavia at the time and unfolding more dramatically in the 1970s at Yugoslavia's student cultural centers. Feminist theorist, artist, and curator Marina Gržinić has repeatedly argued that "the feminist experience in the 1970s laid the foundations for the avant-garde in art and culture in Belgrade and Zagreb."[102] What stands out about Koščević's intervention is not its conceptualization of art through a radical intervention into the institutional space of the gallery—along with a veneration of the aura of a singular artist—but rather its emphasis on common people and their gendered relations. Koščević made the Yugoslav context of the exhibition evident: "At this show you are the creation, you are the figuration, you are the socialistic [sic] realism."[103] This signified New Art Practice's distinctly socialist framework that valued equality among women and men in its ideological foundation. *Exhibition of Women and Men* was about Yugoslav subjects in this specific context of socialism, not universalizing subjects connoting generalities about philosophical shifts in art.

In another context, in Argentina during military dictatorship in 1968, the empty gallery took on an even more profound political meaning when artist Graciela Carnevale confined viewers in the gallery in her now infamous *Acción del Encierro (Lock-Up Action)*.[104] Carnevale's action was aimed at creating art that would force viewers to become bodies of resistance against General Juan Carlos Onganía's dictatorship and resulted in the shutdown of the exhibition. In Yugoslavia, which was under what many would consider a benevolent dictatorship, Koščević's exhibition was neither threatening nor shocking. But using the term "socialist realism" was in itself a provocative gesture toward the Yugoslav government and the larger international art world. Following Clement Greenberg's celebrated denouncement of socialist realism in his 1939 essay "Avant-Garde and Kitsch" in *Partisan Review*, American modernism was strongly invested in following that critique. Social realism was denounced as backwards because of the ways the USSR had instrumentalized the genre to idolize Joseph Stalin, and abstraction was considered the way forward in the immediate post-1945 era. Greenbergian abstraction penetrated museums internationally, being marketed as a universalist and internationalist project, but it was motivated by unspoken and implicit nationalistic, pro-democratic, and capitalist values. The Yugoslavian art academies had also abandoned socialist realism, in part to distinguish themselves from the USSR, given its negative reputation. As Jakovljević has pointed out, the "cultural establishment was quick to marginalize and ridicule its representatives" in the 1950s.[105] However, Jakovljević has shown that this "dethroning" of socialist realism was "incomplete at best."[106] He argues that socialist realism was not merely a style in art and culture, but has to be seen as "a vital part of a political economy" that was "engineered from scratch with a precisely defined purpose and place within society."[107] As such, the process of dethroning was often only surface level and involved new modes of censorship and political manipulation.

Art historian Ješa Denegri has also commented on this tension, recalling how "the political authorities" in Yugoslavia had denigrated abstraction by the early 1960s, a move that had "fatal consequences for the art climate as a whole."[108] The authorities demonized "the entirety of abstract art" and considered it "an unacceptable foreign implant in the supposedly healthy mind of the national culture."[109] In fact, Tito repeatedly expressed his dismay about the development of modernist abstraction, calling it "irreconcilable with our socialist ethics" in his 1963 New Year's speech.[110] Nevertheless in line with a more "progressive" socialist state during the Cold War, abstraction was also to have a socialist function in Yugoslavia, commemorating and celebrating the Yugoslav nation and its heroes, a dogma that experimental artists in Belgrade, Zagreb, and Ljubljana all rejected. Some of those celebratory moments are evident in what Videkanić has called nonaligned modernism, representing "efforts made by the Yugoslavs to move away from the dangers of the growing Cold War divide and at the same time maintain the ideals on which the country was built, namely, antifascism, anti-imperialism, and anticapitalism."[111] Nonaligned modernism was especially evident in state-sponsored art events, such as the Ljubljana Biennale, which as early as the 1950s and into the 1970s invited a large number of non-white and non-Yugoslav artists from Africa, Asia, and the Americas, as well as Egypt, India, Turkey, Japan, and Mexico.[112] Videkanić's research also shows that Yugoslav art was more diverse and included more representation of women in the Ljubljana Biennale than in the German exhibition *documenta*. She notes that the Ljubljana Biennale was exceptional in its "representation of women," which "grew from around thirty in the first several exhibitions to more than seventy-five in 1977, representing around 18 percent of artists."[113] In comparison to the West, "out of 353 artists at documenta in 1964 only seven were women [2 percent], and out of 152 artists [at *documenta*] in 1968 only four were women [2.6 percent]."[114]

She concludes: "From the perspective of the postwar international art scene and its ideological shifts during the twentieth century, the Ljubljana Biennale, in comparison, was an enormously diverse exhibition that preceded calls for diversity in contemporary art that would become central to Western art discourses in the late 1990s." She added: "Ljubljana was ahead of its time."[115]

Despite these important political advances toward racial and gender diversity in the arts in Yugoslavia, the country's avant-garde scene resisted dogmatic and more conservative styles associated with nonaligned cultural production sponsored by the state, and instead pushed against state-endorsed art by introducing experimentation into official art spaces and beyond.[116] Koščević remembers that he wanted to disrupt "the really boring and conservative local art scene," and show his "radical orientation to young artists."[117] In June 1970, Koščević organized *Akcija Total* (*Action Total*), an exhibition-action that took place throughout the city of Zagreb. Koščević wanted to break out of the confines of the gallery, and extend its reach to the broader urban public. Instead of inviting the viewers to come into the gallery, this exhibition would confront them on the streets. Comprised of advertisements and propaganda, Koščević hung black posters featuring nothing but minimal geometric shapes designed by Boris Bućan and Davor Tomičić, and he also distributed leaflets with the heading "The Draft Decree on the Democratization of Art."[118] OZEHA, the official media house of Zagreb, granted Koščević permission to hang his posters throughout Zagreb, authorization that made *Akcija Total* possible.[119] To realize the exhibition, Koščević and other artists went onto the streets and distributed the pamphlets to people going about their everyday business. Koščević explained that he "made a decision to provoke public opinion with *Akcija Total*," and he characterized his motivation as "utopic, nevertheless, but quite nice."[120] He also remembered that "there was no repression (administrative or by police)," and, in fact, the point of his exhibition was not to disrupt Yugoslavian politics.[121] Instead, he placed the emphasis on eradicating the idea of the closed artwork, creating art that "does something other than sit on its ass in a museum," as Claes Oldenburg had written in his 1961 essay, "I am for an Art."[122] *Akcija Total* asked "galleries, museums, exhibition halls, pavilions, … [to] become active art houses, culture houses," not just spaces where "thousands and thousands of images, sculptures, graphics, countless applied art objects, luxury designs" would be stored.[123]

But *Akcija Total*, although open to everyone, centered on the liberation of art from the constraints of institutions and did not consider specifically what such democratization of art might have to do with women. At this time, the cultural template of Yugoslav heroes also included very few women and was, in itself, gendered masculine.[124] Exceptions included sculptures like Antun Augustinčić's *Peace* monument (1952–1954), designed to represent Yugoslavia at the United Nations (UN) Headquarters in New York.[125] According to

Videkanić, Augustinčić superseded the traditional "male figure of a warrior representing political and military prowess with a strong female figure representing leadership toward peace," with the artist's explanation that "there would be more chance for peace if women, instead of men, made political decisions about it."[126] Such attention to the importance of women's contributions is pivotal, especially if one is to consider the symbolic weight of a Yugoslav woman warrior—Jugoslovenka—representing the Yugoslav nation in New York.

In her discussion of photographs of women warriors from the 18th and 19th century in the Balkans, archived in the Fund of the Brothers Manaki in Macedonia, [127] Milevska emphasizes the challenge that comes with analyzing and understanding the image of the warrior woman. She found that one of the most troubling differences between the photographs of warrior men and warrior women is that the women are strictly in static poses with an "absent-minded gaze" that casts "doubt in the reliability of these women, even though they are known historical figures."[128] Milevska also points to Linda Nochlin's discussion of warrior women in *Representing Women* (1999), but notes that Nochlin's examples were based on paintings, not photographs. Milevska argues that photography is as allegorical as painting, "even though we intuitively believe the photographic images are less mediated and therefore closer to *the real.*"[129] For Milevska, this means that in addition to Nochlin's distinguishing between the allegorical and real, the photographs of Balkan women also bring up "the staged."[130] The most fascinating of Milevska's examples is a flag that depicts a woman holding a flag of the Ilinden Republic, the first and short-lived Balkan republic "crushed by the Ottomans" after just ten days in 1903.[131] Milevska likens the woman depicted on the flag—heroically holding a flag—to allegories of women as nation during the French Revolution.[132]

In Augustinčić's vision of Jugoslovenka, she too remains a heroine, an allegory of peace representing the young socialist nation rather than an emancipatory subject, while simultaneously signaling women's leading roles in the formation of Yugoslavia. Ten years later, Augustinčić's *Peace* monument would be reproduced in mirror image on the red hundred-dinar banknote for almost three decades (1965–1993), and as such, it was more of a photographic image that would circulate within Yugoslav society than a sculpture most of the country's citizens would never get to see. It is not without significance that banknotes—because of how they circulate from hand to hand—became an important site of aesthetic and political strategy for mail artists in the Cold War era. Artists often created fake banknotes or altered existing ones, sending them through the mail or attempting to introduce them into fiduciary circulation. As such, banknotes offered a connection to everyday life in the sense that they have actual applications within society in their exchange for goods, while individual artists often transformed them into artworks. In 1990, for example,

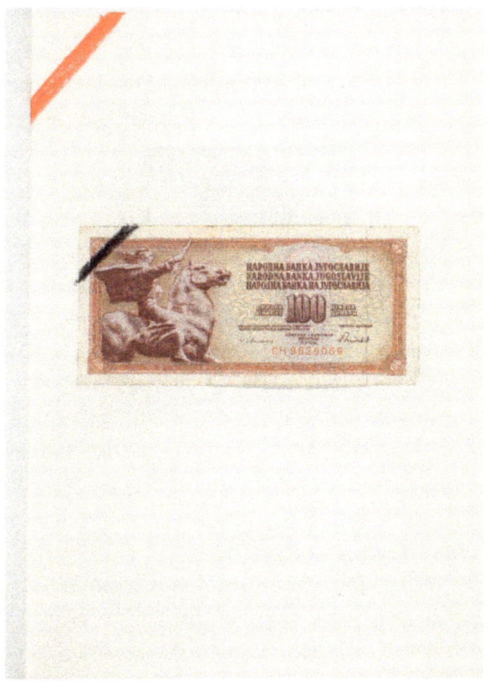

Mladen Stilinović, page in *EX-Maj 75*, 1990.

0.7

a special issue of the samizdat publication *Maj 75* (*EX-Maj 75*) featured a work by Zagreb-based artist Mladen Stilinović in which he used that hundred-dinar bill as an artwork by slightly altering it with the mark of a black line on its upper-left corner, echoed by the same type of line in red on the upper-left corner of the page (Figure 0.7). While Stilinović's conceptual work was highly analytical, here I only want to stress the fact that the actual hundred-dinar bill circulated in this way in the arts, and that in 1990, Stilinović's inclusion of the Yugoslav woman as an advocate for peace was profoundly prophetic. I will return to the discussion of *Maj 75* in Chapter 1, but Stilinović's work in this *Maj 75* issue can be read as anticipating Yugoslav women's crucial role in peace-making efforts during the 1990s Yugoslav wars, such as that of the Belgrade-based feminist and peace activist group Women in Black, which I discuss in Chapter 5. This group of women was on the streets protesting the wars in the early 1990s and organized mass support for rape victims from all the former republics of Yugoslavia, efforts that were loyal to a united Yugoslavia's multiethnic foundation and embrace of transnationalism.

In the case of Augustinčić's *Peace* monument, the banknote carrying this allegorical image of Peace in the form of a warrior Jugoslovenka was a constant marker of Yugoslavia's internationalism, as it referenced its connection to the UN in New York. But submerged in the socialist red color, Jugoslovenka is leading the ideological charge of spreading—and fighting for—socialism, a nationalist political project summed up in the idea of peace on behalf of Tito's Yugoslavia. Augustinčić's *Peace* monument on the hundred-dinar note is allegorical both in the sense that it uses the female body as embodiment of a nation, not unlike other forms of nationalism that came before it, and also as a photograph circulating through the hands of Yugoslav residents for decades, who thus recognize the Yugoslav woman as a lead character in the spread of socialist values of peace internationally. It could be argued that artists in the 1960s and 1970s also sought to touch this everyday sphere with their work and to circulate art, much like a banknote, in novel ways that would be relevant to the society around them in that moment but without interference by the government. Breaking beyond the confines of gendered allegorical instrumentalization in art might have been one side effect of that impulse, even if not yet fully conceptualized.

In that regard, it is worth pointing out that Koščević's *Exhibition of Women and Men* was not heroic; in fact, one might call it banal to its core. What could be more trivial than bodies standing around in an empty space? The lack of heroism offers a way into analyzing aspects of the process of art making—and its publics—rather than the mobilization of an idea or political conviction. *Exhibition of Women and Men* stands out as an exhibition because it could be said that it invited the participants to treat binary gender and its modes of lived embodiment as social construction or "art." "Beware, your eyes are on you," Koščević announced. "You are the body in space, you're [the] body that moves, you are a kinetic sculpture, you are spatial-dynamism. Art is not adjacent to you, it either does not exist or you are the art."[133] By transforming viewers into art, one could argue that Koščević's exhibition posed a tongue-in-cheek hyper-socialist realist approach. Derisive of the political ideology that for various socialist countries necessitated the celebration of socialist realism, Koščević enlivened the concept of socialist realism by inserting the actual people—who made socialism what it is—as art into the gallery space. But this gesture was, at the same time, multivalent: the framing auspices and directives of the space insisted that men and women were equally the makers and subjects of art; they were asked to suspend their inhibitions and consider themselves art, to decide to be art, to exist as art, and in this way re-examine their lives through the lens of artistic experimentation. Their common title was people and art, with only one differentiating function: gender.

Today, we might read Koščević's exhibition as an indication that gender, like the bodies that inhabit and perform it, is a "kinetic sculpture" that changes depending on "spatial dynamism." The curatorial framing invokes the implicit performance of gender. Instead of depicting women as subjects to be looked at (or celebrated as heroines of the nation), *Exhibition of Women and Men* signaled that *art as idea* could be indiscriminate and did not have to favor male over female. This prioritizing of gender as a conceptual intervention, even if unintentional and without a specific political agenda for Koščević, differentiated Yugoslavia from its Western counterparts in avant-garde art. Most importantly, a new reading of Koščević's exhibition opens up the feminist project in Yugoslavia, as well as the unique recognition of gender that was even more palpable in the gendered configurations at the SKC in Belgrade. The SKC's more overt political motivations move the *Exhibition of Women and Men* into an era of change: the recognition of women's voices and agency within the broader Marxist art circles in the cultural spaces of Yugoslavia. There, as elsewhere in the world, a discussion of the position of women in the political project of socialist emancipation was poignantly missing, something Koščević's exhibition also did not address. In this regard, key Yugoslav feminist figures began to intervene not only in the sphere of art, but also in that of pop culture.

Five approaches to Jugoslovenka's feminist performance politics: chapter overviews

"I am Jugoslovenka!" Feminist Performance Politics during and after Yugoslav Socialism is devoted to analyzing the work of feminist leaders as protagonists within the Yugoslav art context, following the bold visual provocation posed by Sanja Iveković's revision of the Yugoslav flag, *Nova Zvijezda (New Star)*, in 1983 (Figure 0.8), in which the artist replaced the signature red socialist star with hair arranged in the triangular shape of a female pubis. By superseding the red star with female genitalia after a decade of feminist work in the 1970s, and just three years after the death of Tito in 1980, Iveković's flag connoted both profound insight and foresight: Yugoslav socialism not only owed its inception to women, but the country and its unity depended on women's leadership to persist, as if to imply that the country ought to have looked to women for emancipatory politics and not the male-centered patriarchal nationalism so pervasive and destructive in the 1980s.[134] To push this analysis even further, it could be argued that *New Star* established feminism's kinship to the transnational and multiethnic politics of socialist Yugoslavia, and that in the 1970s and 1980s it was women who transported this legacy of pacifism, communism, and anti-nationalism and strove for a more just and egalitarian society, as if to replace Yugoslavia's great socialist mantra of "Brotherhood and Unity" with a feminist "Sisterhood and Unity."

This sisterhood, however, was in no way uniform or one-dimensional. As this book shows, the women considered here did not belong to a cohesive movement or a group adhering to the same set of principles. What set these

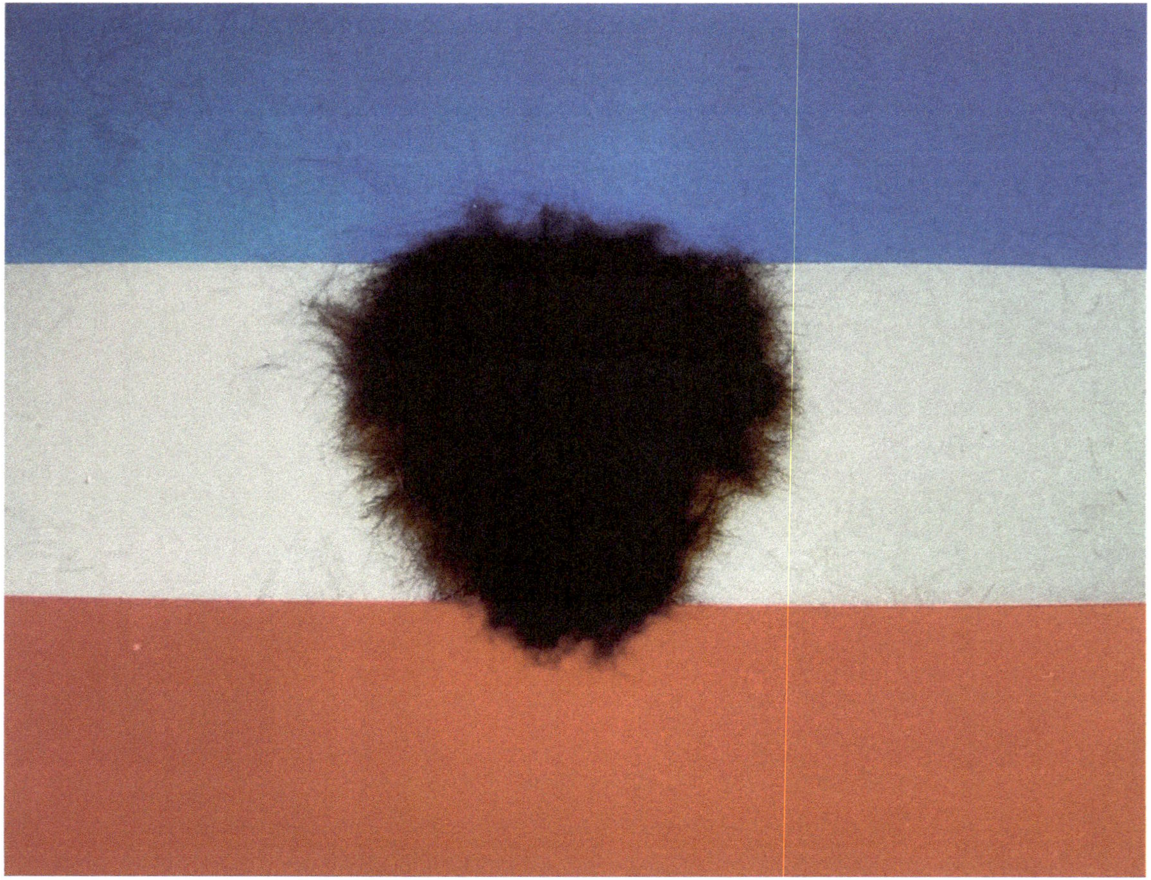

0.8 Sanja Iveković, *New Star*, 1983.
Collage made of printed paper with former Yugoslavia's flag colors. The star is replaced by hair.

women apart from feminists in the West was that they constituted a generation of women whose mothers bore the legacy of partisan resistance to fascism and helped build socialist Yugoslavia and establish its progressive laws for women's rights. Many of those women saw their rights diminish shortly after the establishment of Yugoslavia. But progress for women, such as maternity leave, abortion rights, and literacy, was still unequivocally tied to the Yugoslav project. As such, the generation of women artists, curators, theorists, historians, singers, beauty queens, snipers, and activists discussed in this book inherited the complex cultural legacy of both emancipation and traditionalism from their mothers. This was a contentious relationship that involved a deep political identification with Yugoslav principles of socialist liberation alongside an equally deep mistrust of the patriarchal ideologies that shaped and limited women's experiences in Yugoslavia.

Broadly, the chapters in this book offer case studies of feminist performance politics and emancipatory work within five frames of reference. In Chapter 1, I focus on the avant-garde art circles in the 1970s and early 1980s in major cities, such as Belgrade, Zagreb, and Ljubljana, and single out specific artworks that put the complicated history of feminist resistance into dialogue with performance and body-centered work by women artists. Chapter 2 turns toward three superstar women in culture whose careers were launched in Yugoslavia: Lepa Brena, Esma Redžepova, and Marina Abramović. This chapter discusses these three women's varied relationships to questions of emancipation in Yugoslavia and unfolds the complicated position of Orientalism in Yugoslav culture through their individual performance works. An analysis of the intersection between feminist emancipatory strategies and Orientalism offers insights into how Yugoslavia's brands of "multiculturalism" and transnationalism were uniquely tied to the country's socialist paradigm of an egalitarian society. In Chapter 3, the emergence of a "queer" Jugoslovenka is front and center, including a discussion of her context in the 1980s and her legacy for the twenty-first century. This chapter gives a visual history of the Yugoslav lesbian and queer movement and traces its influences in contemporary visual culture and art, including the surfacing of transgender resistance and queer life in rural areas. Chapter 4 orients itself toward a male-dominated group that has become one of the most well-known collectives coming out of Yugoslavia in the 1980s: Neue Slowenische Kunst (New Slovenian Art, NSK). Offering a feminist critique and rereading of the collective and specific works, Chapter 4 hones in on the principal role of Eda Čufer and the Gledališče Sester Scipion Nasice (Scipion Nasice Sisters Theater, SNST, an NSK subgroup) active in the 1980s. While this chapter reveals the woman question to be a "blind spot" in an otherwise radically critical art collective, it also offers a rereading of NSK's theater subgroup through the lens of gender by honing in on feminine spirituality as a form of covert resistance against state-mandated nationalism.

The last chapter focuses on understanding how the Yugoslav wars impacted Yugoslav feminism and anti-nationalism in the early 1990s and thereafter, including the emergence of one of the most important women activist groups of the region, Women in Black. Centering on women's distressed positions as survivors of civil war and the loss of a homeland, this chapter expands the field of inquiry to include popular images of Yugoslav women during the wars, including beauty contestants and soldiers/snipers. In this regard, Nasta Rojc's self-portrait holding a gun (Figure 0.1), the image with which I began this introduction, holds kinship to the women some eighty years later fighting against patriarchal military aggression. Chapter 5 ends with case studies of women performance artists whose works touch on the wide-ranging challenges Jugoslovenkas face in the post-Yugoslav, postwar, neoliberal space: increased homophobia; immigration nightmares; diasporic loneliness; heightened racism, especially for Roma women; and a return to Yugoslav legacies of emancipatory strength and antifascist resistance.

Notes

1 In 1945, socialist Yugoslavia replaced the Yugoslav monarchy and deposed King Peter II. It was named a Federal People's Republic of Yugoslavia. In 1963, after constitutional reform, it was renamed Socialist Federal Republic of Yugoslavia.

2 For a more comprehensive discussion of homosexuality in Yugoslavia, see Franko Dota interviewed for *Gayten LGBT*. "Kako je bilo biti gej u Jugoslaviji? Pričali smo s čovjekom koji je upravo doktorirao na tu temu," *Gayten LGBT* (October 16, 2017): www.transserbia.org/seksulanost/1301-kako-je-bilo-biti-gej-u-jugoslaviji-pricali-smo-s-covjekom-koji-je-upravo-doktorirao-na-tu-temu (accessed 06/20/2020).

3 Sabrina P. Ramet, "In Tito's Time," in Sabrina Ramet, ed., *Gender Politics in the Western Balkans: Women and Society in Yugoslavia and the Yugoslav Successor States* (University Park: Pennsylvania State University Press, 1999), 96.

4 Jelena Petrović, *Women's Authorship in Interwar Yugoslavia: The Politics of Love and Struggle* (London: Palgrave, 2018), 38.

5 Petrović summarizes the main political point of that first 1936 issue in ibid., 43.

6 Jelena Batinić, *Women and Yugoslav Partisans: A History of World War II Resistance* (Cambridge: Cambridge University Press, 2015), 69.

7 Jasna Jakšić in conversation with the author, June 11, 2019. See also Darija Alujević and Dunja Nekić, "Women's Art Club and Women's Group Exhibitions in Zagreb from 1928 until 1940," *Artl@s Bulletin* 8, no. 1, *Women Artists Shows. Salons. Societies (1870s–1970s)* (2019), article 11. The authors note: "Ljubo Babić (1890–1974) was a Croatian painter, graphic artist, theatrical set and costume designer, teacher, art historian, critic, and museum curator.

As an art critic he was extremely negative in his articles on women in arts, especially in fine arts, and through positions he held in various institutions he effectively undermined the Club's efforts to leave a mark in Croatian art history by excluding its members' oeuvres from subsequent overviews of art history in Yugoslavia." See Chapter 1, endnote 16.

8 Jasna Jakšić in conversation with the author, June 11, 2019.

9 I am indebted to Suzana Tratnik for this detail; she retrieved this information from Dubravka Đurić. Tratnik in e-mail correspondence with the author, March 25, 2020. Translation by the author. The information about the photograph was later confirmed by Đurić and Šuvaković, in an e-mail correspondence with the author, January 27, 2021.

10 Translation by the author.

11 Ann Cvetkovich focuses on the gay and lesbian archives, pointing to the urgency of a "radical archive of emotion in order to document intimacy, sexuality, love, and activism—all areas of experience that are difficult to chronicle through the materials of a traditional archive." See Ann Cvetkovich, *An Archive of Feelings: Trauma, Sexuality, and Lesbian Public Cultures* (Durham, NC: Duke University Press, 2003), 241.

12 Mirjana Karanović, "Yubilej: Ja sam Jugoslovenka," *Peščanik* (December 12, 2018): https://pescanik.net/yubilej-ja-sam-jugoslovenka/ (accessed 12/12/2018). Translation by the author.

13 While the first rituals around the relay baton began in 1945, Tito declared May 25 as "Youth Day" in 1956. Tito was born on May 7, 1892, but his birthday celebration was moved to May 25 to commemorate his escape from a German Nazi attack on May 25, 1944, in Dvar, Bosnia. For more information of Tito and the Youth Day celebration, see "Remembering 25 May, Dan Mladosti (Day of Youth)," on Peter Korchnak's webpage, Remembering Yugoslavia: Journeys through the Memory of a Disappeared Country: https://rememberingyugoslavia.com/dan-mladosti/ (accessed 04/03/2020).

14 Although 1988 was the last time the Youth Day was celebrated, it no longer featured the Youth Baton, the army, or children from elementary school. See Branislav Jakovljević, *Alienation Effects: Performance and Self-Management in Yugoslavia, 1945–91* (Ann Arbor: University of Michigan Press, 2016), 273.

15 Ibid., 35.

16 Ibid., 36.

17 Ibid., 74. Jakovljević discusses his ideas of the baroque state through the work of Spanish literary critic José Antonio Maravall, in particular his book *Culture of the Baroque: Analysis of a Historical Structure* (1975), originally published in Spanish, *La cultura del Barroco* (Barcelona: Ariel, 1975).

18 Ibid.

19 Ibid.

20 Ibid.

21 The Women's Antifascist Front of Yugoslavia was founded in 1942. It was a Yugoslav antifascist organization led by women partisan fighters.

22 Batinić, *Women and Yugoslav Partisans*, 69. Emphasis by Batinić.

23 Ibid. Emphasis by Batinić.

24 Chiara Bonfiglioli's MA thesis, "Remembering the Conference 'Drugarica Zena. Zensko Pitanje—Novi Pristup?'/'Comrade Woman: The Women's Question: A New Approach?' Thirty Years After" (Utrecht University, Women's Studies, 2007/2008), 36. Bonfiglioli's relies on Lydia Sklevicky's research here.

25 Ramet, "In Tito's Time," 94.

26 Ibid.

27 Ibid., 95. Ramet adds here that in 1970s, one of the first things feminists criticized was the education system. For example in Zagreb, the Women and Society group was highly critical of the education system.

28 Rada Iveković and Slavenka Drakulić-Ilić, "YUGOSLAVIA: Neofeminism—and its 'Six Mortal Sins,'" in Robin Morgan, ed., *Sisterhood is Global* (1984; New York: The Feminist Press, 1996), 735.

29 Batinić, *Women and Yugoslav Partisans*, 257.

30 Ibid.

31 Inga Muscio, *Cunt: A Declaration of Independence*, 2nd ed. (Emeryville, CA: Seal Press, 2002), xxiv–xxv.

32 This is important because my sister and I both were young women coming from the Yugoslav context living in Germany as immigrants. We relied on their emancipatory strength in teaching us how to fight unwanted advances by men as we were learning to navigate life in precarious and often unsafe places, such as in a refugee camps and social housing, and we held unpredictable immigration statuses that required frequent moves and offered no stable future.

33 Petrović, *Women's Authorship in Interwar Yugoslavia*, 5.

34 Ibid.

35 Branislava Anđelković and Branislav Dimitrijević, "The Final Decade: Art, Society, Trauma and Normality," in *On Normality: Art in Serbia 1989–2001* (Belgrade: Museum of Contemporary Art, 2005), 101.

36 Bojana Pejić, "And Now Let's Remember … Yugoslavia," in Marina Abramović, *The Cleaner* (Berlin: Hatje Cantz, 2017), 253.

37 Ibid.

38 Ibid.

39 Karol Radziszewski, "Interview with Leonida Kovač," in Karol Radziszewski, ed., "Zagreb: Queering the Museum," special issue *Dik Fagazine* 10 (2016), 76–77. Later in the interview she explains that she had experienced homophobia at the Contemporary Museum of Art in Zagreb, where she worked for fifteen years and "smuggl[ed] queer topics into all of my important exhibits." At the end of her career at the museum, an unnamed male curator at the museum had told her (she paraphrased): "that there had been enough of my lesbian exhibits, and that the Museum was branded with lesbianism because of my lesbian exhibits." See page 76.

40 Leonida Kovač notes that Delimar had made statements like this in public. Radziszewski, "Interview with Leonida Kovač," 60.

41 Translation by the author. I. L., "Žena-hrabrost otišla u legend," *Novosti* (September 14, 2010): www.novosti.rs/vesti/naslovna/aktuelno.69.html: 300102-Zena-hrabrost-otisla-u-legendu (accessed 05/23/2019).

42 Birth name: Željko Ražnatović.

43 Ana Dević, "Theatre of Diversity and Avant-Garde in Late Socialist Yugoslavia and Beyond: Paradoxes of the Disintegration and Cultural Subversion," in Jana Dolečki, Senad Halilbašić, and Stefan Hulfeld, eds., *Theatre in the Context of the Yugoslav Wars* (London: Palgrave Macmillan, 2018), 209.

44 Translation by the author. I. L., "Žena-hrabrost otišla u legend."

45 Translation by the author. Ekipa "Blica," "Heroj otpora koga su svi zaboravili," *Blic* (September 16, 2010): www.blic.rs/vesti/reportaza/heroj-otpora-koga-su-svi-zaboravili/q777vr4 (accessed 05/23/2019).

46 Chiara Bonfiglioli, "Revolutionary Networks: Women's Political and Social Activism in Cold War Italy and Yugoslavia (1945–1957)" (PhD dissertation, Utrecht University, 2012), 26.

47 Ibid.

48 Svetlana Slapšak, "Mein Feminismus ist eine logische Konsequenz von 1968," in Boris Kanzleiter and Krunoslav Stojaković, eds., *1968 in Yugoslawien: Studentendproteste und kutlturelle Avantgarde zwischen 1960 und 1975* (Bonn: Dietz, 2008), 97. Elsewhere, Slapšak identified one of her co-conspirators for this imagined action as "janitor Steve" ("spremač po imenu Steva"), who worked at the university. According to Slapšak, he frequently ridiculed Tito in performances that were extremely popular. She notes that she considered disguising herself as an athlete and stealing a relay baton on Youth Day, and then bringing it to the college yard. See Slapšak, "Kako smo mrzeli Tita," in *Peščanik* (April 6, 2010): https://pescanik.net/kako-smo-mrzeli-tita/ (accessed 06/10/2019).

49 Slapšak, "Mein Feminismus," 97.

50 Bojana Videkanić, "First and Last Emperor: Representations of the President, Bodies of the Youth," in Breda Luthar and Maruša Pušnik, eds., *Remembering Utopia: The Culture of Everyday Life in Yugoslavia* (Washington, DC: New Academic Publishing, 2010), 50–51.

51 Slapšak, "Kako smo mrzeli Tita."

52 Batinić, *Women and Yugoslav Partisans*, 105.

53 Ibid., 113.

54 Ibid., 111.

55 Tito quoted in ibid., 112.

56 Ibid., 123.

57 Ibid., 66.

58 Ibid.

59 Ibid., 137.

60 This dynamic can include gendered violence. In this regard, "femme lesbianism" has become a form of resistance, as well as vulnerability. Rebecca Ann Rugg identifies "femme lesbianism" as "an identity of potential danger and violence." She adds: "Unfortunately, it seems to me that I catch the most fever

for my feminine gender expression from other dykes, the people with whom, for me, the stakes are highest. The risks a feminine person takes in a male dominant culture should not be replayed in dyke communities." See Rebecca Ann Rugg, "How Does She Look?" in Laura Harris and Elizabeth Crocker, eds., *Femme: Feminists, Lesbians and Bad Girls* (New York: Routledge, 2013), 184.

61 Quoted in Batinić, *Women and Yugoslav Partisans*, 65.
62 Petrović, *Women's Authorship*, 40.
63 Ibid.
64 Batinić, *Women and Yugoslav Partisans*, 109.
65 Ibid., 111.
66 Ibid., 113.
67 Petrović, *Women's Authorship*, 40.
68 Slapšak, "Mein Feminismus," 96. The year 1970 is mentioned as the date of censorship in a *Nedeljnik* interview: Svetlana Slapšak, "Svetlana Slapšak: Još sebi čestitam što nisam poštovala Ćosića i Palavestru," *Nedeljnik* (December 22, 2016): https://arhiva.nedeljnik.rs/nedeljnik/portalnews/svetlana-slapsak-jos-sebi-cestitam-sto-nisam-postovala-cosica-i-palavestru (accessed 03/12/2019).
69 Slapšak, "Mein Feminismus," 99.
70 Ibid., 98. Translation by the author.
71 Jakovljević, *Alienation Effects*, 180–181. Here, Jakovljević cites sociologist Mira Bogdanović, who points to the fact that Yugoslavian "dissidence" had little value to the Western anti-USSR propaganda, or what she called the "Cold War industry of anti-communist consciousness." Jakovljević adds: "Being useless in conducting large-scale ideological warfare, the internal critics of Yugoslav socialism were left without the support of the powerful network of the 'Cold War industry of anticommunist consciousness' and were exposed to the winds of internal Yugoslav politics." See *Alienation Effects*, 180.
72 Bonfiglioli, "Revolutionary Networks," 75. Bonfiglioli relies on Jane Slaughter's *Women and the Italian Resistance, 1943–1945.* (Denver, Colorado: Arden Press, 1997).
73 Zsófia Lóránd, *The Feminist Challenge to the Socialist State in Yugoslavia* (London: Palgrave Macmillan, 2018), 94.
74 Slapšak, "Mein Feminismus," 101–102. She identified Neda Nikolić as Bube Rakić's girlfriend.
75 Borka Pavićević, "1941, 1968, 1978, 2018," *Danas* (March 11, 2018): https://www.danas.rs/kolumna/borka-pavicevic/1941-1968-1978-2018/ (accessed 05/23/2019). Translation by the author. Original: "1968. u dvorištu Filozofskog fakulteta, toga se trenutka vrlo dobro sećam, Neda Nikolić je prva rekla nešto o feminizmu i bila je odmah izviždana, to jednostavno nije došlo u obzir i argumenti su bili sledeći: nije sada trenutak, sada se bavimo važnim stvarima, drugo je bila teorijska važnost našeg pokreta, za razliku od feminizma koji je teorijski lagan i beznačajan, i treće – šta se vi žene gurate u prvi red, pa imate sva prava."

76 Vesna Kesić, "Confessions of a Yugo-Nostalgic Witch," in Tanya Renne, ed., *Ana's Land: Sisterhood in Eastern Europe* (Boulder, CO: Westview Press, 1997), 197.

77 Ibid. Kesić gives an explanation of how "pička" could be translated: "a vulgar popular term for women's genitalia." "Pička" is also a term often used like "bitch" in English, but because of the aggressive charge behind kicking in the "pička," "cunt" seems like the most fitting translation here.

78 Jelena Vesić, "The Conference Comrade Woman: Art Program (On Marxism and Feminism and their Mutual Political Discontents)," Parallel Chronologies: An Archive of East European Exhibitions: http://tranzit.org/exhibitionarchive/post_keywords/feminism/ (accessed 03/18/2019).

79 Adriana Zaharijević, "The Strange Case of Yugoslav Feminism: Feminism and Socialism in 'the East,'" in Dijana Jelača, Maša Kolanović, and Danijela Lugarić, eds., *The Cultural Life of Capitalism in Yugoslavia: (Post) Socialism and Its Other* (London: Palgrave Macmillan, 2017), 276.

80 Ibid., 276.

81 Bojana Pejić, "Proletarians of All Countries, Who Washes Your Socks? Equality, Dominance and Difference in Eastern European Art," in Bojana Pejić, ed., *Gender Check: Femininity and Masculinity in the Art of Eastern Europe* (Cologne: Walter König, 2009), 26.

82 Kesić, "Confessions of a Yugo-Nostalgic Witch," 197.

83 Lóránd, *The Feminist Challenge*, 2.

84 Ibid., 2–3.

85 Ibid., 2.

86 Bonfiglioli, "Remembering the Conference," 35.

87 See Batinić, *Women and Yugoslav Partisans*.

88 Slapšak, "Mein Feminismus," 102. Translation by the author.

89 Franko Dota, "An Ambiguous Affair: The Yugoslav Socialist State and its Homosexuals" [Lecture] University of Amsterdam, 2015.

90 Branislav Jakovljević, "The Howling Wilderness of the Maladaptive Struggle in Belgrade in New York," *ARTMargins* 7, no. 2 (June 2018), 23.

91 Ibid.

92 Ibid.

93 Jasna Tijardović identified this photo, taken in Goranka Matić's apartment in Novi Beograd. Tijardović in conversation with the author, July 10, 2019.

94 Suzana Milevska is citing Marina Grzinić here, see "The 'Silkworm Cocoon' Gender Difference and the Impact of Visual Culture on Contemporary Art in the Balkans," in Pejić, ed., *Gender Check*, 231–232.

95 This feminist conference is well documented in Bonfiglioli's "Remembering the Conference." Also, see Lóránd, *The Feminist Challenge*.

96 Cited and translated by Katherine Ann Carl, from *Novine*, No. 8 (1968–1969), 29. In "Aoristic Avant-Garde: Experimental Art in 1960s and 1970s Yugoslavia" (PhD dissertation, State University of New York, Stony Brook, 2009), 59.

97 Davor Matičević, "The Zagreb Circle," in Marijan Susovski, ed., *The New Art Practice in Yugoslavia 1966–1978* (Zagreb: Gallery of Contemporary Art Zagreb, 1978), 23.

98 Ibid.

99 Marijan Susovski, "The Seventies and the Group of Six Artists," in Janka Vukmir, ed., *Grupa Šestorice Autora* (Zagreb: SCCA Zagreb, 1998), 19.

100 Carl, "Aoristic Avant-Garde," 59.

101 See Susovski, ed., *The New Art Practice.*

102 Marina Gržinić, "Feminism and Performance in the Territory of Ex-Yugoslavia," in Laura B. Lengel and John T. Warren, eds., *Casting Gender: Women and Performance in Intercultural Contexts,* Critical Intercultural Communication Studies 7 (New York: Peter Lang, 2005), 165.

103 Carl, "Aoristic Avant-Garde," 59.

104 Translation found on the Hammer Museum's website. The description of the works states: "For this work, Carnevale invited people to the opening of an exhibition; once they were inside the venue, she padlocked the door and left. A passerby broke a window, allowing the visitors to escape. The event took place during the dictatorship of General Juan Carlos Onganía (1966–70), and the police shut it down. Carnevale forced the audience to participate in her work. She replicated the violence of daily life in order to raise the political consciousness of the passive viewer." See "Graciela Carnevale, Acción del encierro (Lock-Up Action)": https://hammer.ucla.edu/radical-women/art/art/accion-del-encierro-lock-up-action (accessed 01/19/2020).

105 Jakovljević, *Alienation Effects,* 94.

106 Ibid. Jakovljević points to the complicated history and tension between socialist modernism and socialist realism in the context of theater, and offers an analysis of literary critic Sveta Lukić's commentary on socialist modernism and socialist realism, 94–95.

107 Ibid., 9.

108 Ješa Denegri, "Inside or Outside 'Socialist Modernism'? Radical Views on the Yugoslav Art Scene, 1950–1970," in Dubravka Đurić and Miško Šuvaković, eds., *Impossible Histories: Historical Avant-Gardes, Neo-Avant-Gardes, and Post-Avant-Gardes in Yugoslavia, 1818–1991* (Cambridge, MA: MIT Press, 2003), 196.

109 Ibid.

110 Tito, quoted by Armin Medosch in "The Scientification of Art? (1962–1963)," in Armin Medosch, *New Tendencies: Art at the Threshold of the Information Revolution (1961–1978)* (Cambridge, MA, and London: MIT Press, 2016), 98.

111 Bojana Videkanić, *Nonaligned Modernism: Socialist Postcolonial Aesthetics in Yugoslavia, 1945–1985* (Montreal: McGill-Queen's University Press, 2019), 3.

112 Ibid., 194.

113 Ibid., 195.

114 Ibid., 195–196.

115 Ibid., 196.

116 Videkanić expands: "The post-war avant-gardes and neo-avant-gardes in Yugoslavia were under the influence of European and Western art, and in that influence they shunned all these efforts to reach out to the NAM [nonaligned] countries. In other words the state, cultural committees and other

bodies were trying to create connections and infrastructure for the artists to come in, but our contemporary curators and artists, those who ran SC and other such galleries, who were organizing international exhibitions were not interested in the kind of art that the artists who were coming in from non-West produced. That art was often representational, it was often based in traditional (folklore practices), also often modernist (in a more traditional sense than what the conceptual and other practices allowed), and in general not expressing the kind of aesthetic ideas that became so prevalent in Yugoslavia in the mid-1960s and later." Videkanić in e-mail correspondence with the author, March 8, 2020.

117 Želimir Koščević in email correspondence with the author, June 6, 2013.

118 The statement: "1. The following is hereby abolished: painting, sculpture, graphic art, applied arts, industrial design, architecture and urban planning. 2. A ban is hereby placed on the following: all activity in the history of art and especially the so-called art criticism. 3. There shall be no exhibitions in galleries, museums or art pavilions." "The Draft Decree on the Democratization of Art" is translated in Matičević, "The Zagreb Circle," 21. Originally published in Croatian on the front page of *Novine Galerija SC* 22 (1970). These three commands were discussed in a longer text elaborating on these points, including an emphasis on anti-institutional art and art for the social good: "Institutionalized forms of presenting art should be gradually phased out. Galleries, museums, exhibition halls, pavilions, must become active art houses, culture houses, their physical properties (covered space) should only be used in the event of rain, snow and other weather disasters ... Cultural, historical, scientific and artistic materials need to be reevaluated according to these criteria, and what may be of general use to be taken out to the tram station, promenade, to night-clubs, factories and department stores. ... The monstrous factory of Yugoslav contemporary art is ... made of the thousands and thousands of images, sculptures, graphics, countless applied art objects, luxury designs, stupid architectural and urban concepts and realizations, and even more stupid 'critical' interpretations, in general it is reminiscent of the purely reactionary action in society which now more than ever needs conceptually powerful art." See *Novine Galerija SC* 22 (1970), 1. Translated from Croatian by the author.

119 Ibid.

120 Ibid.

121 Ibid.

122 Claes Oldenburg, "I am for an Art," in Kristine Stiles and Peter Selz, eds., *Theories and Documents of Contemporary Art: A Sourcebook of Artists' Writings*, rev. and exp. 2nd ed. (Berkeley, Los Angeles, and London: University of California Press, 2012), 385.

123 See *Novine Galerija SC* 22 (1970), 1. Translated from Croatian by the author.

124 Bojana Pejić has noted in her essay on Marina Abramović's *Balkan Baroque* that in 1945 the communists in Belgrade "kept the figure of Jugoslavija standing on one building in Belgrade, but removed the crown from her head!"

See "Balkan Baroque, Balkan Mind," in Adelina von Furstenberg and Steven Henry Madoff, eds., *Marina Abramović: Balkan Epic* (Milan: Skira, 2006), 28.

125 Videkanić, *Nonaligned Modernism*, 3.

126 Ibid.

127 Suzana Milevska, "Gender Difference in the Balkans" (PhD dissertation, Goldsmiths, University of London, 2005). Milevska cites the Regional Historic Archive of Macedonia in Bitola as the source holding the Fund of the Brothers Manaki in Macedonia. See Suzana Milevska, "Gender Difference in the Balkans" (PhD dissertation, Goldsmiths, University of London, 2005), 84.

128 Ibid., 88–89.

129 Ibid., 90.

130 Ibid.

131 Ibid., 91.

132 Ibid.

133 "Izložba žena I muškaraca" ("Exhibition of Women and Men"), *Novine* 8 (1968–1969), 29. Translation by the author.

134 Batinić has written extensively on Yugoslav women's mass political mobilization during World War II and their important contributions to the Yugoslav project. Feminist scholarship in Yugoslavia has, since the 1950s, fought to reinscribe women protagonists into otherwise male-dominated narratives about Yugoslavia. Batinić elucidates how women's roles were gradually diminished during the war and after the establishment of Tito's Yugoslavia. See Batinić, *Women and Yugoslav Partisans*.

Jugoslovenka's body under patriarchal socialism: art and feminist performance politics in Yugoslavia

1

When Bojana Pejić curated the first exhibition addressing gender in Eastern Europe, *Gender Check: Femininity and Masculinity in the Art of Eastern Europe* at mumok (Museum Moderner Kunst Stiftung Ludwig Wien) in Vienna (2009), she commented on the unique history of Yugoslav socialism and its knotty intersection with women's emancipation:

> [We] in Yugoslavia lived a period of high socialism, enjoying sex, drugs and rock 'n' roll and wearing original Levi's jeans. If the Communist Party (in Yugoslavia and elsewhere) emancipated women in many ways, by uprooting illiteracy, improving medical conditions and the child-care system, through paid maternity leave and the right to decide about pregnancy, then in due course it became necessary, as some local feminists saw, to "emancipate the emancipator." This proved not to be easy.[1]

My analysis aims to elucidate how women's struggle for emancipatory strategies in art were undeniably linked to this patriarchal Yugoslav context Pejić describes, and that understandings of the performance and conceptual art movements in Yugoslavia have to account for women's feminist contributions in art and performance history to that moment. Feminist performance politics in the arts during the 1970s and into the 1980s in Yugoslavia demonstrate explicitly that emancipatory resistance did not belong to a cohesive movement of Jugoslovenkas or a group adhering to the same set of principles. The point of the chapter is not to suggest such a cohesion, but to instead illuminate how explorations of resistance through a centering of the female body within patriarchal socialism are key to understanding Yugoslavia's socialist society and its relationship to women in the arts.

The analysis of Yugoslav feminist performance politics in this chapter is mostly limited to the sphere of what was called the "New Art Practice" in the 1970s, a term coined by Belgrade-based art historian Ješa Denegri to describe experimental art practices at the time.[2] Within this extremely rich and wide-ranging movement of experimental art, I single out works that exemplify new directions in feminist performance politics as resistance to patriarchal authority in Yugoslavia. Some of the works discussed also extend into the early 1980s.

Yugoslav women's feminist strategies differed, and they often argued about how they saw the function of art and the role of the artist in Yugoslav socialist society, how they understood their relationship to the socialist regime and its institutions, and how they would go about historically narrating their resistance. They also differed significantly in how they related personally, politically, and professionally to the socialist establishment and its patriarchal foundation, and in their strategies to critique, transform, or embody its ideological tenets. What inevitably linked these women was how boldly they responded to patriarchal forces and social relationships through theoretical and practical experimentations in art. Ultimately, this chapter seeks to excavate the unrecognized ways in which women's concepts of gender, body, and sexuality played out in the Yugoslav avant-garde art context of the 1970s and early 1980s. Their commonalities in privileging the body and performance under Yugoslav socialism inspires my conceptualization of these women as Jugoslovenkas, who, I argue, established gender and sexuality as ubiquitous cultural and personal forces immanent to socialist Yugoslavian and transnational contexts alike.

It is also important to note that the "New Art Practice" is not an exhaustive frame for covering all Yugoslav culture, as it remained primarily tied to major urban areas in Serbia, Croatia, and Slovenia (Belgrade, Zagreb, Novi Sad, and later Ljubljana). Many more women artists existed within this history and more expanded fields of art, such as traditional painting, sculpture, theater, dance, photography, naïve painting, socialist realism, decorative arts, folklore costume design, or hay paintings by women artists such as Lozika Homolja in the small town of Palić, Serbia. It is my hope that the viewpoint of my analyses will encourage further embrace of wide-ranging Jugoslovenkas who challenge the ideological divide between high versus low culture in favor of a more varied narrative of cultural production under Yugoslav socialism. In this chapter, I limit this goal to expanding the history of performance and conceptual art associated with Yugoslavia's New Art Practice.

Beginning first with a discussion of some of the most prominent feminist discontents within the Yugoslav project, I then turn to establishing a context of what I suggest are feminist contributions to the avant-garde cultural work in Yugoslavia in the 1970s into the early 1980s. The second half of the chapter focuses on the emergence of Yugoslav feminist performance politics in the work of individual women artists. The analysis of women's performance and conceptual works does not follow a chronological line but is instead conceptualized around four points of departure, all tied to embodied and performative practices and enveloped in the figure of Jugoslovenka:

1) A consideration of burgeoning feminist performance politics through an analysis of key moments in the arts for Jugoslovenka.

2) Artists contending with the national body as implicitly male, especially in relation to Tito and the ideology of socialism; in this section, I focus on the site of the bed as an exploration of socialist politics in sexism, sexual pleasure, visions of female intimacy in the home, and as a place of emancipation and freedom.
3) Artists situating their bodies within the political discourse of Yugoslav socialism by embracing and critiquing some of the country's most prominent signifiers of power: the Yugoslav socialist flag and Tito himself.
4) Artists introducing the site of women's voices, sounds, and vocalized concerns into an otherwise male-dominated sound and visual scape in the arts.

Burgeoning feminist performance politics: key moments in the arts and culture for Jugoslovenka

While a detailed history of Belgrade's Student Cultural Center (SKC) is beyond the scope of this chapter and book, I want to single out a few events and iconic moments relevant for the history of women's emancipation and performance politics during the 1970s. The 1974 photograph of Marina Abramović, performance artist Joseph Beuys, and Dunja Blažević at the SKC is especially iconic in its display of two extremely well-respected and powerful Yugoslav women in the arts flanking Beuys: on his right, soon to be one of the most important women artists in the international art world, Abramović, and on his left, Blažević, who organized some of the most critical exhibitions and events at the SKC (Figure 1.1). The male bravado of Beuys' presence is thus indicative of the intersection of local Marxist politics with Western male-dominated movements toward art and social change. This photograph also shows the importance of Yugoslav women in the emergence of transgressive and politically charged performance and conceptual art in Yugoslavia.

Blažević led Belgrade's SKC in the 1970s (1971–1979) with a political agenda that often critiqued the socialist state and its cultural policies and introduced women's leadership into art exhibitions, conferences, catalogue texts, and performances.[3] She was, according to Branislav Dimitrijević, "oriented towards the idea of [the] SKC as a 'meeting point' of radical youth culture and the political establishment," and exemplified "those progressive and younger communist [e.g. socialist] officials who tried to be sensitive to the idea that the 'new society' should bring up 'new art' too."[4] Jakovljević has noted that within student and activist circles, the SKC "was one of very few tangible gains made by Belgrade students in their June 1968 uprising."[5] In an interview with Zsófia Lóránd, Blažević remembered a conflict she had with the Central Committee, when they pushed to replace the first director of the SKC, Petar Ignjatović, who had been a key protagonist in the 1968 student protests. Along with five other program directors at the SKC, Blažević "protested against the decision

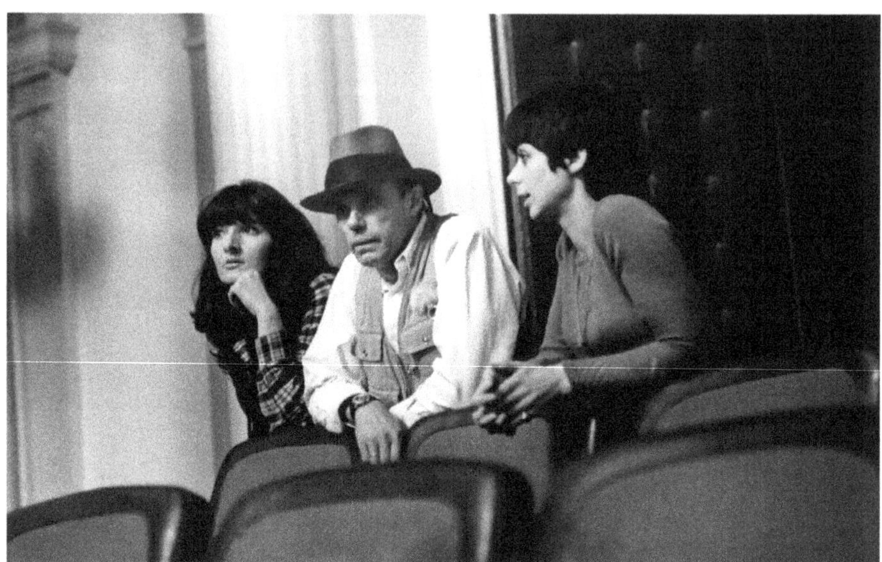

1.1   Marina Abramović with Joseph Beuys and Dunja Blažević at the Student Cultural Center, Belgrade, 1974.

based on the lack of professional knowledge of those making the decision."[6] She recalled: "'So, we sent the CC representative away, we were not afraid at all.'"[7]

Blažević began in 1972 to organize the famous April Meetings, attracting numerous international artists, including Beuys, Gina Pane, and Ana Mendieta. The SKC quickly developed an international reputation for performance art, in large measure due to the respect garnered by Raša Todosijević, Zoran Popović, Neša Paripović, Gergelj Urkom, Abramović, and Era Milivojević, artists known as the Group of Six, who Blažević supported through her curatorial leadership. Other women leaders and organizers included Biljana Tomić and Bojana Pejić. Tomić had a history of organizing ephemeral and performative works at the Belgrade International Experimental Theater Festival (BITEF), a curatorial objective she later continued at the SKC. Experimentation and highly symbolic actions at BITEF demonstrated the urgency artists felt to formulate a visual and corporeal language enacting alternatives to the status quo. At the heart of such conceptual artworks were techniques that Tomić would insist were created to change perception.[8]

During the April Meeting in 1975, Blažević, Tomić, and Pejić organized one of the first explicitly feminist events at the SKC: a dialogue called "Women in Art" that focused on the relationship between women and social change with specific emphasis on culture, revolution, and capitalism (Figure 1.2).[9]

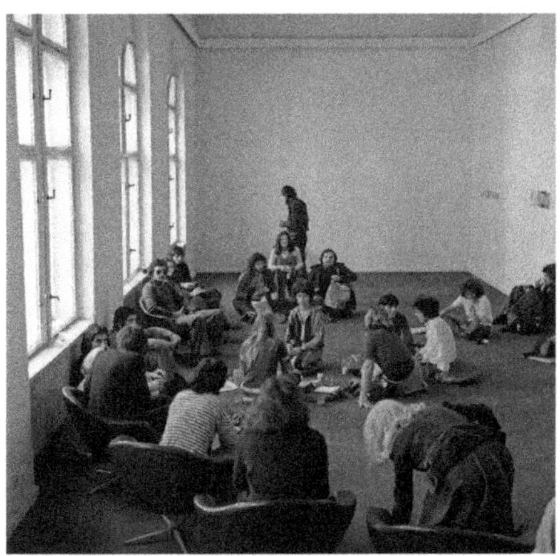

Nebojša Čanković, *Women and Art Discussion*, Student Cultural Center, Belgrade, 1975.   **1.2**

One of the main points of discussion happened on April 9, with the head-line: "Discussion of Claim: An Artwork by this Art-Ess [woman artist] is as Good as an Artwork by a Man."[10] Participants included women artists from Yugoslavia alongside visiting artists Iole de Freitas (a Brazilian artist based in Italy), Natalia LL (Poland), and Ulrike Rosenbach (Germany).[11] According to Dragica Vukadinović, who began working as an assistant to Biljana Tomić at the SKC in 1971, this discussion was a catalyst for a feminist approach to art and organized more formal and designated forums for the discussion of women in art.[12]

Abramović admired Blažević's capacity to introduce Belgrade artists to the international art world:

> Dunja was not just anyone. She was an art historian, extremely bright, and rich. She was a Croatian and her father was the Minister of Culture of Croatia in that time when everything was fine with the republics. So it was incredibly important because whatever she was doing there, she had the background and the protection of the party. We [the SKC] became the island of the freedom of experiment in art in the middle of the old things. It was really like a miracle.[13]

Blažević's political commitment to a socially critical and artistically rigorous art is best documented in her organization of the seminal *Oktobar 75* meeting/ exhibition in 1975. *Oktobar 75* functioned as an alternative to the official Yugoslav *October Salon* (*Oktobarski Salon*), bringing together SKC artists and curators for a "collective re-thinking of the potential of the principles of 'self-management' in the field of culture, through either the affirmative or critical positioning."[14] Blažević criticized the Yugoslavian government for its strict policies regarding the distribution or acknowledgment of "new" art:

> Art should be changed! As long as we leave art alone and keep on transferring works of art from studios to depots and basements by means of social regulations and mechanisms, storing them, like stillborn children, for the benefit of our cultural offspring, or while we keep on creating, through the private market, our own variant of the nouveau riche or kleinbürgers,[15] art will remain a social appendage, something serving no useful purpose, but something it is not decent or cultured to be without.[16]

Blažević's play on the maternal body—coerced into bearing "stillborn children"—signaled a disdain for the paternalistic and patriarchal construction of creativity by the socialist leadership, which relegated artists of all genders to becoming reproductive agents for the state. In her biting logic, such oppressive mediocrity in vision can only produce artworks that have died before they even enter this world.

This contempt from feeling used by the state would find even more piercing expression three years later at the SKC, when Blažević organized the conference "Drug-ca Žena. Žensko Pitanje. Novi Pristup?" with feminist sociologist Žarana Papić. Drug-ca is shorthand for "drugarica," which translates to "female comrade" (or "comrade-ess") in English.[17] The fully translated title is "Comrade Woman: The Woman Question: A New Approach?"[18] Other organizers included Dragica Vukadinović, Jasmina Tešanović, and Nada Ler-Sofronić,[19] as well as the assistant for the SKC Gallery, Pejić. The "Drug-ca Žena" conference plan states at one point:

> Woman lived through her history reduced to only *one activity* (biological and socializing [sic] reproduction) and to one limited *social space* (the private domain of the family). The institution of marriage and family became the exact reflection of the allienated [sic] social relation between the sexes representing thus the *only* and *"natural"* vocation, veiling all forms of her factual impotence and hindering all other possibilities.[20]

The metaphor of reproduction is therefore critical in thinking about the patriarchal construction of art and labor and the ways in which it imposes unjust limitations on women. One other section in the "Drug-ca Žena" conference plan stands out. It asks: "what are the practical, social, and individual elements of the new ~~woman's~~ [crossed out and overwritten with the word] *feminist* consciousness, what does the new private/public behaviour consist [of] and what are its characteristics?"[21]

While I do not know who crossed out "woman's" and substituted "feminist," nor when that edit occurred, the switch is nevertheless telling, indicating a shift from an essentializing emphasis on womanhood to a more recognizable political project of feminist liberation. This 1978 conference sparked feminist organizing across the various republics of Yugoslavia and internationally and raised awareness of just how much Yugoslav socialism had ignored and failed women.[22] "I thought that the laws of the Socialist Federal Republic of Yugoslavia were great," Vukadinović remembers. "I wasn't aware that the praxis was different. … During and after the conference I began to understand that the situation was not so great."[23] Jelena Vesić notes that the conference "was considered as a form of 'internal critique' of the Yugoslav system, stemming from the feminist, but also from socialist premises."[24]

Pejić has commented on the meeting's influence on the Western participants. The list of invited participants included such feminist trailblazers as Julia Kristeva, Susan Sontag, Luce Irigaray, Alice Schwarzer, Simone de Beauvoir, and Lucy Lippard. She remembers that women who came from the West "objected to the presence of men in the conference room" and "could not understand that women in Yugoslavia have certain freedoms unimaginable in the West (same salaries as their male colleagues, right to abortion, etc.)."[25] In her discussion of the clashes between the Western feminists and Yugoslav feminists, feminist art historian and curator Ivana Bago has argued that women in Yugoslavia used "the strategy of mimicry" indiscernible for Western feminists, a feminism "in 'disguise,' submerged in the benevolence of a popular women's magazine [*Bazaar*] that predominantly addressed fashion, travel, and culinary needs."[26] Those who published in *Bazaar* were also at the conference and Yugoslav women were accused of being too made up, for example, wearing lipstick and sporting painted nails. Bonfiglioli's study of the conference emphasizes the ways in which cultural differences and similarities could account for whether or not the participants identified as feminists.[27] For example, Sofija Trivunac, a journalist from Belgrade at the time, remembered that "she felt judged by some foreign feminists because of her look," adding: "I have to say that a lot of us were saying 'oh no, no no, we are not feminists, we just want equal rights.'"[28] One of the reasons some Yugoslav women did not want to identify with the Western feminists had to do with a common stereotype of equating feminists with supposedly unattractive or butch lesbians. Trivunac's explanation exposes this antagonism: "Especially when you see somebody coming from England who looks like a horrifying butch, and you sit there with [painted] nails and they look at you like *ouaah* [expression of disgust]."[29] This Yugoslav woman's homophobic reading of a butch feminist from England effortlessly collided with an equal distaste and disregard by Western feminists for an "East European woman" who had her nails done for this international feminist gathering.

Feminist art historian and curator Katja Kobolt has theorized nails were "the corneous membrane between a self and others" and "a projection screen for both."[30] Kobolt suggests that patronizing attitudes toward women's painted nails are deeply connected to the colonial and capitalist underpinnings of the United States and other Western countries. She states: "It seems that only in the 1970s, in the wake of the international loan politics, which raised the culture of consumption also in some of the socialist countries, the image of a working, peasant 'socialist' woman began to convert into 'femme.'"[31] But this "femme" Jugoslovenka (Trivunac) was not welcomed by Western feminists—not even in her city of residence on the occasion of a feminist conference—as she had painted nails and wore make-up, which to British eyes looked like a stereotypical American woman shown in beauty and fashion magazines, made for consumption and to please a male gaze. In this regard, it is noteworthy that as early as 1972, the "American magazine *Penthouse* announced the opening of a hotel in socialist Yugoslavia called The Penthouse Adriatic Club / Haludovo Palace Hotel with a cover girl covering her breasts with polished nails."[32] Prevailing "construction[s] of 'Eastern-Europeanness'" with respect to nail culture, according to Kobolt, have resulted in "negative stereotypes of 'Eastern European women', used in the USA to depict Melania Trump" and others.[33] Nails are connected to a cultural colonization that reveals tensions with patriarchal power and complicates coherent narratives about feminism and socialism in Yugoslavia. Paradoxical, complex, and "femme," Yugoslav feminism shifts in significance depending on the vantage point. And while Pejić would diagnose "the legacy of this meeting" as "simply nonexistent" for the arts during the time because it was mostly attended by "sociologists and theoreticians,"[34] some three decades later the "Drug-ca Žena" conference would enter the canon of feminist art history.[35] And only three years after "Drug-ca Žena," on the occasion of Rada Đuričin's 1981 monologue performance of Erica Jong's feminist novel *Fear of Flying*, a poster design by Mirko Ilić visually paid homage to the feminist resistance expressed in the red nails of "Drug-ca Žena"'s local feminists: a fist with a raised middle finger, the nail manicured and painted red, an image powerfully characterizing the emancipatory strength of Yugoslav feminism as distinctly femme and defiant (Figure 1.3).

The "Drug-ca Žena" conference was also accompanied by *Drug-ca Žena (Comrade Woman)*, an exhibition at the SKC solely focused on women (Figure 1.4).[36] This 1978 exhibition was curated by Goranka Matić and Nebojša Čanković and included headshots of women with fictional data based on a questionnaire designed by Matić that focused on "desires and imagination of a 'better world'" made into captions accompanying the headshots.[37] In one photograph (not depicted in the examples here), Matić included a simulacrum of a self-portrait in which she embodied the likeness of an archetypal lesbian or butch feminist whom she called Ira Fasbinder, "a thirty-year-old Madam of the Brothel in Budapest."[38] Vesić emphasizes Matić's butch appearance: "A young woman with short hair, dressed in a tie, a neat shirt, waistcoat, and jacket, with a cigarette hanging from the corner of her mouth."[39] Performing a visual and

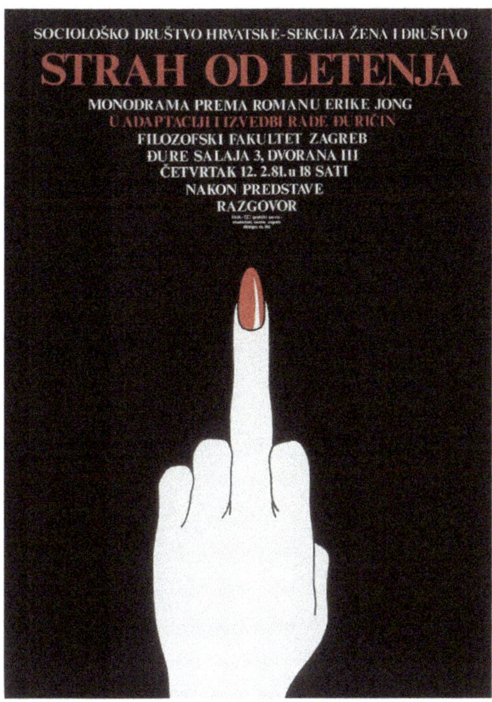

Mirko Ilić, poster for monologue by Rada Đuričin, based on Erica Jong's *Fear of Flying* 1.3
(*Strah od letenja*), produced by the Women and Society section of the Croatian
Sociological Association, 1981.

libidinal kinship with the notorious West German bisexual filmmaker Rainer
Werner Fassbinder and embodying the sexual prowess and bravado of a butch
lesbian pimp from the heart of Central Europe, Matić challenged gender
expectations while also heralding a Yugoslav femininity not bound to traditional gender roles, such as socialist expectations of motherhood or honest
work. Instead, the emancipation of Jugoslovenka here has a dual purpose: for
Matić herself, who makes her own image, and for Ira Fasbinder, whose pride
in her sex work and underground life spills out of the image.

It is important to note that this feminist exhibition had been preceded
two years earlier by an action titled *Why Do Women Not Catcall Men?* (1976),
involving copies of a poster hung all over Belgrade, including the university and other cultural buildings.[40] Organized by feminist sociologist Žarana
Papić and political scientist Ivan Vejvoda, this was an activist action using
the language of conceptual art: simple and to the point. Dragan Stojanovski,
who designed the poster, printed the question in capital letters in the center
of a white sheet of paper. It was a confrontation with unaddressed sexism

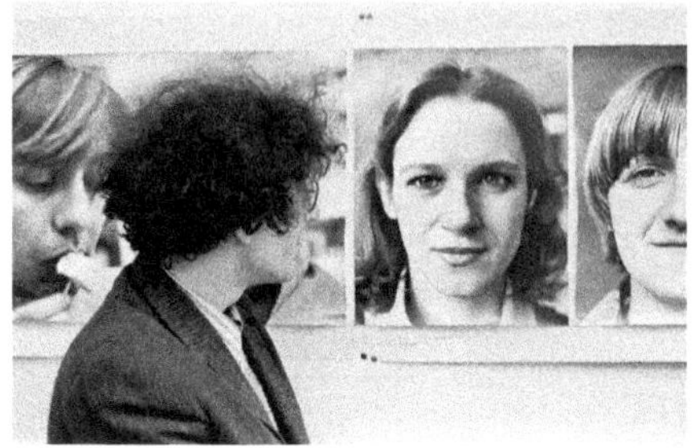

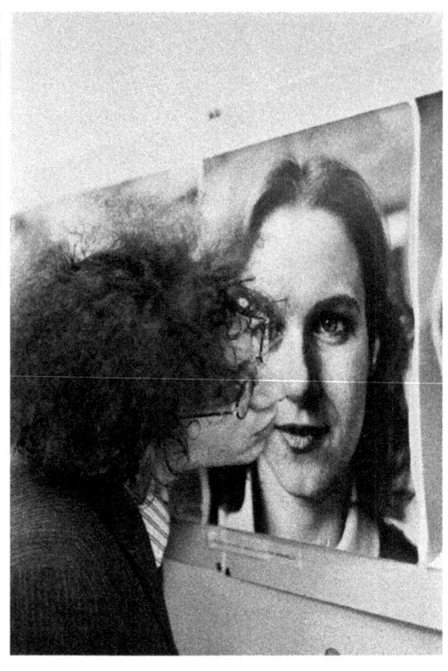

1.4–1.5   Nebojša Čanković, photos taken during the opening of *Comrade Woman*, Student Cultural Center, Belgrade, 1978.

in Yugoslavia, which was just as prevalent as in any other nation despite socialism's promise for a more egalitarian society. As Lóránd succinctly notes, feminists shared "a deep disappointment with leftist political ideologies, be it the New Left in Western capitalism or the state's distorted Marxist agenda in Eastern Europe."[41]

The question posed by the poster campaign in 1976 was still relevant two years later; one of the documentary photos of the *Comrade Woman* exhibition opening shows just how prevalent the objectification of women was and continued to be. The photograph depicts journalist Milorad Miša Pavlović, a male visitor to the exhibition, leaning in to kiss the photograph of Marinela Koželj directly on her lips (Figure 1.5).[42]

At the time, Koželj was becoming known as performance artist Raša Todosijević's elegant and beautiful wife, who remained stoic and quiet while enduring multiple violations from him during his performances, such as his 1977–1978 series *Was ist Kunst? (What is Art?)*[43] She had also served as Todosijević's "found object" for the first SKC exhibition, curated by Blažević in 1972, when he exhibited her as a mute living object in *Drangularium*. In a sardonic twist of fate, Koželj became an object again in *Comrade Woman*. Pavlović's act of kissing her photograph constituted what some might have considered an amusing intervention in the dynamic of the barrier between the art object and the gallery viewer, a welcome breakdown of the barrier between art and life—a reading that owes much to the fetishization of the merging of art and life in the history of performance art. But a feminist analysis of this penetration of the gap between art and life entails recognizing the specter of patriarchal disregard for women's work, women's art, and women themselves, as his gesture effectively elevates sexism and the objectification of women in the guise of playfulness.

And yet one significant exception is noteworthy. In a 1973 photo performance shot in Tašmajdan Park—considered one of the early performance works in the oeuvre of the Belgrade Group of Six Artists—Popović hid his body behind artist Sally Holman, who was visiting Belgrade (Figures 1.6–1.7). By making himself small, Popović stepped aside and foregrounded a woman's body, her presence, and her actions. Holman was Richard Demarco's assistant at the time and came to Yugoslavia to meet artists who were invited for the Edinburgh Art Festival that same year.[44] Popović showed slides of this photo performance with Holman in Edinburgh, along with *Axioms*, which would become one of his most famous works. The Edinburgh Art Festival became a watershed event in the history of performance art, especially because of its inclusion of East European artists and because it premiered Marina Abramović's infamous *Rhythm 10* performance. But it is significant that a Yugoslav working-class artist made the most profound statement about gender. *Skrivanje iza Sally Holman* (*Hiding behind Sally Holman*) privileged the body of Sally Holman, who in some photos appears happy and is laughing, while in others she sits calmly on the grass, smoking a cigarette. Sometimes she is shown looking directly into the camera with a somber expression. In all the images, Popović's body lurks behind her, sometimes almost not visible at all, while other times he is unable to make himself small enough to disappear. The struggle to hide behind her and the failure to do so entirely—to remain

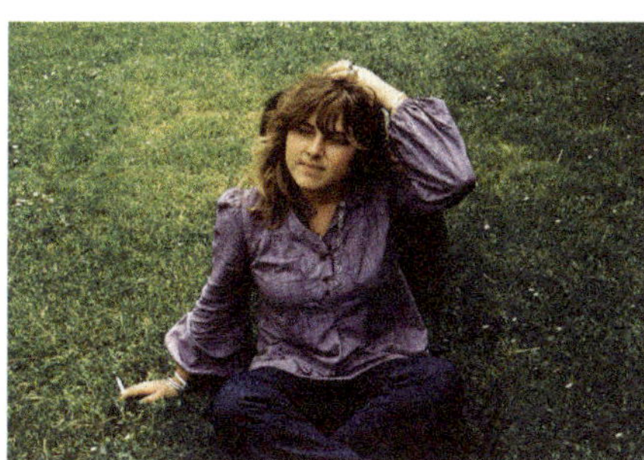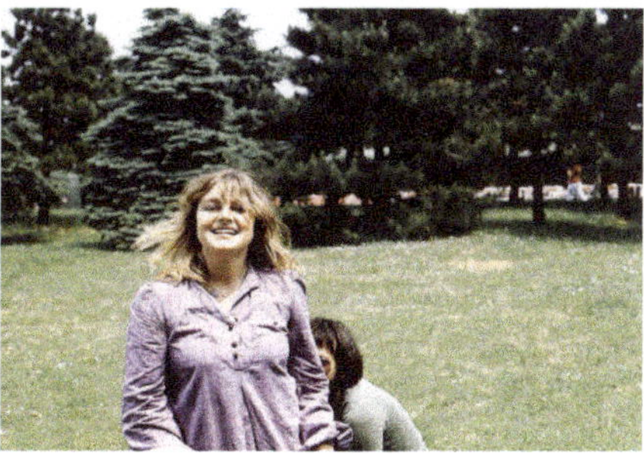

Zoran Popović, *Hiding behind Sally Holman*, Tašmajdan Park, Belgrade, 1973. Photographs of a performance.   **1.6–1.7**

hidden—highlighted the specter of male dominance while being simultaneously an unusually progressive and poetic intervention within an otherwise male-dominated art world. By doing so, Popović reversed the iconography of the macho East European artist, who here is nothing but an inadequate jester, hiding behind a woman. And yet, one must also acknowledge the fact that Holman represented a "Westerner," a British gallerist who overpowers and outshines an East European performance artist.

While Popović's action is remarkable, it is less remarked in the literature how many women remained hidden in the shadows of their husbands from the 1970s until today, including Marinela Koželj and others such as Branka Stipančić and Vlasta Delimar. With the enduring patriarchal structure in the arts in Yugoslavia, and elsewhere, it is not surprising that women like Stipančić took on supporting roles, such as becoming art historians and curators who supported their husbands and male partners' careers, or carrying the brunt of the production of some of the collaborative works. Koželj's fate was even more indicative of this trend, as she was mostly reduced to the renown of being Todosijević's beautiful wife, despite the fact that she was an integral part of his practice and an artist in her own right. As such, women's emancipatory strategies varied in strength and purpose, and some might argue that there was a willingness among women to enable such second-class status of women's work. Kate Manne has described this type of "subordination" by women as part of the logic of misogyny, which is especially operative "in the context of familial or intimate relations."[45] She explains:

> A social milieu counts as patriarchal insofar as certain kinds of institutions or social structures both proliferate and enjoy widespread support within it—from, for example, the state, as well as broader cultural sources, such as material resources, communal values, cultural narratives, media and artistic depictions … These patriarchal institutions … will be such that all or most women are positioned as subordinate in relation to some man or men therein ….[46]

While the history of the region has embraced narratives that privilege men above all, this book attempts to track down some of those repressed and forgotten feminist moments, understudied and unrecognized in the arts, whether by men or women who upheld patriarchal power. While much valuable scholarship has honed in on the Zagreb-based art collective of all-male artists, known as the Group of Six Authors (Grupa Šestorice Autora), I want to instead point to work by women who were marginalized around the collective in collaborative works that are relevant for the history of feminism in Yugoslavia.

The work of the Group of Six Authors emerged with their first action in May 1975; they included Boris Demur, Željko Jerman, Vlado Martek, Mladen Stilinović, Sven Stilinović, and Fedor Vučemilović. The group created "exhibitions-actions"[47] and also produced the samizdat publication *Maj 75*.

Stipančić would become a seminal figure in theorizing and historicizing the group's work, and her writing was foundational for Mladen Stilinović's international success. The Group of Six Authors began to exhibit actions and artworks in public squares all over the former Yugoslavia in 1975. Stipančić characterized their actions as embracing "the style of guerrilla warfare, the tactics of constant disturbance … a resistance full of a critical spirit and imagination, simultaneously derisive and joyful."[48] They used town squares, public spaces for leisure activities, housing areas that lacked any cultural life, and also universities.[49] But unlike "guerrilla warfare," these artists made sure to obtain police consent for every action, which was mostly granted, despite leading critics' regular dismissal of their art.[50]

Calling themselves "authors" rather than "artists," the Group of Six Authors distinguished themselves from the Group of Six at the SKC in Belgrade, but more importantly, they emphasized the prominence of writing and poetry in their individual and collective work. Like the art collective Gorgona in Zagreb before them, they also self-published, calling their publication *Maj 75* (1978–1984), with each edition organized around a letter of the alphabet. *Maj 75* served as a publication as well as an alternative exhibition format that became especially popular through such experimental art forms as mail art, which, as an art form, was collaborative, interactive, and often included international participation. As one mail art manifesto urged: "Mail art is not objects going through the mail, but artists establishing direct *contact* with other artists, sharing ideas and experiences, all over the world."[51] It was also an art form associated with the East, trapped within the local socialist context of the Cold War, which was not the experience of Yugoslav artists. Yugoslav artists did not have "a parallel culture of samizdat publications or underground art actions" associated with more repressive regimes, such as those of the Soviet Union or Hungary.[52] Nevertheless, Yugoslav artists participated in mail art events and exhibitions in the early 1970s, with Miroljub Todorović organizing his *Signalist Explorations 1.* exhibition at the SKC in 1973, as well as the mail art activities of the Bosch+Bosch art members from Subotica, including Katalin Ladik.

Although *Maj 75* shared a similar visual language and material manifestation of a zine with mail art, it was mainly distributed among friends and colleagues, as well as being mailed to artists abroad. Treating *Maj 75* as an alternative but no less critical exhibition site, I want to single out two issues of the publication that I argue mark noteworthy moments in the history of women's representation and the subject of women's bodies within the visual field of art in Yugoslavia. Although Zagreb-based artist Vlasta Delimar worked independently on performance, collage, and photography, she also collaborated often with the Group of Six Authors in Zagreb and contributed to *Maj 75* (1978–1984). She was the only woman associated with the group who ended up married to two of its members, first Željko Jerman and then Vlado Martek. Delimar produced *Maj 75* collaboratively with Jerman in his atelier, using silk-screens and inserting pages with artworks by individual artists. She was most involved in producing the magazine, and as such took on the role of maintaining the groups' material productivity, a role often ascribed to women and criticized in Mierle Laderman Ukeles's famous "Maintenance Art Manifesto 1969!"[53] Darko Šimičić has also emphasized the general "patriarchal nature of the cultural and social space" in avant-garde publishing in magazines from the 1920s onward, which included only a "small number of women artists."[54] In 1981, when it was time for the letter F edition, Delimar would change that history by conceptualizing and editing a special issue dedicated to women artists, *Maj 75 F*.[55] The issue featured twelve works by women artists, including Edita Schubert, Bogdanka Poznanović, and Duba Sambolec (Figures 1.8–1.10).

In general, many of the contributions in *Maj 75* included actual objects incorporated into the publication, such as pencils, fabric, and other items that could be touched and that transformed the samizdat publication into a sculpture. Schubert's geometric play with the triangle functioning as a foldout for an otherwise disguised face played with haptic elements, the triangle also suggesting the visual language of female genitalia (Figure 1.8). Poznanović's interactive spiral commanded reader participation, an invitation to touch and make contact with the center of the spiral, which she identified as art (Figure 1.9). But this art is directed by the lunar cycle marked above and the sphere

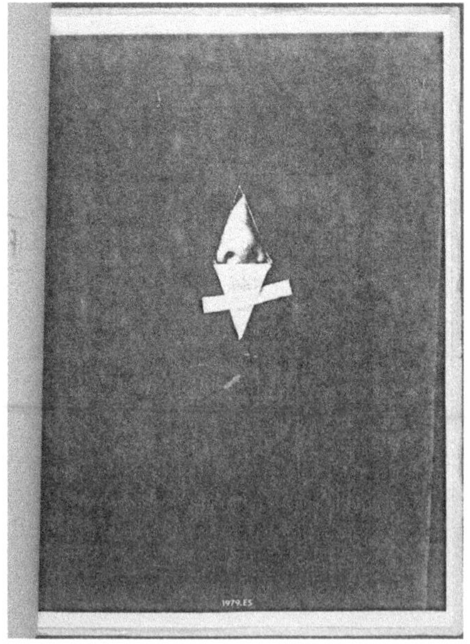

1.8   Edita Schubert, page in *Maj 75 F*, 1981.

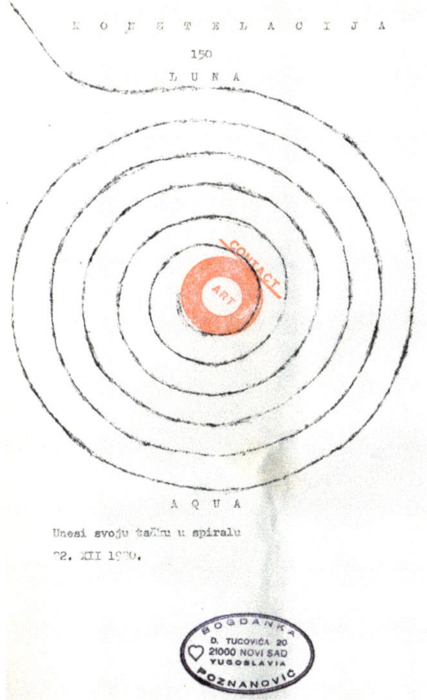

Bogdanka Poznanović, page in *Maj 75 F*, 1981.   **1.9**

of water below. As Inga Muscio and other feminists have argued, the moon represents "the *psychic* with all women who have ever bled on this planet";[56] while other artists, such as Susan Hiller, have explored lunar cycles in relationship to womanhood (in Hiller's case, pregnancy) in their conceptual and performance works. The color red at the center connoting "art" might be read as Poznanović's celebration of female creation in the menstrual cycles. Below, she stated: "Insert your dot into a spiral." It asks the viewer to not only penetrate the surface of the page, but also to enter the cycle of life, echoed in the spiral. Sambolec's work in the *F* issue of *Maj 75* shows a stamp in bold red marking the piece "FRAGILE," with a sewing needle piercing through the thin paper of the publication (Figure 1.10). Leaking vaginas, noses that come out of the pages through triangular orifices, and the evocation of fragility demarcate the issue's concern with the female body as a site of creativity and emancipated interaction through art.

Breda Beban's and Rada Čupić's contributions to *Maj 75 F* most poignantly show two contrasting emphases on the female body: on Beban's page, it is front and center, while on Čupić's page the woman's body disappears, visually subsumed by the socialist home (Figures 1.11–1.12). In a black-and-white photograph of the artist Xeroxed on paper, Beban meticulously draws

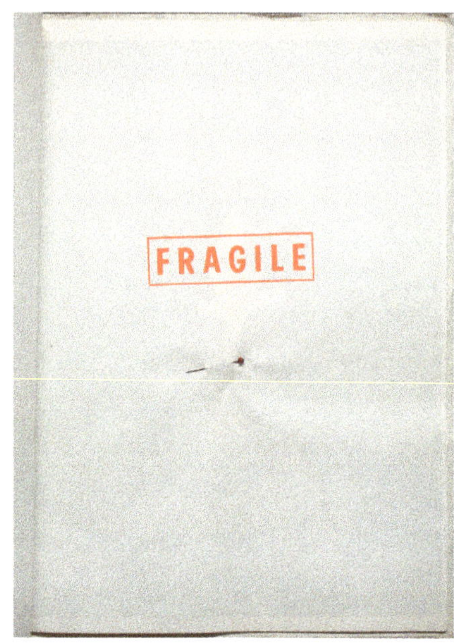

1.10   Duba Sambolec, page in *Maj 75 F*, 1981.

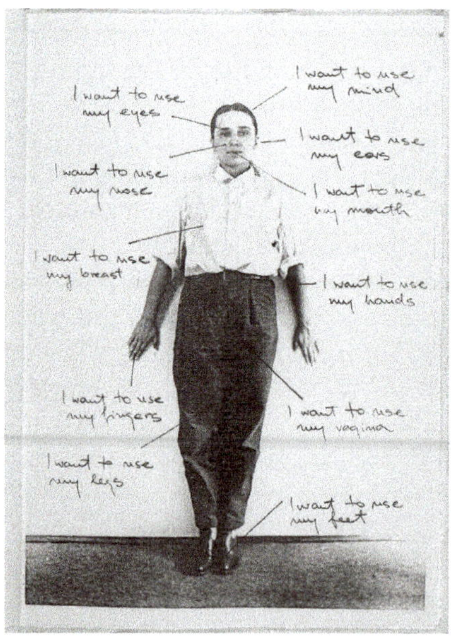

1.11   Breda Beban, page in *Maj 75 F*, 1981.

Rada Čupić, page in *Maj 75 F*, 1981.   **1.12**

lines on the image pointing to different parts of her body that she wants to use: her nose, her eyes, her mind, her ears, her mouth, her hands, her vagina, her feet, her legs, her fingers, and her breasts (Figure 1.11). Dressed in a white button-up blouse and standing against the wall with a perfectly centered pony tail, high-rise pants fastened with a belt, and shiny leather shoes, Beban looks directly at the readers. Her appearance implies that she is professional and ready, but her words remind us that she is longing to have sovereignty over her own body. Beban's, along with the other women's contributions to *Maj 75 F*, collapsed questions of women's corporeality onto the theoretically dense and male-dominated conceptual art ideas coming out of the 1960s and 1970s. Women's bodies are signaled as sites of feminist politics that resist being subsumed by universalist political and artistic projects.

The universalist element of the project of socialism is represented by the red star, which historically has connected various iterations of socialism over different times and geographical locations. Čupić's photograph of a tiny house in the middle of an otherwise empty page, marked by a large red star in the middle, leaves a suffocating and anticlimactic mood (Figure 1.12). Instead of women warriors, women reclaiming their bodies, or even women with their comrades working in factories, Čupić's contribution to *Maj F*—identified as a "private house in a village in Vojvodina," the northern autonomous province of Serbia—is small in scale and seems to confine the topic of womanhood to the home.[57] That sense of discomfort at first glance is precisely why it is such a thought-provoking feminist contribution in the Yugoslav context. Upon closer examination, it turns out that the red star is actually part of a Yugoslav flag painted on the entire front face of the house, with a faded blue stripe on top, and a red stripe on the bottom, which almost looks like a fence. Calling the home "private" while marking it with the Yugoslav flag strengthens the connection between the state (public) and the home (private), which in this case seem to be one and the same.

According to Čupić, she made this piece to commemorate "the courage of a woman, a widow with three small children," who during World War II had built shelters under her house for antifascist partisans. This was in Čurug, a village that served as an underground base for many antifascist fighters.[58] The original house is no longer standing, but the owner of the house that was built in its stead on the same site painted it like a flag as part of what Čupić calls "his incredible courage and awareness of the need for resistance." To add an additional level of respect, she enclosed the photographed house in a "circle" and "pulsating line," which for her "speak of eternal motion and rest … taken from the structure of the atom."[59] Contemplating the political weight of the widow's bravery, and the villager's veneration for that history in light of today's political landscape, Čupić provocatively noted that for her, this work brings up "the question [of] how much we are ready to sacrifice today."[60]

And yet, from a feminist point of view, the work might read as completely antithetical to the celebration of women's contributions to antifascist liberation at the root of Čupić's concept for this *Maj 75 F* issue. Without knowing the context, the flower surrounding the tiny house on the page might be indicative of the prison that a home can be. Here, that prison is marked by the ideology of the nation and its flag imposed on the house, and the imagined women's bodies still confined within gendered roles of cooking and tending to children. In that reading, the problem of patriarchal oppression is marked as a decidedly nationalist one, even if in a socialist context. But here I am influenced by Manne's analysis again, in which she notes how women's bodies as fetus-carrying subjects are already always burdened by men's entitlement to ownership, much like a house or other property. Manne notes that the prominent "analogy between a mother's womb and a dominant man's home-cum-haven—or safe space [for men's misogyny]—has long been part of patriarchal ideology."[61] As such, it could be argued that Čupić's tiny home marked by the socialist patriarchy is also a moment of embodied and claustrophobic gender-specific pain under nationalism. But as is often the case with Yugoslav socialism, the story is a more complicated one; once we consider the historical connection to women's antifascist resistance, this Western feminist reading begins to unravel. What does remain clear, however, is that the ideology of nationalism haunted Yugoslavia, even as a unified country.

In analyzing Beban's body politic and offering two opposing readings of Čupić's contribution to *Maj 75 F*, as I have done, we are tasked with contemplating three forms of emancipatory liberation in Yugoslavia: one through the focus on agency over one's body; a second through historical emphasis on women's antifascist liberation in Yugoslavia and the many unknown stories of their courage, manifest in specific local architectures and their stories; and a third, contingent on a contemporary feminist reading, through an exposing of the erasure of the female body subsumed within the socialist, patriarchal home, marked by nationalism.

I want to point to one more work relevant to this line of thinking in *Maj 75 L* (1983), which featured a work by Delimar with a photograph of a vagina with painted drops of blood projecting from the image. The black-and-white photograph was covered with a solid black square sheet, requiring viewers to lift the black square in order to see it (Figures 1.13–1.14). The question of menstruation is critical to this work. The samizdat magazine, requiring a more intimate relation by being handed from one to the next, was by the very nature of this work disturbed by corporeal content, such as women's body fluids.

With its implicit illicitness and its use of the black square as a cover for the vagina, however, this work anticipated canonical feminist works from the

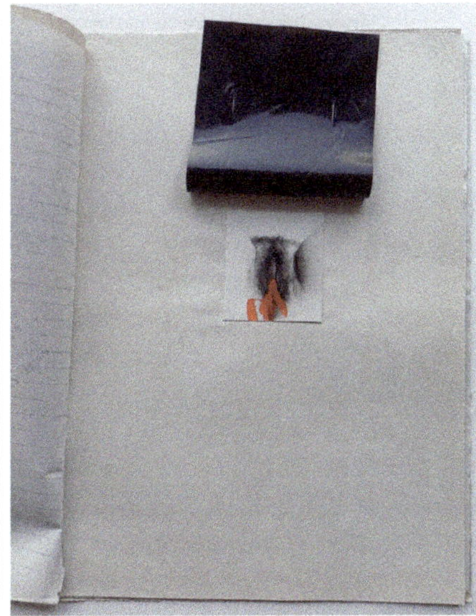

Vlasta Delimar, pages from *Maj 75 L*, 1983.   **1.13–1.14**

region that would come decades later. In her 2001 performance *I'LL BE YOUR ANGEL*, for example, Tanja Ostojić accompanied renowned curator and director Harald Szeemann as his unofficial (and unsolicited) escort at the opening of the 49th Venice Biennale. Szeemann was tasked with the responsibility of "opening" Ostojić's exhibition as he was supposedly the only person who could pronounce that "the 'hidden Malevich' in between Ostojić's legs" was art.[62] Whether or not Szeemann had actually seen her pubic hair, which she had shaved in the shape of Kazimir Malevich's Black Square, remains unknown. The connection I draw to Delimar is that Ostojić referenced both the black square and her own vagina as art. And she did so in a manner similar to samizdat of this period when she distributed postcards that bore the image of her shaved Venus hill, *Black Square on White* (2001), at the Venice Biennale. I revisit Ostojić's *Hidden Malevich* in Chapter 5.

Delimar had no trepidation about the circulation of her images and the titillating possibility that she might be touched and played with through the metonym of her photographs. She even proclaimed in the title of a series of works that "*I Love Dick*," *Volim Kurac* (1982).[63] Photographed with naked men while holding their penises in her hands,[64] Delimar frequently exhibited sexually explicit acts both in performance and two-dimensional works. Her unapologetic declaration of love for sex, pleasure, and the penis ran counter to some feminist theoretical and political interventions that considered such imagery to belong to the objectification of women. But what we consider feminist has changed over time, and now we can and must read Delimar's contributions to *Maj 75* as an important moment for Yugoslav women's artworks and their visibility, a precursor to more celebrated feminist performances that would come out of this region in the 1990s and 2000s. It also reminds us that the work coming out of the New Art Practice was a far cry from stereotypical and heroic depictions of Yugoslav women as partisans, mothers, and allegories of peace. Instead, we see sexually explicit, aesthetically innovative images of women made by women for exploratory, potentially transformative interaction with the public.

Performance and emancipatory ideas around sexual liberation have to be put in context with the glaring fact that women's bodies, of course, were readily available for male consumption within pornographic works in Yugoslavia at the time. But the story is also more complicated than one might first assume, and is extremely relevant to any discussion of feminism in former Yugoslavia. While it might be hard to imagine that a Yugoslav magazine flaunting pornographic images of naked women on the cover could have become an important platform for Yugoslav feminist thought, the country's most famous pornographic magazine *Start* employed some of the most important feminists in Yugoslavia. Slavenka Drakulić and Vesna Kesić are just two authors who worked at the magazine for decades. Established in 1969, *Start* was read widely within cultural circles and became an important publication for intellectual discourses around Marxism, state politics, gender, and sexuality. During the 1970s and 1980s, it received a lot of pushback from the reigning political elite, and was, according to Kesić, "mostly anti-Communist, particularly anti-Soviet."[65] *Start's* independence from the Communist Party also meant that it mostly "represented a marginalized political minority"; despite this position, it "was tolerated by the regime and was influential in promoting cultural values, standards, and lifestyles that differed from those of the dominant party-state ideology."[66] Lóránd's research shows that *Start* was far more than a porno magazine. Rather, it actively engaged feminist international debates about the sexual revolution, with *Start* publishing everything from Kesić's review of the "Drug-ca" conference at the SKC in November 1978, to reviews of books by and interviews with some of the most well-known Western feminists, such as Simone de Beauvoir, Betty Friedan, Germaine Greer, Shere Hite, Erica Jong, Julia Kristeva, and Gloria Steinem. This material was published alongside reviews of very well-respected male theorists such as Roland Barthes and Eric Hobsbawm. *Start* also printed articles clearly conscious of and in critical conversation with feminism and pornographic imagery, with titles such as "History Has a Male Gender" (1979), "How to Undress Pornography" (1980), "The Long War of the Naked Venus" (1980), "Woman Without Clothes" (1981), "The Feminist New Wave" (1981), "Everything About Sexuality: The Hite Report on Male Sexuality" (1981), and "Isn't Pornography Cynical?" (1982).[67]

Yugoslav feminists fiercely debated questions of pornography, warning against its demonization, given that anti-pornographic discourses often discourage any engagement with sexual liberation.[68] At the same time, feminists published in *Start* did not draw a causal relationship between pornography and sexual liberation and equally warned against the violent objectification of women in pornography. Kesić's words most succinctly sum up the impetus for these debates: "Feminists do not put pornography on trial because it shows sex and the human body, but because it does it in an unscrupulous and dehumanised way, usually combined with psychological and physical violence against women."[69] It would be false to assume that the male editorial team was in support of this feminist work. To the contrary, it was feminist authors who had to push to create a feminist space in *Start*. For example, editors wanted to name Kesić's 1978 article on the first feminist conference in Eastern Europe "Old Hag Feminism" ("Trle babe feminizam"), which the author fought against vehemently.[70] But there were many more instances of this sexism behind the scenes of the publication, such as Kesić's recollection of the conflict surrounding the publishing of a Shere Hite interview: "[Hite] said something ironic about male sexuality in the interview, about which my editor told me: we cannot attack our readership, and our readership is male. So I said, but you attack your female readers all the time. I had to fight for every line."[71]

Later, when Kesić came into conflict with American lawyer and writer Catharine MacKinnon's anti-pornographic agenda projected on the war in Bosnia in the 1990s (see Chapter 5), she incisively remarked:

> This occurred in a society where the holy virgin, the devoted, self-sacrificing mother and wife, and the heroic partisan woman (who does the washing for her comrades) were the dominant stereotypes and role models for women. To understand that *Start*'s objectives were radical, initial steps toward changing Yugoslavian society's confining, narrow view of women, cultural differences must be recognized. With such an understanding, it is then possible to see that American theories on sex and pornography may not be appropriately applied in the Yugoslavian context.[72]

While *Start* principally featured stereotypical pornographic shots of naked women similar to American pornographic magazines, it was also a space for illustrations that showed women's sexual agency beyond the figure of the virgin, mother, and partisan hero in the Yugoslav context. Two illustrations by Mirko Ilić in *Start* (Figures 1.15–1.16) show the influence of concurrent feminist debates on the journal's visual content, which challenged and changed

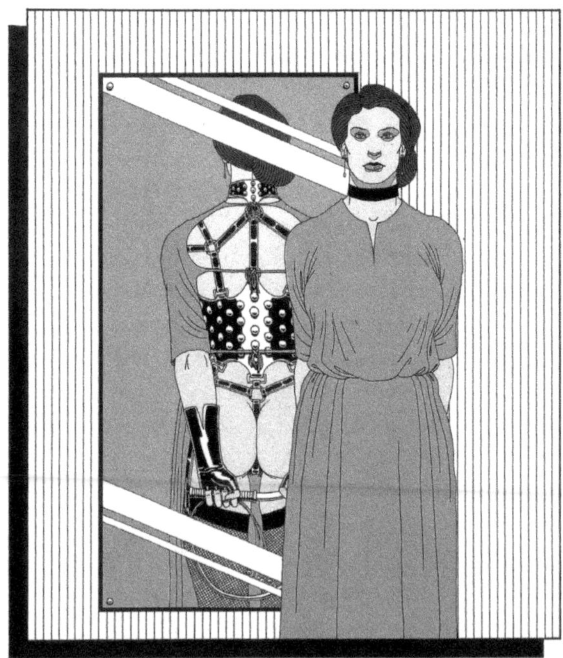

1.15   Mirko Ilić, *The Ideology of Our Girl*, illustration for *Start Magazine* 269 (May 16, 1979).

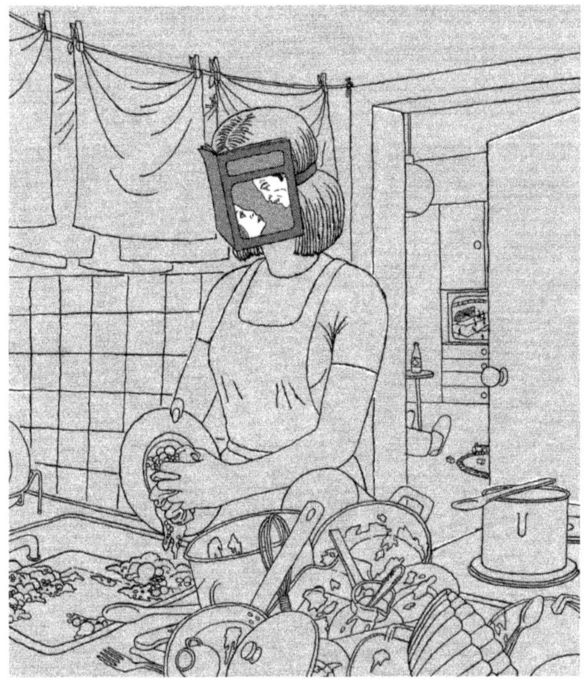

Mirko Ilić, *Why Women Like Fairytales,* illustration for *Start Magazine* 299 (July 9, 1980).   **1.16**

the visual icon of the Yugoslav woman to expose the narrow parameters of her life and offer visual provocations of her emancipation from the domestic heteronormative socialist sphere.[73]

In the first illustration, we see a gorgeous, composed woman in a monochromatic flowing dress staring directly at the viewer (Figure 1.15). The image was titled *Ideologija Naše Cure* (*The Ideology of Our Girl*), and it was paired with Veselko Tenžera's text about the "phenomenon of nudity as a medium" and "the dual morality of 'consuming' this phenomenon."[74] Behind her, a mirror shows the exposed back of her respectable dress, showing she is a dominatrix with a flogger in her hands, latex gloves, a thong, and a studded leather corset. The signature dog collar on her neck only reveals itself as such in the mirror, carefully tucked below her hair arranged in a neat bun. She is a modern version of the fourteenth-century sculpture *Madam World* (*Frau Welt*) from the portal of the St. Sebaldus Church in Nuremberg, which visualized the woman of the world as "seductive and physically corrupt," wearing an identical dress concealing the front of her body, with an opening in the back revealing a diseased and decaying body.[75] Sander L. Gilman links *Madam World* to visualizations of the contagious syphilitic woman during the

Enlightenment, showing "the female as the image of the source of infection" and men as victims of the disease.[76] In this modern version of the Yugoslav woman, she is not physically diseased, but morally perverted, a perversion she can pass on to others, who "consume" this "dual morality." As the carrier of her moral and sexual deviance, she comes to personify a new type of contagion in Yugoslav society: a sexually deviant and liberated, sexy woman, desired by her *Start* audience.

The second illustration is titled *Zašto Žene Vole Bajke* (*Why Women Like Fairytales*),[77] and shows a woman washing the dishes, with clothes drying in the same room, and an open door behind her revealing a tiny slice of the living room (Figure 1.16). This is enough to allow us to discern that there is a man resting on a couch, having a drink, and watching sports. The woman, by contrast, has an open book strapped to the front of her face, obstructing her vision without hindering her ability to do the dishes. Its cover features the profile of a woman and man about to kiss. This small insight into her domestic life renders the dutiful wife faceless, smothered by illusory romance stories that keep her chained to domestic chores whose labor is discounted. Both of these images show a diagnostic portrait of the Yugoslav woman: a dominatrix who hides her sexual desires beneath a veneer of respectability within the private sphere, and a housewife who is lost in romantic fantasy that facilitates her submission to domestic labor. And both point to women's bodies as sights of oppression, desire, and need for liberation.

In bed with socialism: contending with the national body as implicitly male

Just as the private house in Vojvodina adorned with the red star marked a tension between and merging of the private and public sphere, the "bed" is part of women's domestic space which is burdened with expectations of submission to patriarchal paradigms of social and biological reproduction. This section considers women's works that resist such imposition by conceptually probing questions of "being in bed" with socialism and its patriarchal charge. I begin with Sanja Iveković because she has been internationally recognized as the most outspoken, powerful feminist artist of Zagreb, who systemically scrutinized the sexist bedrock of political ideology within Yugoslav media and the arts. Like many feminists of her time, she worked in a predominantly male-dominated art scene and was not an opponent of socialism per se, but rather was disenchanted with the patriarchal erasure of women and their agency in the Yugoslav project. Using her own body, performance, drawings, sculpture, collage, research-based projects, film, and participatory works, Iveković aimed to unfold intricate as well as banal forms of sexism, with a sustained commitment to other women's experiences that remains unmatched to this day. Iveković's practice explored the many nuances of gendered experience. Across her work, women were not painted as victims but instead as complicated subjects with sexual agency.

In her collage, *He is Looking at Me All the Time*, c.1979, she thematized the omnipresence, threat, and invasiveness of the specter of a male political leader in the bedroom: this work featured a black-and-white photograph of Tito placed immediately above a drawing of a female figure in bed, who has a surprised and worried facial expression and is trying to cover her naked body with a much-too-short blanket that bears the hammer and sickle insignia, leaving her legs exposed (Figure 1.17). Through the deliberate use of humor, Iveković's collage made palpable the sense of Tito as the male gaze incarnate, an omnipresent dictator who sexualizes and controls women, invades their privacy, and objectifies them, be it in the bedroom, the school, or the office, pervading public and private spaces alike.

Iveković renders this trenchant critique in the style of a sweet, simple line drawing, akin to a child's private drawing. The playfulness of an otherwise sober feminist critique is methodical here, as the collage also suggests a libidinal relationship between Yugoslav socialism and its women, Jugoslovenkas. What the scanty blanket signals is the shortcomings of Yugoslav socialism's promises for women: the blanket is positioned like a proletariat flag. Its horizontal use exacerbates the failings of the horizontally oriented egalitarianism of socialism, unable to protect women from patriarchal invasion and sexualization. The official state ideology, under the veneer of emancipation and gender equality, reasserted the status of the woman as sexual object, both privately and publicly. The flag itself becomes an erotic symbol instrumentalized to sexualize women in the name of socialist ideology, which decreed that its citizens owed their bodies to the state, the revolution, and their leader.

The image of the father of the people, as powerful as Tito's, was inevitably also libidinally heteronormative: a potent, domineering symbol of national masculinity—for women to desire, and for men to never fully attain. In the atmosphere of new political promise, institutional relationships, and supposed sexual freedoms, the 1970s were an era in which male bosses could still assert their discriminatory dominance over their female colleagues and employees.[78] In fact, as is well known, many of the women artists principally had access to male-dominated art exhibitions and actions through their personal relationships and marriages to men.[79] Finally, Tito himself, charming with a smirk that was the signature of his perceived sex appeal, was a notorious womanizer and had been married numerous times. But by conceptualizing this work as a performance, Iveković also linked women's sexuality, the attractiveness of the beloved lifetime leader and his threatening power, and women's lack of privacy to an emancipatory urgency to escape the president's gaze—and most importantly—to reclaim one's body.

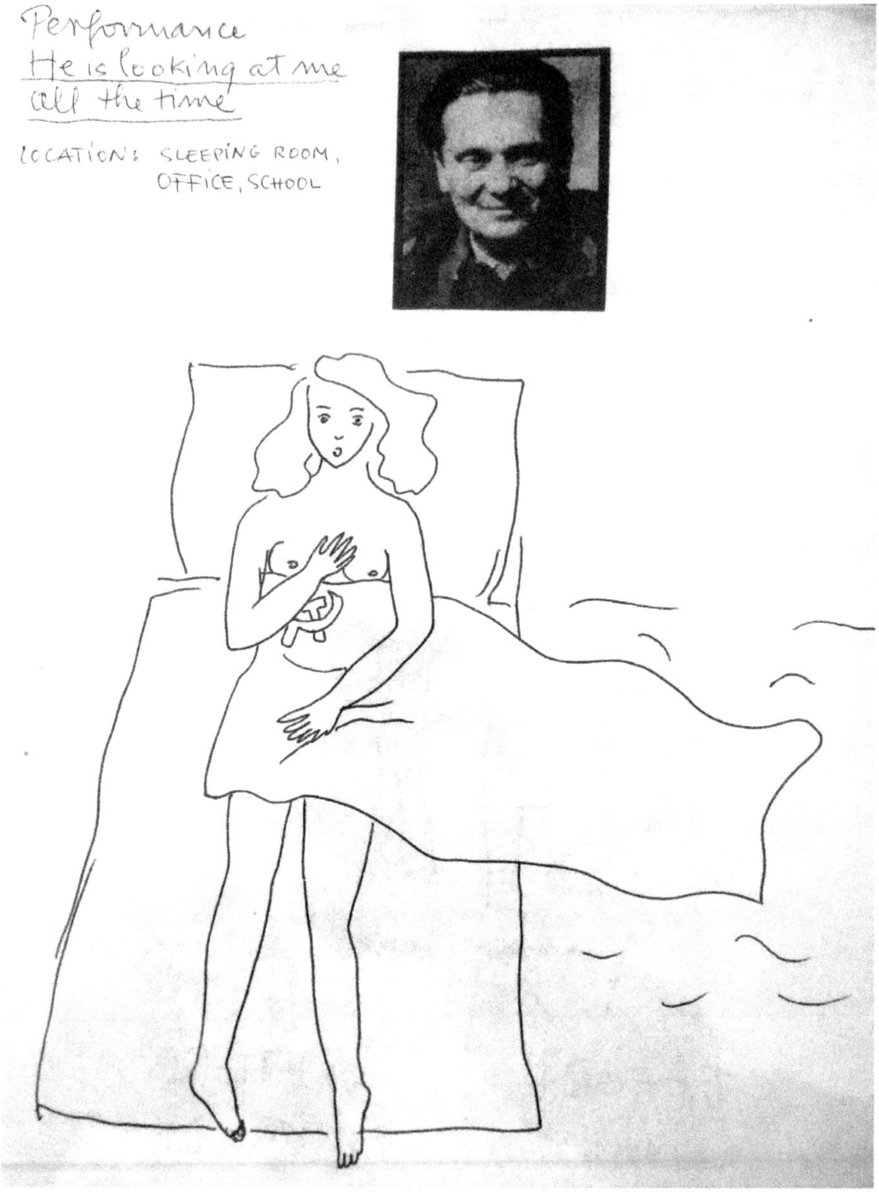

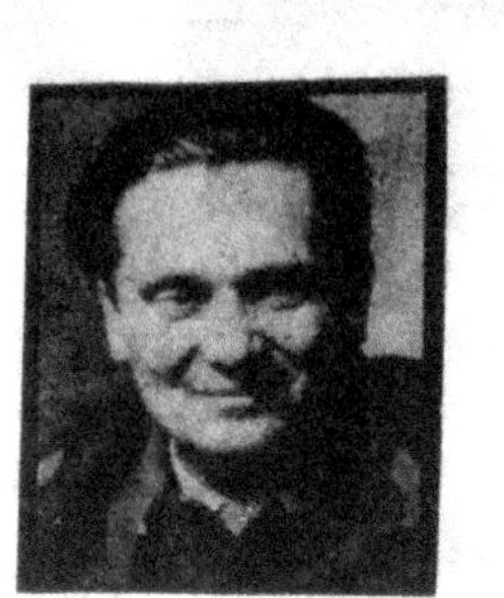

1.17   Sanja Iveković, *He Is Looking at Me All the Time*, c.1979. Drawing and script for performance.

But what about going to bed alone? Or pleasuring oneself? In her now iconic action *Trokut* (*Triangle*), Iveković set herself up on the balcony of her apartment during a visit by Tito to Zagreb in 1979. Reclining on a bench, Iveković deliberately provoked the attention of security personnel on the nearby rooftops surrounding her apartment, assuming that the officers would observe her with binoculars and alert the police that something was amiss. Wearing an American T-shirt while reading a book, sipping whiskey, and gesticulating as if masturbating, she incited the police to make her leave the balcony and stop her "disgraceful" behavior. This intentional "act of disobedience," as Branka Stipančić has called it, revealed the Yugoslavian government's security measures forbidding citizens from viewing the president from their windows or balconies.[80] But Iveković inverted the gaze, confronting the watchdogs of the state with her own calculated measures of counter-surveillance and exposing the regime's fear of a woman who threatens their control by ignoring the president, reading a book on Marxism, drinking whiskey in broad daylight, and pleasuring herself.[81] In addition, the threat also lies in her suggestion as to what really happens in the domestic sphere: not nurturing, homemaking, and child-rearing, but instead explorations of sexuality and positionings of the body right on the porous line between the private and public, both literally and symbolically. It took less than eighteen minutes for the police to intervene and stop her private act in a public, highly politicized and surveyed space. Reading Marx (erotically) in *Trokut* is an act of self-love, subverting the patriarchal expectation of how Marxism may have shaped her generation of women as indoctrinated worshippers of the paternalistic leader, and instead showing a woman who boldly critiques and parodies the regime using their own central text: a Jugoslovenka who loves herself and socialism more than her president.

For Iveković, feminist art was not just about analysis, but about changing perceptions, raising awareness, and pushing for change. As early as the mid-1970s, Iveković rigorously analyzed advertisements and propaganda material on TV and in newspapers "to enact," as Bago has argued, "a transformation from woman as object of representation to autonomous artistic subject."[82] In her *Tragedija Jedne Venere* (*Tragedy of a Venus*) series (1975) (Figure 1.18), she made twenty-five photomontages pairing her personal photographs with clippings she collected from the magazine *Duga*, which put out a special issue on Hollywood star Marilyn Monroe in 1975 with the title "Tragedy of a Venus."[83] These pairings were less about judgment of women and more about revealing women's shared modes of embodying compulsory beauty standards, whether in commercially or privately produced photographs. "Iveković does not adopt a condescending attitude whereby art is presented as superior to other occupations," Bago notes. "She points to their co-dependencies and relations, and to her own entanglements with the dominant ideals of female

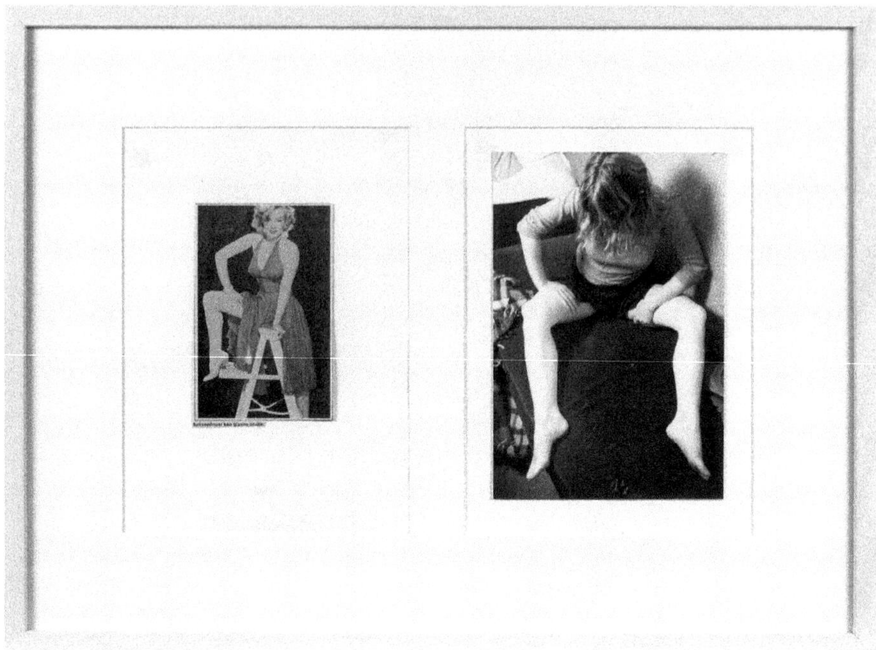

1.18   Sanja Iveković, *Tragedy of a Venus*, 1975.

beauty and 'femininity,' while at the same time submitting such ideals to critical deconstruction."[84] These deconstructions serve in the spirit of emancipatory liberation within the socialist state, not against it. As noted, Iveković supported socialist political ideals but was invested in exposing how patriarchal leadership obstructed women's possibilities for liberation and social mobility. In one of the pairings, we see Iveković sitting with spread legs on a bed or sofa, mimicking Monroe's same posture on a ladder. The metaphorical affinity is potently clear, as the ascension of women in their careers and society so frequently depends on their willingness to go to bed with the right people, usually men.

The site of the bed would become central to another artist from Croatia discussed in the section "Burgeoning feminist performance politics," slightly younger than Iveković and entering the scene toward the end of the 1970s: Delimar. Her conceptual use of the bed is antithetical to Iveković's in the sense that she fully embraces it as a site of pleasure, disregarding the patriarchal violence with which that site is marked. Furthermore, Delimar unabashedly celebrates the male body and exclaims her desire and love for heterosexual sex in her work. Not surprisingly, compared to Abramović and Iveković, Delimar has proven a less marketable artist to Western and local audiences. This is most likely due to the fact that she explicitly embodied and performed women's erotic desires, challenging the paradigms of normative sexuality within the arts while paradoxically resisting alliance with feminism.

Delimar's time in bed with socialism is a complicated and contested story with loose ends and incoherent narratives, which makes her work especially potent with meaning. Delimar is renowned in Croatia but has been ignored internationally for a long time. Ljiljana Kolešnik characterizes Delimar's work, which relies on highly sexualized "intuitive feminism," as "a unique phenomenon in our country that had no parallel even then, and there is none today."[85] Her work has been left out of most exhibitions on performance and other kinds of art from Eastern Europe and especially the Balkans, with the exception of Bojana Pejić's exhibition *Gender Check* at mumok in Vienna (2009). Delimar was also omitted from IRWIN's book *East Art Map* (2006) and Piotr Piotrowski's survey of Yugoslav art from 1945 to 1989, *In the Shadow of Yalta* (2009).[86] She often does not appear in other important surveys of the region. Similar to the generally negative reception that dogged Carolee Schneemann up until the final years of her life, Delimar has been charged with producing pornographic, narcissistic, exhibitionist work that is too sexually explicit.

In her 1981 *Vizualni Orgazam* (*Visual Orgasm*), Delimar libidinally charges the site of the bed under socialism (Figure 1.19). Arranged as a grid of twelve black-and-white photographs of the artist's face grimacing in pleasure during masturbation, the images show Delimar on her back in a bed with her head on a large white pillow. The grid lines are made of soft blue embroidery, while her lips are painted pinkish-red. In my view, this added coloration evokes the colors of the Yugoslav flag: blue and white stripes with a red star in the middle. Yet clearly the pinkish-red lips stand in for a different political agenda than the red socialist star in the Yugoslav flag: not socialist brotherhood and unity, and not even its imagined feminist equivalent of sisterhood. Instead, Delimar's *Visual Orgasm* is a radical investment in individual women's right to joy and sexual pleasure, wrapped in delicate embroidery, with the moaning mouth at the center of this reconfigured, iconic political emblem.

Despite these emphases on her own emancipatory sexual liberation, Delimar never identified as a feminist. As her art openly proclaims a desire and love for men, it has also often been interpreted as misogynistic.[87] This familiar charge echoes Belgrade's 1978 feminist conference when British "butch" women looked down on Yugoslav feminists for having painted nails and wearing lipstick. Accusations of women who flaunted their sexuality as perpetrators of patriarchal misogyny were a common point of conflict in feminist circles in Yugoslavia as well as the West in the late 1970s. In this context, pornography and pornographic imagery, along with sexual liberation, became divisive elements in feminist circles. In the USA, Andrea Dworkin is the most outspoken critic of pornography within feminist discourses. Along

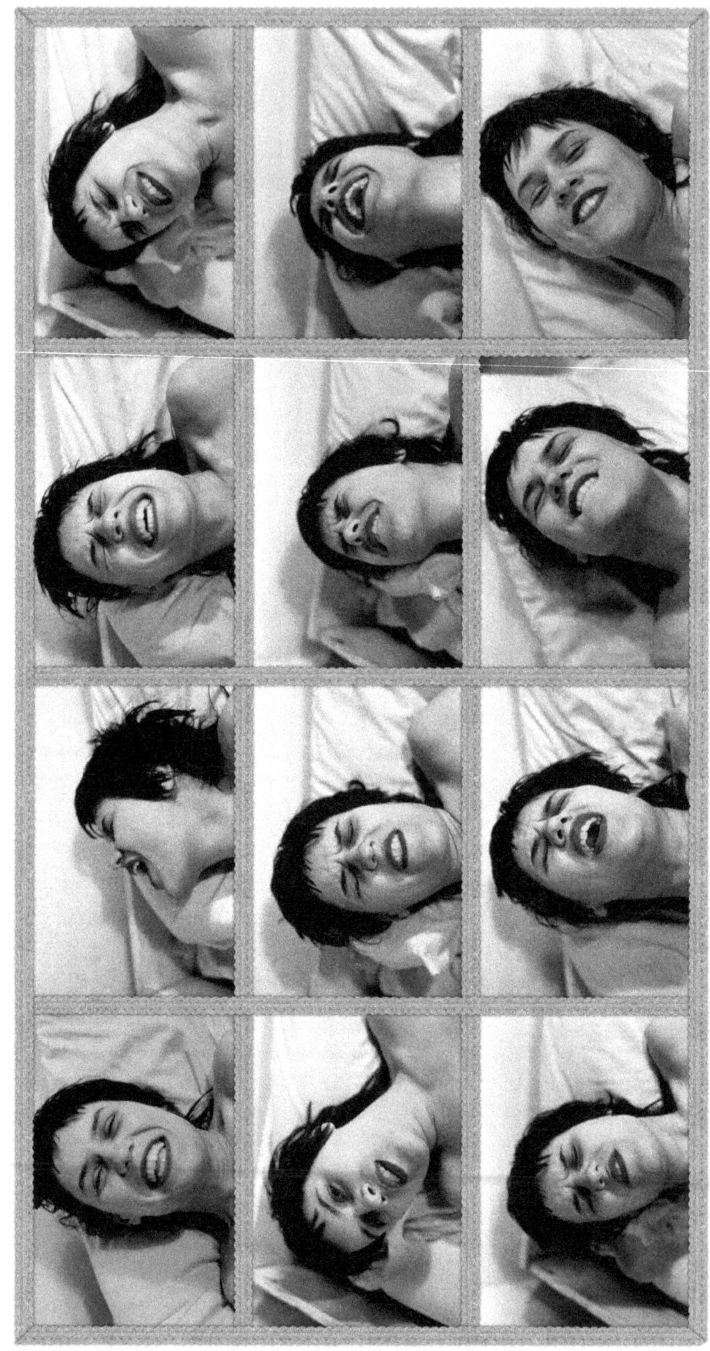

1.19 Vlasta Delimar, *Visual Orgasm*, 1981.

with organizations such as Women Against Violence in Pornography and Media and Women Against Pornography arising in the later 1970s, Dworkin and Susan Brownmiller "were holding conferences, conducting research, and developing theories about the harm pornography posed to women."[88] Dworkin considered pornography to represent a "new terrorism" in forms of "death threats to a female population in rebellion ... against male sexual authority" that was invested in the humiliation of women.[89] Writers for *Start* magazine such as Slavenka Drakulić and Kesić defended pornography and pornographic imagery in part because conservatism, or "bourgeois moral-ity," toward sexual liberation often pretends to protect women but actually oppresses them even more with projections of purity and motherhood. At the same time, neither Drakulić nor Kesić thought that the simple act of nudity could bring any liberation. In 1980, Drakulić wrote in *Start*:

> The erotic magazines, which have such a revolutionary function, created a general euphoria around the so-called sexual revolution, a euphoria in which they don't see the forest from the tree, creating an illusion that despite all, the naked female body testifies of some sort of a liberation of women [sic]. By this logic, porn magazines would be the major [fertile ground] for feminism.[90]

Drakulić's critique of the misleading euphoric response to the celebration of female sexuality within the frame of the male gaze is accurate. Liberation does not occur through the replication of negative stereotypes and the objectifica-tion of women. But we have seen over time in feminist discourses that women persistently find their own language of emancipation and empowerment within the repressive visual economy of sexual exploitation. A recent example is Lorene Scafaria's film *Hustlers* (2019), which focuses on sex workers and red-light district dancers who con their wealthy Wall Street clients. The film was decried for replicating misogynist emphases on beautiful and sexy bodies, but also celebrated by feminists for the ways in which the characters—overwhelmingly women of color—exhibited sex-positive agency over their own bodies and formed a collective resistance against their morally and politi-cally corrupt patrons, as well as the system that props those men up and holds women down. These patrons are exposed for their entitlement, both in exploit-ing women's bodies and the world through capitalist greed. As such, it is important to caution against one-dimensional negative appellations of women selling their bodies to a male audience because such dismissive perspectives ignore or purposefully reject the unprecedented ways in which taking agency over one's own body can manifest. What's more, viewing empowered women in art and film influences female viewers. A critique of women who flaunt their sexuality often falls into the trap of assuming a male viewer, or worse, assum-ing that women are already so victimized that they inherently lack the ability to see through patriarchal oppression. Worst of all, such critiques can also result in erasing the possibility of female pleasure. Delimar's works embody a feminist performance politics because she claimed pleasure for herself and confronted female sexuality without shame or fear of moral condemnation, from both women and men. In my interview with Delimar, she explained: "It's strange that women couldn't recognize that I am on their side and that I am working on myself for women."[91] She added: "Everybody has to fight for themselves. If you don't learn to fight for yourself, you won't have the strength to fight for others."[92] This fight for oneself, according to Delimar, is linked to pleasure: "I am interested in women's autonomy in owning their pleasures. I am always trying to convey the message: women, enjoy yourselves."[93]

Asserting her sexuality was feminist in a social context where deep conservatism and sexism in the socialist left pervaded social and political life, Slapšak has pointed out how notorious womanizers like the politician Dragoljub Mićunović frequently made comments during his public lectures about how there were "too many women wearing make-up and dressed up in his audience."[94] The control over women's bodies by socialist politicians and intellectuals, including Praxis leftist Mihailo Marković, haunts the memories of many feminists. Feminist theorist Vesna Kesić remembers that Marković was, overall, tolerant of the new feminist movement, but in contrast to Mićunović, requested of women, "'Could you please look more feminine?'"[95] It is within this political context that we must understand Delimar's deliberate embrace of her own desires. On the surface, the moment of her moan can be read as a simple affirmation of women's pleasure. Yet, intensified by her laughter, the biting of her lips, her turning head and unkempt hair pressed against the pillow, as well as her squinting eyes, Delimar's joyous and courageous embrace of her private pleasure was as much an intervention against the male-dominated art scene as it was a political statement that prioritized women's sexual independence. In its advocacy of women's sexual pleasures, the grid-like structure of *Visual Orgasm*—denoting women's labor in its use of embroidery—can also be read as breaking through the social and political constraints put on women and their pleasures in Yugoslavia at the time.

In another work from 1985, Delimar took to task male bravado by inverting the commonplace missionary position of male bodies situated between women's spread legs and objectifying her male lover (Figure 1.20). With a cutout of her naked torso and face placed in the center, including the fragment of her lover's hairy leg lifted up with his foot resting on the side of her face, her confident and satisfied facial expression underscores the position of the man beneath her serving at her pleasure. The photograph is adorned by a veil-like material echoing that of a wedding dress, but here in amplified punk fashion typical of the 1980s, it is glued to a wrinkled piece of shiny black fabric (or paper), while a golden paper most likely taken from a pack of cigarettes blankets the lower part of her body and that of her lover. The gold reappears

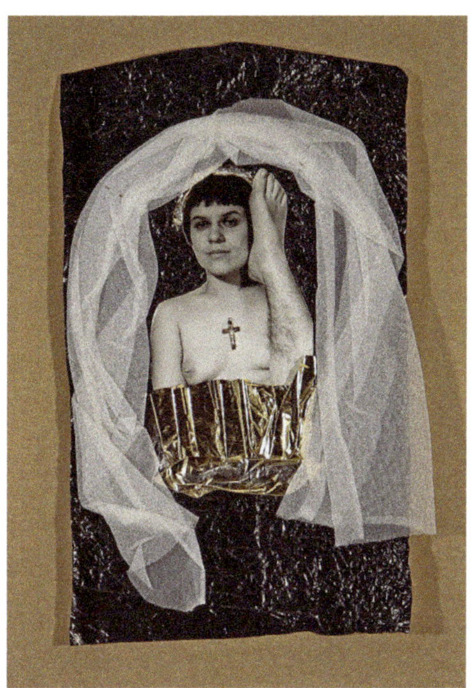

Vlasta Delimar, *Untitled*, 1985. **1.20**

in the crucifix of the Catholic Church between her breasts, a strategic place-ment which, along with the halo-like veil and the golden-brown background, also plays with imageries of the Madonna, who here clearly is simultaneously whore, a dichotomy frequently explored in feminist thought. Art theorist and conceptual artist Miško Šuvaković has commented on this connection to Catholic religious imagery, noting that Delimar's work marks a "break-through" in our understanding of "sin" with all its "otherwise invisible ideo-logical folds, promises, and prohibitions."[96] I am also reminded of Iveković's spread legs in *Tragedy of a Venus*, a gesture that in Delimar's work is neither tragic nor reserved for women: Delimar's men spread their legs for her—flexible and submissive—as she is a different Madonna who embraces tabooed sexual desire and takes what she wants in bed. The threat to patriarchy becomes most explicit in Delimar's work, as the bed in socialism is transformed into the site of female creativity—not biological creation (or nationalist reproduc-tion)—where the intimate and private gain political significance when shared without inhibition as art. In this way, Delimar's embrace of female sexuality generated new narratives and possibilities for pleasure and reversed gender roles during socialism.

The site of the bed as one of gender role reversals and female creativity could also transcend the question of sexism and sexual pleasure altogether, if we instead considered the gendered site of the home and bed with a new emphasis on political harmony. Much like Iveković, art historian and curator Jasna Tijardović believed in the Marxist promise of intellectual and artistic growth. This political idea manifested itself in a photo performance developed and recorded by her and her husband, conceptual artist Zoran Popović, in 1973, which featured a small red star and Popović and Tijardović as protagonists. But here, the engagement with socialism and the intimate sphere of their gender-egalitarian home takes on new meaning. Titled *Rad Sa Crvenom Zvezdom* (*Work with the Red Star*), Tijardović and Popović document one another as they each handle a small red star across more than thirty photographs.[97]

These photos were first shown during a "farewell party" exhibition for the couple on February 13, 1974, organized by the SKC, before their departure for New York.[98] In two striking images from the series, published in 2007 by the Cultural Center Belgrade on the occasion of Popović's exhibition *Vremenski Radovi 1973–2006* (*Time Works 1973–2006*), Tijardović is shown lying down in the couple's apartment on Bulevar Oktobarske Revolucije 52a in Belgrade (Figures 1.21–1.22). In one of the images, Tijardović is on the bed in a fetal position, gently holding—and contemplating—the tiny red star in her left palm; in the other image, Tijardović reclines on the same bed, laughing exuberantly, fully dressed in blue jeans, a blue blouse, and white socks; she is on her back with her arms behind her head, her right foot resting on her angled knee, and the small red star stuck to the bottom of her right foot. The signature blue jeans, which were frequently worn by counter-culture Yugoslav youth, along with the red star and white (or cream) hand-knitted coverlet, visually connect Tijardović to the country's red-white-blue colors, marking her as distinctly Yugoslav. The emancipatory power of this image is deepened by the way in which her joyous laughter—visually conjuring up Delimar's pleasure—is captured by the sunlight coming through the windows, leaving traces of gridded shadows along the bed, walls, and floor. These shadows, like the grid structuring Delimar's photographs in *Visual Orgasm*, evoke the specter of the horizontal bars of the Yugoslav flag, in the middle of which lies the red star.

The Yugoslav flag was the conceptual foundation for a silhouette portrait of Tijardović by Popović in 1971, when the artist inserted the contours of her body into the horizontal middle-white stripe of the flag for a tempera drawing, *Jasna Tijardović: Jugoslovenska Zastava* (*Jasna Tijardović: Yugoslav Flag*) (Figure 1.23). Popović made the drawing on March 8, 1971, on International Women's Day, a critical holiday in Yugoslavia honoring women workers across the nation and worldwide. Tijardović appears as Jugoslovenka personified, with the Yugoslav red star crowning her vaginal area, her face emerging

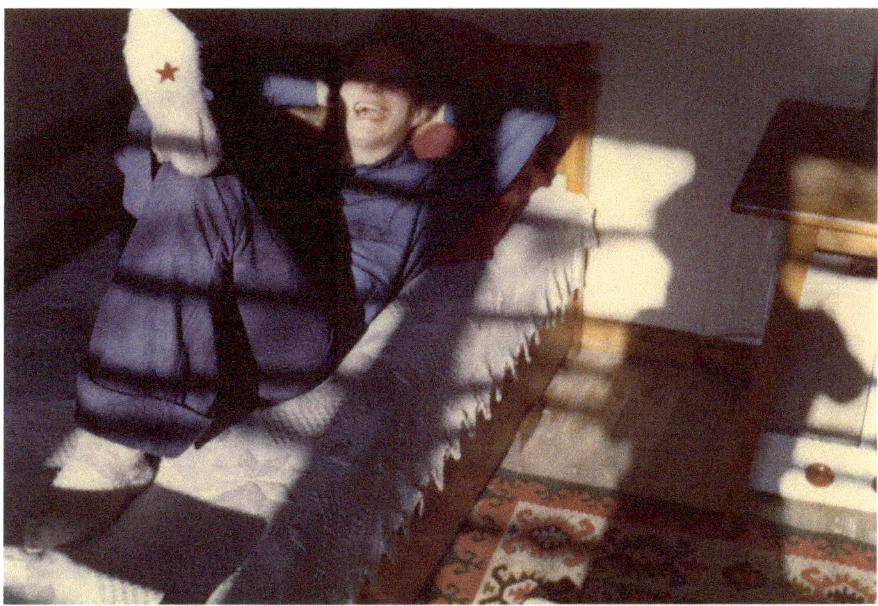

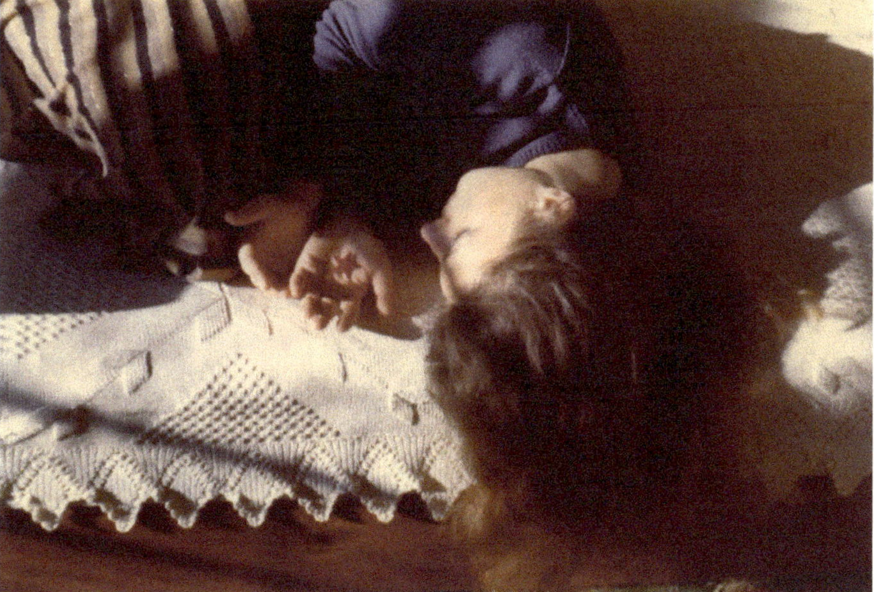

Zoran Popović in collaboration with Jasna Tijardović, *Work with the Red Star*, Boulevard of the October Revolution 52a, Belgrade, 1973. Photo–performance.	**1.21–1.22**

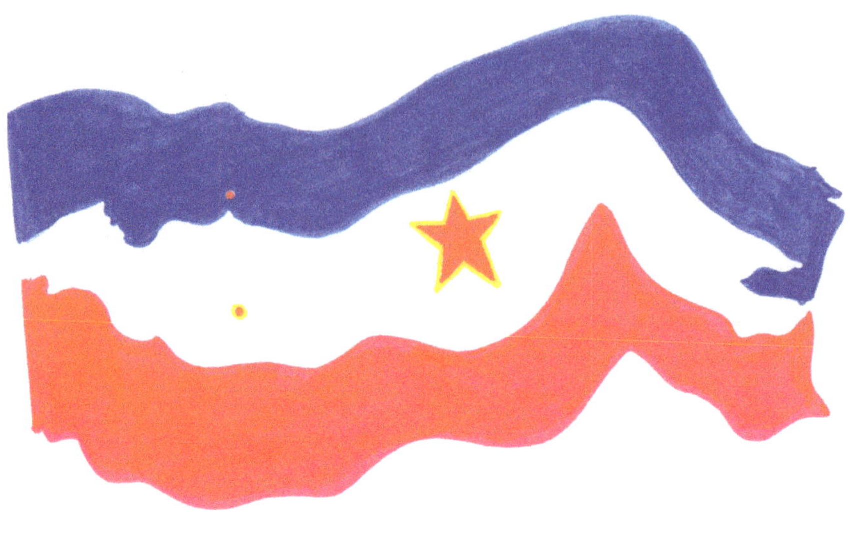

1.23   Zoran Popović, *Jasna Tijardović: Yugoslav Flag*, tempera drawing created in the painting studio of the Home of the Yugoslav People's Army (JNA Home), Zagreb, March 8, 1971.

in profile in the blue color, and her legs elegantly crossed. Like Delimar, she lies horizontally within this flag; her mouth is slightly open but in an ambiguous way. While the joy spills off every frame in Delimar's *Visual Orgasm*, Tijardović's moan appears almost as if trapped in the flag, with her arms disappearing in her silhouette. Drawn by her lover, who was living in the military barracks at the time, this homage to both Tijardović and his country suggests the paradoxical trappings of the more women-oriented Yugoslav state: the framework of the nationalistic flag here honors the woman at its very center, but it does so by relegating her body to the horizontal—lying down—position, and consigning the star—her power—between her legs.

Despite the emphasis on her sex, there is no libidinally charged masturbatory joy in the flag, just as there is none in the photographs showing Tijardović on the bed in Belgrade. Returning once more to *Work with the Red Star*, the bed here is also a site that reflects the modesty of the home, indicating a rejection of the elitism of the red bourgeoisie of the nouveau riche or what Blažević called *kleinbürger* (Figures 1.21–1.22). The hand-knitted coverlet, like Delimar's embroidery, signals women's labor and creativity. Tijardović was herself a curator and art historian active in the SKC scene, boldly intervening in discussions with a feminist and Marxist critique of the state and its alternative student cultural center. But in these photographs, Tijardović reminds us that art and politics are part of everyday life, and that they can be transformative for the body and the sphere of the private home—two realms often associated with women. Here, the site of the bed is not a point from which to critique sexism in socialist society, or to embrace emancipatory desire. Instead, Tijardović's resting and joyous body, as she played with the star, allowed her to transform her emancipatory performativity into a political gesture privileging gentleness and care. Like Iveković and Delimar, she converted the patriarchal site of the bed—in which women are usually expected to serve their husbands and reproduce for the nation—into a site of feminist emancipation through performative and contemplative activities that bore none of the typical masculinized bravado of activism nor the reference to the celebrated "warrior" women partisans of World War II. The shadow of her husband Popović, who took the photographs, aligned with that of the window's grid cast upon the bed, offers a poignant reminder that women in Marxist circles were still subject to the male gaze and control. But as in his action with Sally Holman (see the section "Burgeoning feminist performance politics"), he is only a shadow and Tijardović is neither sex object nor objectified. She is recorded in her simple play with the star on the bed—her political context—which she nurtures, making potently clear that Jugoslovenkas had much more to offer than their bodies and their beauty.

But what about bringing the bed into the gallery space? How might taking the bed out of familiar private homes and into the public change how we understand what "going to bed" with socialism means? In *Oslobadjanje Glasa* (*Freeing the Voice*),[99] Marina Abramović performed an action that included lying on a makeshift bed on her back and screaming for three hours in front of an audience during the April Meeting in 1975 (Figure 1.24). The score read:

I lie on the floor with my head tilted backward.

Performance

I scream until I lose my voice.[100]

With her eyes wide open and lying down with her legs up, Abramović turned her scream into a tormented howl, one that induced empathy in the viewer, who witnessed and heard what might be described as the primal scream of women's experience, from giving birth to rape, from war to murder and oppression. But these interpretations are contemporary projections that were referenced nowhere in the action, as the work itself was non-referential and centered on the female body as a raw instrument of endurance, vocalization,

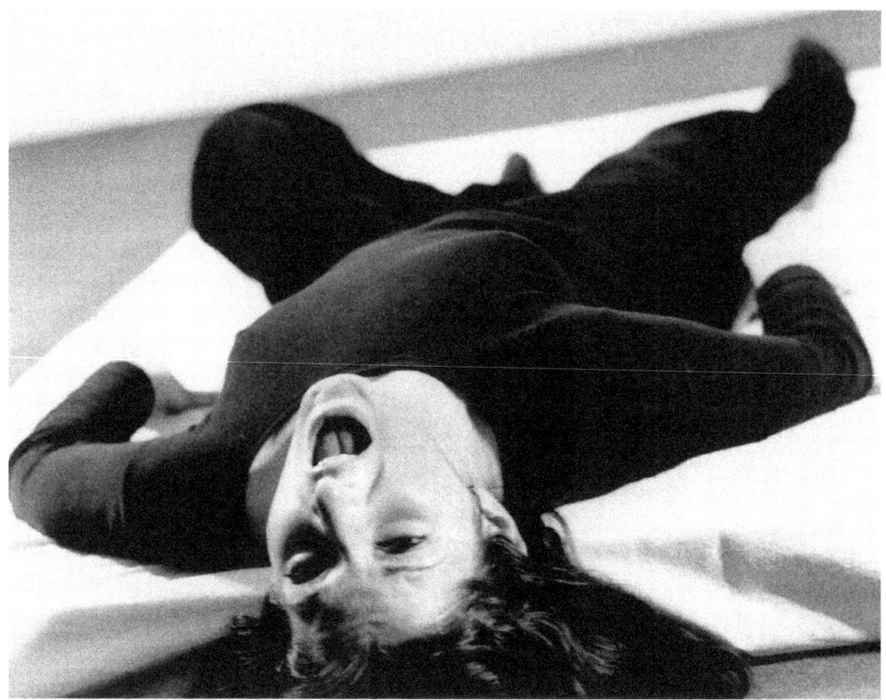

1.24   Marina Abramović, *Freeing the Voice*, performance (3 hours). Student Cultural Center, Belgrade, 1975.

and agency. It must be understood that Abramović's extreme body works were out of character with her male colleagues at SKC, the Group of Six, with the exception, to some degree, of those of Todosijević.[101] Moreover, Abramović did not identify as a feminist at the time and has been committed to such a disavowal ever since. Nonetheless, both Pejić and Šuvaković propose that some of Abramović's work "could be read in feminist terms," though the artist does not have a feminist agenda.[102] The display of total control through complete submission to the strictures of her own body characterizes Abramović's body works, a conceptual and corporeal strategy that bore the emotional and psychic intensity of a woman, an aesthetic otherwise absent at the SKC.

Only five years earlier, inspired by the American artist Raphael Montañez Ortiz's *Self-Destruction* performance at the Destruction in Art Symposium in London in 1966, psychologist and psychiatric social worker Arthur Janov published his best-selling book, *Primal Scream* (1970).[103] Janov argued that "screaming" would release the pain resulting from a traumatic wound buried in the unconscious. The emphasis on releasing psychic pain through bodily action was of prevalent concern to artists in the 1960s and 1970s, especially feminists, and while Janov's therapeutic approach was widely undertaken by such artists as John Lennon and Yoko Ono, it was equally widely contested as ineffective by psychologists. Nonetheless, by reducing her experience to an animalistic howl, Abramović felt that she had "freed" her "voice."

In her vulnerable position of lying on the bed for everyone to see, the extreme minimalism of Abramović's endurance piece also spoke to what she calls her "spartan" convictions, an aesthetic marking both intense admiration of her mother's partisan strength and a rebellious inversion of it. In her 2016 memoir *Walk through Walls*, Abramović repeatedly mentions her "headstrong nature, as a daughter of tough partisans," and the "walk-through-walls tough-ness [her] parents had passed along to [her]," which she termed "Spartan determination."[104] But her constant mention of her mother, Danica Abramović (née Rosić), as a source of discipline and strength, deeply resonates with my own experience of feminist empowerment through the influence of my Yugo-slav mother and grandmother discussed in the Introduction. In the simplest terms, the Spartans were a warrior people whose women were more emanci-pated than in any other place in the ancient Greek world, and who were cel-ebrated as superb athlete warriors.[105] The Spartans' reduced aesthetic—austerity and lack of comforts—was in the service of the state, for which the idea of the warrior was the body politic.

Abramović's identification with spartanism also points to her controversial and often contradictory stands on her socialist background. Time and again, Abramović has expressed her disgust for the "Communist dictatorship" and its "perpetual shortages of everything, drabness everywhere" and has called Yugoslavia "a dark place."[106] However contested Abramović's declarations about communism in the region have been by art historians over time,[107] the idea of austerity and lack of comforts was conceptually tied to both her mother and the Yugoslav project. She writes extensively about her mother, and how as an artist she owed the rigor of her practice to her. According to Abramović, Danica Abramović was an "ambivalent Communist, but … a tough one" who never screamed and who could endure a lot of pain. "Nobody has, and nobody ever will hear me scream," Abramović quotes her mother saying. She adds: "I learned my self-discipline from her."[108] In contrast to her mother, then, Abramović screamed the entire time, though ultimately to experiment with disciplining her bodily faculties.

Abramović's self-proclaimed self-discipline and "spartan" aesthetic translated into a work that left her alone in bed. Unlike the other examples described, Abramović's going to bed with socialism is decidedly solitary here, self-referential, and an act of endurance through which the artist filters all the violence of gender and socialism into her body. Abramović's howl on the bed lacks a coherent narrative or testimony; it does not directly reference the ideology of socialism, but nevertheless it is intensely communal. Despite her self-contained action, her emancipatory performance politics emanate from her by making her voice, throat, and body, tensely horizontal and upside-down, the instrument of vocalizing pain from the site of the bed in front of a witnessing public. In her process of freeing her voice, Abramović does not require the imagined presence of a male partner, not even in the form of an implied narrative. Her body and howl are not restrained by the Yugoslav flag. But she does want an audience, one that she leaves no choice but to feel the vibrations of her painful sounds, even decades later, watching the performance as a recording. Abramović contends with the masculine national body by expunging it and becoming her own instrument of meaning making.

Absorbing the power of the Yugoslav socialist flag and its leader: points of resistance and emancipation

In a portrait of Iveković by Dalibor Martinis, we see Iveković standing in front of seventeen Yugoslav flags (Figure 1.25). The way in which the artist looks straight into the camera solidifies my reading of Iveković as a self-confident, young Jugoslovenka with her own ambition for and vision of socialism. This

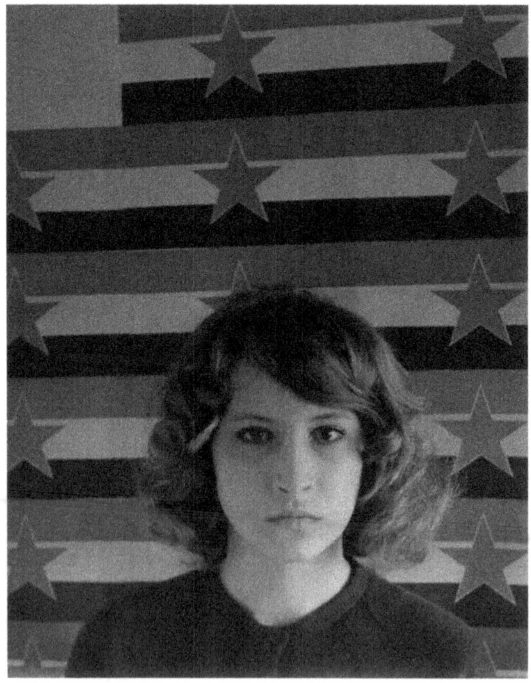

1.25 Sanja Iveković, 1975. Photograph by Dalibor Martinis.

photograph also points to the fact that the iconography of the Yugoslav state became an important place of conceptual and performative intervention for women artists. Instead of exploring conceptual and performance works that embraced state socialism by serving a type of state feminism, in this section I want to briefly single out those who challenged the symbolism of the state through a form of emancipatory performance politics and who used distinctly Yugoslav markers: the socialist flag or Tito.

While the examples of performance works related to the site of the bed by Iveković, Delimar, Tijardović, and Abramović all engage with at least one of these two markers of Yugoslav national identity, I want to turn briefly to an artist here who I have not discussed yet, but who was one of the first women in Yugoslavia to openly use her own body as art in conceptual, performance, and mail artworks: Katalin Ladik. Her works as a poet, actress, and performance and sound artist have marked her as one of the most important avant-garde artists to come out of Yugoslavia and Eastern Europe in general. Working since the late 1960s, Ladik performed in Belgrade and Zagreb regularly, but she was based in Novi Sad, Vojvodina, which was an autonomous province in Serbia with a large Hungarian population. Within the context of international performance art by women, Ladik's artistic approach reflected her ability to push the woman's body and its unbridled voice into yet new "forbidden" territories. In an action in Vienna in 1975, *Identifikacija* (*Identification*), the artist stood behind an imposingly large hanging Yugoslav flag on the impressive neoclassical building of the Academy of Fine Arts in Vienna (Figure 1.26).

Here, her head is eclipsed by the flag, connoting in one simple action both a symbolic decapitation of women, and in a more geopolitical sense, that women's ideas, expressions, and voices had become forbidden or occluded territories under the national flag of Yugoslavia. In a second photo, she shows her head in front of the flag, playing here symbolically with the re-emergence and disappearance of women before and behind the flag (Figure 1.27). One might read this action as a provocation for the state to consider its role in repressing women's leadership in the socialist state despite its progress toward equality. That same year, she also made a paper collage titled *Laž Papir* (*Cheating Paper*) that can be read as a visual equivalent of the feminist critiques of the Yugoslav project during the time (Figure 1.28)—namely, that Yugoslavia was only equal and fair on paper, and that it had abandoned its initial mission to support women and their work.

Ladik was outspoken about her position as a woman and artist in the Yugoslav state. In the 1981 February issue of *Start* she noted:

> I have radically aligned myself with a particular artistic worldview—my whole life is a synthesis of performances, like public undressing, announcing my death, and accidental occurrences. Doing all this, I tempt both myself and my

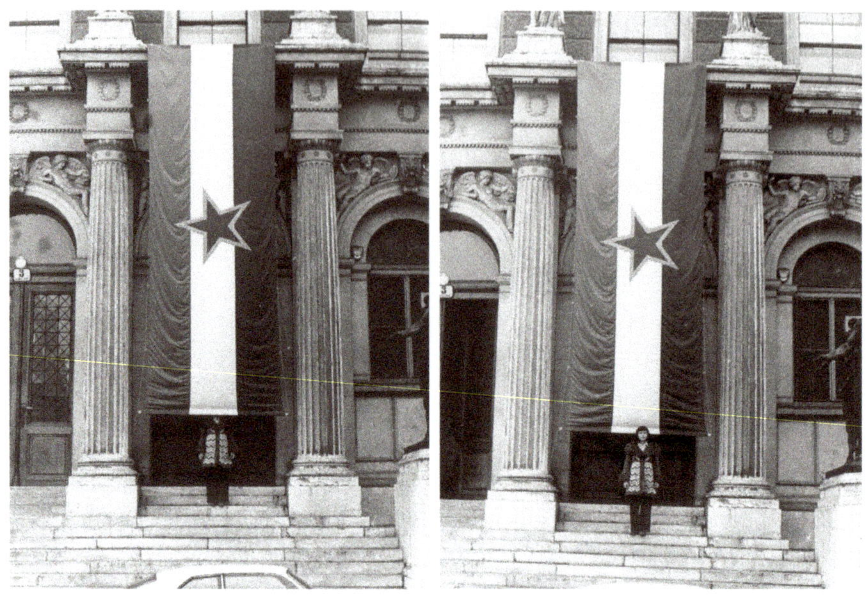

1.26–1.27 Katalin Ladik, *Identification*, Akademie der bildenden Künste Wien, 1975. Gelatin silver prints.

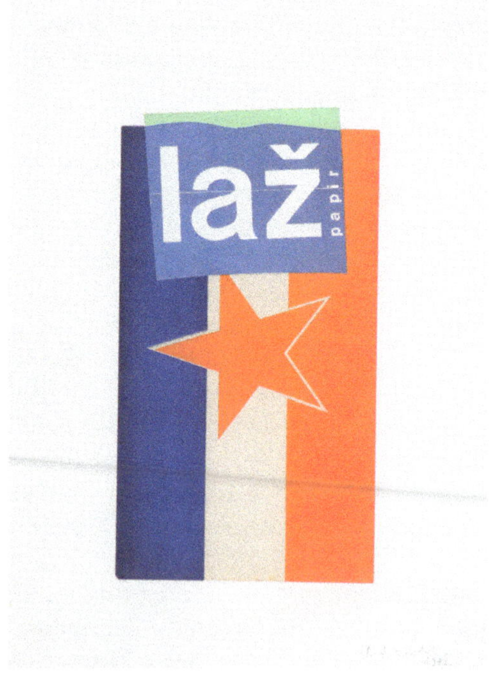

1.28 Katalin Ladik, *Cheating Paper*, 1973. Collage, paper.

surroundings and thus affirm myself, because everything I had been doing was an attempt at self-discovery. Meanwhile, I have never idealized myself. I accepted all aspects and contradictions—both these gilded nude photographs and the need to maintain this illusion for the audience, including my real life in Novi Sad (…) where I support myself and my son with minimal resources. I consider everything I do socially, ethnically and geographically justified, bearing in mind that two hundred kilometers south or east, or two hundred kilometers north or west, everything would be different.[109]

Ladik traces the geography of her country and collapses it with the condition of her life as a mother struggling to make ends meet and pushing her art toward self-discovery, regardless of any contradictions or reproaches. Ladik, even in 2021, is one of the most prolific artists in the region, but her work was not immediately well received during the 1980s and 1990s. Reflecting on the Hungarian situation in the 1990s, Hungarian art historian Edit András blamed the "pollution and poisonous gases like Eastern European sexism whose heavy smell permeates every layer and sphere of society" for the negative reception of Ladik's work.[110] For her, such a condition leads to "the instant ostracizing and professional discrediting of anyone said to be associated with gender or feminism-related issues—methods and devices [of the oppression of women] that have long become unacceptable in the West."[111] While András rightly points to the discrepancy of reception and production of feminist thought and action between East and West, neither "territory" has even come close to eradicating patriarchy and its destructive mechanisms of oppression. Surely Ladik's pointed critique of Yugoslav nationhood—along with her enigmatic charisma as an experimental poet, performer, artist, and intellectual—were in part what barred her from reaching international acclaim at the time.

Delimar's resistance to the dogmas of Yugoslav socialism—relegated to pornography or narcissism instead of being recognized for its political dimensions—is pivotal to understanding the feminist strength of her work. Here, I want to point to two more works by Delimar, one which directly references Tito in a performance, and another which rejects the state socialist program of women warriors. In 1980, it became very clear to Delimar that she could not escape her own political context for the sake of self-expression, pleasure, or her art practice. Unlike Ladik and Iveković, Delimar created no overt political work commenting on Yugoslavia and its politics. Similarly to Abramović, Delimar focused on herself and her career. When her first solo performance was scheduled for the spring of 1980 at the SC Gallery in Zagreb, it was put on "on hold" for months because of Tito's hospitalization and impending death. She remembered that it was not clear if or when he would die, and that Tito and his political sphere intruded on her ability to make and present her work as a young artist. "There was a huge hysteria then in

Yugoslavia," she noted. "Everybody was afraid of what will happen when Tito dies." She added: "To me, that was so absurd, so senseless. As a young woman I thought: why should I care so much about this old man? All I wanted to do is work."[112] Tito died on May 4, 1980, but she would have to wait a few more months "until the situation calmed down in the nation." When she finally did her performance, she presented herself like a mannequin, stripping in the gallery in front of people until she ended up nude. A photograph of the performance shows her standing naked against a wall (Figure 1.29).

She decided to add words to the photograph to commemorate the circumstances of her performance, ultimately writing (and later calling the work): "Ovo sam bila ja 1980 kada je umro drug Tito" ("This was me in 1980 when comrade Tito died"). She explained: "Tito had put me through such an ordeal to do this performance, I had to add it to the work."[113] Despite her frustration with politics and politicians, her words still express a tender relationship with Yugoslavia's leader, "comrade Tito." Tito's "special type of charm," as she called it in our conversation, had an important influence on the ways in which Yugoslav society dealt with sexuality.[114] Delimar took as inspiration Tito's and other men's narcissism and decided that if men can be narcissists, so can she.

For Delimar, this advocacy for women's pleasure was a universalist project removed from any geographic context or national project. She noted:

> Yes, I was born in Yugoslavia, not Croatia. That is an important distinction. But I wouldn't say that I am Jugoslovenka. I do not want to identify with any regime or state. It doesn't matter to me if I am Croatian, Yugoslav, or from Zagreb. Why must I identify with an idea of a people that doesn't interest me at all? [115]

Delimar's rejection of the term Jugoslovenka or any other nationalist marker speaks to her sense of emancipation from nationalist political projects. This reaction also corresponds with her critical engagement with militarist machismo,[116] which she thematizes in her 1982 collage, *Žena Nije Ratnik* (*Woman is Not a Warrior*) (Figure 1.30).

In the work, Delimar offered a visual argument against the celebration of women partisans and warriors. She pierced two black-and-white images of her genitalia and a bloody leaf with a long needle diagonally on a hand-cut, rectangular piece of transparent black fabric. The black fabric is adorned with a small white ribbon on the upper-right corner, along with violet letters spelling out "žena nije ratnik" (woman is not a warrior) at the bottom, all of which are framed in a wooden box. Like the lesbian pacifist movement that would come to the foreground after 1985 in Slovenia (see Chapter 3), Delimar resisted narratives of warrior women and instead embraced the vulnerability of the female body empowered by a categorical rejection of women as warriors. The categories "feminist" and "Jugoslovenka" are both complicated by

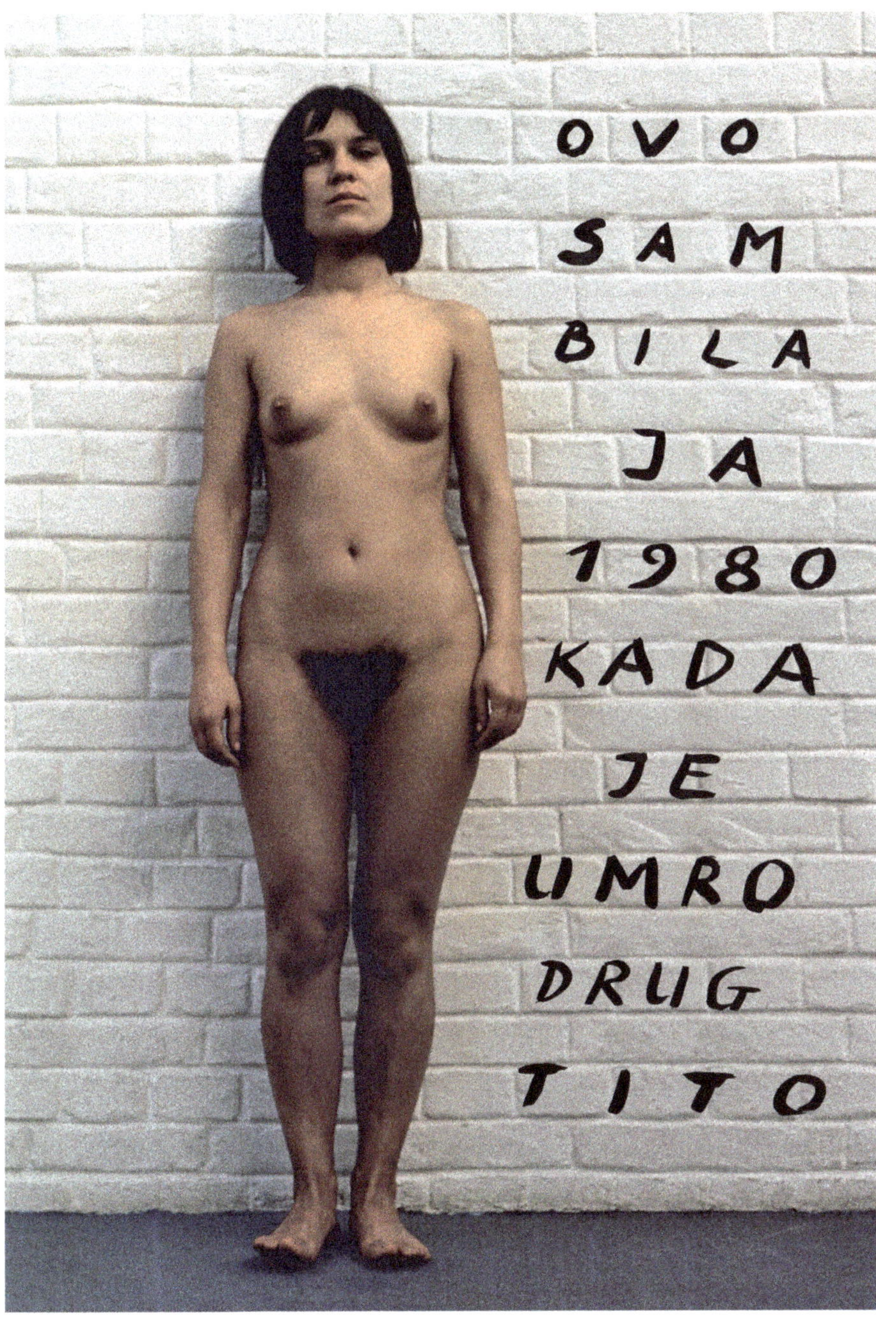

Vlasta Delimar, *This Was Me in 1980 When Comrade Tito Died*, 1980.   **1.29**

1.30   Vlasta Delimar, *Woman Is Not a Warrior*, 1982.

Delimar's work, as they are inherently part of it despite her rejection: like two sides of a medallion. She rejects those labels while they are integrally part of the society in which she lived and created her work. The penetrating stitch into her genitalia is painful to view, and instantly reminds us just how much bodies—especially women's bodies—suffer in war. The white ribbon exacerbates the sense of loss of innocence and youth, while the violet letters soothe an anxious onlooker with a message of peace. To this day, Delimar believes that if women had risen to power in the 1990s, things would have unfolded very differently.[117]

Disturbing the sound of silence: contending with the male voice of socialism

The most critical sound artist in Yugoslavia was Ladik, who must be acknowledged first as a performance artist whose sound works and naked body penetrated an otherwise male-dominated sphere of art. As Hungarian as she was Yugoslavian, Ladik possessed a double national identity, which was typical for the multicultural region of Vojvodina (and other parts of Yugoslavia) and also marked the transnationalism of Jugoslovenka: women artists who came from different republics but nevertheless shared diverse cultural backgrounds within a united Yugoslavia.[118] According to Šuvaković, Yugoslavia operated as "a kind of 'intermediary zone'" during the Cold War, which permitted artists to move around. Along with members of the group Bosch+Bosch (based in Subotica and Novi Sad), who created experimental actions and publications all over Eastern Europe, Ladik frequently visited Budapest and staged performances at the Chapel Studio, Hungarian mail and conceptual artist György Galántai's famous clandestine performance and conceptual art space.[119] Šuvaković has argued that Bosch+Bosch as a group was "a real mediator in the communication of Central European artistic practices, ranging from neo-avant-garde to conceptual art."[120] Vojvodina itself was a particularly good fit for such an intermediary zone for Hungarians as it was very close to the border and had previously been Hungarian territory during the Habsburg Empire.[121]

Galántai, who had visited Subotica, was in regular contact with the Bosch+Bosch members and held an exhibition in 1973 titled *Jugoszláv Kollégák* (*Yugoslavian Colleagues*) at the Chapel.[122] By then, Ladik was already well known in both Yugoslavia and Hungary. Between 1973 and 1977 she exhibited regularly at the SKC in Belgrade. She was particularly known for Shaman poem performances, in which she appeared nearly nude, her body covered only with a strip of fur that left one breast exposed (Figure 1.31). Ladik performed a kind of ritualistic dance while singing and playing bagpipes and other ancient instruments. Šuvaković has characterized Ladik's work as "behavioral pro-feminist conceptual art," arguing that the artist "problematized and provoked sexual, political and cultural identity, the norms and horizons of understanding the role and function of the artist in socialist society."[123] While her art was welcomed and respected in Yugoslavia, she was considered narcissistic and an exhibitionistic "poetess" in Hungary.[124]

In *Šamanska Pesma* (*Shaman Poem*) (1970), Ladik's exposure of the female body, its movements, and "voice" specifically as embodied emission—unkempt and uncontrolled by language but instead operating as experimental sound—brought the creative potential of a woman's body to view. Her embrace of a performatively primitive, ersatz "cave woman"—not unusual, say, for the Hollywood film industry at the time—was "too much" (too low brow) to be accepted and respected as art for many in Hungary. Perhaps Ladik exposed a fear of exploring the fact that, as Alain Badiou has noted, "the body, qua body, is capable of art," and that "dance is precisely what shows us that the body is capable of art."[125] Ladik's vocal performance indeed expands Badiou's conviction that dance is a "sensitivity possessed by each and every one of us," and that it "answers, after its own fashion, Spinoza's question: What is a body as such capable of?"[126] Ladik's "primitivist" approach provoked the boundaries of what was considered "cultured" and "acceptable" in the art world and

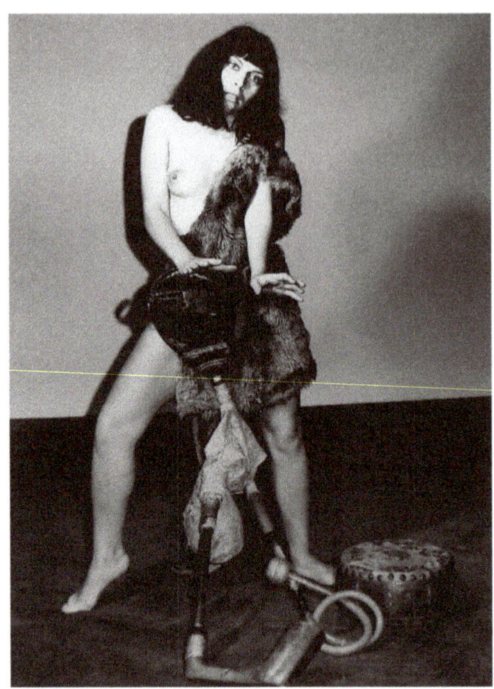

1.31   Katalin Ladik, *Shaman Poem*, performance in Novi Sad, Serbia, 1970.

beyond, a strategy historically rooted in a critique of Western colonial domination by early twentieth-century artists such as Alfred Jarry in the West and Ljubomir Micić and his Zenitism in the East.[127] Exhibiting the "primitive" body from Vojvodina—a region culturally entangled in the shifting borders between the Balkans and the West—Ladik embodied the "Other," a body inscribed by the no-man's land of national identity, while simultaneously also embodying the figure of Jugoslovenka. In addition, as a woman, Ladik may have evoked the greatest provocation by enunciating her otherness in the primordial vocalization and corporeal movement of female bodies, making known what French feminist philosopher Luce Irigaray has claimed in her book *In the Beginning, She Was*: "[I]n the beginning it is a she—nature, woman, Goddess—who inspires a sage with the truth."[128] In this way, Ladik recuperates the primitive as a site of ancient wisdom, a repository of an inaccessible other knowledge conveyed through embodiment, performance, and experimental sound. This recuperation places the body of an unapologetically Balkan woman, poet, and performer at the center of artistic intervention.

Iveković takes the socialist female body and places it at the center of media. In her experimental work in video and performance, Iveković investigates how the female body is politicized under state socialism and its embrace of

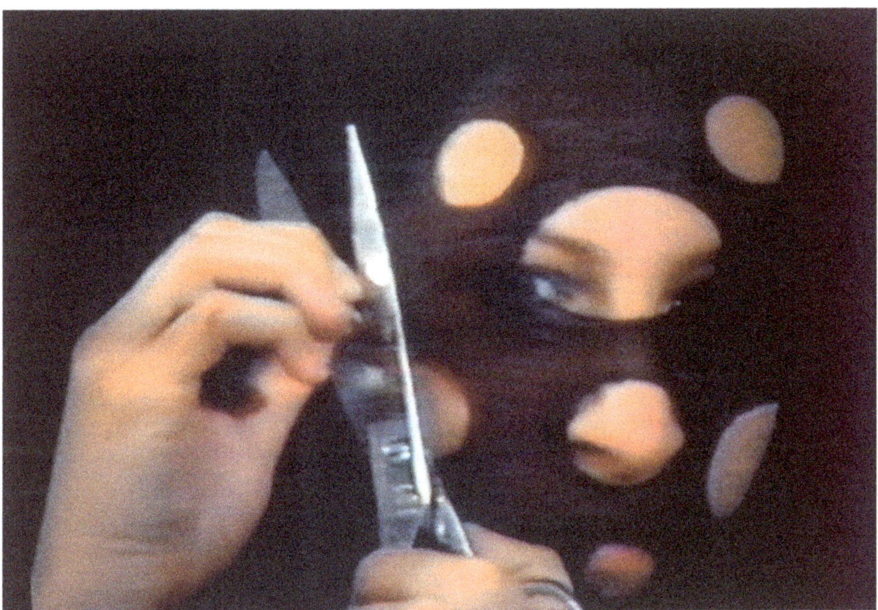

Sanja Iveković, *Personal Cuts*, 1982.   **1.32**
Video, 3:40

Western capitalist media. This process within the framework of socialist and capitalist consumer culture objectified and erased women's voices in favor of male narratives. In 1982, Iveković made *Personal Cuts*, a video collage involving footage of the artist cutting holes into black tights wrapped around her head, interlaced with split-second recordings of advertisements, news clips, and other propaganda (Figure 1.32). Sound is central in this work, as every time the camera shows Iveković about to make a cut, the film is silent, save for the ambient noises of her body and cars passing in the background. The moment she cuts, the sound of the scissors is eclipsed by male sounds coming from TV recordings: men speaking in advertisements, men acting as commentators on political documentary footage, and men singing popular songs.

In many ways, *Osobni Rezovi* (*Personal Cuts*) was an extension of a twelve-minute video she had made eight years earlier in 1974, *Slatko Naslije* (*Sweet Violence*), which appropriated multiple commercials, overlain by Iveković with black vertical gridlines. One, for Black Cats brand stockings, showed women walking down the street being admired by men, with a male narrator posing the rhetorical question: "Why are these men turning their heads?" The implicit answer, of course, is the women's legs in Black Cat tights. In another clip, the male narrator of the commercial notes that love can only begin if you have confidence, while the image shows a woman walking into a room, looking lost, until she finds her male date. The woman is mute. They exchange glances, and then her face transforms into the deodorant, Rexona, solidifying compulsory patriarchal and heterosexual expectations: buying hygiene products will help a woman land a date and keep a man. I would like to draw attention to the fact that the grid of black lines, overlying women's bodies, echo the window shades in Tijardović's intimate portrait with the red star and Delimar's grid in *Visual Orgasm*; but here, they are starkly oppressive and indicative of women's imprisonment by cultural objectification on TV. In *Personal Cuts*, Iveković manifests this suffocating expectation for women by using the black tights to obfuscate her face, like that of a bank robber, but she remains mute. This evocation of invisibility and silence suggests both the protections of anonymity while also welcoming associations with criminality. Iveković casts off this armor, methodically cutting holes into the tights with scissors, eventually revealing her entire face, but remains silent to the very end. Lóránd rightly interprets the black tights over her head as a "mask imposed on the individual through media, history or a political regime" and characterizes the artist as "not liberated" and instead "more and more desperate" as the performance continues.[129] In between each cut, Iveković shows various advertisements, including commercials for beds and women's nightgowns, as well as a pair running with the relay baton during Yugoslavia's Youth Day celebration, bringing us squarely back to the beginning of this book, when I discuss Slapšak's fantasy of stealing the relay baton (see the Introduction). In this way, Iveković's own face becomes the political site for negotiating the gendered violence of visual culture in which socialism and capitalism collide: Yugoslavia's unique socialism and its embrace of capitalist media culture, unabashedly celebrating consumption and money through the bodies of women. As Iveković gains sight and becomes visible, she also sacrifices more agency through her exposure. At the same time, her silence marks her resilience in enduring her position of vulnerability and erasure.

In another silent performance that involved disguising her face, *Übung Macht den Meister* (*Practice Makes a Master*) (1982), the artist danced to a song, wearing a little black business or cocktail dress, high heels, and a white plastic bag over her head. She repeatedly collapsed and got up again while one of Marilyn Monroe's songs from the movie *Bus Stop* played, in conjunction with "the jarring clamor of guns and other machines from video games, recorded by the artist in New York the previous year."[130] As art historian and curator Tom Holert observed, Iveković became a "performing body—defaced, decapitated," but a body that "speaks, though deprived of a voice [that] incorporates the secret of a somewhat obscene ... knowledge of violence directed against women."[131] As one without facial identity and despite her effort to gain control over herself, Iveković performed as one unable to communicate, a silenced woman struggling to stand. What additionally stands out in this performance, however, is Iveković's use of Monroe's song, again a symbol of violent and misogynistic American capitalism and its greed conjoined with patriarchal socialism in her Yugoslav context, a combination that results in the artist's body becoming the site of colliding ideologies, ultimately resulting in her collapse.

A year earlier, Iveković made her silence paradoxically the vocalizing and mediating agent in her work. In *Nessie* (1981), Iveković lay on a large table for twenty minutes with a camera resting on her stomach and a microphone augmenting the sound of her breathing (Figure 1.33):

> A large table is placed in the middle of a square room so that only a small space remains for the audience. A video monitor that transmits a live image is placed near the entrance of the room. The performance begins when the artist lies down on the table and places a camera on her stomach. She holds a microphone close to her mouth so as to amplify the sounds of her breathing. She breathes as deeply as possible, holding her breath as long as she can before taking another deep breath. This causes an up and down movement of the camera, which is constantly focused on the visitors. As the zoom button is pressed, the video image comprises only the hands, chest and heads of one or two persons. The artist slowly moves around until she returns to her starting point.[132]

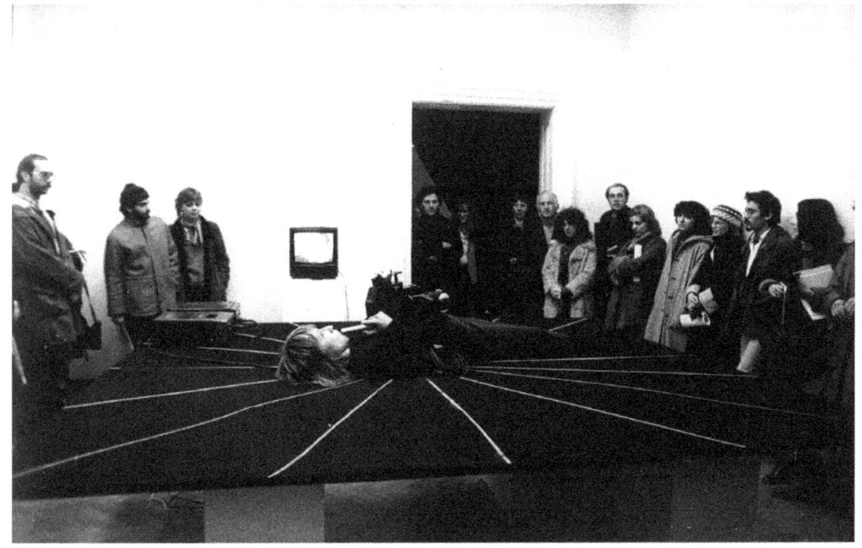

Sanja Iveković, *Nessie*, 1981. Performance at the Gallery of Contemporary Art, Zagreb.   **1.33**

The video is in color, while the documentary photographs of the performance are in black and white. Like these two iterations of the performance—one mediated by the artist's camera in color and one mediated by documentary footage showing the artist in action—the work itself has two dimensions in which a feminist reading of sound is significant. As an artist, Iveković forces her body into the center of the room not only to be looked at but to be heard, even if only through the sounds of her breathing. Her breathing influences what the camera, and by extension, she and her viewers see, which are limited glimpses of people's clothes and torsos, along with half of their faces. Magnifying the importance of her living and breathing body, she makes her own body the agent of mediation, a process the public simultaneously could observe on the TV screen, and which now we can see in the final footage. At one point, the sounds of her breathing merge with the sounds of the equipment, marking the technological innovation of film and media as female and disrupting the male-dominated canon, which readily silences women's contributions.

Returning once more to Abramović, whose *Freeing the Voice* could be equally relevant for this section, I want to point to one work that embraces through sound what Tijardović called "the ritual of pain" in women's performance work in Belgrade.[133] Tijardović identified three artists who performed in Belgrade and who embodied women's performance art: Gina Pane, Ana Mendieta,[134] and Abramović, all of whom embraced pain in their practice in response to the fact "that the woman's body was publicly controlled."[135] Abramović, however, was the only local artist in Belgrade who tested the limits of her female body. In *Ritam 10 (Rhythm 10)* (1973), Abramović knelt on the floor, stabbing the flesh between her fingers with a set of knives (Figure 1.34). Photographs of her performance show knives alongside tape recorders, which she used to capture and replay the sound of the cuts. As she wrote in her score:

> I place 2 tape recorders with microphones on the floor. I turn on the first recorder. I take the first knife and stab in between the fingers of my left hand as fast as possible. Every time I cut myself, I change the knife. When I've used all of the knives (all the rhythms), I rewind the tape recorder. I listen to the recording of the first part of the performance. I concentrate.[136]

While listening to the first set of cuts, she synchronizes her cutting motions in the same rhythm as the tape, now having constructed two sets of cutting sounds, one on tape and one in action, both captured on the second tape recorder. She ends the performance by rewinding the last recording, listening to it, and finally leaving the knives on the floor.

Abramović performed the first version of her work *Rhythm 10* alongside pieces by Urkom and Todosijević, at Richard Demarco's exhibition *Eight Yugoslav Artists* in Edinburgh in 1973. Without vocalizing pain, the embodiment of pain is transmitted through the cutting sounds, which the artist mediated

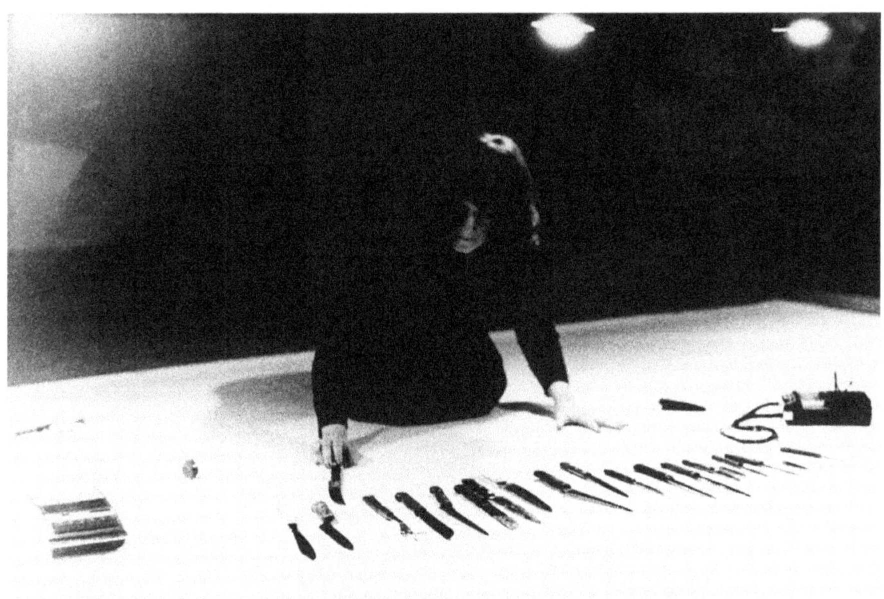

Marina Abramović, *Rhythm 10*, performance (1 hour), Museo d'Arte Contemporanea   **1.34**
Villa Borghese, Rome, 1973.

with technology, her body, and a controlled emphasis on her body's motions. Abramović does not look to collective political pain, the relation to media, or the erasure of women's voices; instead, she relies only on her own body as the measure of endurance and the maker of sound.

In 1975, Abramović created a work that is most easily read through a feminist lens, and that also significantly featured sound. In *Art Must Be Beautiful, Artist Must Be Beautiful*, which she performed at the Charlottenburg Art Festival in Copenhagen, Denmark (Figure 1.35), she repeatedly exclaimed the words of the title while violently brushing her hair until her scalp bled.

Abramović was also accosted by a woman who walked up to the artist and grabbed her, "first by the hand, and then by the hair," Abramović remembers. "I pushed her away, continued and eventually finished my 'happening.'"[137] Abramović continued her performance but she felt that the woman's intrusion had ruined her "happening." For Abramović, her art once again had more weight than the participation of a viewer. This understanding of the audience's agency starkly contrasts with Koščević's 1969 *Exhibition of Women and Men* (see Introduction), as Abramović's focus is on her own experience, despite the fact that the repeated sentences she utters with violent undertones of her body being beaten and hurt—"art must be beautiful, artist must be beautiful"—address a collective, albeit gendered, problem of suffering in the arts.

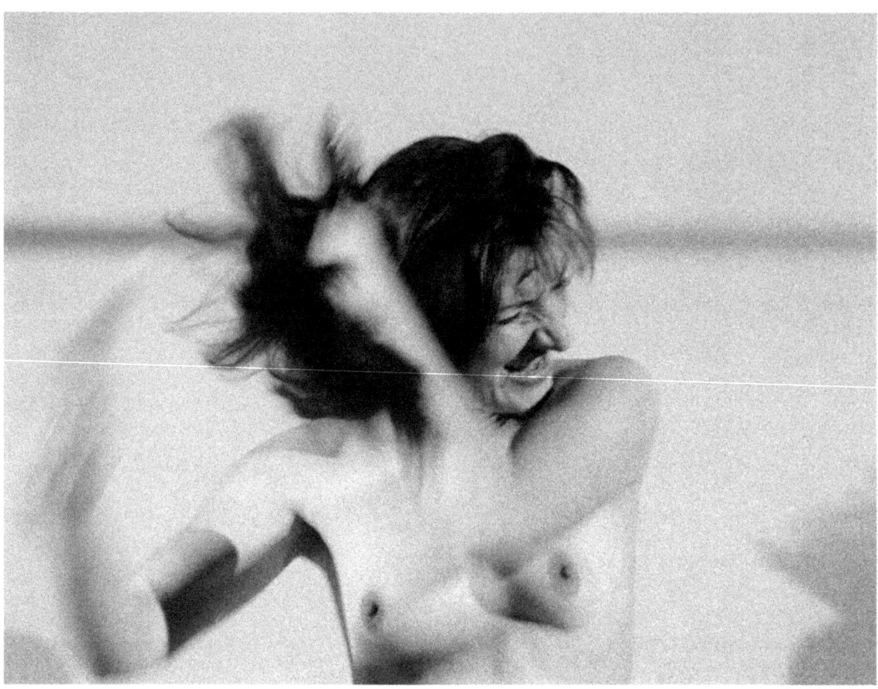

1.35 Marina Abramović, *Art Must Be Beautiful, Artist Must Be Beautiful*, performance (1 hour), Charlottenburg Art Festival, Copenhagen, Denmark, 1975.

The clash between her and the participant also illustrates the tensions in feminist interventions discussed throughout the entire chapter: while Abramović empowered herself in this action, the woman's intrusion was apparently motivated by her impulse to save Abramović from the violence she was imposing on herself. In her quest to "save" Abramović, she ultimately also violated her. It is this kind of chaotic power struggle that makes Abramović's work an important voice in the discourse of feminist performance art, capturing the irresolvable paradoxes of gender identity and experience in the arts under Yugoslav patriarchy.

I want to end by revisiting an even more complicated figure, Marinela Koželj, an artist who has primarily been left out of histories of performance, largely due to the fact that she was the partner of a much more famous artist, Todosijević. While Todosijević's actions have been attributed to him as author, I suggest we look at Koželj as a co-author, whose position in their shared actions I want to highlight here to open up a feminist recontextualization of their performances. Returning once more to Manne's discussion of misogyny, she explicates that women are often pushed into performing not only mother roles and emotional care for men, but also the "cool" girlfriend who appears to have chosen her fate of subservient work for her male partner.[138] As noted in the section "Burgeoning feminist performance politics," Koželj was regularly featured as a silent and stoic body during Todosijević's aggressive actions: screaming at Koželj, smearing her face, and objectifying her as his artwork under the category "found object."[139] Manne suggests that "this seamless appearance is almost inevitably deceptive, since more or less subtly hostile, threatening, and punitive norm-enforcement mechanisms will be standing at the ready, or operating in the background, should these 'soft' forms of social power prove insufficient for upholding them."[140] In the following I want to show how in *Pijenje Vode: Inversizije, Imitacije i Kontrasti* (*Drinking Water: Inversions, Imitations, and Contrasts*), Todosijević and Koželj exhibit this very hostility as the foundation of Yugoslav misogyny and patriarchy, where Koželj's silence becomes operative in unhinging the male ego and upsetting Todosijević's masculinity.

In *Drinking Water* at the 1974 SKC April Meeting—the same April Meeting of Abramović's burning star performance (*Rhythm 5*)—the bearded and bare-chested Todosijević grabbed a carp weighing 1.2 kilos and threw it "in front of the public." A large, white board illustrated with words and phrases written in black capital letters, such as "PRESUMPTION ABOUT—ART" and "DECISION AS ART," served as the backdrop for this action. Over thirty-five minutes, Todosijević drank twenty-six glasses of water and attempted "to harmonize the rhythm of swallowing with the rhythm of the dying fish breathing on the floor."[141] As the fish gasped for its life, needing water to breathe, Todosijević drank water and followed the pace of the animal's attempts to breathe with the pace of his own swallowing efforts. This soon resulted in Todosijević vomiting water and gasping for air. Prior to the performance, Todosijević scattered powdered violet pigment on the tablecloth covering the table at which he sat consuming water. The pigment discolored the white cloth as it became saturated with water and vomit.[142] Todosijević continued his action until almost all the cloth was stained with the violet pigment and the fish died.[143] Koželj sat next to him the entire time with a stoic expression throughout the performance (Figure 1.36).

The compliant Koželj sat strategically in front of the right side of the board featuring the phrases and names: DECISION AS ART; R. MUTT—1917; DISINFECTION 1974; MARINELA; JOSEPHINE BEUYS; T. D. RASA. Neatly dressed and calm, Koželj provided a visual manifestation of self-restraint and composure, in stark contrast to the struggling, vomiting god-like artist and the dying fish. Viewers could find solace in Koželj's personification of the norm (seated, calm, dressed), but also empathize with her painful position as a witness prevented from intervening. She was the concrete manifestation of the "stability" in Todosijević's battle and his "disinfection." Todosijević placed Marcel Duchamp in the same role for having initiated the concept of the

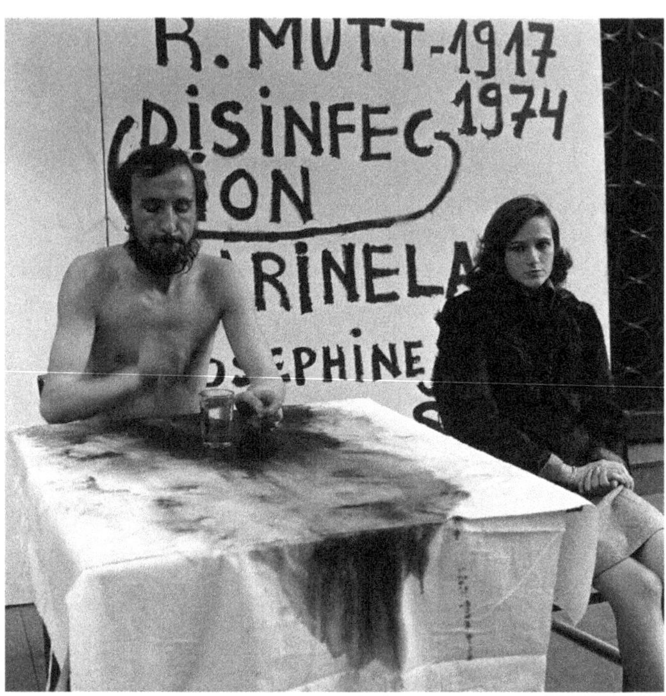

1.36   Raša Todosijević and Marinela Koželj, *Drinking Water: Inversions, Imitations, and Contrasts*, performance, April Meeting, Student Cultural Center, Belgrade, 1974.

readymade in 1913 with the *Bicycle Wheel*. Indeed, Todosijević's indebtedness to Duchamp, and perhaps even his female alter ego, Rrose Sélavy, further reminds us of his exhibition of Koželj's body two years earlier, when he had her sit on a chair as his artwork—a "found object"— for the first SKC exhibition called *Drangularium* (curated by Blažević in 1972). While one could argue that Todosijević's collaboration with Koželj helped remedy an absence of women artists in the SKC exhibition space, and more broadly, in the history of art, he also blatantly objectified her. In this female representation through objectification, Todosijević's battle with water begs a feminist examination, as does Koželj's silence. For Koželj chose to stay silent, a silence that amplified Todosijević's struggles with water and survival.

In her book *Marine Lover of Friedrich Nietzsche*, published in 1980 but written during the period when Koželj and Todosijević were regularly performing together, Irigaray began to examine how water, as an uncontrollable and immeasurable substance, has always been understood through the phallic emphasis on solidity and containment driven by a fear of fluidity, that is, the fear of women. "But (I) no longer wish to return into you," Irigaray wrote to Nietzsche in *Marine Lover*. "As soon as I am inside, you vomit me up again."[144]

Irigaray's insights help elucidate that in their art action Todosijević consumed and purged himself of water, signifying the patriarchal impossibility of understanding women's experiences, while Koželj deliberately denied him access to that knowledge. The incongruence between his masculinity and her femininity is played out in his violent and loud vomiting, which Koželj as a woman is equipped to endure without trouble. But another reading of her strength echoes more nefarious elements of misogyny. Manne has noted that women's ability to endure is linked to "the strength of her resolve to keep her promises" of upholding her male partner's importance. Manne adds, "women's power, strength, and agency may be highly valued, when she is standing behind a great man as the 'great woman' in the background."[145] Koželj manifests both emancipatory strength in unsettling the struggling male artist with her resolve, while also embodying the misogynistic conditions under which women develop the strength to remain silent.

Todosijević posed his masculinity against the femininity of Koželj who serves as witness and whose sensitivity mediates his violence, disinfects presumptions about art, and inspires the male artist to feminize himself, in the multiple forms of what Todosijević described on his wall text as "Josephine Beuys" (Joseph Beuys' anima),[146] Marcel Duchamp (doubled in Rrose Sélavy), and Todosijević's own feminine mirror image, "Marinela" (Koželj). Vesić has noted "'critical art' created inside the socialist state can only be the representation of an individual rebel in totalitarian society (stereotypically represented through the skinny body of the [male] performer in the gloomy alternative (art) space)."[147] Todosijević embodied every aspect of this myth including contrasting his loud vomiting and aggression with the soundlessness of a woman, Koželj, as the passive observer and the one observed. But Koželj's presence also allowed the breaking of gender boundaries on the conceptual level, marked on the board behind Todosijević and embodied in his visceral struggle with water.

It is within this context that we must scrutinize another set of performances orchestrated by Todosijević and Koželj, in which Todosijević would receive no answer from Koželj to his question (and the title of a long series of actions): *Was ist Kunst?* (*What is Art?*) series (1977–1978). In this powerful series, the artist incessantly whispered, grunted, screamed, begged, whined, and asked the question "Was ist Kunst?" while looking at the impassive Koželj (his partner/double and representative of women). Despite his plea for an answer, Koželj ignored Todosijević's screams and remained silent. Irigaray's reproach to Friedrich Nietzsche's silence and his apparent inability to hear and to answer a woman is worthy of note in this context:

Are you waiting for me to scream out so loudly in distress that the wall of your deafness is broken down? For me to call you out farther than the farthest recesses you frequent? Out of your circle? […] Endlessly, you turn back to that enigmatic question, but you never go on, you leave it still in the dark: who is she? who am I? How is that difference marked?[148]

The difference is marked clearly in sound during *Drinking Water* and *Was ist Kunst?* Sound is operative in Todosijević's struggle as a male artist, both with water and with the question of the patriarchal identity of art, embodied in the silent and silenced body of Koželj. The battle was as much with himself as it was an encounter with the ethical and aesthetic dilemmas of art and their role in society, all played out within the public space of the SKC under the power-fully silent gaze of Koželj. The SKC served as the space where Todosijević could display the violence, failures, and struggles of his masculinity, all the while using his body to elevate the intimate relationship with his female partner in art and life within the public realm. Koželj, unlike Abramović, chose silence as a form of resistance and resilience. In many ways, these works bring us back full circle to questions of gender and sexuality in *Exhibition of Women and Men*, reminding us that patriarchal assumptions were prevalent not only socially but in the work of men, whose works weighed upon—and silenced—women. As such, gender was not only positioned toward feminism, but it was a frame that silently haunted the performance work men made—and women supported—in Yugoslavia.

Conclusion: Yugoslavia's other (female) body

While my book begins with the Youth Day processions that outline Tito's national body across geographical lines of the young, unified, and decidedly male socialist state, I want to conclude Chapter 1 with an alternative vision of the gender of Yugoslavia. In "Homeland as a Form of Women's Disloyalty," Biljana Regodić thinks back to Yugoslavia as a country that is female, one that is reflected in her own body:

> My body is my biggest trap. … When I think about my country, when I search for it, I find it in the boundaries of my body. My country spreads along my body, reaches the boundaries of my senses, searching for colors, for sights, for smells and sounds. Inside my body I carry the coast of Istria, with the grass rushing into the sea, the politeness of the local people; the walls of the ancient town of Motovun woven into the rocky hills behind the coast; the trees of Slovenia on the road to Porec; the sounds of Bascarsija on a sunny morning; the face of an Albanian who, in Sarajevo, talks lovingly about Belgrade the very moment that the war begins; the heated cobblestones of Stradun; the sounds of different languages in a summer camp in Makarska; Slavonian villages like swans in blue-green waters; the vineyards on the slopes of Macedonia; the silence in Ravanica; the liveliness of impoverished Kosovo, swarming with

children; huge snowflakes about the fir trees of Zlatibor and the closeness of starlit waterfalls in the night; the sand of Sutumore; skies, skies across Vojvodina, the endless rich soil, crows, rains, frosts, and wheat. … Peace is the possibility to realize one's country. To make it grow. To discover new colors. To find out that countless forms of existence are within it.[149]

Regodić shifts the identification of Yugoslavia from the inscription of Tito onto the nation and instead discovered its contours within her own body. This profession for the love of her country is not imposed upon her by political patriarchy, but it comes from the landscape she claims for herself, and she identifies as herself. And yet, she also feels trapped by it. This paradoxical tension brings us back to the female Yugoslav body, Jugoslovenka, whose position within twentieth-century socialism and feminism remains unique, at times contradictory, and complex. Regodić's words echo some of the key analytical points in this chapter, including the exploration of the boundaries of women's senses and bodies; new ways of interpreting and generating sight; an embrace of silence and its disturbance as a site of resistance and resilience; and even, paradoxically, the trapped private sphere as a site of antifascist liberation in Čupić's contribution to *Maj F*—a knotty complexity unfastened in Regodić's euphoric embrace of skies and possibilities of the region. Lastly, there is the idea of peace, which for Regodić only occurs when one can "realize" one's country: "To make it grow. To discover new colors. To find out that countless forms of existence are within it."

It was the aim of this chapter to show the multiplicity of existences within the Yugoslav project and to privilege a feminist vision of those existences. In the Introduction, I summon Slapšak's imaginary feminist performance of stealing her leader's power to mark the revolutionary, confident, and contrarian spirit of Jugoslovenka central to the argument of this book. It is important to remember that none of the Yugoslav women described in this chapter were interested in being transformed into Tito worshippers. They may have gone to bed with socialism, but they did not marry its patriarch—symbolically, politically, or otherwise. The fact that women led the most important art spaces, were chief voices in the department of philosophy, and commanded the indictment of Yugoslavian socialism for misogynistic policies and practices is key and sets them apart from many of their Western colleagues, as these forms of resistance informed and characterized feminist interventions long after the official end of Yugoslavia in the 1990s. But research on the region also reveals tensions between feminist dogmas, feminist experimentations, feminist stereotypes, and women's own subordination to patriarchy, all of which counter a coherent and chronological narrative of a feminist art history in Yugoslavia. Instead, this chapter highlights feminist performance politics within the avant-garde space of art and performance in the late 1960s,

1970s, and into the early 1980s, where questions of gender and sexuality began to take hold in multiple and contradictory forms, nevertheless amounting to remarkable contributions to the cultural discussions about women's embodied experiences in a male-centered society, which I broadly call feminist. The sphere of art offered women a unique space in which they could explore forms to expose such injustices, finding forms of resistance by using their bodies, celebrating their bodies, and thematizing the repression of their bodies. The body of Yugoslavia was not just Tito or the muscled socialist worker, but very much that of Jugoslovenka breaking into the sphere of male-dominated art discourses; it was that way due to the work of women, and their mothers and grandmothers, regardless of whether or not they pushed the frame of feminism.

Notes

1 Bojana Pejić, "Proletarians of All Countries, Who Washes Your Socks? Equality, Dominance and Difference in Eastern European Art," in Bojana Pejić, ed., *Gender Check: Femininity and Masculinity in the Art of Eastern Europe* (Cologne: Walter König, 2009), 23.

2 The term "New Art Practice" was used broadly to discuss conceptual and performance works in Yugoslavia at the time. Marijan Susovski's 1978 exhibition, *The New Art Practice in Yugoslavia 1966–1978* (*Nova Umjetnička Praksa 1966–1978*) at the Gallery of Contemporary Art Zagreb is one of the most important references in art history. See Marijan Susovski, ed., *The New Art Practice in Yugoslavia 1966–1978* (Zagreb: Gallery of Contemporary Art Zagreb, 1978). There are slight variations in the translation and use of the term, such as "New Artistic Practice." See Jelena Vesić, "'New Artistic Practice' in Former Yugoslavia: From Leftist Critique of Socialist Bureaucracy to the Post-Communist Artifact in Neo-Liberal Institution Art," in the catalogue of Prelom kolektiv and ŠKUC Gallery's exhibition: *SKC in ŠKUC: The Case of Students' Cultural Centre in 1970s: SKC and Political Practices of Art* (Ljubljana: ŠKUC Gallery, 2008).

3 Blažević served as the SKC's gallery's artistic director from 1971 to 1975, and as the director of the center from 1975 to 1979. See Branislav Jakovljević, *Alienation Effects. Performance and Self-Management in Yugoslavia, 1945–91* (Ann Arbor: University of Michigan Press, 2016), 145.

4 Branislav Dimitrijević, "Altered Identities: Goran Đorđević as an Artist, SKC as an Institution," *PRELOM Journal for Images and Politics* 8 (Fall 2006), 243.

5 Jakovljević, *Alienation Effects*, 145.

6 Zsófia Lóránd, *The Feminist Challenge to the Socialist State in Yugoslavia* (London: Palgrave Macmillan, 2018), 93.

7 Blažević quoted in ibid.

8 Biljana Tomić in conversation with the author, August 4, 2011, Belgrade, Serbia.

9 Jelena Vesić, "The Conference Comrade Woman: Art Program (On Marxism and Feminism and their Mutual Political Discontents)," Parallel Chronologies: An Archive of East European Exhibitions: http://tranzit.org/exhibitionarchive/the-conference-comrade-woman-art-program/ (accessed 05/18/2019).

10 Dragica Vukadinović in e-mail correspondence with the author, July 12, 2019. Translation by Vukadinović, amended by author.

11 The participants included: Gislind Nabakowski, Katharina Sieverding, Ulrike Rosenbach, Iole de Freitas, Nicol Gravier, Natalia LL, Marina Abramović, Borka Pavićević, Nena Baljković, Irina Subotić, Ida Biard, Biljana Tomić, Jasna Tijardović, Jadranka Vinterhalter, and Dunja Blažević.

12 Vukadinović in e-mail correspondence with the author, July 12, 2019.

13 Marina Abramović in conversation with Kristine Stiles, 17 April 2007, New York City. Cited in Stiles' "Cloud with Its Shadow," in Kristine Stiles, Klaus Biesenbach and Chrissie Iles, *Marina Abramović* (London and New York: Phaidon, 2008), 33–95, quote 136n62.

14 Jelena Vesić, "Oktobar 75," in *SKC in ŠKUC*, 5.

15 *Kleinbürger* was the German expression for petty bourgeoisie, a term frequently used by radical activists such as Ulrike Meinhof of the Red Army Faction.

16 Dunja Blažević, "Art as a Form of Ownership Awareness," in *SKC in ŠKUC*, 7.

17 Chiara Bonfiglioli, "Feminist Translations in a Socialist Context: The Case of Yugoslavia," *Gender and History* 30, no. 1 (March 2018), 241.

18 Ibid.

19 Lóránd, *The Feminist Challenge*, 32.

20 Comrade Woman flyer—reproduced on the website Parallel Chronologies: An Archive of East European Exhibitions: http://tranzit.org/exhibitionarchive/wp-content/uploads/2015/02/woman-comrade-report.pdf (accessed 06/18/2019).

21 Ibid. Page three of the Comrade Woman flyer shows the manually crossed-out word "women's," which was replaced with "feminist" (in handwritten script). Emphasis added.

22 Slavenka Drakulić quoted in Lóránd, *The Feminist Challenge*, 33.

23 Vukadinović quoted in ibid.

24 Vesić, "The Conference Comrade Woman."

25 Hedwig Turai, "Bojana Pejić on Gender and Feminism in Eastern European Art (Interview)," in Katrin Kivimaa, ed., *Working with Feminism: Curating and Exhibitions in Eastern Europe* (Tallinn: Tallinn University Press, 2012), 200.

26 Ivana Bago, "The Question of Female Guilt in Sanja Iveković's Art: From Yugoslav Beauty Pageants to Wartime Witch-Hunts," *Calvert* 22 (2013), 75.

27 Chiara Bonfiglioli, "Remembering the Conference 'Drugarica Zena. Zensko Pitanje—Novi Pristup?'/'Comrade Woman: The Women's Question: A New Approach?' Thirty Years After" (MA thesis, Utrecht University, Women's Studies, 2007/2008), 87–90.

28 Ibid., 88.

29 Ibid.

30 Katja Kobolt, "Nailstories," in Jasmina Tumbas, Corina Apostol, and Vladan Jeremić, eds., *ArtLeaks Gazette 5: Patriarchy Over and Out: Discourse Made Manifest* (ArtLeaks, 2019), 126.

31 Ibid.

32 Ibid.

33 Ibid., 123.

34 The names of participants are listed on the Comrade Woman flyer.

35 The most comprehensive source is Bonfiglioli's 2007/2008 MA thesis, "Remembering the Conference." In addition, please see Lóránd, *The Feminist Challenge*, and Vesić, "The Conference Comrade Woman," cited throughout this chapter.

36 Vesić, "The Conference Comrade Woman."

37 Ibid.

38 Ibid.

39 Ibid. To view the photograph, please visit Staša Rosić, "Goranka Matić: Posle četrdeset godina, baterije su se ispraznile," *Euronews Srbija* (May 27, 2021): https://www.euronews.rs/magazin/poznati/1823/goranka-matic-posle-cetrdeset-godina-baterije-su-se-ispraznile/vest (accessed 06/05/2021).

40 The poster is reproduced in Lóránd, *The Feminist Challenge*, 95.

41 Ibid., 48.

42 Dragica Vukadinović identified the man as Milorad Miša Pavlović, a journalist. He worked closely with SKC in those years. Vukadinović in conversation with the author, July 13, 2019.

43 The focus on Koželj's beauty is evident in the fact that one of the most frequent questions I have been asked about her since I first met her in 2007 has been: "Is she still as beautiful?" Many others often noted: "She was so beautiful back then."

44 Jasna Tijardović in conversation with the author, October 13, 2019.

45 Kate Manne, *Down Girl: The Logic of Misogyny* (Oxford: Oxford University Press, 2018), 46.

46 Ibid, 45.

47 Mladen Stilinović has been credited with coining the term "exhibitions-actions." See Vlado Martek, "Rococo Biographies," in Janka Vukmir, ed., *Grupa Šestorice Autora* (Zagreb: SCCA Zagreb, 1998), 10.

48 Branka Stipančić, "This is Not My World," in Vukmir, ed., *Grupa Šestorice Autora*, 101.

49 Miško Šuvaković, "The Post-Avant-Garde: The Group of Six Artists 1975–1978 and After," in Vukmir, ed., *Grupa Šestorice Autora*, 69.

50 Janka Vukmir, "Conceptual Co-Existance," in Vukmir, ed., *Grupa Šestorice Autora*, 29.

51 John Held Jr., "The Mail Art Exhibition: Personal Worlds to Cultural Strategies," in Annmarie Chandler and Norie Neumark, eds., *At a Distance: Precursors to Art and Activism on the Internet* (Cambridge, MA: MIT Press, 2005), 101; emphasis added.

52 Jakovljević, *Alienation Effects*, 180.

53 Vlasta Delimar in conversation with the author, June 12, 2019.

54 Darko Šimičić, "From Zenit to Mental Space Avant-Garde, Neo-Avant-Garde, and Post-Avant-Garde Magazines and Books in Yugoslavia, 1921–1987," in Dubravka Đurić and Miško Šuvaković, eds., *Impossible Histories: Historical Avant-Gardes, Neo-Avant-Gardes, and Post-Avant-Gardes in Yugoslavia, 1818–1991* (Cambridge, MA: MIT Press, 2003), 296.

55 Artists included in this issue were: Breda Beban, Rada Čupić, Vlasta Delimar, Sanja Iveković, Jasna Jurum, Vesna Miksić, Vesna Pokas, Bogdanka Poznanović, Duba Sambolec, Edita Schubert, Branka Stanković, and Iris Vučemilović.

56 Inga Muscio, *Cunt: A Declaration of Independence*, 2nd ed. (Emeryville, CA: Seal Press, 2002), 23.

57 Rada Čupić has noted that this work was created as a small excursion into conceptual art under the influence of Professor Bogdanka Poznanivić. In e-mail correspondence with the author, February 14, 2021.

58 Ibid., February 20, 2021.

59 Ibid., February 18, 2021.

60 Ibid., February 20, 2021.

61 Manne, *Down Girl*, 101.

62 Marina Gržinić, "Tanja Ostojić: 'Yes it's Fucking Political'—Skunk Anansie," in Tanja Ostojić, ed., *Strategies of Success/Curators Series 2001–2003* (Bourges: La Box; Belgrade: SKC, 2004), 15.

63 *Maj 75 H* (1982), for example, featured a work by Delimar which simply had "VOLIM KURAC" in typed black bold letters in caps, under which Delimar had signed her name with a blue pen.

64 *Maj 75 K* (1983) features a photograph of Delimar holding two penises, which she called "Ja S Dva Kurca," and another artwork identified as a work by Delimar and Jarman which features two photographs: on top, a photo of Jarman's face pleasuring a woman's genitalia (it is implied that it is Delimar's body), and a photo at the bottom showing Delimar in profile with a penis in her mouth (implied that it is Jarman's).

65 Vesna Kesić, "A Response to Catharine MacKinnon's Article 'Turning Rape into Pornography: Postmodern Genocide,'" *Hastings Women's L. R.* 5 (1994), 272.

66 Ibid.

67 Translations of the essays' titles are adopted from Lóránd's *The Feminist Challenge*.

68 Ibid., 155.

69 Quoted in ibid. Originally published in Vesna Kesić, "Nije li pornogra ja cinična?"/"Isn't Pornography Cynical?" *Start* 355 (August 28, 1982), 75.

70 Lóránd translates it to "old, ugly woman's feminism," but I prefer using "hag" here because of its kinship to folklore and the Middle Ages. See Lóránd, *The Feminist Challenge*, 149.

71 Vesna Kesić quoted in ibid. In turn, the male editorial team published nude photographs of Hite just a few weeks after the interview, which resulted in a scandal that included Hite writing a letter demanding an apology. See Lóránd, *The Feminist Challenge*, 154.

72 Kesić, "A Response to Catharine MacKinnon's Article," 272–273.

73 I am indebted to feminist art historian and curator Ivana Bago, who first showed me these illustrations in 2012 when we were both graduate students at Duke University. She had found them while she served on the research team for Bojana Pejić's *Gender Check* exhibition.

74 Original text: "Ideologija nase cure. Ilustracija uz tekst Veselka Tenžere o 'fenomenu' golotinje kao medije [pa i *Start*], i o dvojnom moralu 'konzumiranja' te pojave." See *Start Magazine*, no. 269 (May 16, 1979). Translation by the author.

75 Sander L. Gilman, *Disease and Representation: Images of Illness from Madness to AIDS* (Ithaca, NY: Cornell University Press, 1988), 252–255. Thanks to Damien Keane for pointing out this connection to Gilman's text.

76 Ibid.

77 In *Start*, no. 299 (July 9, 1980). Translation by the author.

78 Research on the question of sexism at the workplace is burdened by the limitations of oral histories and women's understandable hesitation to share details about the actual experiences of abuse. Rory Archer and Goran Musić discuss the significance of fieldwork and offer one case of oral history that illustrates at least in part sexual harassment in the workplace. "For example, sisters Mirjana and Gordana spoke about working in a Belgrade wood processing collective in the 1970s and 1980s. They recalled sexual harassment by managers and the trials of single parenthood in the self-managing workplace. Mirjana's experience of joining and subsequently leaving the League of Communists reveal how some of the permutations of class and gender were experienced. As a cleaner and courier, she was encouraged to join the party in her workplace to bolster the numbers of rank and file workers. By 1985, however, Mirjana was extremely embittered by management who she believed were defrauding the collective and lying to the workers. Furthermore, she considered that her role as a party member was more of a burden than a privilege." See Rory Archer and Goran Musić, "Approaching the Socialist Factory and its Workforce: Considerations from Fieldwork in (former) Yugoslavia," *Labor History* 58, no. 1 (2017), 57–58.

79 See Ivana Bago, "Sanja Iveković. Becoming Woman Artist," in Lina Džuverović, ed., *Sanja Iveković. Unknown Heroine* (London: Calvert 22, 2012), 49–64.

80 Branka Stipančić, "Body Language in Croatian Art," in Zdenka Badovinac, ed., *The Body and the East: From the 1960s to the Present* (Cambridge, MA, and London: MIT Press, 1998), 59.

81 British Marxist sociologist Tom Bottomore's *Elites and Society* (1964).

82 Bago, "The Question of Female Guilt," 64.

83 Nataša Ilić and Kathrin Rhomberg, eds., *Sanja Iveković: Selected Works* (Barcelona: Fundacio Antoni Tapies, 2008), 52.

84 Ibid., 70.

85 Ljiljana Kolešnik, "Intuitivni feminizam Vlaste Delimar [Vlasta Delimar's Intuitive Feminism]," *Quorum, Časopis za Književnost* 13, no. 4 (1997), 197. Translation by the author.

86 See IRWIN, ed., *East Art Map: Contemporary Art and Eastern Europe* (Cambridge, MA, and London: MIT Press, 2006) and *Piotr Piotrowski, in the Shadow of Yalta: Art and the Avant-Garde in Eastern Europe, 1945–1989* (London: Reaktion Books, 2009).

87 Kolešnik discusses this contested position of being deemed too narcissist and too sexual to be taken seriously by feminists. Lóránd has also written extensively about the debates around sexual revolution and feminism in Yugoslavia. See Zsófia Lóránd, "'A Politically Non-Dangerous Revolution is Not a Revolution': Critical Readings of the Concept of Sexual Revolution by Yugoslav Feminists in the 1970s," *European Review of History: Revue Uropéenne d'Histoire* 22, no. 1 (2015), 120–137. See also Leigh Ann Wheeler, "'Handmaiden of the Pornographer, Champion of Free Speech: The American Civil Liberties Union and Sexual Expression in the 1970s and 1980s," in Carolyn Bronstein and Whitney Strub, eds., *Porno Chic and the Sex Wars: American Sexual Representation in the 1970s* (Amherst: University of Massachusetts Press, 2016), 237.

88 Ibid.

89 Ibid.

90 Quoted and translated in Lóránd, "A Politically Non-Dangerous Revolution,'" 129. The original text can be found at Slavenka Drakulić, "Dugi rat nage venere [The Long War of the Naked Venus]," *Start* 303 (September 3, 1980), 18–20. Quote amended by the author.

91 Delimar in conversation with the author, June 12, 2019.

92 Ibid.

93 Ibid.

94 Svetlana Slapšak, "Mein Feminismus ist eine logische Konsequenz von 1968," in Boris Kanzleiter and Krunoslav Stojaković, eds., *1968 in Yugoslawien: Studentendproteste und kutlturelle Avantgarde zwischen 1960 und 1975* (Bonn: Dietz, 2008), 93. Translation by the author.

95 Lóránd, *The Feminist Challenge*, 32.

96 Miško Šuvaković, "You Can't Find a Woman, Can You? An Essay on Performers' Theme-Questioning of Politics, Body and Sex in Vlasta Delimar's Deed," in Miško Šuvaković, Marijan Špoljar, and Vlado Martek, *Vlasta Delimar: Monografija Performans* (Zagreb: Areagrafika, 2003), 68. Original quote amended by the author.

97 Only nine of those photographs remain today. Zoran Popović in email correspondence with the author, May 22, 2013.

98 Zoran Popović provided the scans of the official invitation postcards from the SKC, which featured one of his photographs on the front. Email correspondence with the author, May 22, 2013. This series was also exhibited in the *1 & 1* exhibition at the SKC gallery in 1974, an exhibition that showed the works of couples and collaborators, including Belgrade-based Raša Todosijević and Marinela Koželj. The catalogue for this exhibition is accessible at the archive of the Museum of Contemporary Art in Belgrade, Serbia. Both of these Belgrade couples have remained together, supporting each other throughout numerous decades.

99 This action was part of her 1975 trilogy of performances titled *Freeing the Voice*, *Freeing the Memory*, and *Freeing the Body*.

100 Marina Abramović, "Freeing the Voice," in Klaus Biesenbach, *Marina Abramović: The Artist is Present* (New York: MOMA, 2010), 84.

101 Todosijević was well known for performances that included an emphasis on his own body in relation to objects such as a dying fish in *Drinking Water* (1974), or the artist enacting violence on women, such as in his series, *Was ist Kunst?* (1976–1981) and *Vive La France—Vive La Tyranie* (*Long Live France—Long Live Tyrany*) (1979).

102 Quote from Bojana Pejić, "Marina Abramović," in mumok, ed., *Kontakt … Works from the Collection of Erste Bank Group* (Vienna and Cologne: Museum Moderner Kunst Stiftung Ludwig, Buchhandlung Walther König, 2006), 83. For Šuvaković's comments on Abramović, see Miško Šuvaković, *Konceptualna Umetnost* (Novi Sad: Muzej Savremene Umetnosti Vojvodine, 2007), 265.

103 Kristine Stiles, "Synopsis of the Destruction in Art Symposium (DIAS) and Its Theoretical Significance," *The Act* 1 (Spring 1987), 22–31.

104 Marina Abramović, *Walk through Walls: A Memoir* (New York: Three Rivers Press, 2016), 142, 183–184, and 11.

105 For a more in-depth discussion of women's rights in Sparta, see Sarah B. Pomeroy, *Spartan Women* (Oxford: Oxford University Press, 2002).

106 Abramović, *Walk through Walls*, 2.

107 See Bojana Pejić, "And Now Let's Remember … Yugoslavia," in Marina Abramović, *The Cleaner* (Berlin: Hatje Cantz, 2017), 250–259.

108 Ibid., 11.

109 Quoted and translated in Miško Šuvaković, "The Power of a Woman: Katalin Ladik. Narratives of Interpretation, of Subjectification, Women and Art between the Cold War and Transition in Central Europe," in Dragomir Ugren, ed., *The Power of a Woman: Katalin Ladik* (Novi Sad: Museum of Contemporary Art Vojvodina in Novi Sad, 2010), 17. Originally printed in Vesna Kesić, "Katalin Ladik: JA SAM JAVNA ŽENA [I AM A PUBLIC WOMAN]," *Start* (February 28, 1981), 72–73.

110 Edit András, "Gender Minefields," *n.paradoxa* 11 (1999), 8: www.ktpress.co.uk/nparadoxa-issue-details.asp?issueid=11 (accessed 05/06/2019).

111 Ibid.

112 Delimar in conversation with the author, June 12, 2019.

113 Ibid.

114 Ibid.

115 Ibid.

116 In 1999, Delimar met Milan Božić, a soldier with whom she began to collaborate and engage with the question of gender and war in works such as *Conversation with a Warrior or the Woman Has Disappeared* at the Culture Factory, Zagreb. See Delimar's chronology in Martina Munivrana, ed., *This is I. Retrospective Exhibition 1979–2014* (Zagreb: Museum of Contemporary Art, 2014), 23.

117 Vlasta Delimar in conversation with the author, June 12, 2019.

118 Ladik left Yugoslavia during the war in 1992 and settled in Budapest, where she lives and works today.

119 Other members of Bosch+Bosch included Attila Csernik, László Kerekes, Slavko Matković, László Szalma, Bálint Szombathy, and Ante Vukov.

120 Šuvaković, "The Power of a Woman," 51.

121 For example, Galántai's visit to Subotica in 1972 for an exhibition brought about an experience that starkly contrasted with that of Hungarian socialism: "I loved it there and was thinking: why was Hungary so bad? Why could it not adopt more of Tito's socialism?" Galántai in conversation with the author, December 21, 2011, Artpool Art Research Center, Budapest, Hungary.

122 Participants included József Ács, Ferenc Baráth, Attila Csernik, Gábor Ifjú, József Markulik, Slavko Matković, József Smit, Bálint Szombathy.

123 Šuvaković, *Konceptualna Umetnost*, 259. Translation by the author.

124 Beáta Hock, "Gendered Artistic Positions and Social Voices: Politics, Cinema, and the Visual Arts: In State-Socialist and Post-Socialist Hungary" (PhD thesis, Central European University, Budapest, 2009), 227. The doctoral dissertation was later published as a book. See Beáta Hock, *Gendered Artistic Positions and Social Voices: Politics, Cinema, and the Visual Arts: In State-Socialist and Post-Socialist Hungary* (Stuttgart: Steiner, 2013).

125 Alain Badiou, "Dance as Metaphor for Thought," in Alain Badiou, *Handbook of Inaesthetics*, trans. Alberto Toscano (Stanford, CA: Stanford University Press, 2005), 69–70.

126 Ibid.

127 Patricia Leighten and Mark Antliff have pointed out the connection between anarchism and primitivism, outlining the four factors characteristic of primitivist critique of Western colonial practices: time/space, gender, race, and class. In their analysis, Leighten and Antliff argued that the political dimension of the artists' critique was both complicit with, and ran counter to, the enlightenment logic of colonialism. See Patricia Leighten and Mark Antliff, "Primitive," in Robert Nelson and Richard Schiff, eds., *Critical Terms for Art History* (Chicago: University of Chicago Press, 2003), 217–233; and Patricia Leighten, "Colonialism, L'art negre, and 'Les Demoiselles d'Avignon,'" in Christopher Green, ed., *Picasso's "Les Demoiselles d'Avignon"* (Cambridge: Cambridge University Press, 2001), 77–103. In the Balkans, Ljubomir Micić's Zenitism constituted one effort to protect the Balkan culture from Western enlightenment in the early twentieth century, paralleling international Dadaist practices but situating them in the non-Western Balkan context with his concept of the "Barbarogenius." See Dubravka Đurić, "Radical Poetic Practices: Concrete and Visual Poetry in the Avant-Garde and Neo-Avant-Garde," in Đurić and Šuvaković, eds., *Impossible Histories*, 64–95.

128 See Luce Irigaray, *In the Beginning, She Was* (London and New York: Bloomsbury Academic, 2013), 2.

129 Lóránd, *The Feminist Challenge*, 124.

130 See *Practice Makes a Master*: https://www.moma.org/interactives/exhibitions/2011/sanjaivekovic/#practice-makes-a-master (accessed 08/13/2021). See also Sanja Iveković, "Übung Macht den Meister (Practice Makes a Master, 1982)," in Ilić and Rhomberg, eds., *Sanja Iveković*, 134.

131 Tom Holert, "Face-Shifting: Violence and Expression in the Work of Sanja Iveković," in Ilić and Rhomberg, eds., *Sanja Iveković*, 27.

132 Ilić and Rhomberg, eds., *Sanja Iveković*, 122.

133 Jasna Tijardović-Popović, "Performance Art in Belgrade in the 70s: On the Exhibition of Photo-Documentation and Photographs," in *Performance/1968–1978* (Belgrade: Gallery Beograd, 2006), 30.

134 Ana Mendieta did a performance at the SKC gallery in 1976.

135 Tijardović-Popović, "Performance Art in Belgrade in the 70s," 30.

136 *Rhythm 10* description in Abramović, *The Cleaner*, 68.

137 "Marina Abramović in Conversation with Radovan Gajić, 1974," in Stiles, Biesenbach, and Iles, *Marina Abramović*, 125. It seems that this interview is wrongly dated, as the performance to which Abramović refers took place in 1975. A decade earlier, in 1965, Allan Kaprow had outlined the parameters of happenings in his *Untitled Guidelines for Happenings*, emphasizing its aim as the dissolution of the line between art and life, as well as that between the artist and audience: "*It follows that audiences should be eliminated entirely. All the elements—people, space, the particular materials and character of the environment, time—can in this way be integrated*" (original emphasis). See Allan Kaprow, "Guidelines for Happenings," in Kristine Stiles and Peter Selz, eds., *Theories and Documents of Contemporary Art: A Sourcebook of Artists' Writings*, rev. and exp. 2nd ed. (Berkeley, Los Angeles, and London: University of California Press, 2012), 837.

138 Manne, *Down Girl*, 47.

139 Since around 2014, Todosijević has begun to push Koželj's role more into the foreground on social media, for example regularly sharing images of Koželj's artwork, as well as marking their co-authorship of performances by identifying images of performances from the 1970s at their common work.

140 Manne, *Down Girl*, 47.

141 Part of this section of the essay has previously been published in Jasmina Tumbas, "Decision as Art: Performance in the Balkans," in Katalin Cseh-Varga and Adam Czirak, eds., *Performing Arts in the Second Public Sphere: Event-Based Art in Late Socialist Europe* (Basingstoke: Palgrave Macmillan, 2018), 184–201. Todosijević's statement about *Drinking Water* was cited in Sretenović, *Was ist Kunst? Art as Social Practice*, 59.

142 Todosijević, in *Was ist Kunst?*, 59.

143 Ibid.

144 Luce Irigaray, *Marine Lover of Friedrich Nietzsche*, trans., Gillian C. Gill (New York: Columbia University Press, 1991), 12; originally published in 1980 as *Amante marine de Friedrich Nietzsche* (Paris: Minuit).

145 Manne, *Down Girl*, 118.

146 Joseph Beuys had sent Todosijević a letter which he signed "Josephine Beuys." Todosijević also distributed pamphlets in 1973 at the Edinburgh Festival with "Josephine Beuys" written on them, supposedly in protest against the fame of Beuys.

147 Vesić, "'New Artistic Practice,'" 4.

148 Irigaray, *Marine Lover*, 12 and 67.

149 Biljana Regodić, "Homeland as a Form of Women's Disloyalty," in Tanya Renne, ed., *Ana's Land: Sisterhood in Eastern Europe* (Boulder, CO: Westview Press, 1997), 176.

Marina Abramović, Lepa Brena, and Esma Redžepova: socialist nation, Orientalism, and Yugoslav legacy

Three of the most significant celebrities to come out of the Federation of Yugoslavia during its last decades were women who were prominent within the field of culture: in the sphere of avant-garde visual and performance art, artist Marina Abramović; and as performers and businesspeople in the popular music sphere, singers Lepa Brena and Esma Redžepova. All three women were "firsts" in their fields, achieving breakthroughs previously unattainable for women within the Yugoslav context. While Abramović changed the history of performance art in the elite echelons of the local and global art world from the late 1970s on, Lepa Brena conquered popular culture, starting out in the small *kafanas* (bars or restaurants that played live music) of Yugoslavia before erupting into a megastar who toured sold-out stadiums in neighboring social-ist states in the 1980s with unprecedented and lasting success. Achieving international stature and exposure, and earning the title Queen of Romani music,[1] Redžepova, the third of this powerful set of Jugoslovenkas, began her career much earlier than both Abramović and Brena. Already at age eighteen, she found herself singing in front of none other than Marshal Tito in 1961 during the legendary first Non-Aligned Movement Conference in Belgrade.[2] In 1976, Redžepova, along with her mentor/husband Stevo Teodosievski, per-formed in front of Indira Gandhi in Chandigarh, India, representing Yugosla-via at the first World Festival of Romani Songs and Music, where they were dubbed "King and Queen of Romani* Music," a designation that marked Redžepova's fame in Yugoslavia and internationally until the end of her life in 2016.[3] All three women would come to represent Yugoslavia in divergent ways during the socialist period and after, attesting once again to the many ways that the feminist legacy of Yugoslavia manifested in complex and often irrec-oncilable ways in the bodies and emancipatory performative actions of suc-cessful female cultural icons.

In the case of Abramović and Brena, the socialist female body would become iconic in its ability to transport political ideology on an international scale. On the one hand, Brena herself became a substitute for the by-then departed Tito (d. 1980)—who had symbolized a united Yugoslavia—broadcasting the image of an independent woman and internationally known star who came to represent the more "open" and "free" Yugoslav socialist state for the people of Bulgaria and Romania in the 1980s. On the other hand, in the 1990s, she became a source of nostalgic identification with the shattered nation of Yugoslavia.[4] Abramović's symbolic relationship with Yugoslavia was less affirmative; early in her career, the artist's 1975 departure from Yugoslavia spurred unceasing art historical speculations in North Atlantic spheres about the lack of freedom and darkness of communism in the East, due in no small part to the artist's repeated emphasis on the bleakness of life in socialist Yugoslavia. Her mental and bodily endurance, particularly in performances that demand stamina in the face of deprivation, and her will to innovate and push boundaries in the arts, have often been linked by both Western critics and the artist herself to her Yugoslav partisan parents and her harsher coming-of-age experiences under socialism.[5] Experiencing acclaim and rejection, both women had difficult relationships to their local contexts, especially during and after the Yugoslav wars, which might explain in part why both ended up moving to the United States. But they have also had spectacular returns to the capital of the former federation in fall and winter 2019: Abramović's first solo show since 1975, *The Cleaner*, opened in Belgrade at the Museum of Contemporary Art, and Lepa Brena became the central figure through whose life the legacy and destruction of socialism in Yugoslavia had been memorialized in the theatrical performance and musical *Lepa Brena Project*, spearheaded by a new generation of queer and feminist dramaturges, actors, and choreographers.

Originally from Skopje, Macedonia, and as the most famous Romani woman singer in the world, Redžepova would complicate the embodiment of Yugoslavia, representing her socialist home worldwide in more than 20,000 concerts, a third of which benefitted humanitarian causes. While Brena and Abramović presented as white East European women making it big beyond the Yugoslav borders—Brena as a pop folk icon and Abramović as a communist expatriate and acclaimed performance artist—Redžepova's body signaled a much less white and more exotic and discriminated against constituent body of people in Yugoslavia, namely the Roma population. As such, Redžepova's emancipatory strategies were subject to an additional barrier—not just the communist East, but struggles around gender and race within the Yugoslav borders. The first woman performer on TV to be of Romani origin and proudly wear "dimije" pants, often derogatorily referred to as "Harem or Muslim pants," Redžepova visually and performatively showed her loyalties to the Romani people, the Muslim traditions integral to the Yugoslav region, and her embrace of traditional values in modern times.[6] At the same time, she was also extremely relatable to Yugoslav audiences and could switch into Western clothing, singing, and performing styles. Redžepova's success was unprecedented for a Romani woman living in Yugoslavia at that time, as women singers with that ethnic background faced racial discrimination and were stigmatized as "easy women" in both Yugoslav and Romani culture.[7]

As a socialist nation thriving under the influence of intersecting traditions—ranging from the Habsburg and Ottoman empires to the extensive cultural wealth of Roma and Sinti, as well as the bedrock of Marxist ethics during the partisan revolution, and nonalignment cultural exchanges between some ninety "Third World" countries involving leaders from India, Africa, Latin America, and the Middle East[8]—Yugoslavia's brand of multicultural Orientalism was an integral part of Yugoslav culture. Outmoded today, the term multiculturalism is nevertheless extremely useful for understanding the convergences of different religions, ethnicities, and cultural foundations in the emancipatory performances of Abramović, Brena, and Redžepova. While many of the feminists discussed in this book railed against the climate of state-imposed patriarchy, this chapter is about feminist cultural production that interacts with something much more ancient and enduring: the dynamic juncture of folk culture and ethnic identity, and local tensions based on race, including racial stereotypes imported from the West, religion, and ethnicity in Yugoslavia. The cases of Abramović, Brena, and Redžepova complicate the history of feminist resistance in the region, because their bodies and practices reveal how the matrix of gender, sexuality, Orientalism, and folk culture are all bound up in a uniquely Yugoslav notion of multiculturalism.

This chapter singles out these three women artists because their emancipatory performances were able to transfuse the legacies of an extraordinary combination of cultural forces in differing and sometimes even conflicting ways during and after Yugoslav socialism. Rather than offering a biographical sketch of each artist, the following approaches their feminist performance strategies around three interrelated questions: (1) How did they represent their relationship to the socialist nation and Tito? (2) How and when was the complicated legacy of Orientalism in Yugoslavia and the Balkan region a tool for emancipatory performance in each of their respective careers? (3) In what ways did they come to represent the legacy of Yugoslavia during and after the wars of the 1990s? While these points of comparison are anything but exhaustive, this chapter seeks to shed light on the multivalent legacy of feminist performance in the Yugoslav project through the bodies and performances of these three megastars of culture. Ultimately, Redžepova, Abramović, and Brena are undeniably linked to Yugoslavia through the launch of their careers and subsequent nostalgic returns, even if through denunciations, lamentations, or sentimental longings; they are Jugoslovenkas in their own right and have shaped their respective fields in unparalleled ways.

Marina Abramović: Jugoslovenka in the West

Despite a troubled and often distanced relationship to her place of birth, Abramović's half-century-spanning oeuvre has represented her connection to the socialist nation that raised her—sometimes in obscure but more often in recognizable ways. Beginning with her Belgrade performance works that centered on communist symbols, one of which I will discuss in more detail, Abramović's art frequently parades her socialist background, such as when she posed in what could be considered a communist Pietà wearing a grandiose red dress with her then partner in life and art, Ulay (Frank Uwe Laysiepen), laying in her arms, in their 1983 *Anima Mundi (Pietà)* performance;[9] or in 1995, in *The Onion*, when she tortured herself by eating an onion and described how tired she was of being "ashamed about the war in Yugoslavia" while tears streamed down her face.[10] Even in her durational performance during her retrospective at the Museum of Modern Art in New York, *The Artist is Present* (2010), she wore red, white, and blue dresses, connoting the colors of the Yugoslav flag and incidentally also the colors of her new home, the United States of America.

However, no other work represents her complicated relationship to the socialist country more intensely than her most famous performance from the 1970s, *Ritam 5 (Rhythm 5)* (1974), at the Student Cultural Center (SKC) in Belgrade (Figure 2.1). A characteristic bodily action, the performance begins with the artist lying down (Chapter 1)—this time inside a burning star evocative of the Yugoslav flag. Abramović privileged Yugoslav national iconography in her work and here placed her own body in the center of that body politic. On the grounds of the SKC was a wooden five-point star structure, the outline of which was filled with one hundred liters of gasoline that she had lit on fire. Abramović ritually cut her hair and nails and threw the clippings into the fire, stepped into the center of the star and laid down while the flames consumed the oxygen around her. As the performance progressed, she visibly suffered from a lack of oxygen and eventually passed out. Among others, Joseph Beuys, who had met Abramović at Demarco's Edinburgh Festival in 1973 (Chapter 1), watched the artist as she lost consciousness. Those witnessing this felt a need to rescue the artist, and two artists, Gergelj Urkom and Radomir Damnjan, eventually did so, pulling her from the flaming star and ending her performance.

In Chapter 1, I discussed Abramović's personal relationship to the ideology of socialism through the figure of her mother, Danica Abramović (née Rosić).

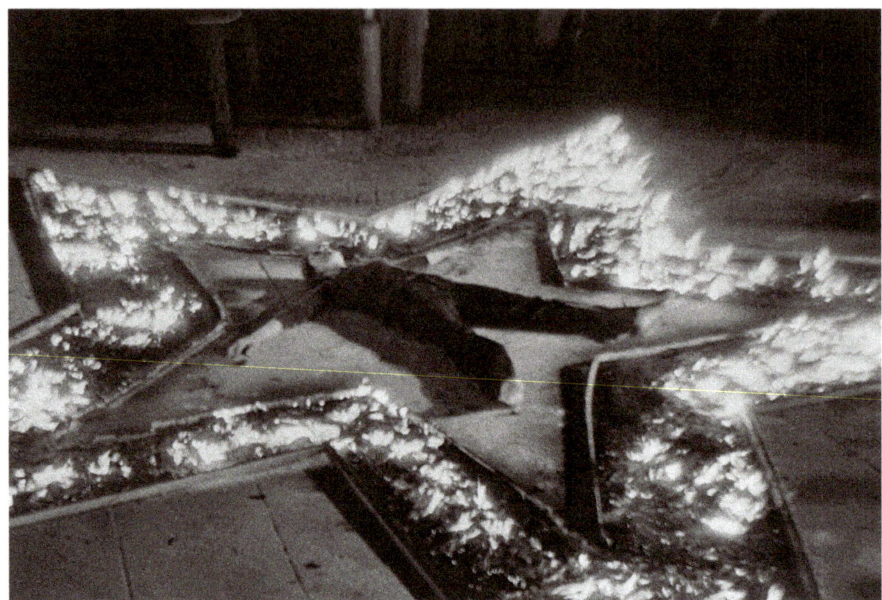

2.1   Marina Abramović, *Rhythm 5*, performance (90 minutes), Student Cultural Center, Belgrade, 1974.

Abramović's own recollections often echo narratives of suffocation by her mother's strict socialist values, and by extension, the socialist state's narrow vision for life and art. On a surface level, Abramović's action could be read as rendering the flaming star a symbol of psychic and physical suffocation under Yugoslav socialism. But Jakovljević suggests that such readings "oversimplify" when viewing the burning star solely "as a symbol of violence perpetrated by the socialist state or the burning up of the revolutionary ideals of the Left."[11] I want to add a different perspective to the work, one which considers it through the matrices of gender and the state, that is, through the figure of Jugoslovenka in the arts. This work powerfully embodies and represents how the communist star collided in tension with the female body. If we turn the narrative of the destructive and suffocating burning star on its head, and instead consider the fundamental strength of a star in space, whose inherent condition is to burn, Abramović situated herself within the nucleus of an extremely powerful force: the iconography of Yugoslav socialism. As an artist interested in energy throughout her entire career, one might think about how stars combine elements through nuclear fusion and release energy in a form visible in the sky as light. In *Rhythm 5*, a Yugoslav woman is at the center of that transformation of matter into energy, a powerful position that is out of reach for most of her audience, not because they could not—but because they would not—put their own bodies in that same place. Abramović's will and decision to put her body in danger translates into a test of survival, iconographically potent with emancipatory meaning: the courage and endurance of Jugoslovenka.

But the story has an additional element that complicates such a heroic reading of *Rhythm 5*. Abramović had to be rescued, and she was saved by two men. Following the logic of Yugoslav women as embodied in Abramović's courageous action, one might read her loss of consciousness as dramatizing the perfunctory misogyny Yugoslav women have to endure, while also insisting on creating a space for her to control her world within the boundaries of art. Abramović vehemently rejected any intrusion into her work, male or female. In *Lips of Thomas* (1976), just two years after *Rhythm 5*, Abramović cut a pentagram into her stomach, bled profusely, and lay on a crucifix-shaped ice block with a heater pointed at her wounds. Again, it was an endurance piece that the audience, including feminist artist Valie Export, could not endure witnessing without intervening. Viewers removed the ice block, and Abramović was taken to the hospital.[12] Similarly, in her infamous *Ritam o* (*Rhythm 0*) action in Italy (1974), the artist surrendered her body to the mercy of gallery visitors—allowing them to do whatever they permitted themselves to do to her using any of seventy-two objects, some potentially lethal, such as a gun, while others like honey, grapes, and a feather posed no threat. Abramović further intended and attempted to control the length of the performance at exactly six hours, regardless of any intervention.

If the artist did not want to be rescued, she chose to rescue herself, over and over again, staging dangerous performances in which she continually defied death. In her defiance, as on the bed during *Freeing the Voice* (Chapter 1), she is an agent of individuality disinterested in sharing the space inside the star with others. *Rhythm 5* pushes us to consider how the socialist ideology of collectivism and Abramović's philosophy of individualism collide. It might seem that feminism is at odds with individuality. Even if dismissed as egocentric, Abramović's self-promotion and self-enclosure did what many male artists have done unquestioned for decades. Similar to how Vlasta Delimar's work collides with feminism (Chapters 1 and 3), it is not relevant whether or not Abramović's feminism is appealing; Abramović's work must be acknowledged as its own branch of empowerment and emancipation, rooted in her female body, even if she disputes this. The body lying in the burning star, by now an iconic image representing performance art in the 1970s, put a Yugoslav woman's search for emancipatory performance in art at the forefront of performance and feminist art history. In a photograph from 1977, we see the artist wearing a partisan cap with the signature red star, looking directly at the camera (Figure 2.2). Abramović appears as a partisan Jugoslovenka, a warrior, who sought her own way.

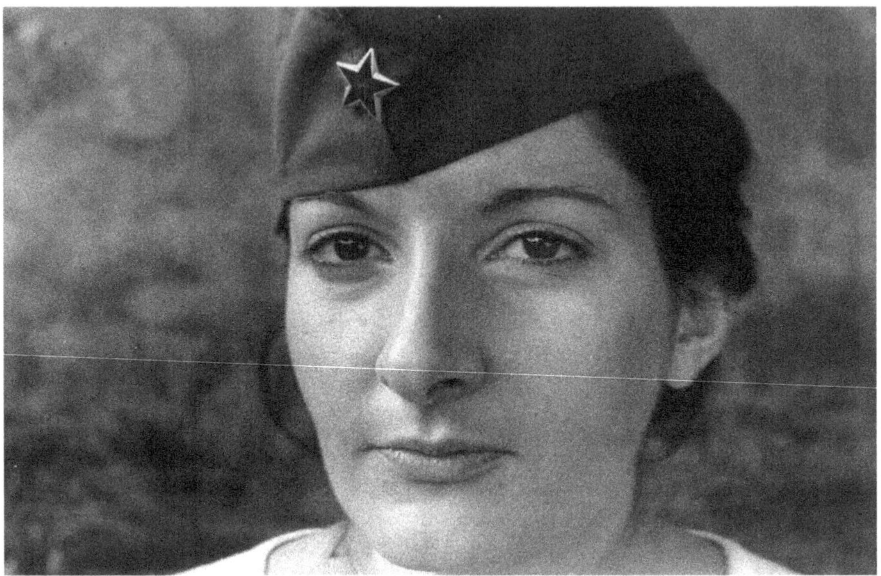

2.2   Marina Abramović in partisan cap, 1977.

Abramović returned to the iconography of the communist star in 1976 with *Lips of Thomas*, featuring a blood-red pentagram. While the connection might seem tenuous, Abramović affirmed the connection in 2005 when she reperformed the work for *7 Easy Pieces* at the Solomon R. Guggenheim Museum by wearing the Yugoslav partisan hat and appearing in the guise of a Yugoslav patriot. Abramović's difficult relationship to her birthplace is expressed in what Bojana Pejić calls the "diasporic self," a flexible identity that lets her assume different personas, most prominent in *Balkan Baroque* (see Figures 2.3–2.4).[13] At the 1997 Venice Biennale, Abramović won the Golden Lion for her performance and installation *Balkan Baroque*, presented in the Italian pavilion's international group show. She had been invited to exhibit in the Yugoslav pavilion (then administered by Serbia and Montenegro), but her proposal was rejected in part for its explicit references to the genocidal violence of the Yugoslav wars. Abramović sat among bloody cow bones for four days, six hours every day, cleaning them incessantly while singing songs from Serbia and Croatia, as well as a Russian ballad.[14] On both of the side walls, the artist installed large screens with video projections that showed interviews of her parents, both committed partisans who fought in World War II under Tito. Two copper sinks and one copper bath filled with water served as furnishings in the otherwise barren room. A video projection of her performing the Wolf Rat poem, in which she narrates—through metaphors—how the Balkans transform humans into killing machines, was installed behind the pile of

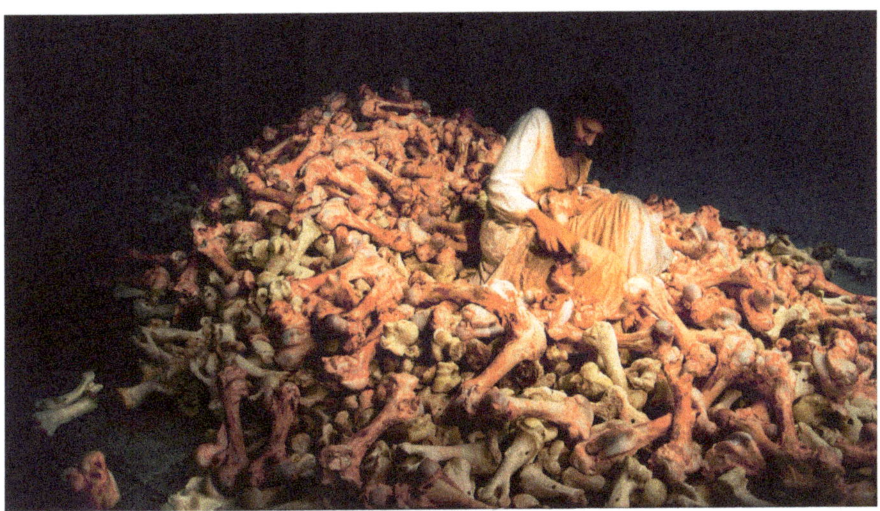

Marina Abramović, *Balkan Baroque I*, performance (4 days, 6 hours), 47th Venice Biennale June 1997.

2.3

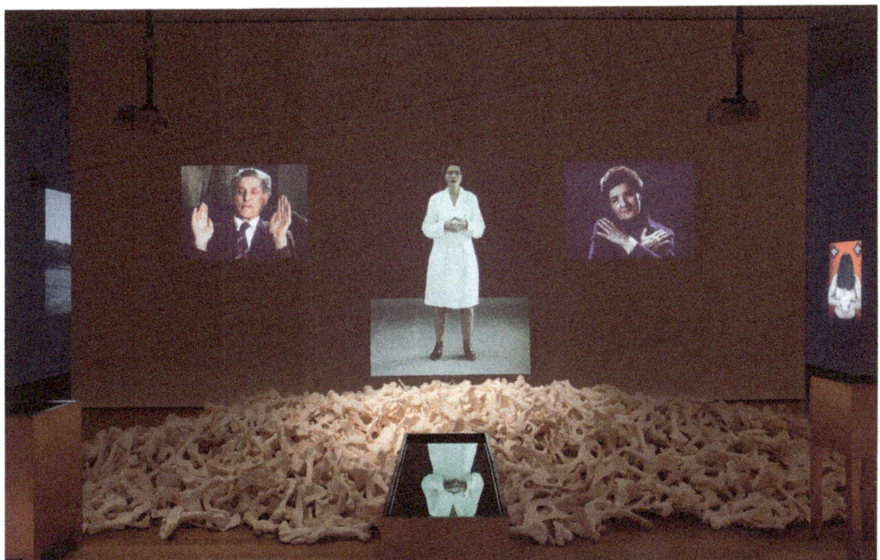

Installation view of *Balkan Baroque* at the exhibition *Marina Abramović: The Artist Is Present*, March 14–May 31, 2010.

2.4

bones. Abramović's *Balkan Baroque* stands as an extraordinary moment of mourning for the destruction of Yugoslavia, by a daughter of antifascist partisan fighters who left her homeland two decades prior, revealing the artist's deep connection to her country of origin. Pejić connects the artist's mourning to the regional folk tradition of professional singers, "narikačas," women who mourn the dead at funerals with songs (also known as dirges).[15] Pejić pushes the connection to Yugoslavia even further when she likens Abramović to "the national allegory of Yugoslavia: the mother who mourns 'her' dead and 'her' nation."[16] In 1997, Abramović becomes the most visible Yugoslav woman in contemporary art.

But *Balkan Baroque* has also been criticized for exploiting negative ethnic stereotypes of the Balkans as an inherently violent backwater. When the artist presents the Wolf Rat poem, she first appears in a white coat as a zoologist explaining how rats are tortured and trained to kill one another, an explanation which ends with a comment on how the wolf rat is created in the Balkans. At the end, Abramović removes her white coat, pulls a red scarf from her décolletage, and dances frantically to Hungarian Apollónia Kovács's Romani folk. Provocatively, Abramović performs this dance clumsily, reminding viewers that she was not raised in the Yugoslav folklore traditions that are more prevalent in the rural areas of southeastern Europe, where people practice them as part of their culture. The dance's potency lies in the fact that while Abramović acknowledges its role in her culture and gives it a global stage, this connection to her homeland is undercut by her amateurish performance, amplifying the tenuousness of her ties to the very country she mourns.

In *Count on Us* (2004), Abramović revisited the space of childhood and mourning when she featured two young singers wearing black uniforms and singing old folklore songs with angelic voices against stunning red backgrounds that evoke her socialist past (Figure 2.5). Projected on opposing screens, the boy and girl sing ballads alone, while on a third channel projected between them, Abramović, with a skeleton on her back, directs a children's choir in a performance of the United Nations (UN) anthem, sung in Serbo-Croatian. For Pejić, Abramović is drawing an important contrast with the historical fact that Yugoslavia was a founding member of the UN while the UN also played an important role in the republic's dissolution. Yugoslavia's denigration during the wars led the region to be renamed "the Balkans."[17] The longing to understand the position of Yugoslavia in the global chaos of violence seems to be at the center of Abramović's practice after the Yugoslav wars, as are the symbols of Yugoslavia, most potently the star. Seeing the artist in a skeleton costume performing with a choir of children—making a large star on the floor and also directing them to sing—seems to signify that any leader who "directs" a mass of innocent youth will inevitably lead them to death. Abramović's difficult relationship with the former Yugoslavia and its demise

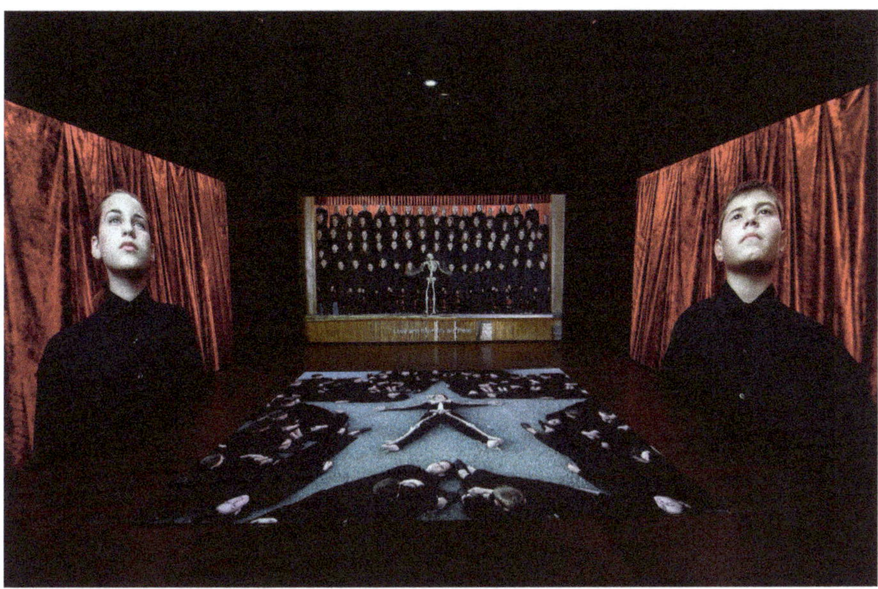

Marina Abramović, *Count on Us*, four-channel video installation (12 minutes), Museum
of Contemporary Art, Belgrade, 2003.   **2.5**

is complicated by the artist's courage in facing the pain and loss of her homeland and its continual haunting images of death.

In Abramović's works through the 1990s, erotics and sexual desire are not
central to her identification with Yugoslavia. That changed in 2004, however,
when the artist was photographed holding Tito's portrait—the only instance,
to my knowledge, of Abramović directly referencing Tito visually in her work
(Figure 2.6). In this photograph, Abramović appears in black tights wearing
high heels with her hair loose to her shoulders. Her seemingly unclothed
breasts and abdomen are hidden behind a painted portrait of Tito, who had
been dead for twenty-four years at the time of the photograph. Abramović's
outfit introduces sexuality to the image, evoking something absent in the
highly official portrait of Tito. This work spurred an increase of eroticism
in the artist's treatment of her homeland in the ensuing decades, beginning
with the moving-image work *Balkan Erotic Epic* (2005), which revives interest in regional folklore and mysticism that would mark Yugoslavia—and the
artist's abandoned and now lost homeland—as distinctly *Balkan* and *Oriental*
(Figure 2.7).

In *Balkan Erotic Epic*, Abramović's sexuality is linked to the Yugoslav
region, yet steeped in stereotypes that border on what might be understood
in the West as primitive perversions: naked men fornicating with dirt, women

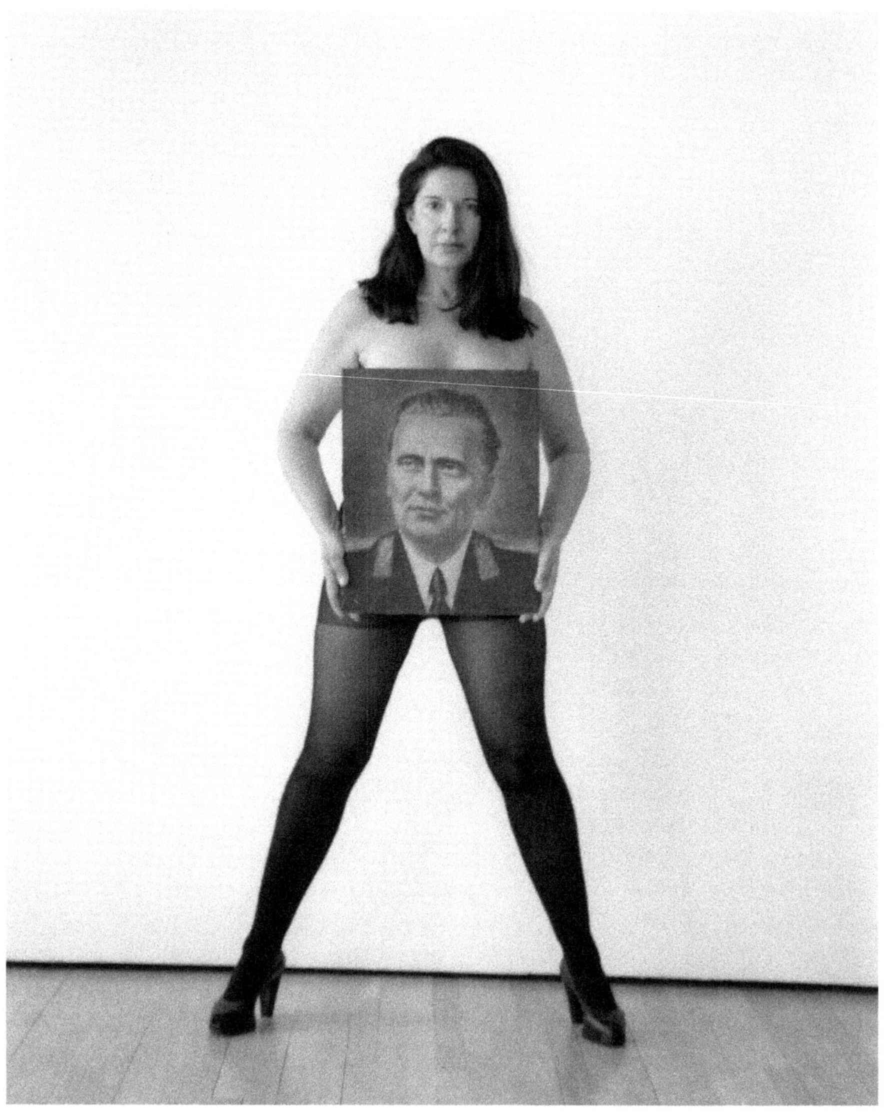

2.6   Marina Abramović, *Portrait with Tito*, photograph, 2004.

of all ages in traditional dresses offering their bare breasts to the heavens while spreading their naked legs toward the earth, and men, also in traditional garb, flaunting erections. While rightly critiqued for employing sensationalist self-exoticization and for exploiting Orientalist prejudices against the region, *Balkan Erotic Epic* also marked the artist's libidinal ties to Yugoslavia some

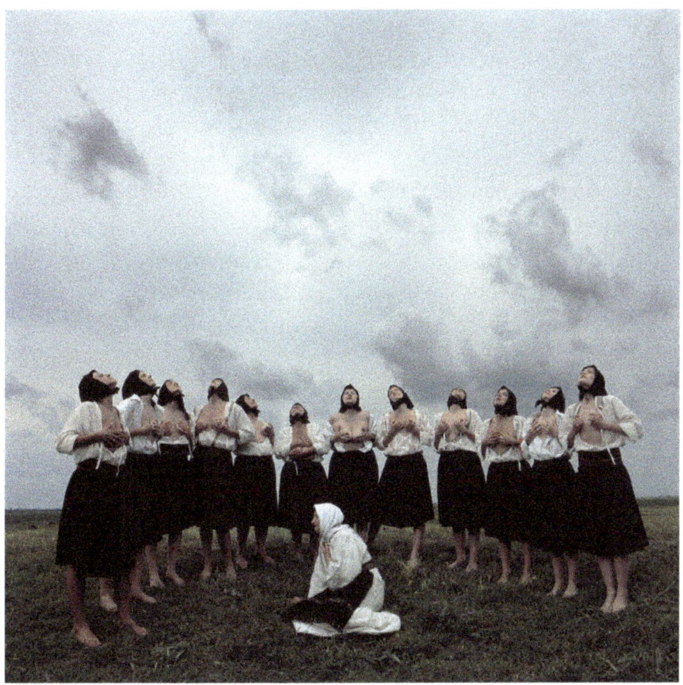

Marina Abramović, *Women Massaging Breasts*, from the series *Balkan Erotic Epic*, 2005,   **2.7**
C-print, Serbia.

fourteen years after the disintegration of the country and some thirty years after her emigration.

According to Abramović, she was attempting to counter the negative and hostile relationship to Balkan sexuality. She noted: "I was thinking that sex is healthy in this country. Food is good and sex is healthy. Everything else is fucked up, but this is another story. And I was thinking 'OK, let's see where this sexual kind of attitude comes from.'"[18] Relying on her research into the history of pagan rituals in the region, Abramović asked stars in the pornography business to re-enact some of those rituals, such as men fornicating with the earth and women exposing their vaginas and massaging their bare breasts. On a separate screen in the installation, Abramović, with a deadpan expression and dressed in black, explains how these acts belonged to old Balkan traditions aimed at guaranteeing successful harvests, protecting children from evil, and finding a man to marry. She elaborates on a number of practices that involve male and female genitals in order to tame the earth and reconnect with nature. Knowing very well that she would be wounding national pride with this work, Abramović deliberately used traditional folklore garments, which would leave male and female genitals exposed. She also invited two prominent women from the region to participate: Serbian actress Olivera Katarina, whose role as the Romani woman Lenče in Aleksandar Petrović's 1967 film *Skupljači Perja* (*I Even Met Happy Gypsies*) is one of the most venerated performances in Yugoslav film history; and Svetlana Spajić, a singer and performer of Serbian traditional music, folklore, and dance. Katarina, an actress not of Roma origin, reminds us that Romani women were and still are underrepresented in Yugoslavia and post-Yugoslavia. Spajić's participation in Abramović's piece signals the end of Yugoslavia and the emphasis on regional nationalism. Abramović begins to embrace her "homeland" in the early 2000s, but does so through a more pointed embrace of her Serbian and Montenegrin, not Yugoslav, background.

Lepa Brena: the original Jugoslovenka

A 2014 headline of the Serbian daily tabloid newspaper *Blic* announced: "Instead of Tito, Lepa Brena has arrived" ("Umesto Tita stigla Lepa Brena").[19] This provocative headline, while having an ordinary foundation in actual events—Brena was staying in one of Tito's former apartments in Novi Sad in preparation for a concert—hinted at a more loaded hypothesis: decades after Tito's death, and the death of his country, Brena had replaced the political leader in her embodiment of his legacy of socialist Yugoslavia. Despite the fact that Brena comes from a Muslim family, and is originally from Bosnia and now lives in Serbia—an enemy country to Croatia during the wars in the 1990s—Brena successfully united an audience in Croatia in December 2019 when she performed her song "Jugoslovenka" in front of an energetic and enthusiastic crowd screaming, "Ja Sam Jugoslovenka!" Croatian generals and right-wing politicians had boycotted the concert in advance, but the people in the stadium were ready for reconciliation and a celebration of a united Yugoslavia—and not just a united Yugoslavia, but a Yugoslavia united in the figure of Jugoslovenka, embodied by Brena and her song.

An accomplished singer, businesswoman, and cultural icon in former Yugoslavia, Brena first became a singing sensation in the Yugoslav music scene of the 1980s. At that time, Yugoslavia was heading into economic decline, which was accompanied by a harsh drop in the spirit of Yugoslav unity and identity. An antidote to such demoralization, Brena's energy served as a "ready-made commercialized transnationalism," according to theorist Uroš Čvoro, that quickly replaced Tito's Yugoslav motto of "brotherhood and unity."[20] Čvoro summarizes the wide appeal of Brena' witty, light-hearted, but simultaneously emotionally accessible lyrics, which revolutionized folk music: children were drawn to her humor and "simplistic lyrics"; men to "her revealing clothes and use of playful sexual innuendo in her lyrics"; and women to "her public personality and music," which "reflected female empowerment and independence."[21] Most importantly, she also showed that success was possible for women, and that in general, people could move up in the socialist system during a time when the economic situation was becoming more and more dire.[22]

It was unprecedented for a female artist to have such a broad reach and following in the region, and no other solo performer—male or female—has had comparable success since. But Čvoro's characterization of Brena's success as relying on a "ready-made" and "commercialized" mode of artistic success across the different Yugoslav republics also subtly undermines the strength of her originality and know-how. Placed in contrast to something supposedly more serious, like Tito's "brotherhood and unity," Čvoro's portrayal of Brena as merely a shallow brand of socialism in lieu of more serious political convictions relies on a gendered assumption about political ideologies and their implementation. From what we have learned about the history of gender relations in socialist Yugoslavia, the socialist brotherhood mostly understood its unity in relation to patriarchal bonds, and, as such, always had the advantage of considering itself the more "serious" and more important approach to shaping Yugoslav society while ignoring and erasing women's contributions. However, one might consider Čvoro's comparing young Brena, only in her twenties in the 1980s, with someone as extraordinary as Tito as the ultimate testament to her emancipatory power and ability to move the masses.

The sexist context under which Brena rose to fame makes it even clearer why her success was due to her ability to navigate the male-dominated music scene of Yugoslavia. The comedian Minimaks has been credited with giving her the name "Lepa" when she first appeared on his show in 1982, an event which contributed significantly to her success as a performer.[23] Minimaks's show reached the homes of everyday Yugoslav women, including my mother, Eržebet Tumbas. She remembered how "Minimaks was known as a mean comedian who often disgraced his guests and was sexually crass and inappropriate with women. He tried to humiliate Lepa Brena, but she was so smart and quick to respond to his jabs, she outwitted him on the spot. Watching her was an inspiration and made me respect her as a woman instantly."[24] To illustrate just how difficult it might have been for a woman like Brena to navigate her career, four photos by Zoran Trbović from 1982 show Minimaks visibly harassing the young singer (see Figures 2.8–2.11).

Wedged between Minimaks and rock singer Seid Memić Vajta, both dressed in black suits, Brena smiles with discernible discomfort as Minimaks places his hand on her breast and waist. At the same time, his eyes are fixed on her breasts as he looks at her grinning. In the next shot, we see Brena push his hand away, but this does not seem to dissuade him, as his head is now even closer to her face and shoulder, and in the third shot, he is touching her shoulder as she smiles with embarrassment and leans away from him. *XXZ*

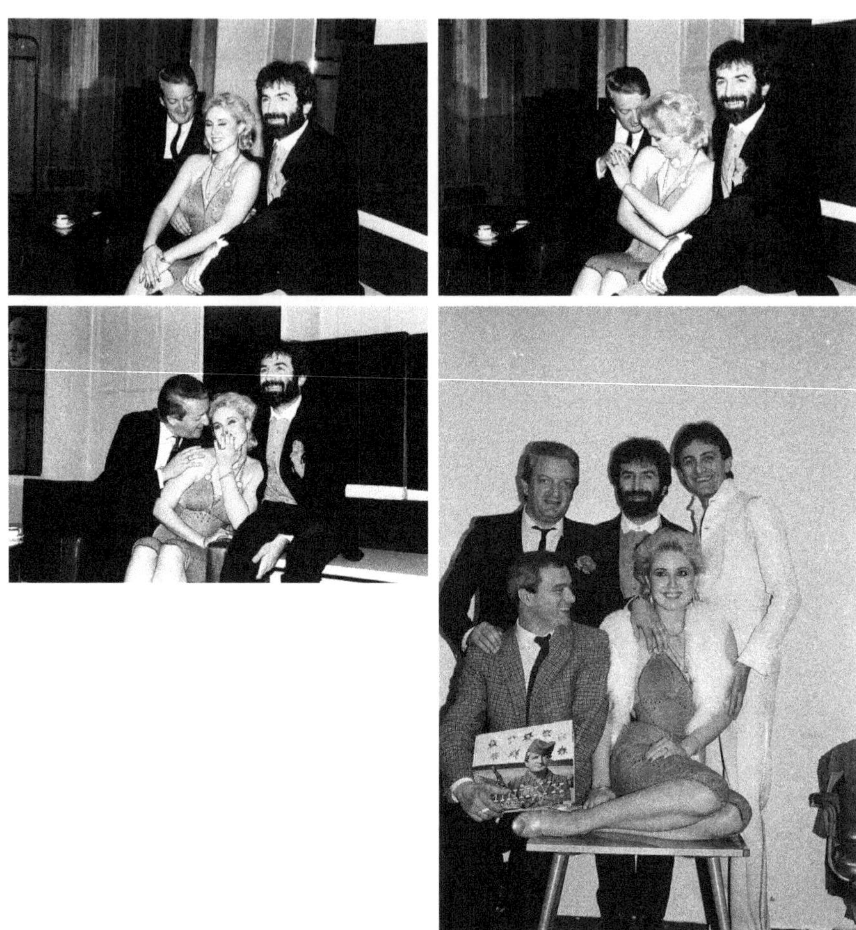

2.8–2.11   Zoran Trbović, Lepa Brena with Minimaks and Seid Memić Vajta at Dom Sindikata, Belgrade, 1982. Photographs.

Magazin, which featured these images in 2018, noted that "an atmosphere of carelessness approaching childhood joy has remained recorded on these photo documents," and that "this looks like a period of innocence before the storm."[25] The photos are also titled individually, and the second photo's description touches on Minimaks's transgression by characterizing him as "aggressive" and Seid Memić Vajta (sitting to her left) as "smiling," while not mentioning Brena at all.[26] The third photo is labeled "Hajde da se volimo" ("Let's love each other"), alluding to Brena's hit film and song from the late 1980s. In another shot from the same night, Brena is seated on a coffee table with her legs together in an elegant pose. Again, she is closely surrounded by grinning men touching her, with Minimaks's left hand standing out as the most obtrusive, resting on her right shoulder and touching the strap of her dress near her breasts. Actor Momčilo Stanišić is holding Minimaks's new record at the time, *Zlatna Ploča*, reminding us that Brena's career was in constant competition with the careers of men like Minimaks, who felt entitled to touch and demean her.

This set of images illustrates the sexist context in which Brena had to operate and which posed a challenge to her success. Even though she exploited her status as a sex symbol in music, as could be said about any major female pop star, such as Madonna or Beyoncé, her emancipatory performance politics must also be recognized in her ability to find empowerment in her own body despite being the subject of unwanted advances. Brena has never commented publicly on these photos (to my knowledge), but we know since the #MeToo movement how prevalent experiences of harassment were and continue to be for women in any social context, particularly in the media industry. One important difference to the #MeToo cases here, however, is that these unwanted advances were in public and practically normalized, even if many people might have considered Minimaks's behavior to be in bad taste at the time. What's worse, it is entirely conceivable that many more blamed Brena for facilitating such bad behavior.

What we do know is that it was difficult for Brena to convince her parents to let her sing when she was young. In a 2014 interview, she recalled her parents constantly referring to her gender as the main problem: "What? How are you going to be a singer? You are still a child, you are not even an adult yet, you are a woman!"[27] Brena resisted. "I never liked that discrimination," she remarked. "It seems, it was always part of my life since I was born and was always posed as a 'problem' to me. But my response was: What problem? I simply was not willing to accept the idea of being a woman as a problem."[28]

Brena was not a vocal feminist in the 1980s, but her behavior spoke volumes. The co-director and writer of the *Lepa Brena Project*, Olga Dimitrijević, has pointed to how she experienced Brena's embodiment of strength and emancipation when growing up in Yugoslavia:

For me, in Brena's movie [series] *Hajde da Se Volimo*—Brena is a feminist legacy, especially in the first part of the series [1987]. At least for my generation, because we were sitting there, watching that film, and she is beating up guys, she is jumping from the bridge, she is flying the plane, she can do everything, and plays the video game. And you don't read it as, "ah Lepa Brena is [just] playing a video game." No, you read it as: Lepa Brena can do *everything*. And you identify yourself with a woman who can do *everything*. For me, that is a huge pop cultural feminist legacy.[29]

Feminism was a decisive subtext that penetrated the cultural landscape of Yugoslavia, and Brena did indeed change identities and characters in her songs and videos. To do so, her music often merged her sexuality, ethnic background, and Yugoslavia's entanglements with Orientalist tropes. Most bizarrely, and interestingly, in her 1985 song "Šeki Šeki" ("Sheikh Sheikh") we see a low-budget video production featuring Brena in a tightly fitted burgundy sequinned dress with her back exposed. She is surrounded by her band members from Slatki Greh, who are dressed in fake sheikh outfits. While on the surface Brena sings about bringing the sheikh to bankruptcy because of her beauty, Čvoro offers an astute analysis of the politics at play:

> The song takes the form of a dialogue between Brena and the sheikh with references to foreign finance, sexuality as commodity, and the use of female sexuality as empowerment (…) the song's historical background of the early eighties' recession, caused partly by the global oil crisis, also suggested that the sheikh's "help" is a reference to the extravagant foreign loans that bankrolled Yugoslavia throughout the seventies and stopped in the eighties, causing an economic crisis. Despite the song's grim subject, its upbeat tempo and tongue-in-cheek orientalist lyrics create an image of Yugoslavia defined through the nexus of sexuality and ideology. The references to the sheikh's help suggest that Yugoslavia was willing to "sell itself" economically to gain superficial ideological independence of non-alignment. It also suggests that this was done willingly and aligned with the general self-exoticizing perception of Yugoslavia as a nation of opportunistic swindlers operating within the grey zone of self-management.[30]

In Čvoro's analysis, Brena's body is both a symbol for Yugoslavia and a profound critique of the recklessness with which the socialist leaders in the 1980s sold themselves out under the veneer of political emancipation. She is also a stand-in for the knotty racial politics of Yugoslavia, which Čvoro points to by linking her to the troubled ideological foundation of nonalignment socialism in Yugoslavia. But the song's lyrics manifest additional tensions in Yugoslav culture, specifically those that touch on gender and race. Brena plays the seductress who remains aloof and in charge, knowing her power over the man who only has material goods to share. The fake sheikh pleads with her to "increase the rhythm of my heart." He adds: "I won't ask how much it costs," alluding to the trope that a beautiful woman is always paid for at great cost to the man. But Brena resists this monetization: "Oh, I am not that way. I don't need riches. I only need you for my fortune (or happiness). Ducats are cursed."[31] At another point, she indicates that the sheikh is trying to "solve my problems" with big bags of jewelry, which is clearly a futile endeavor. Another subtext that haunts the song is the fact that Brena is "white," and therefore more desirable. The fake sheikh notes how much he admires her "white" face, clearly indicating his preference for a white woman. But in this tacky caricature that is culturally prejudiced, one might surmise that underneath the sheikh costume he is as white as she is. To make matters worse, an unknown Black servant is also in the video, holding a handheld fan in the background and dancing the entire time. Brena's "Šeki Šeki" reminds us that Yugoslavia's status as a nonaligned country, and its history with the Ottoman Empire, opened it up to more racial and cultural diversity; but racism, along with sexism, was still an underlying part of Yugoslav culture.

In her 1989 video *Robinja* (*Slave*), Brena finds herself at the Hagia Sophia and in markets in Istanbul, trapped in a sadomasochistic (S&M) relationship with a lover, displaying what feminist theorist and anthropologist Žarana Papić diagnosed as a "new visual culture of femininity that plays with, and freely disposes of, [the ideas of] strength and weakness."[32] This play with S&M also marks the inversion of the "essence of traditional femininity" and of women being subordinate to and dependent on men for recognition as individuals.[33] The man in the video is anonymous, a no-name player in Brena's elaborate game with Orientalist tropes that also signified the Yugoslav woman's unique position of being part of both the Orient and the Occident. Both sexist and sexualized spaces for women, these collided worlds can and must be navigated by one and the same woman: Brena. Brena's practice as an emancipated woman embodied these many diverse facets of Yugoslav socialism, which might also explain why her music and varied self-presentation were so relatable to her audiences, who were surrounded by this cultural diversity in Yugoslavia. Papić considered Lepa Brena a "significant political phenomenon of the former Yugoslavia, something like a peaceful communist body," a "princess" in a "fairy tale," with her "blonde" hair embodying an unthreatening representation of something akin to a "Yugoslav dream."[34] Papić elaborates: "This dream [of Yugoslavia as a country] also had many dark elements, but its people did not want to, or could not, see it."[35] It could be said that Brena's emancipatory strength in the video relied on these problematic markers of difference to stand out as feminist strengths, reminding us how deeply feminism itself is often implicated in other forms of injustices.

Brena maintained an air of fun and light-heartedness in her incorporation of folk and Orientalist tropes as well as more difficult subject matters, a characteristic of her work that speaks to her ability to adjust to her times and connect with her audiences. In a 2017 interview, she was challenged to comment on accusations of "having changed" over time, to which she responded:

> I changed myself [over and over again] because I definitely know that I love this work very much. And I know that I have to send a beautiful message to people. That is simply my task. But the thing that is most important to me is that I enjoy it all [the work]. Because if I don't enjoy it, then it's for nothing.

> Because I don't need parties, or anything else, I just need to feel good when I
> am doing this work, and to have a good energy with my audience.[36]

Her versatility in finding ways to enjoy her own work and connect with audiences becomes palpable when considering that in the same year as "Šeki Šeki," Brena released one of her signature songs connecting her to Yugoslavia as a political project. For her 1985 duet with Miroslav Ilić, "Živela Jugoslavija" ("Long Live Yugoslavia"), the music video was staged in front of the Museum of Yugoslavia in Belgrade, which is set on a hill overlooking the city and which holds Marshal Tito's grave and artifacts from the Yugoslav period. The video featured Brena and Ilić singing the song surrounded by musicians, children's music groups dressed identically and acting as dancers and a choir, among a huge audience of fans standing on the descending steps, singing along with raised arms. At various moments, the video cuts to aerial scenes of Belgrade and the concert, showing dancers in folklore costumes in the Yugoslav flag colors of blue, red, and white, and dancing to the song in a circle in front of the museum. The video is also spliced with images of the Yugoslav flag undulating in the air, and Brena and Ilić raising their hands entwined together. The video features none of her overtly sexualized performances. Nor does it capitalize on her humor. Rather, Brena appears as a dignified singer representing the country politically.

Looking at the video today—especially the close-up of their entwined hands lifted in the sky symbolizing unity, peace, and strength—makes for a disturbing and also touching moment, knowing that only five years later the country would be divided by brutal civil war. The same feeling might arise when considering the very optimistic lyrics of the song, which call Yugoslavia "the land of peace, the land of Tito," proclaim "we love you our mother (Yugoslavia)," and pledge "we will not give you to anyone, long live Yugoslavia!"[37] On the surface, the song reads like a propaganda piece for Yugoslavia. But considering the fact that ethno-religious tensions were already on the rise, as was political and economic corruption throughout the republics, this song can also be seen as a form of resistance to that right-wing takeover and eventual fragmentation of the formerly peaceful and united country. Although Yugoslavia broke apart due to the rise of patriarchal nationalism, Brena held to her promise of not giving Yugoslavia to anyone, preserving across her career a belief in a unified Yugoslavia.

Brena's unique command over her audiences also speaks to the political power of her work as *the* self-proclaimed Jugoslovenka in 1989. Returning to Lepa Brena's 2019 concert, one of the most common images from the event shows Brena sitting inside a large, glittery star, the signature marker of Yugoslav socialism; but the red color of communism is replaced with luxurious gold, celebrating her commercial success. During the concert, she was suspended slowly from above and greeted with hysterical clapping by the crowd. If Abramović's body signified the energetic force of feminine power at the nucleus of the socialist star in the 1970s, then Brena today is the sustained embodiment of that cultural phenomenon of feminist socialism—in all its complications and contradictions— that is unmistakable in her performance politics, which have remained loyal to Yugoslavia for four decades. These two women's bodies inside the star—one feeling suffocated and oppressed and resisting it, another feeling empowered and catapulted into "star"dom—remarkably reveal the wide-ranging legacy of women's emancipation in Yugoslavia.

Brena's "Jugoslovenka" song deliberately celebrated the beauty of her multiethnic, multinational, and multicultural background. The song's production itself consciously sought to embody a wide-ranging inclusivity, in that it featured Brena, born in the Yugoslav republic of Bosnia-Herzegovina and at the time living in the Serbian city of Belgrade, with three well-known multiethnic singers from the 1980s: Croatian pop star Vlado Kalember, Montenegrin pop star Daniel Popović, and Bosnian Muslim rock star Alen Islamović. Her self-representation as an embodiment of all these multiple ethnicities and religions, along with her rejection of nationalism, had dire consequences for the artist: a song that was a chart-topping hit in 1989 stood just a decade later as a fraught anthem that amplified the divide between former Yugoslavians who still believed in a greater Yugoslavia and those who favored the national independence of the former republics. Brena's earlier and continued identification with Yugoslavia and her self-proclaimed position as a Jugoslovenka became most volatile during what Zlatan Delić characterized as a "collective paranoia of nationalism and ensuing violence" in the early 1990s, leaving Brena "stripped of her country" and her popularity, and tied to what was suddenly "the past." He adds that "the populist groundswell that hoisted her as a Yugoslav icon soon resurfaced in the overwhelming readiness to annihilate her, indifferent to the ethical intricacies of wartime."[38] The impulse to punish Brena was most pronounced during what was called the "Brčko affair," when the singer was spotted in 1993 performing for Serbian frontline forces in a Serbian Army uniform, which represented "the ultimate betrayal of her Yugoslavism, particularly in her native Bosnia."[39] Crucially, it must be noted that she allegedly made a pact with the Serbian Army to perform for them in exchange for freeing her parents, who were under siege in her hometown (Brčko) at the time.[40] While the circumstances of the "Brčko affair" remain obscure, one might suspect that Brena, as a private person and as a public Jugoslovenka, learned firsthand how painful the disintegration of her cherished Yugoslavia was, and how deeply her own fame was implicated in the destruction of its unifying legacy.

What if we recognized the fact that as a singer, she was able to save her parents by performing; something many of us would be willing to do to keep our loved ones out of harm's way? What if we recognized that even though the populists and nationalists tried to "annihilate" her career along with Yugoslavia, she, and the idea of Yugoslavia, remained relevant? What if, instead of accepting negative interpretations of Brena, such as the characterization of her transnationalism as being solely invested in commercialized efforts to capitalize on people's emotions, we considered the possibility that she may have made those artistic choices sincerely? And that in fact, they might have been deeply politically charged gestures attached to the possibility of unity in former Yugoslavia? Even as recently as 2017, Brena said that "Music doesn't have a passport. Music doesn't have a border."[41] In both her work and her life, this Jugoslovenka was instrumental in exposing the inextricable links between the rise of nationalism and the swell in patriarchal violence during this period, while at the same time wielding her power as a feminist icon in the service of resistance against the impending genocides and wars.

It is noteworthy that Brena's Zagreb concert in 2019 also reached other audiences beyond the stadium: many in the Yugoslav diaspora, and those still living in the region of former Yugoslavia, were watching YouTube videos of her concert with astonishment and with bated breath. Could it be true? Could the younger and older generations of former Yugoslavs come together in this song and feel united again? After all the carnage, the hatred, the divisions, and economic catastrophes, could there really still be a hope for Yugoslavia? In the comment section for the YouTube video of Brena performing "Ja Sam Jugoslovenka," which went viral as soon as the concert aired, one self-identified Jugoslovenka from Novi Sad noted euphorically:

> After Belgrade [Serbia] Skopje [Macedonia] and middle of Zagreb [Croatia]! So much singing and there will be even more singing [of the song, Jugoslovenka]! Everything is obvious … Long live Yugoslavia! Greetings to all good people, from a Jugoslovenka from Novi Sad [Vojvodina] Long live Yugoslavia![42]

This enthusiastic statement was followed by a heart emoji, a heart-eyed smiley face, and clapping hands emoji. The ellipses after "everything is obvious" are striking and indicate that, for the writer, the time for Jugoslovenka is now. And indeed, just days after Lepa Brena's performance, in December 2019, the Belgrade International Experimental Theater Festival (BITEF) opened its *Lepa Brena Project* show, dedicating it entirely to the legacy of Yugoslav socialism through the embodiment of different stages of Lepa Brena's career. Directed by Vladimir Aleksić and Olga Dimitrijević, the play was conceptualized around five types of Lepa Brenas (Figure 2.12):

> Brena, the Builder[43] (played by Jovana Gavrilović, written by Vedrana Klepica)
>
> Brena, the Business Woman (played by Jasna Đuričić, written by Maja Pelević)

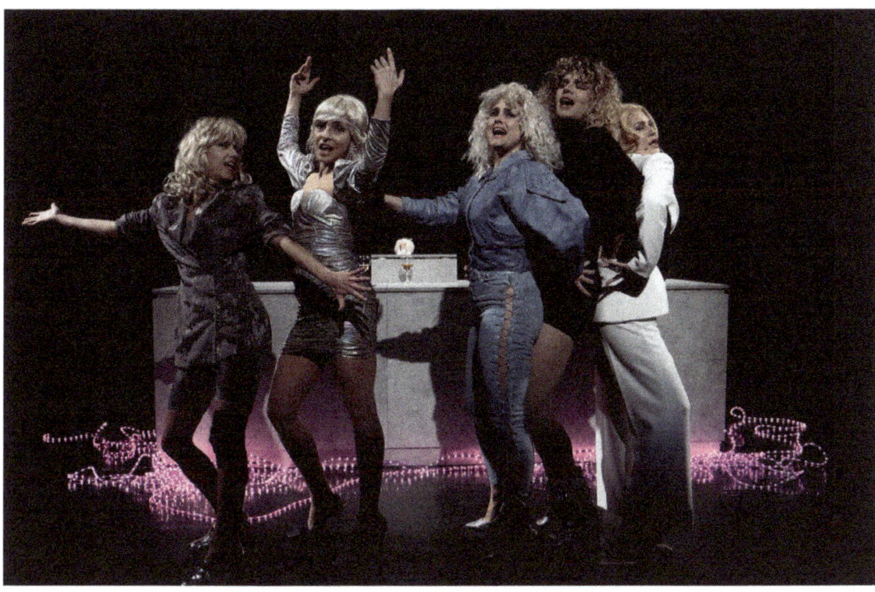

The Five Lepa Brenas in the *Lepa Brena Project*, 2019. BITEF Theatre, Belgrade.   **2.12**
Photograph by Jelena Janković.

Brena, of Songs (played by Jelena Ilić, written by Olga Dimitrijević)

Brena, the Yugoslav (played by Tamara Krcunović, written by Tanja Šljivar)

Brena, of Sexuality (played by Ivan Marković, written by Slobodan Obradović)

The poster for the show features a Barbie-like body, collaged together to account for these five personalities (Figure 2.13): extremely long legs, referring to Brena's 1982 song "Duge Noge" ("Long Legs"); a microphone instead of a face; a Yugoslav socialist cap and a big, blonde ponytail; a hammer in her right hand and a purse in her left; a shiny silver skirt, along with sparkly jewelry and black high heels. And instead of her eyes, or her face, she has one eye, apparently taken from a banknote. As she is captured mid-walk, her body is adorned with a large pink star in the background. While the turn to the pink-colored star (instead of red) recalls the Serbian radio and TV music station Pink, it also magnifies the importance of Brena's reception in the queer community. One of the five Brenas, Brena of Sexuality, is played by a male actor. Dimitrijević noted that "in the whole network of signs, it somehow signifies the trans, drag and the cross-dressing existence—actually that queer life on the margins—it is inscribed in the script [of Lepa Brena's life]."[44]

When walking into the space, the audience is greeted by only one Brena, with her body turned away, sitting next to a Yugoslav flag. She is surrounded

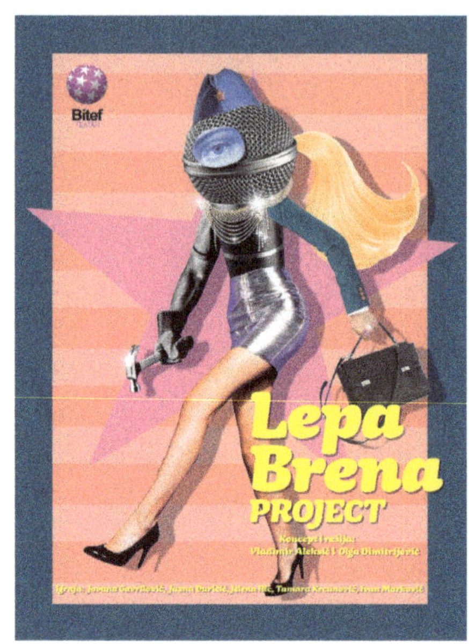

2.13   *Lepa Brena Project* poster, 2019. BITEF, Belgrade. Designed by McCann Belgrade.

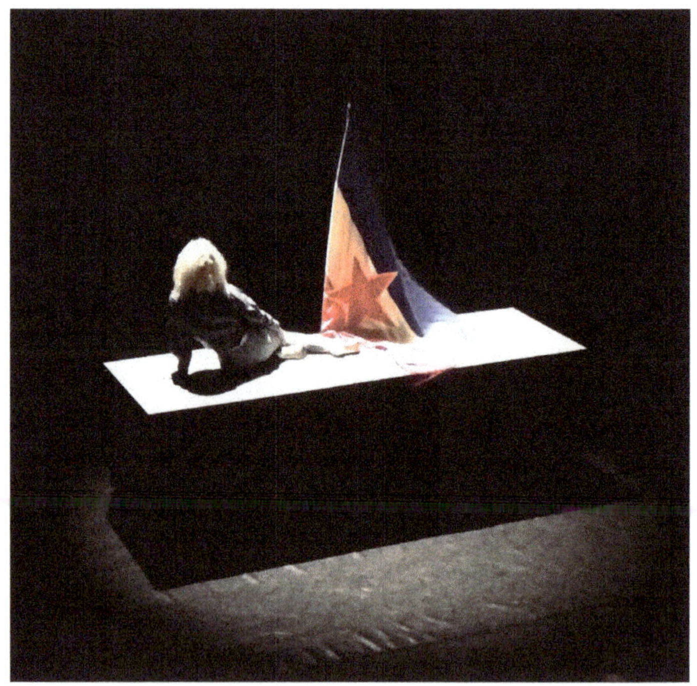

2.14   *Lepa Brena Project*, 2019. BITEF, Belgrade.

by darkness as she sits in total silence (Figure 2.14). The entire play is a musical that engages with the history of Yugoslavia through the ups and downs of Brena's career, as well as the ups and downs of the country. Brena, who attended the performance, spoke afterward to the *Lepa Brena Project* actors and the press: "You made a chronology, a retrospective of all the things we survived, what was happening to a nation, or what happened with these twenty-five million people who need [she gestures with her hand] 1) love, 2) (state) support, 3) and a good job." She then added in English: "All you need is love, yes? Love and money!"[45]

Years before the *Lepa Brena Project*, Brena stated that it was precisely her wish to reach this new generation: "to touch a young generation of people who weren't even born in that country; for them to still feel so deeply those emotions associated with Yugoslavia." She added: "I always wanted to touch the youth (…) I wanted to pull them into this story."[46] As the self-anointed Jugoslovenka, Brena continues the legacy of women's emancipatory power in Yugoslavia. For new generations of artists and playwrights, it seems she has become a more important icon of socialist history than Tito himself, offering new insights into Yugoslavia's radical past and becoming the embodiment of a return to the transnational alliances and respect that were so imperative for the feminist movement of Yugoslavia.

Esma Redžepova: Romani Jugoslovenka

While a production like the *Lepa Brena Project* suggests a move to historicize Brena's career, such attention has not been given to Esma Redžepova. In fact, since her death in 2016, the North Macedonian government has exhibited no interest in honoring her legacy or history for the country. This is especially troubling given her long list of "firsts," which cultural anthropologist and folklorist Carol Silverman succinctly summarizes:

> Esma was the first Balkan Romani musician (male or female) to achieve commercial success in the non-Romani world; she was the first openly identified Romani singer to perform in the Romani and Macedonian languages for non-Roma; she was the first female Romani artist to record in Yugoslavia; and she was the first Macedonian woman (Romani or non-Romani) to perform on television.[47]

Redžepova's emancipatory power remains understudied to this day, due to the continued discrimination against Roma in Europe and the ignorance about Roma in North America. In fact, it was thanks to Redžepova's non-Romani partner Teodosievski, who worked for the radio station in Skopje at the time and who pushed for the representation of Romani women, that Redžepova had a launchpad to the kind of celebrity she achieved, allowing her to overcome the lack of recognition typically experienced by women of color or women from marginalized cultures.[48] Redžepova's position as an outsider in the Yugoslav socialist state was palpable for her, even if she was later accepted and celebrated. She recalls how

> I was the first Rom to sing in the Romani language. It was actually historical, that Yugoslavia was the first place to broadcast Romani songs on the radio. It was kind of a shame to sing in Romani in my time; many singers hid the fact that they were Romani. When I came out singing my own songs in Romani, many came out after me. …
>
> Our Romani women were afraid at the time to say they were Roma—they said they were Turkish, Macedonian, Albanian, anything but Roma. … After the cleansings of World War II, Roma were afraid for their lives and at no time would admit they were Roma.[49]

This statement makes clear that Yugoslavia's multiculturalism had an embedded hierarchy of racial representation operating in subtle ways to undermine racial equity within the country. Roma, who had been murdered en masse all over Europe during the Holocaust—including in several concentration camps within the territory of Yugoslavia—never received reparations or acknowledgment for the genocide they endured and only slowly began to trust the newly formed socialist state. While Roma still faced discrimination, Tito's socialist system implemented policies that were much more open, such as desegregating schools and securing employment for Roma, earning Tito a positive reputation in Roma communities. During and after the wars in the 1990s, the Roma population experienced an upsurge of racial violence, discrimination, expulsion, and segregation. Many Roma living in the former Yugoslav region today lament the loss of socialism and Tito for this reason (see Chapter 5). Redžepova, too, was an avid supporter of Tito, who was a huge fan of her music, especially her version of the song "Čaje Šukarije" ("Beautiful Woman"), a hit that swept the entire Yugoslav nation and the world.

Redžepova's embrace of Romani languages and styles, along with frequent performances in Yugoslav dialects and languages delivered at the request of Tito, made her a key cultural representative of Muslim and Romani women under Yugoslav socialism. It is important to note here that Redžepova represented a limited image of Roma women, as she resisted the prejudices and stigmatized roles projected onto Romani women as seductive and available women in the patriarchal, macho bar culture of Yugoslavia. In fact, the Lenče character in *I Even Met Happy Gypsies* (1967), played by Olivera Katarina (whom Abramović featured in *Balkan Erotic Epic*), embodies many of these stereotypes. Redžepova's rejection of sexualized performances was linked to the degradation of Roma women, who were often treated as second-class citizens in non-Romani communities. Redžepova's older sister, for example, had sung in *kafanas*, which was considered a disgrace for the family because marriage was then the preferred role for women.[50] A woman singing alone in a *kafana* was considered loose, as she would inevitably provoke unwanted attention.

Redžepova did not want to get married at an early age, and she also refused to perform in *kafanas* because she sought to be respected as a serious musician. Ana Hofman has noted how "being a *kafana* entertainer was recognized in public discourses as the opposite of being a respected music professional."[51] Redžepova favored more respected and elite venues. In this way, she and Abramović—albeit for different reasons—moved away from "the everyday/common people," while Brena, whose career was launched in *kafanas*, remained tied to the rural classes through her witty, sexualized, and folkloristic style.

Like Brena, Redžepova knew from an early age that she wanted to be a singer, despite the fact that her family, too, was avidly against it. In an interview from 2016, she remembered that she had threatened to kill herself if her family did not let her sing.[52] In another instance, when discussing the pressures for women to get married, Redžepova responded with an implicit critique of the patriarchal model of marriage that made women into servants: "I don't want to be a servant," she said, "I want to be an artist."[53]

For Redžepova to rise as an artist, she had to find a language so she could be both Yugoslav and Roma at the same time, a strategic engagement that would become the definitive marker of her feminist performance politics and her status as Jugoslovenka. Unlike Abramović and Brena, Redžepova's engagement with Orientalism as a performer was a given; as a Romani woman, she was already racially distinctive in the Yugoslav population. According to Silverman, "Roma Orientalize themselves when necessary for marketing purposes."[54] Here, it is imperative to recognize that Silverman, as I, place no value judgment on such "self-Orientalization" for profit, or for any other reason. In fact, the most frequent negative charges projected on contemporary artists of Romani descent are rooted in racist, narrow expectations for Roma, especially Roma women, to represent themselves in certain ways, such as "playing guitar or dancing."[55] Marika Schmiedt in Austria vehemently rejects being labeled as a "Roma artist" because of the highly racially charged and discriminatory subtext of such categorizations. In addition, as Silverman has pointed out, "Roma have had few opportunities to alter their imagery and discourse because they have never been in control of their representations."[56] Consequently, Redžepova faced challenges on three fronts: first, as a woman, she had to fight for her right to be emancipated and ascend in the patriarchal music business that venerated the sexual exploitation of women; second, as a Romani woman, who was "the first" to create a language of self-representation and expression in the Yugoslav public; and third, as one who also had to validate her status as a Yugoslav woman (Jugoslovenka) within the dominant culture of South Slavic East Europeans. Redžepova's emancipatory performance politics became a stand-in for "her" people, the Roma people, but also for Yugoslavia.

In 1977, she made an album with the Teodosievski ensemble (her husband's band), called *Kroz Jugoslaviju* (*Across Yugoslavia*), for which the artist was photographed in different folklore costumes representing the multiculturalism of Yugoslavia.[57] Silverman sums up the political importance of Redžepova's performative photoshoot: "She embodied Tito's principle of 'bratstvo i [j] edinstvo' (brotherhood and unity) by performing the music of all the ethnic groups in Yugoslavia."[58] Her versatility as a unique Romani Jugoslovenka, who could slip into different folklore personalities while remaining distinctly herself in all of them, was calculated and tied to her success. And while she is smiling in all the photographs on *Kroz Jugoslaviju*, her voice was so profoundly distinctive, and with such depth of pathos, that her music was never regarded as shallow pop or folk music. For example, Garth Cartwright recalls that one local Roma living in the Macedonian city Shutka had attested to Redžepova's reputation as a singer of the people, of "the village [Roma] and all the suffering we have known."[59] Suffering was one way that the Yugoslav audiences also connected to her music; for the South Slav population, with its marginal status in Europe, also identified as outsiders to the West.[60] In this way, Yugoslav audience members could identify their own sense of marginalization through the embodiment of Redžepova's strength in bridging so many different cultural facets of Yugoslavia, including the two big ones: the Orient and the Occident.

As a performer and singer who could carry the weight of "knowing" and accurately articulate the suffering of the most marginalized (ethnic Roma) within an already marginalized population in Europe (the multiple ethnicities that made up the united Yugoslav nation), Redžepova became one of the most respected singers in Yugoslavia. She frequently performed in prestigious concert halls in Yugoslavia and Europe, as well as in the United States, including at Carnegie Hall. To return once more to the idea of suffering: according to Redžepova, one of Tito's favorite songs was her 1974 hit, "Zašto si me majko rodila" ("Why Did You Give Birth to Me, Mother?"), a song that expresses both longing for the mother and also disappointment over her "never" seeing her own child. Tito might have seen some parts of his own life reflected in this song. He and his first wife, Pelagija Belousova from Russia, had four children, of which only one survived: their son Žarko. When Tito was arrested in 1928 for communist activities, Belousova moved back to Stalinist Russia and ended up in prison herself, sending their only son to live in institutions while Tito was away.[61] It is worth noting that Tito was in his late twenties when he met Belousova, then fourteen years old; Tito married her a year later, in 1919. Although Tito was a proponent of women's rights, he was also part of a culture that normalized expectations for young, adolescent women to serve as wives and child bearers.

Redžepova's husband, nineteen years her senior, met the young singer when she was thirteen. While it is not clear when they became lovers, he swiftly became her manager, and they married in 1968, when she was in her twenties. He carefully facilitated Redžepova's self-presentation, insisting that she had to be "likable" to her Yugoslav and European (read: non-Roma) audience. Consequently, Redžepova delivered on a level that most female pop stars of color had to, particularly Black women in the USA (e.g. Tina Turner, Beyoncé), especially at the beginning of their careers. To make sure she was relatable to "all women," photoshoots of Redžepova often included her wearing different "modern clothing," as can be seen in a set of photographs on the cover of her 1970 single, "Odžačar, Odžačar/Pjesma Šeher Sarajevu" (Figure 2.15).

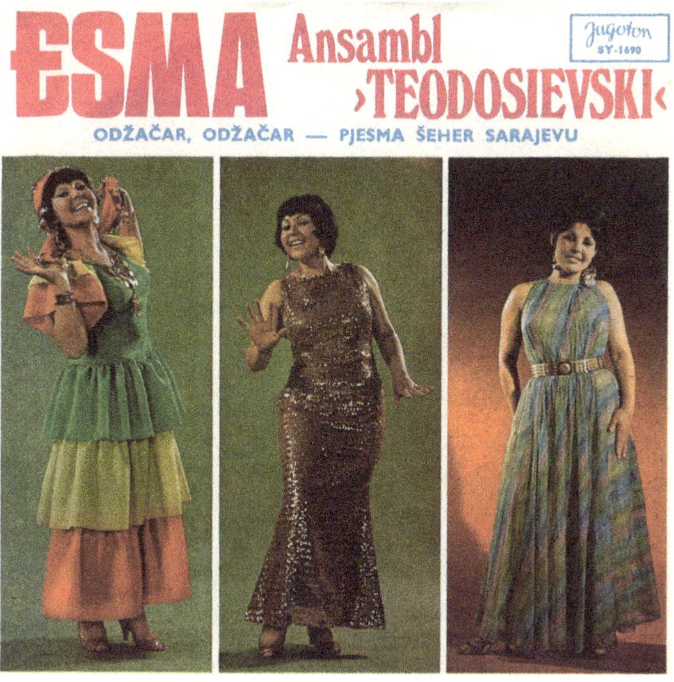

Esma Redžepova and Ansambl Teodosievski, "Odžačar, Odžačar/Pjesma Šeher Sarajevu." Single, Jugoton, 1970. Album cover.   **2.15**

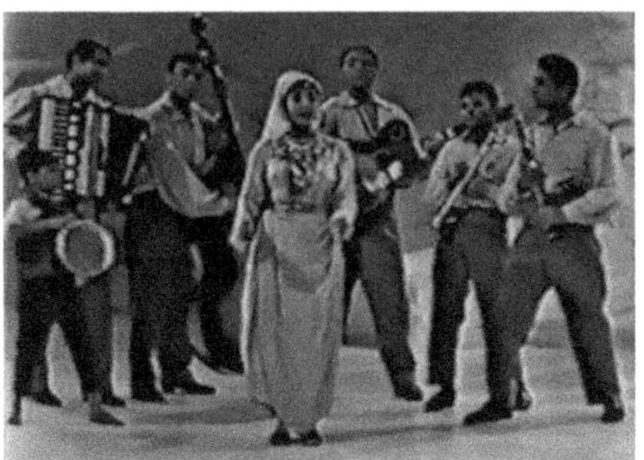 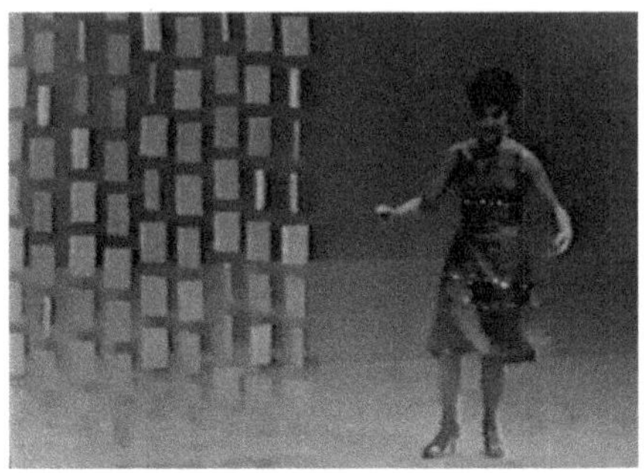

2.16   Esma Redžepova and Ansambl Teodosievski, performing "Čaje Šukarije" for Austrian Public Broadcasting, 1965. Film still. Rebroadcast on Macedonian National Television.

Esma Redžepova and Ansambl Teodosievski, performing "Romano Horo" for Austrian Public Broadcasting, 1965. Film still. Rebroadcast on Macedonian National Television.

In these three photographs, Redžepova shows her comfort and ease at slipping into these different roles. She heightened that embodiment of versatility when she performed on Austrian television in 1965, where she first appeared in her signature dimije pants singing "Čaje Šukarije," then switched into "Western" clothing for "Romano Horo" ("Roma Dance") and began to dance the twist, which was, as Silverman notes, the most popular dancing style at the time (see Figures 2.16-2.17).[62]

While some might consider this a form of "whitewashing," the particular context of coming from Yugoslavia with its brand of multiculturalism might shed light on her willingness to play with these two embodiments as she pleased. Why must she only perform wearing dimije pants? As Patricia Leighten and Mark Antliff have argued, the desire to keep non-Western cultures locked in a particular time and space has long been part of modernist discourse on primitivist art and culture.[63] Expecting Redžepova to perform her otherness in fixed terms echoes this impulse to control representation, so frequently projected onto women, especially women of color. Redžepova's ability to transform her body was an emancipatory strategy that was enabled by her Yugoslav background, a place where the Orient and the Occident were constant fixtures of everyday life. In an album cover from 1980, we see these two worlds manifest: Redžepova is wearing a top and headscarf in the signature colors of the Yugoslav flag, and she is adorned with golden jewelry and make-up (Figure 2.18). Here, she becomes the total embodiment of an ethnic Roma woman in the Balkans who also and simultaneously represents Jugoslovenka, a singularly critical part of Yugoslav art and culture.

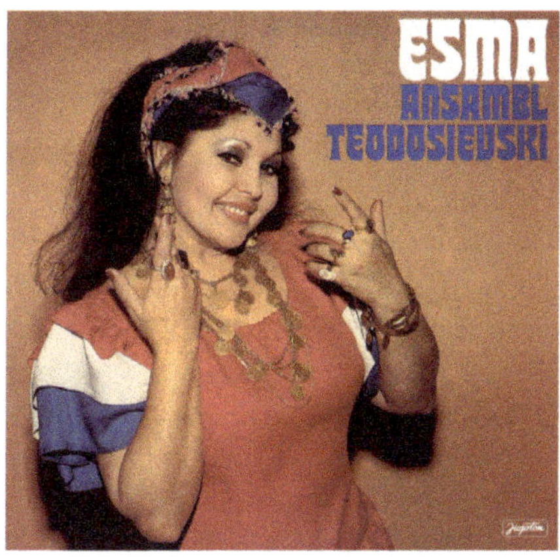

Esma Redžepova and Ansambl Teodosievski, compilation, Jugoton, 1980. Album   **2.18**
cover.

It is no surprise then that Redžepova, some three decades later during the Yugoslav wars, became an important marker of that pan-ethnic solidarity. As a person living in the diaspora, I remember going to the "Yugoslav Club" in Hachen, Germany, in 1991. The club had existed since the 1960s, when my grandmother was a guest worker there, and as refugees my family sought connection and a feeling of home there. Walking in, an enormous Yugoslav flag hung on the wall. Inevitably, Redžepova's "Čaje Šukarije" would be played at the height of the night, for every celebration, with people coming together to dance in huge circles, holding hands entwined up in the air. I cannot help but think of Lepa Brena and Miroslav Ilić holding up their hands together in "Živela Jugoslavija"; in 1991—in that small Yugoslav club—this gesture was an even more devastating statement on the impending destruction of Yugoslav solidarity. As the wars progressed, the Yugoslav club became non-operational because of nationalist tensions.

Redžepova's 1977 album, *Kroz Jugoslaviju* (*Across Yugoslavia*), was re-released in 1990, and also circulated as a cassette on the black market, a copy of which my father, Petar Tumbas, somehow secured in Germany. My mother, Eržebet Tumbas, remembered how listening to that cassette during wartime was extremely emotional, but also gave her and my father hope that the ethnic conflict would cease, and that we could return home to a multicultural and open Yugoslavia.[64] That never happened; but Redžepova remained an important figure representing Yugoslav unity and diversity, while also being crowned one of the most talented singers in the world. And despite her fame, this Jugoslovenka was open to talk to anyone, including me, when I attended one of her last concerts in 2016 at the Bellefield Hall Auditorium in Pittsburgh. Starstruck and singing every word of every song, I attended the concert with the Palestinian musician Jiryis Murkus Ballan, who incidentally also knew her music: his aunt, Amal Murkus, had performed with Redžepova in 2002 in Austria for the ARTE-produced music film dedicated to celebrating "women's voices, the beautiful voices of the 20th century" in what was called the "Festival of the Last Prima Donnas."[65]

Redžepova represented a connective tissue not only in Yugoslavia, but across the world, including the Middle East. The fact that the tickets to her concert only cost $10 left us embarrassed, ashamed to have paid such a low price to see a legend of music history. But such is the fate of the Romani Jugoslovenka: extraordinary but underrecognized.

Conclusion

Abramović, Brena, and Redžepova share the site of their socialist nation as the place that launched their international careers. They also remained successful and relevant long after the breakup of Yugoslavia, when many others in the cultural sector went under. Despite sexist stereotypes and inequalities haunting their individual practices throughout their entire careers, these three women represent a uniquely Yugoslav form of feminist, emancipatory performance politics centered on their embodied, highly celebrated, and remarkably distinctive works. Each manifested a different facet of a distinctively Yugoslav multicultural landscape in art and music: Abramović returning after the wars to her roots in sensational performances that revealed her complicated and tenuous relationship to her homeland; Brena as the blonde woman whose hypersexualized and racially charged performances flaunted Tito's open socialism; and Redžepova as the Romani Jugoslovenka, whose talent as a performer and singer introduced and legitimized Romani culture within the Yugoslav cultural spheres across all classes and republics.

Notes

1 In reality, she has mostly been referred to as the "Queen of *Gypsy music," but the term "*Gypsy" since then has been contested as a derogatory classification, often associated with racist stereotypes and sweeping generalizations made by non-Romani populations.

2 This biographical information remains unconfirmed in the literature I consulted, but in an interview with Milan Jevtić in 2016, Redžepova noted that she performed at the first Non-Aligned Movement (NAM) conference and that she sang in front of Tito in 1961. Born in 1948, Redžepova would have

been eighteen years old, but during the interview she noted she was thirteen at the time. I assume that she might have incorrectly remembered her age at the event. Her discussion of this experience at the first NAM conference can be seen in Milan Jevtić's interview with Redžepova for MIC Kopernikus on September 5, 2016: www.youtube.com/watch?v=b_HXr4dffzY (accessed 8/6/2020). The YouTube link has since been changed to private. For inquiries regarding the video, see www.kopernikus.rs (accessed 3/12/2021), or https:// tvkcn.net (accessed 8/18/2021).

3 Carol Silverman, *Romani Routes: Cultural Politics and Balkan Music in Diaspora* (Oxford: Oxford University Press, 2012), 211. For example, *The Guardian*'s obituary bore the title: "Esma Redžepova Obituary: Singer Known as 'Queen of the Gypsies' Who Spoke Out on Issues Affecting Europe's Roma People," see www.theguardian.com/world/2016/dec/14/esma-redzepova-obituary (accessed 8/6/2020); the BBC wrote "Esma Redzepova, Macedonia's 'Romany Music Queen', Dies at 73," see www.bbc.com/news/world-europe-38283554 (accessed 8/6/2020); the *Washington Post* wrote "Esma Redzepova, 'Queen of Gypsy Music,' dies at 73," see www.washingtonpost.com/entertainment/ music/esma-redzepova-queen-of-gypsy-music-dies-at-73/2016/12/13/d2752d5 6-c153–11e6–9a51-cd56ea1c2bb7_story.html (accessed 8/6/2020); and *Novosti* announced "ODLAZAK KRALJICE ROMSKE MUZIKE: Preminula Esma Redžepova [The Departure of the Queen of Romani Music: Esma Redžepova Has Passed Away]," see www.novosti.rs/vesti/scena.147.html:639391- ODLAZAK-KRALjICE-ROMSKE-MUZIKE-Preminula-Esma-Redzepova (accessed 8/6/2020).

4 Catherine Baker sees "Jugoslovenka" as standing in for a representation of Croatia, not Yugoslavia, because of the song's emphasis on the coastal line and Pannonian hair. See Catherine Baker, *Sounds of the Borderland: Popular Music, War and Nationalism in Croatia since 1991* (London: Taylor & Francis, 2016), 43. Zlatan Delić notes that Lepa Brena was a lot more than a national fantasy, a "'phantasm' of Yugoslavism." In Lacanian terms, Delić considers Brena to have functioned as "a screen that conceals something quite primary." He adds: "I argue that this is how Brena held onto the Yugoslav dream amid the erosion of communal ties and the impending carnage at the turn of the 1990s." See Zlatan Delić, "Fantasy, Sexuality, and Yugoslavism in Lepa Brena's Music," in Danijela Š. Beard and Ljerka V. Rasmussen, eds., *Made in Yugoslavia: Studies in Popular Music* (New York: Routledge, 2020), 158.

5 See Marina Abramović, *Walk through Walls: A Memoir* (New York: Three Rivers Press, 2016).

6 Silverman, *Romani Routes*, 208.

7 In the supplementary information for chapter 10 of *Romani Routes*, an online platform for the book provided by Oxford University Press, Silverman writes: "The professional singing of female Balkan Roma is associated with sexuality because the voice and body are displayed for men for remuneration." She adds: "Roma regard most professional female singers as loose and lacking decorum, an attitude echoed by non-Romani audiences." Silverman notes that,

in part, this sexist judgment is enforced by the fact that "women vocalists often receive tips in a tactile fashion, as when drunk and sweaty male patrons paste bills to their foreheads and other body parts." See https://global.oup.com/us/companion.websites/9780195300949/ (accessed 08/27/2021).

8 By 1961, at the NAM conference in Belgrade, countries with representatives included Afghanistan, Algeria, Burma, Cambodia, Cuba, Cyprus, Ethiopia, Ghana, Guinea, India, Indonesia, Iran, Lebanon, Mali, Morocco, Nepal, Saudi Arabia, Somalia, Sri Lanka, Sudan, Tunisia, the United Arab Republic, Yemen, and Yugoslavia.

9 In religious imagery, the Pietà represents Virgin Mary holding the dead body of Jesus Christ on her lap or in her arms.

10 Klaus Biesenbach, *Marina Abramović: The Artist is Present* (New York: Museum of Modern Art, 2010), 156.

11 Branislav Jakovljević, *Alienation Effects: Performance and Self-Management in Yugoslavia, 1945–91* (Ann Arbor: University of Michigan Press, 2016), 179.

12 James Westcott, *When Marina Abramović Dies: A Biography* (Cambridge, MA, and London: MIT Press, 2010), 82.

13 Bojana Pejić, "And Now, Let's Remember … Yugoslavia," in Marina Abramović, *The Cleaner* (Stockholm: Moderna Museet; Berlin: Hatje Cantz Verlag, 2017), 250–259. I published my analysis of *Balkan Baroque* and *Count on Us* when I had the chance to view and review Abramović's solo exhibition, *The Cleaner*, at the Museum of Contemporary Art in Belgrade (2019–2020). See "Solo and Ensemble," *Art in America* 108, no. 3 (March 2020), 60–65.

14 Bojana Pejić, "Balkan Baroque, Balkan Mind," in Adelina von Furstenberg and Steven Henry Madoff, eds., *Marina Abramović: Balkan Epic* (Milan: Skira, 2006), 28.

15 Ibid.

16 Pejić, "And Now, Let's Remember … Yugoslavia," 256.

17 Ibid., 250–251.

18 Fredrik Carlström and Marina Abramović, "A Conversation on Balkan Erotic Epic," in von Furstenberg and Henry Madoff, eds., *Marina Abramović: Balkan Epic*, 66.

19 "Umesto Tita stigla Lepa Brena," *Blic* (February 13, 2014): www.blic.rs/zabava/vesti/umesto-tita-stigla-lepa-brena/wjx1lmh (accessed 06/07/2019).

20 Uroš Čvoro, *Turbo-Folk Music and Cultural Representations of National Identity in Former Yugoslavia* (Farnham: Ashgate, 2014), 48.

21 Ibid., 29.

22 Ibid., 29–30.

23 Lepa Brena has credited her basketball coach for calling her "Brena." Her birth name is Fahreta Živojinović, but her coach had difficulty pronouncing her name, so he named her after a "beauty" he knew. See "Lepa Brena: Ne stidim se muslimanskog porekla," *Novosti* (March 4, 2014): www.novosti.rs/vesti/spektakl.147.html:481139-Lepa-Brena-Ne-stidim-se-muslimanskog-porekla (accessed 06/07/2019).

24 Eržebet Tumbas in conversation with the author, June 15, 2018.

25 "Ekskluzivno: Retro fotografije Lepe Brene, sredinom osamdesetih. Galerija: Sitnije, Cile, sitnije," *XXZMagazin* (March 20, 2018): www.xxzmagazin.com/fotogalerija/sitnije-cile-sitnije (accessed 06/15/2018). Translation by the author.

26 The photos have the following descriptions: Fig. 2.8: Reinforcement has arrived ("Stiglo pojačanje"): Milovan Ilić (Minimaks) with singers; Fig. 2.9: Don't touch: aggressive ("Ne pipati: Nasrtljivi") Milovan (Minimaks) and a smiling Seid; Fig. 2.10: Let's love each other ("Hajde da se volimo"): Minimaks, Brena, Seid. Fig. 2.11: Milovan Ilić (Minimaks), Seid Memić, and Big Lale (top); Momčilo Stanišić and Lepa Brena, 1982. See ibid. Translation by the author.

27 Lepa Brena interviewed on *Iz Profila TV Grand* (May 13, 2014): www.youtube.com/watch?v=uRVEk9RItOc (accessed 06/03/2019).

28 Ibid.

29 Olga Dimitrijević in conversation with the author, December 25, 2019.

30 Čvoro, *Turbo-Folk Music*, 48–49.

31 Translation by the author.

32 Žarana Papić, "Dvostruka prisutnost žena: snaga i slabost žena u masovnim medijima," *Gledišta* 1–2 (1990), 143–147. Reprinted for Adriana Zaharijević and Daša Ivanović, *Žarana Papić. Tekstovi 1977–2002* (Belgrade: Centar za Studije Roda i Politike, Fakultet Političkih Nauka, 2012), 146. Translation by the author.

33 Ibid.

34 Žarana Papić, "Europa nakon 1989: etnički ratovi, fašizacija života i politika tijela u Srbiji," *Treća* 3, nos. 1–2 (2001), 30–46. Reprinted for Zaharijević and Ivanović, *Žarana Papić*, 367. Translation by the author.

35 Ibid.

36 Lepa Brena speaking in *Lepa Brena se rasplakala zbog susreta sa Slatkim Grehom*, on Happy TV (Nacionalna Televizija Happy) (December 3, 2017): www.youtube.com/watch?v=5ymBNAj3sLc (accessed 06/03/2019).

37 Translation by the author.

38 Delić, "Fantasy, Sexuality, and Yugoslavism," 159.

39 Ibid.

40 Ibid.

41 Brena speaking in *Lepa Brena se rasplakala zbog susreta sa Slatkim Grehom*.

42 Bojana Vatić, comment on YouTube video, December 14, 2019. Original comment: "Posle Beograda Skopija i u sred Zagreba! Peva se I pevaće se sve više! Sve se vidi … Živela Jugoslavija! Pozdrav svim dobrim ljudima od Jugoslovenke iz Novog Sada."

43 Original description amended by the author. In the translated program leaflet, she is listed as "Brena the Buildings."

44 Dimitrijević in conversation with the author, December 25, 2019.

45 Translation by the author. Prva TV (December 19, 2019): "Lepa Brena—Exkluziv—Premijera predstave 'LEPA BRENA PROJECT'": www.youtube.com/watch?v=ntW4rfQ9Z2o (accessed 12/25/2019).

46 Brena speaking in *Lepa Brena se rasplakala zbog susreta sa Slatkim Grehom*.

47 Silverman, *Romani Routes*, 205.

48 Stevo Teodosievski quoted in Silverman: "Some of the top officials from Radio Skopje's communist party leadership thought they needed me to know that it would be better for the show to have a participant of Macedonian nationality. I was then, just like now, devoid of any nationalistic preconceptions. I consider myself a cosmopolitan." See Silverman, *Romani Routes*, 207.

49 Ibid., 206–207.

50 Ibid., 203.

51 Ana Hofman, "Music (as) Labour: Professional Musicianship, Affective Labour and Gender in Socialist Yugoslavia," *Ethnomusicology Forum* 24, no. 1 (April 2015), 34.

52 Interview in 2016. Stevo Teodosievski "discovered" her in 1957, when she was only thirteen years old, after a singing competition, which she won. He asked her family if he could manage her career as a singer, and the parents agreed under the condition that she would never perform in the *kafana* scene. According to Redžepova, Teodosievski honored this request.

53 Silverman, *Romani Routes*, 204.

54 Ibid., 208.

55 When I presented a paper on Selma Selman's performance art at the annual College Art Association conference in 2016, one of the audience members accused Selman of exploiting her Roma background as an artist; they also suggested that Selman should "dance" or "play music" when performing to more authentically represent her race. This is just one example of the many that thread through academic and non-academic discourse on the history of Roma in art and culture.

56 Silverman, *Romani Routes*, 208.

57 Esma Redžepova with Ansambl Teodosievski. *Kroz Jugoslaviju (Across Yugoslavia)* (1977) featured Redžepova in numerous Yugoslav folklore costumes: Macedonian, Slovenian, Serbian, Croatian, and Bosnian. The images can be viewed at "Esma*—Kroz Jugoslaviju," on Discogs website: www.discogs.com/Esma-Kroz-Jugoslaviju/release/3257789 (accessed 01/20/2021).

58 Silverman, *Romani Routes*, 210.

59 Garth Cartwright, "Among the Gypsies," *World Literature Today* 80, no. 3 (May–June 2006), 54.

60 Dina Iordanova suggests that "the compassion exhibited for the plight of the Roma is often a parabolical expression for the (suppressed) self-pitying attitude of the dominant group, who may be dominant in one context, but feels subservient in another." See Dina Iordanova, *Cinema of Flames: Balkan Film, Culture and Media* (London: BFI Publishing, 2002), 216.

61 Tone Bringa, "The Peaceful Death of Tito and Violent End of Yugoslavia," in John Borneman, ed., *Death of the Father: An Anthropology of the End in Political Authority* (New York: Berghahn Books, 2004), 160.

62 Silverman, *Romani Routes*, 210.

63 See Patricia Leighten and Mark Antliff, "Primitive," in Robert Nelson and Richard Schiff, eds., *Critical Terms for Art History* (Chicago: University of Chicago Press, 2003), 217–233.

64 Eržebet Tumbas in conversation with the author, June 19, 2020.
65 André Heller organized and produced this concert and film, which featured appearances by women singers from all over the world, including Haris Alexiou, Cristina Branco, Dee Dee Bridgewater, Ami Koita, Amal Murkus, Noa, Jessye Norman, Esma Redžepova, Sainkho, and Lina Sastri. Amal Murkus in conversation with this author, February 23, 2021.

3   Queer Jugoslovenka

The most sexually transgressive decade of socialist Yugoslavia, the 1980s, was a time when challenging compulsory heterosexuality politics and attendant gender roles became central to performative art practices in the alternative cultural scenes of Ljubljana. Questions of feminist and queer sexuality were a pervasive subtext and were often extremely overt themes in art, popular culture, and activism in the Yugoslav republic of Slovenia, with the punk as well as gay and lesbian underground scenes in Ljubljana marking a decisively political transformation for the arts centered on questions of gender and sexuality as modes of resistance. Remembering that extraordinary time in Yugoslavia, Slovenian artist and theorist Marina Gržinić summarized the period in the following way:

> The emergence of Slovenian punk in 1977, along with the first coming out of the gay scene in 1984 (the Magnus Festival organised in the ŠKUC Gallery) represented something entirely new and different behind the Iron Curtain in Europe. These two movements (punk and homosexuality) transformed us into urban entities; they opened up the possibility of conceptualising anti-authoritativeness, different sexuality, the anti-hegemonic battle against patriarchy and chauvinism, normalisation of everyday life, and the revolt against depoliticisation. [...] We stood and embraced the position of political lesbianism with the cyberfeminism and transfeminism to come. Therefore, the explicit lesbian, drag, and transsexual sequences (from blow jobs to peep-show dancing) were politically conceptualised, and the aims were political demands and visibility for homosexuals and to operate against the official heterosexist socialist reality.[1]

These new emphases on individual sex and sexual liberation in punk, alternative art, and music scenes were deeply influenced by similar underground trends in London, but instead of resisting capitalism and a conservative government, the Yugoslav LGBTQ youth confronted the "official heterosexist socialist reality," the morally corrupt and (in their view) hypocritical Yugoslav state for hijacking and perverting socialism's potential for liberation and equality.[2] In the midst of the threat of nuclear war and ascending nationalist tendencies in Yugoslavia, the feminist, lesbian, and peace movements together became one of the principal forces laying the groundwork for feminist activism against the wars in the 1990s. This combination of emergent feminist, LGBT, sex-positive, and anti-war movements in the arts resulted in sexually charged performance works that confronted and exposed the roots of patriarchal violence in the Yugoslav state and its dangerous vitality in the nationalist rhetoric of Yugoslavia as a whole and in its republics.

Women continued to be marginalized as they had been in the 1970s, despite their extensive and generative resistance work in the alternative scenes throughout the 1980s. This chapter hones in on women's explorations of their gender power in music, avant-garde art circles, and performance art. Focusing on performance, video, and photographical works by music groups as well as prominent women artists such as Zemira Alajbegović, Gržinić and Aina Šmid, and Vlasta Delimar, this chapter highlights how Yugoslav emancipatory performance politics and liberatory plays on gender performance pushed for the embrace of women's desires in spite of unceasing patriarchal domination in Yugoslavia.

Analyzing the significance of emancipatory and sexually charged politics for the immediate postwar context in Yugoslavia, the chapter also considers the seminal role of Merlinka, a well-known transgender woman and sex worker in Belgrade, featured in director Želimir Žilnik's *Marble Ass* (1995). This film was one of the earliest from the region to feature an affirmative image of trans identity and Merlinka became a symbol of peace and resistance. The chapter ends with artist Helena Janečić, whose emphasis on the question of gay life within rural areas of former Yugoslavia, along with her own desire in her *Horny Dyke* series, pays homage to the untold legacies of lesbian Yugoslav women in love.

This chapter's focus on the groundbreaking creative and emancipatory role of women, non-normative sexuality, and the embrace of erotic pleasure in Yugoslavia aims to show just how deeply "the East" of Europe has been misunderstood, desexualized, and defeminized. Feminist scholars such as Kristen R. Ghodsee have persistently argued that women living in socialist countries throughout Europe had "better sex" and "economic independence" than women in capitalist societies.[3] I want to move a step further, to merge the question of women's sexual pleasure and sexual liberation with that of homosexual and trans pleasures; moreover, these questions are also deeply tied to sexual liberation theories *within* the socialist Yugoslav context, many of which aimed to provoke a different relationship to politics, culture, and the body in Yugoslavia. Here, I want to summon Herbert Marcuse's impression of Yugoslavia; he had visited Yugoslavia's Korčula Summer School, run by the Marxist humanist philosophical movement Praxis on the Croatian island of Korčula in 1968.[4] The following year, Marcuse published *An Essay on Liberation*, where his descriptions echoed the spirit and fashions of Yugoslav youth:

> The aesthetic as the possible form of a free society appears ... Where the hatred of the young bursts into laughter and song, mixing the barricade and the dance floor, love, play and heroism. And the young also attach the esprit de sérieux in the socialist camp: miniskirts against the apparatchiks, rock 'n' roll against Soviet Realism. The insistence that a socialist society can and ought to be light, pretty, playful, that these qualities are essential elements of freedom, the faith in the rationality of the imagination, the demand for a new morality and culture—does this great anti-authoritarian rebellion indicate a new dimension and a direction of radical change, the appearance of new agents of radical change, and a new vision of socialism in its qualitative difference from the established societies?[5]

Marcuse's words regarding the embrace of miniskirts, laughter, and the "prettiness" of things as evidence of a radical "faith in the rationality of the imagination," paint a picture of a fundamentally "feminine" resistance in Yugoslavia. Marcuse's rhetoric also pinpoints characteristics readily weaponized against women to discredit their ideas, competence, and needs. The Yugoslav socialist youth's steadfast "demand for a new morality and culture"[6] would in fact find its peak in the 1980s through the courageous efforts of feminists, lesbians, and homosexual men, the latter of whom to this day face the social stigma of being "failed" men, derogatorily feminized as "sissies" in both the West and the East. I theorize art performances, character development in film, and the activism of minoritarian groups as the last bastion of socialist Yugoslavia's political-libidinal commitment to an anti-capitalist, peaceful, non-patriarchal, and just society. Jugoslovenkas are here manifested in images and embodiments of effeminate male homosexuality, lesbian politics, feminist performances, sexually liberated artwork, and an open embrace of transsexuality and sex work as a healing force counteracting chauvinist state power.

I begin with a 1984 image of Zemira Alajbegović, a leading female performer of the industrial-punk band Borghesia in Slovenia, coupled with one film still from Gržinić and artist Šmid's 1990 video *Bilocations*, because they respectively represent the early and final stages of 1980s Yugoslavia (see Figures 3.1–3.2). I consider this decade as Yugoslavia's interregnum between two patriarchal strands of regimes: first Tito's socialism, which fastened the six Yugoslav republics (and two autonomous regions) together, but lost its cohesion with the leader's death in 1980; and second, the rise of various nationalisms that ended in war and solidified and deepened misogyny and hostility toward non-heteronormative sexualities by the early 1990s. It is also no coincidence that both of these images are from the Slovenian context, as the queer revolt within

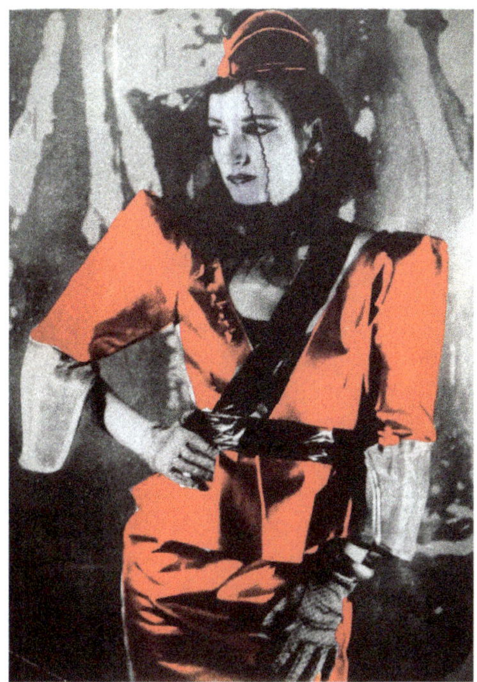

Zemira Alajbegović, *Young Prisoners Performance*, 1984. Colored photograph by Jane Štravs.   **3.1**

the Yugoslav alternative scenes originated in Ljubljana, a city that had a very different set of conditions than the art worlds of Belgrade or Zagreb, two crucial centers for avant-garde art in the 1970s. Ljubljana's Student Cultural Center, ŠKUC, was much less established in the arts at that point. With a few exceptions, its underground centers were led by artists, musicians, and curators who did not have powerful family ties to the communist elite. ŠKUC was under much more financial strain than the centers in Zagreb and Belgrade.[7] But here, too, female leadership was key, with Gržinić and Barbara Borčić serving as artistic directors of ŠKUC Gallery from 1982 to 1986, the most formative period for the avant-garde art scene at the time. Not only did ŠKUC Gallery present transgressive local art and performance works from Ljubljana that had been rejected at every "respectable" art space, its female curators also organized the first exhibitions in Slovenia to feature conceptual and performance art from Belgrade and Zagreb, such as works by Vlasta Delimar, Raša Todosijević, and Tomislav Gotovac, which all confronted issues of gender, state politics, and liberation.[8] The young generation of artists and musicians in Ljubljana built their art practices on these Yugoslav artists' political works, developed a new visual language in defiance of respectability politics, and expanded avant-garde art to intersect with music, video, and performance in order to push against prevailing norms of gender and sexuality in an unprecedented way.

The colored black-and-white photograph of Alajbegović, titled *Zemira, Performans Mladi Zaporniki* (*Zemira, Young Prisoners Performance*), shows her in one of her performances with Borghesia, a musical act closely associated with the alternative art scenes that grew out of the experimental FV 112/115 Theater, such as Disko FV club, FV Video, Disko Študent, the Šiška Youth Center, Kersnikova (Club K4), and FV Založba (a publishing house and music label). Borghesia members organized much of what FV generated in underground art, theater, performance, music, and publishing during the decade. FV was fundamental in creating "significant shifts ... on the margins of society under socialism, shifts that made it possible for the first gay and lesbian clubs, independent publishing houses, multimedia groups, and other forms of creativity in the subculture to function."[9] Alajbegović independently became an important figure in supporting and penetrating the male-dominated gay scene around Borghesia in the early 1980s. Similarly, Gržinić supplemented her work as an artist, theorist, and curator at ŠKUC Gallery by editing many alternative magazines, including *VIKS* and its legendary 1984 issue "Homosexuality in Culture."

Borghesia became infamous for its sadomasochistic (S&M) performances, embrace of homosexual erotics, and genderqueer interventions, as well as for screening pornography during performances. Alajbegović was an essential and charismatic performer within Borghesia: often naked in her performances, she appeared as a dominatrix, leather queen, or simply a sexy woman who dared to do and take what she wanted. In the *Young Prisoner's Performance* (1984) photo, however, she is wearing what could be read as a tightly-fitted women's dress, with a signature communist hat, both over-painted in red. Black duct tape tightens her waist and extends diagonally across her chest. A vertical line cuts across her face. Her right hand rests on her hip, much like a fashion model's, and she looks pensively to the side. Her gloves, too, insinuate a fashionista. The red color marks the politics of her world; her symbolic clothing connotes a socialist politics, but this is troubled by the title *Young Prisoners*, a song and set of performances by Borghesia that spanned several years (1984–1989).[10] In the photograph, Alajbegović reminds us of a well-dressed *drugarica*, a term which was first used for Yugoslav female comrades who fought as antifascist communist partisans in World War II. The red color of her dress and the signature communist uniform hat confirm the mark of socialism on her identity. In contrast, the duct tape, the ominous black-and-white background, the scribbled line across her face, along with her facial expression, makes one wonder if the icon of a Yugoslav *drugarica*—Jugoslovenka—is ever complete without an emancipatory and feminist spirit of resistance. Decades later, Alajbegović commented:

> There is an inherent contradiction: on the one hand, it was normal to criticize a system which was fossilized, it ran out of ideas, and was endlessly repeating certain phrases—we portrayed that well in our videos, for example. On the other hand, it was very important for us and our activism and we believed in the socialist postulates of art and culture for the masses. … That's why we were basing our work on the Russian activist art. That was a utopian project. It seems to me that back then we were all utopians—not only us in FV, but all of us believed that things can change only for the better. [...] We all felt a sort of solidarity, because we all had a common enemy, which was the socialist regime we were surrounded by. At that point perhaps it was less repressive, but it was equally boring and omnipresent. … The [socialist] iconography was very powerful; it was ideal both for theater and video. We used it a lot, we joked with it, with the partisans and that revolutionary poetry. It was ideal for video art, with those kilometers of recordings and speeches. It's very powerful iconography.[11]

Emancipatory power refuses the typifying gesture of replication and reassertion bound up with socialist iconography, instead laying its iconographic weight as fashion on the female body. In line with this reading, the duct tape could be understood as mimicking a soldier's magazine belt wrapped across Alajbegović's chest; but since she is unarmed, this is simply military chic. Furthermore, the red costume that outshines her black-and-white face and body marks her indeed as a Young Prisoner, indicative of women being trapped by ideology. If pushed in another direction, this image of Alajbegović can also be viewed as the female personification of Yugoslavia itself, held together with duct tape in the 1980s and carried by the elegant strength of women, who nevertheless would be permanently marked by the explosion of patriarchal violence soon to come.

The political significance of the socialist woman would become even more pivotal in Marina Gržinić and Aina Šmid's video work *Bilocations* (1990) (Figures 3.2–3.3), which marks the end of the decade, just before the wars began. Gržinić and Šmid used footage that TV Slovenia had filmed in the South Serbian autonomous region of Kosovo during the uprisings that followed Slobodan Milošević's crackdown on basic human rights for Kosovo Albanians.[12] TV Slovenia did not air this material at the time; *Bilocations* as an artwork and as a work of televisual media uniquely bore witness to the injustices happening in Kosovo. It is part of an even smaller group of works (the only one to my knowledge) that centered the politics of *looking* at the conflict—the political gaze—within the agency of the socialist woman. In addition to the TV footage, Gržinić and Šmid filmed classical ballet dancer Mateja Rebolj—let's call her

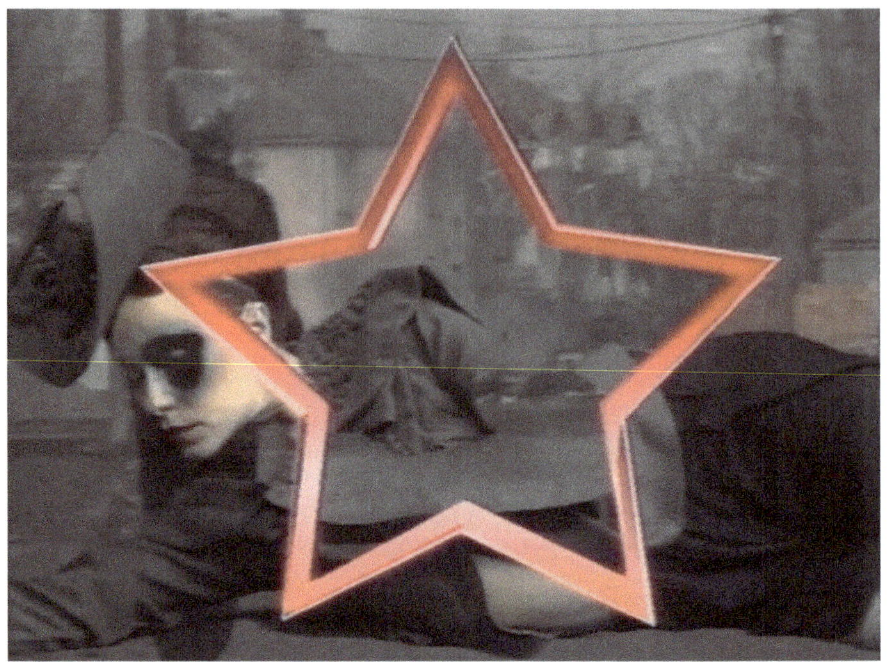

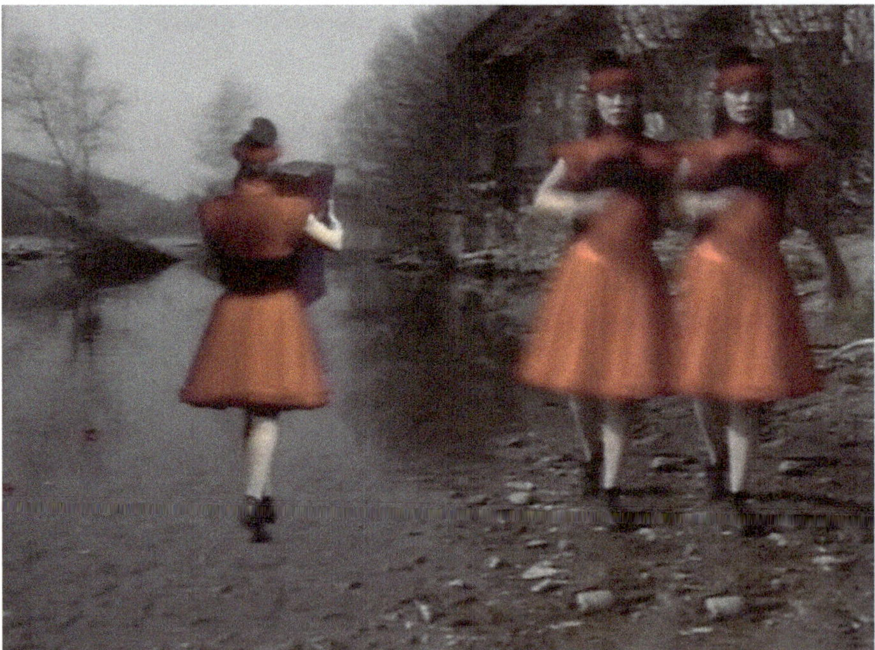

3.2–3.3 Marina Gržinić and Aina Šmid, *Bilocations*, 1990. Video stills.

Jugoslovenka—in Ljubljana on an abandoned farm and at the Astronomical Geophysical Observatory in Golovec. The figure is "bilocated"—a neologism created by the artists that they define as "the residence of the body and soul in two different places at the same time—simultaneously."[13] The film uses chroma key technology, a technique often employed in newscasting because it allows the display of multiple layers on top of one another, to erase parts of various layers and allow others to be viewed beneath, and vice versa. It was also an important strategy in video art of the time, particularly for political groups such as the video collective Paper Tiger TV coming out of New York in the 1980s. Here, the bilocated figure of Jugoslovenka is the main subject of the chroma key technique, playing upon her dual embodiment in the following way: (a) a woman-warrior, sometimes solo, sometimes tripled in chroma key, moving through landscapes and artificial videoscapes, wearing a bright-red dress designed to look like a modern-day folkloristic Balkan warrior outfit, or a variant of a Russian Kazachok (Cossack) costume; (b) a fashion model lying horizontally across the screen, wearing a high-fashion modern grey suit and superimposed on scenes of conflict from Kosovo. Both iterations of the same woman, bilocated, render time and space fragmented and chaotic, while maintaining positions of visionary power.

Using a dance that imitates Japanese Noh theater, the warrior-woman in red never speaks a word, yet she is crucial to the narrative structure of the film.[14] For example, she ends up reviving what appears to be an incapacitated man lying in the forest with a ritualistic dance and a tight grip on the back of his neck, pulling him upwards and compelling him to walk, without making a sound. Here, she reminds me of the archetypal *junakinja*, a Yugoslav female fighter who "'do[es] not quail before obstacles.'"[15] The man recites passages from Roland Barthes's *A Lover's Discourse: Fragments* (1977) throughout the film.[16] Jugoslovenka's soundless, mechanical body moves through space and becomes an important marker of plot changes across disparate scenes. In one scene, she climbs up a ladder in a planetarium and opens up the dome for him. He, the inquisitor who asks about the fate of deportees in Dachau and heartbroken lovers, ends up looking at the world through the telescope, a fantasy of optical omniscience mediated by the warrior-woman's soundless efforts and labor. Further, her journey to open up this vision and the world has been haunted by a red sign she passed during her climb up the ladder, bearing only the name of the notorious, murderous Nazi doctor Mengele. According to Gržinić, the artists had serendipitously found a Mengele tractor on the abandoned farm where they filmed *Bilocations*, which had also been the site of the farm machinery business run by relatives of the Nazi doctor (who to this day remain silent about their notorious relative).[17] Male vision here is layered in meaning, interrelating genocidal violence and patriarchal gaze, facilitated by the tireless background work and help of the socialist woman. Silent as it is, Jugoslovenka's labor also implies her complicity. Gržinić and Šmid thus avoid making absolute or pure the figure of the socialist woman.

This prophetic exposure of genocide performed in the name of patriarchal ideals and interests becomes embodied in a different but no less potent way through the figure of the fashion model in grey: the scenes of violence in Kosovo behind her are visible past the outline of her body, as well as through a round area around her left eye, erased from her face, as several other parts of her body are also effaced. The grey color of her clothes echoes the dark, industrial, polluted ground of Kosovo, accentuating the contrasting cleanliness of her guise and white skin. As the sequence goes on, every sensuous move of her hand across her body erases more of it to reveal what is happening behind her. As politicians in black suits arrive and leave in a Mercedes Benz— one of Tito's favorite car models—on the streets of the uprisings in the working-class district of Kosovo, the dull grey ground is pierced by the bright red of a tiny Mercedes Benz logo at the front of the hood of the car, signaling the nefarious branding of socialist ideology by corrupt politicians to cloak their nationalist and genocidal politics. The red color adorning the Mercedes Benz also foretells the bloody wars and violent capitalism to come, as this was the car manufacturer most venerated by Adolph Hitler. Gržinić points to the grotesque collapse of the model's body with this political landscape, noting that the corruption "was inserted in her eye, her intestines, and other parts of her body."[18] Complicating the Tito-body-landscape discussed in the Introduction, it could be said that Gržinić and Šmid not only reclaim the gaze, but they reclaim space by re-gendering the Yugoslav territory as female. "These are pictures on the body of the former Yugoslavia," Gržinić asserts, "where our memories become both psychotic and erotic."[19]

As her bilocation illustrates, the eroticism of the socialist female body, contrasted with and connected to male-driven psychosis, is able to transform more than one reality. Bearing this weight of socialist transformation as warrior, fashion model, or queer S&M dominatrix, Jugoslovenka is fashionable and looks stunning even in a conflict zone. Her beauty and libidinal impulse, however, are anything but surface level: she is a vision and a visionary within the political landscape. To quote Gržinić once more: "The men are talking, but actually the vision of the future and the vision of history is in the head and in the body of the woman."[20] Here Jugoslovenka becomes the figure through which we can best understand what happened in the Yugoslavian underground culture of the 1980s and what was to come in the 1990s.

Homo-Jugoslovenka: lesbianism, homoeroticism, and S&M in Yugoslav urban culture

As a fertile intersection of performance, music, theater, video, and theory, underground avant-garde culture in Ljubljana produced some of the most important strides for LGBTQ subculture in the Balkan region. In fact, Gržinić has noted that the alternative culture of the 1980s skipped straight to queer cultural expression without waiting for feminism to get there through theory.[21] The examples in this chapter from the 1980s emphasize works that took the critique of heteronormativity even further than *Start* magazine's visual and literary debates, and that intervened in more radical ways than feminist thought did in the 1970s (see Chapter 1), when writers such as Jasenka Kodrnja still wrote about homosexuality and S&M as a threat to feminism and patholo-gized non-normative sexualities.[22] In 1984, Borghesia collaborated with Gržinić in a video for their song "Cindy," an homage to the feminist work of Cindy Sherman featuring tableau-vivant performances by Gržinić, Alajbegović, and the openly gay and S&M fashion-wearing Borghesia frontman Aldo Ivančić. Gržinić had already produced work around the question of same-sex and trans desire with Šmid in their 1982 *Icons of Glamour, Echoes of Death*, where one of the protagonists is a drag king who dons a dildo between their legs.[23] In that film, as in *Cindy*, the performers "strike poses" that embody unknown identities and play with liberation and emancipation while express-ing exhibitionistic pleasure.

For Gržinić, "Video becomes a conscious means for examining the politics of female pleasure."[24] Gržinić appears as a kind of cyborgian punk ballerina, wearing a white dress that reveals her breasts, while Alajbegović and Ivančić merely wear what seem to be identical black panties.[25] However, what stands out in this elaborate music video is the lesbian eroticism between Gržinić and Alajbegović. In one scene, we see Gržinić lying on the ground, her legs spread and Alajbegović standing right above her; in another, the two bare-breasted women are in the kitchen, turned toward each other, ignoring an overflowing pot on the stove (Figure 3.4). Signifying resistance to their imposed roles as women in the kitchen, the pot also seems to point to something brewing and

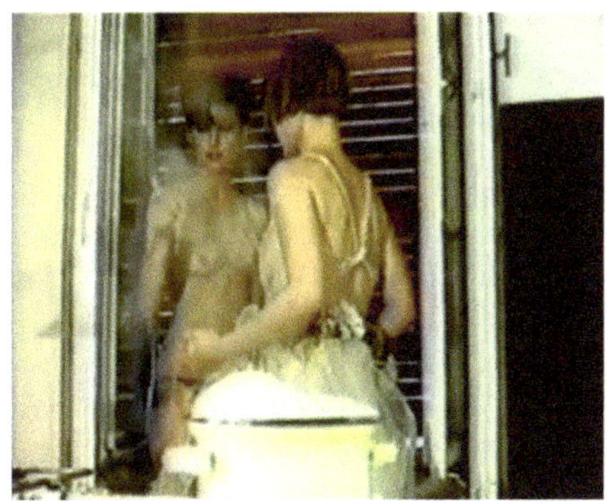

Marina Gržinić, *Cindy*, still of tableau-vivant performances with Zemira Alajbegović for Borghesia's music video, 1984. **3.4**

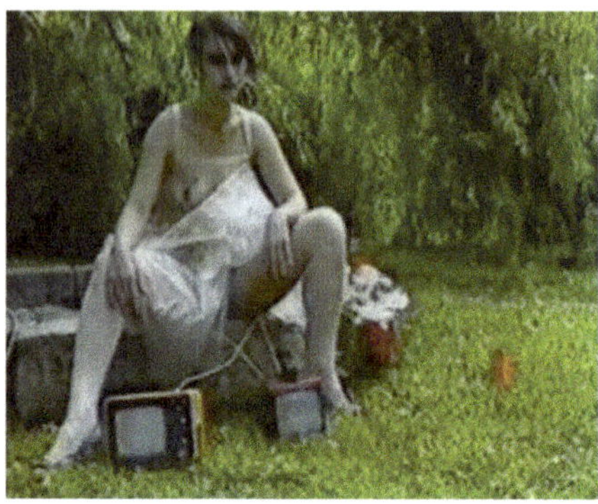

3.5   Marina Gržinić, *Cindy*, still of tableau-vivant performances for Borghesia's music video, 1984.

overflowing in that disobedient atmosphere: their queer sexuality. At one point, Gržinić slowly turns her head toward the viewer, reminding us that she knows she is being watched, and that she is in charge of her own gaze. In another remarkable moment, Gržinić sits on the edge of the pool with spread legs, from which two small television screens with long wires protrude (Figure 3.5). The small TVs visually linked with wires to her spread legs are reminiscent of umbilical cords attached to newborns, here acting as conduits between her body and media art. The green grassy background intensifies this cyborgian Jugoslovenka's out-of-placeness: she defies the traditional image of a Venus in nature, and instead poses in a messy white dress with defiance and confidence linked to the biomechatronic devices that make up her sexual difference. One TV is off, while the other one accentuates her female gender with an image of double-X chromosomes. In these multiple layers of emancipatory sexuality and feminist performance in *Cindy*, we see an answer to *Start* magazine's critique of women's confinement in the home (Chapter 1): do away with the heteronormative matrix of power and transform the domestic sphere into one of queer desire, leisure, resistance, and feminist subjectivity. Woman is not an object of a male illustrator here; she embodies her own subjectivity, and she does so in defiance of normative gender roles and concomitant delimited sexual desires.

Although male homosexuality was more visible in the Slovenian underground scene, lesbian politics became an important part of the political gay subculture in the arts at FV and ŠKUC. The London gay and lesbian documentary film *Framed Youth: The Revenge of the Teenage Perverts* (1983) was screened in Ljubljana in 1984. Censored in Canada at the time, it passed the censors without a problem in Yugoslavia.[26] That same year, Yugoslavia's first gay organization, Magnus, was founded and created the first exhibition centered on homosexuality in Yugoslavia. *Homoseksualnost in Kultura* (*Homosexuality in Culture*) included a display of art and magazines for gays and lesbians, such as the UK lesbian/feminist magazine *Spare Rib*'s 1982 special issue "Peace Not Quiet," which featured multiple essays on the peace movement. The black cover of this issue bore various anti-war and anti-nuclear power slogans on circles resembling pin-up badges, as well as anti-capitalist and pro-feminist slogans: "Fall Out with Thatcher," "Women's Day for Disarmament," "Jobs Not Bombs," and "Resist the War Machine." The exhibition also featured sexually explicit content and gay porno magazines. Suzana Tratnik, lesbian poet and founding member of the first lesbian group in Yugoslavia in 1985, Lesbian Lilit, a group that became more established in 1987, with its offshoot ŠKUC-LL, remembered that although the exhibition had presented mostly male homosexuality "[i]t opened up a new field of sexuality and homosexuality." She added that ŠKUC and the underground punk/art movements "were spaces of freedom, variety and diversity of sexuality and as well spaces of courage. … Women have been present here in a very strong way, creative and active. It was the information that 'women can do it' no matter what others think. … Women did it."[27]

One of the most important documents for the LGBTQ history of socialist Yugoslavia, Gržinić's 1984 *VIKS* issue "Homosexuality in Culture" highlighted women as being at the center of Yugoslav homosexuality by featuring a high-contrast image of a woman on its bright, pinkish-red cover, morphing the socialist red color into a gay pink. Diverse gay content filled the entire issue, spotlighting queer icons such as Rosa von Praunheim alongside images of drag queens and tips for using condoms, as well as a reproduction of Dušan Mandič's 1984 graffiti work, *Back to the USA*, which boldly stated: "1968 is over. 1983 is over. Future is between your legs." The issue concluded with the same pinkish-red colored reproduction of gay artist Tom of Finland's erotic drawing of two men, one positioned *between the legs* of the other. Provocatively printed on top of a chart of prisoner markings in Nazi concentration camps, this homoeroticism paired with the traumatic history of the Holocaust intensified the political charge leveled by the LGBTQ subculture against the Yugoslav establishment. While similar to how the Slovenian group Neue Slowenische Kunst (NSK) drew parallels between socialism and fascism (see Chapter 4), here, *VIKS* notably went beyond by positing gender and sexuality at the forefront of that critique.

A year before "Homosexuality in Culture," Gržinić and Bogdan Lešnik also edited a special issue for *VIKS* magazine titled "Nasilje In Reprezentacija" (Violence and Represenation) which, among other things, explored S&M and lesbian desire. Two of the November 1983 essays/interviews were accompanied by images of women kissing and in S&M poses (see Figures 3.6–3.8). An essay by Andreas Spengler on S&M and its subcultures was published among a set

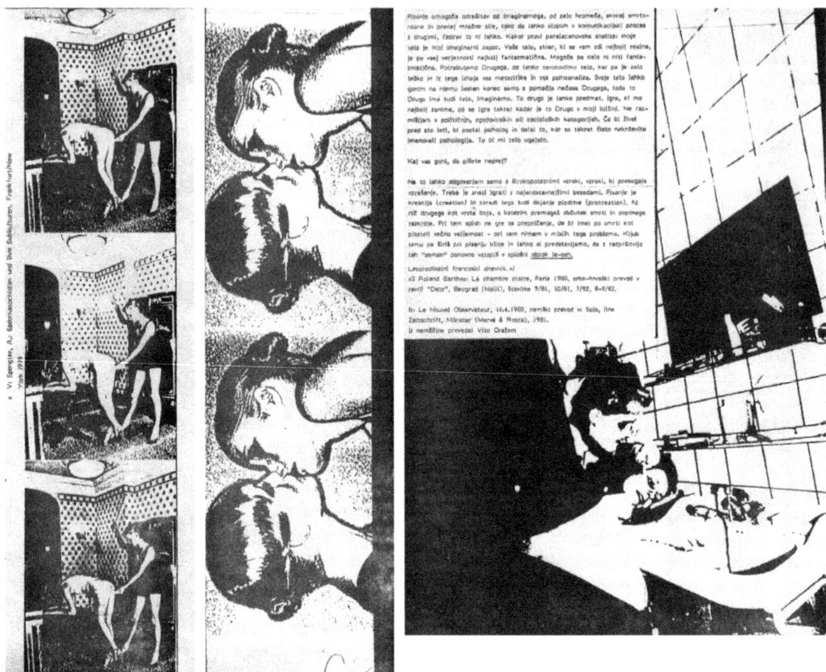

3.6–3.8   *VIKS* magazine illustrations in the special *VIKS* magazine issue: "Violence and Representation," November 1983 (pages 6, 14–15, and 16).

of images of a woman spanking another woman, while a translated interview with Roland Barthes discussing S&M was flanked by women kissing as well as an erotic scene of a woman mounting another woman over the edge of a bathtub.

One of the images showing two women in a bathroom, one dominating the other, came from a collaborative project by Šmid, Gržinić and Barbara Borčić, exhibited at ŠKUC Gallery the year prior, in 1982 (Figure 3.8). The invitation for this project emphasized ideas of submission and liberation as forms of exposing repression; in other words, an embrace of S&M in Yugoslav youth culture at the time: "They attract attention to themselves; they represent an expression of powerlessness and a kind of power—the power to disclose." Borčić elaborates:

> The scenes of "unnatural" sexuality problematized the connection of the social mechanisms of domination with the libidinal structure of individuals and they aroused a discomfort. The project somehow materialized one of the specific features of the subcultural/alternative art production in the context of the Ljubljana alternative scene of the early 1980s, namely, the disclosure of the

ideological apparatuses of the state and the marginal and taboo themes coupled with an ideological/aesthetic effect.[28]

Such early engagements with S&M and lesbian sexuality cannot be underestimated in their political and cultural significance. Borčić's description of the political stakes of the work also demonstrates that women artists in the alternative scenes of Ljubljana felt emboldened to push against the government's dominant heteronormative and conservative bias.

Although lesbians worked hand in hand with feminists in building a women's movement, it would take four more years for lesbians to organize and gain some recognition through Lesbian Lilit in Slovenia (1987) and two more years for the first lesbian group, Lila Initiative, to form in Zagreb (1989). Male homosexuality had much more prominence in activist and intellectual discourses. For example, *Potkulture* (*Subcultures*) in Belgrade published an issue dedicated to homosexuality in 1987, featuring numerous essays from local and international writers, but it only featured one article on lesbian sexuality by Slađana Marković.[29] Activist, DJ, and writer Nataša Sukič recalls the struggle for lesbian representation:

> It was of course obvious that a "woman" was immediately a problem, even more a woman's sexuality, for socialism. Precisely, what I was mentioning, this dissident art scene, the subculture, that started in the first place to discuss the body in relation to sexuality was a provocation. It presented the politicization of the homosexual body in that social context. Now, female sexuality was in an even more problematic position, if we make a relation toward a gay sexuality. The gay body was seen as [a] bigger "threat" for that social order, but on the other side the lesbian body did not even exist.[30]

Lesbian activist, writer, and organizer Lepa Mladenović similarly recalled how difficult and anxiety-provoking it was to do even the simplest thing, such as getting a hotel room with a lover:

> How loud could a lesbian couple be in the 1980s in a hotel in Eastern Europe? How many lesbians recognize even to this day the phenomenon of "restricted breath," preventing any sound of lesbian lust from coming out of the body. How many recognize "swallowed orgasm" [sic] so that the silence of desire maintains "the denial of existence." If no one hears, then it does not exist: not the parents next door nor the neighbours next hall nor the hotel guests behind the wall [sic], if there are any. There was a total absence of representation of lesbian lovemaking in the images of Eastern European societies. Nothing. No traces of a history of women loving women, no kisses of two women, no erotic touch, not even cultural symbolism of the clitoris. Simone de Beauvoir was asking herself already in the 1970s in her philosophical manner whether women existed at all. What could, then, lesbians expect?[31]

Defying this absence of lesbian visibility, there were still some Yugoslav women in visual art, performance, and music who were instrumental in foregrounding the female body as a site of lesbian desire and positing lesbian desire as emancipation and resistance. In 1983, the musician Xenia released the pop hit "Moja Prijateljica" (My Girlfriend), in which she openly celebrated her girlfriend's head-turning beauty and proclaimed "I'm so proud!"[32] The following year, synth-pop music band Videosex, with its frontwoman Anja Rupel, released "Ana" on their album *Videosex 84* (1984), which spoke to the "forbidden" nature of female-on-female desire: "Ana, you're well aware/ What you do to me is forbidden here [in our country]/You're well aware of that/What you do to me is forbidden for us." Rupel here speaks of intense, hidden, and repressed desires that are "forbidden" and that lead to powerful, contradictory feelings of attraction to the other woman, as well as self-hate, a wish to be extinguished, and the relief of finally being seen. "A secret made of stone was set free … I wish I didn't exist … Ana, why do I love you like crazy?"[33] In a black-and-white PR photo from that time, circulating to this day on the web, Rupel dons a butch attire and seductive gaze, a lesbian undertone which speaks to how Yugoslav women in the underground scene in Ljubljana did not shy away from addressing gender and sexuality in their work and fashion.[34] Videosex played frequently in the alternative spaces, such as Disco Študent and Šiška Youth Center, and was oriented toward the Yugoslav youth and international trends in music and art. The cover of *Videosex 84*, for example, looked like an airmail envelope to be sent around the world, its stamp representing a shattered window. The idea of shattered glass would be picked up in the next album, *Lacrimae Christi*, which included a song called "Stakleno Nebo" (Glass Sky) where Rupel proclaimed: "The sky, made of glass, got broken … I want you, I need you, I want you to awaken my dream."[35] As the song progresses, the singer reveals that she dreamed of the glass being broken, and she is asking her lover, whose gender remains unknown, to make her dream into a reality (awaken her from the dream). She feels confined and hindered in her room, trapped behind the glass of her window, able to see the outdoors but know it is beyond her reach. On the small stamp featured on the album *Videosex 84*, the window is half-broken, with the intact glass reflecting blue skies and clouds.[36] Thinking of the proverbial glass ceiling used by feminists to characterize the limits to women's abilities to ascend beyond a certain point, here the broken window indicates that this young woman has found a way to escape her confines. The visual language mimics a significant motif in René Magritte's surrealist paintings, further amplifying that an embrace of her dream and imagination—the waking dream come to life—was her way out. And what's more, this escape was predicated on following her desires.

In 1985, Karlowy Vary, with frontwoman Varja Orlić, released their album *La Femme*, featuring Orlić bathed in blue light on the cover.[37] Their unreleased album from 1984, *Haotika*, shows Orlić as a mysterious and androgynous woman, who four years later would be described in *Polet* as the "Prva Dama Undergrounda" ("First Lady of the Underground"); she sang in an unusually "low, male voice" and dressed in masculine clothing on the back cover of *Haotika*.[38] Varja Orlić, along with Anja Rupel and Xenia, show us that the circulation of women's emancipated music and self-images was indicative of Yugoslav socialism's more open feminist and queer subculture, in which these Jugoslovenkas could rise as cultural icons of emancipatory joy and gender resistance, as well as pioneers of openly embraced homosexuality.

Female sexuality and lesbianism gradually became integrated more systematically into Yugoslav feminist publishing in 1985 when sociologist and activist Mojca Dobnikar edited the anthology *About Women and Women's Movements* (printed in early 1986), and a translation of Anne Koedt's "The Lesbian Movement and Feminism" (1985) was published in the supplemental section "*Pogledi*" (*Perspectives*) in *Mladina*.[39] This March 7, 1985 *Pogledi* supplement focused on questions related to "Marxism, dialectical sexism, self-managing masculinity, and revolutionary feminism."[40] The cover of the *Pogledi* supplement featured an altered version of Albrecht Dürer's *Women's Bath* (*c.*1496), which scholars consider to be the first study of the nude to use multiple naked bodies without religious narrative or symbology (Figure 3.9).[41] While Dürer's *Men's Bathhouse* (1496–1497) has become an often referenced work in the history of homoerotic art, *Women's Bath* has received much less attention in straight or gay art history (Figure 3.10). Here, it is also important to remember the scandal regarding soccer player Miran Šarović appearing nude in the music magazine *Polet*, which resulted in censorship and controversy, a topic Slavenka Drakulić addressed in a confrontational article, "Men Are Something Different," she wrote in *Start* in 1980.[42] Drakulić called out the Yugoslav press for their conservative and sexist attitudes toward women who readily appear naked in magazines, but also charged *Start* magazine with hypocrisy for mostly reproducing naked images of Western women, as "our girls do not get undressed, they are chaste, only the girls in the rotten West do that."[43] By reproducing Dürer's print in *Pogledi*, the feminists made a visual argument for solidarity among women and their arrival on the local scene: naked, together, and busy in activities of self-care, a clever provocation against the male-dominated Marxist political scene.

One more element is noteworthy here: the change in the figure of the "peeping Tom" from the original. In Dürer's work, we can see an ajar door in the back with a man staring at the women, with one foot stepping into the space. In the 1985 *Pogledi* version, the invasive gaze is signaled more dramatically with a bearded man looking in the window on the right side. Unlike the Dürer version, he is on the outside. As early as the 1970s, John Berger and Laura Mulvey had parsed the ways in which the gaze in art and cinema, always

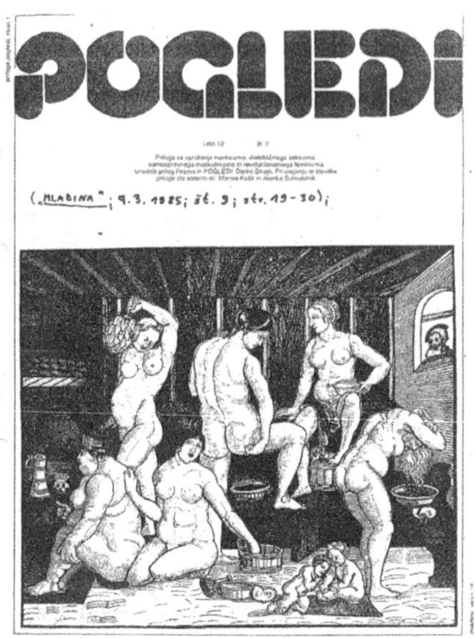

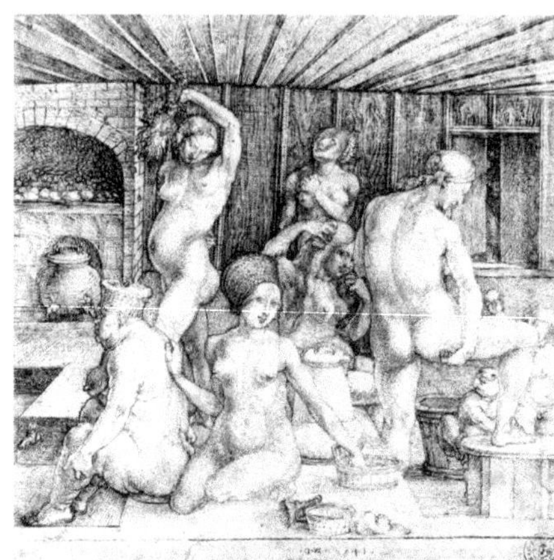

3.9   Cover of *Pogledi* in *Mladina*, March 7, 1985.

Albrecht Dürer, *Women's Bath*, c.1496.

assumed to be male, incessantly and moralistically castigates yet solicits women's nudity. And let us remember that Sanja Iveković had played with the idea of the "peeping Tom" in a number of her works including *Trokut* (1979) and *He's Always Looking at Me* (*c.*1979) (see Chapter 1), both of which are precisely linked to socialist leaders (especially Tito) invading and violating women's privacy. The fact that the peeping Tom in *Pogledi* looks a little like Karl Marx intensifies the political dimension of this intrusion while increasing its comedic power, as the women in the print pay no attention to the old man. As such, the reproduction of this altered Dürer print in *Pogledi* might have served as a signpost that women in Yugoslavia had begun to carve out spaces for themselves in which they were concerned with women, not men, where, indeed, men were clearly excluded, indicating that women were taking the lead in alternative culture, such as with the founding of Lilit that same spring.

Less than a month after *Pogledi*'s Dürer cover, Lilit organized its first "women only" event at Club K4 (Figure 3.11), which was held in the discotheque on April 3, 1985. The poster advertising the event was designed by Veronika Jona Rev using angular typography in the post-punk goth style typical of the subculture at the time. The poster introduced what would become the signature emblem of Lilit, a triangle in the shape of "L i" doubled in a mirror image (Li-Li) with a "T" in the middle, making up the word Lilit. Between the two Ls, Rev added the Venus symbol representing the female sex. The triangle is flanked by two athletic, naked women in profile wearing white panties and holding hands at the bottom of the triangle. Significantly, these two women also hold a hammer and sickle at the top of the triangle, marking this feminist group as distinctly socialist in its political ambition. According to Mojca Dobnikar, they symbolized "a mutual mirroring among women," but with an added element of irony: "you can see that the two women are not very feminine, they are half naked and yet they raise the hammer and the sickle so high."[44] Harkening back to the masculinized ethos of carrying Tito's relay baton on Youth Day through the Yugoslav land to mark it male (see the Introduction), this logo played with the erasure of the feminine body in socialism while it embraced the veneration of socialism as a political direction for feminism.

The poster announces that this will be the first discussion of female sexuality, and that the meeting will feature music, watercolors, and foreign magazines. Most importantly, the bottom of the poster offers an invitation for everyone to rethink how "our world could be different." Although "everybody" is invited, the event is marked as being exclusive for women: "samo za žene," a phrase also translated into three other languages: French ("seulement pour les femmes"), English ("only for women") and German ("nur für Frauen"), each separated again by the Venus symbol. The same poster design was used for a talk on "The German and Berlin Feminist and Lesbian Movements" by Barbara Martin from West Germany (Figure 3.12), organized by Lilit at ŠKUC the following year in April, and for Zagreb-based Lydia Sklevicky's talk that May on "Emancipated Integration or Integrated Emancipation." The decision to make the posters multilingual exemplified just how much the Yugoslav feminists were interested in building networks across national boundaries and within multiple cultural contexts, here focusing on those that already had well-established feminist networks in the West. Drakulić's visit to the United States in 1982, along with her and Rada Iveković's contributions to the renowned 1984 *Sisterhood is Global* anthology, also marked Yugoslav feminists as internationalists. Moreover, while Iveković's essay mainly focused on diagnosing the "patriarchal Balkan mentality" operative in Yugoslavia and its oppression of women, Iveković also briefly mentioned homosexuality, a decision that suggests that sexual orientation was already a priority for Yugoslav feminism at the time. She noted: "Homosexuals, both woman and men, also joined to analyze the problems of oppression they face."[45]

By 1987, the October issue of *Mladina* flaunted the words "LJUBIMO ŽENSKE" ("We love women") on the cover, along with two large intertwined symbols for women at the center, held by two identical women with long black ponytails kissing, while the background featured the same image of two

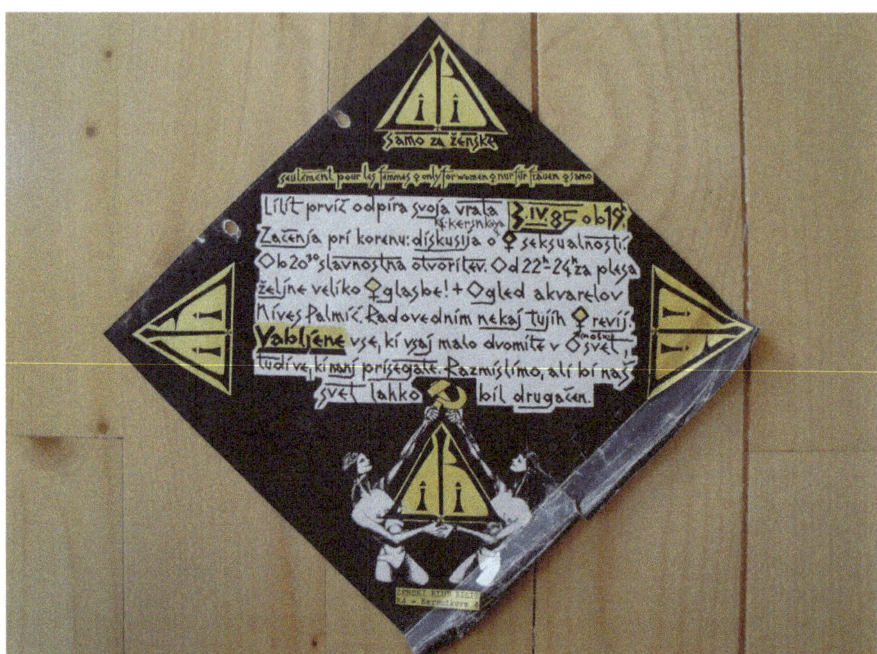

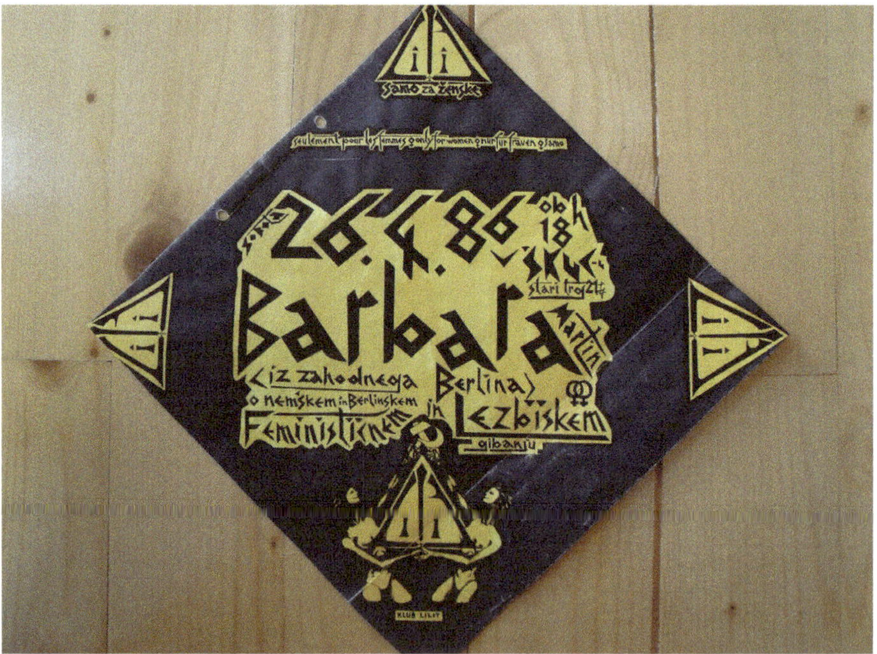

3.11–3.12   Lilit posters, 1985 and 1986. Designed by Veronika Jona Rev.

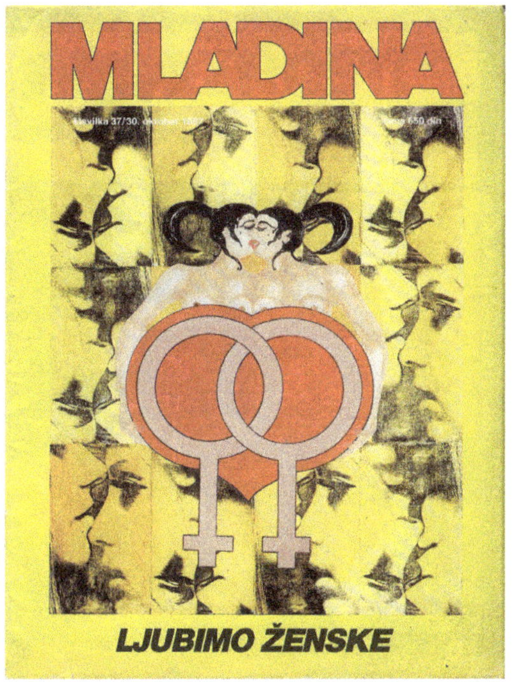

Mladina 37, cover, October 1987. Designed by Veronika Jona Rev.   **3.13**

women's faces intimately touching, reproduced ten times, with every other variation flipped so it was upside down (Figure 3.13).

This busy cover of *Mladina* made clear that lesbian sexuality was a topic at the forefront of Yugoslav youth culture. This issue of *Mladina* also featured the newly written manifesto of Lesbian Lilit, again in the supplemental section *Pogledi*, which reproduced the repeated photograph from *Mladina*'s cover on the *Pogledi* cover, but this time only once, in high resolution and flanked by the headline, "A Few Things about Women Loving Women" (Figure 3.14). Upon a closer look, the now-enlarged photo reveals a third female face behind the two women, visually arguing that love between women might transgress the normative idea of two partners.[46] A short statement below the photograph, which noted that "female disclosures of identity and love for women" were so rare in Yugoslav society that they were mostly ignored, further amplified this play on the hidden aspects of lesbian desire and culture. This now legendary *Mladina* issue featured numerous essays on lesbianism, including Radicalesbians's "The Woman Identified Woman," International Lesbian Information Service and CoC Amsterdam's "Ten Questions about Lesbianism," and "The

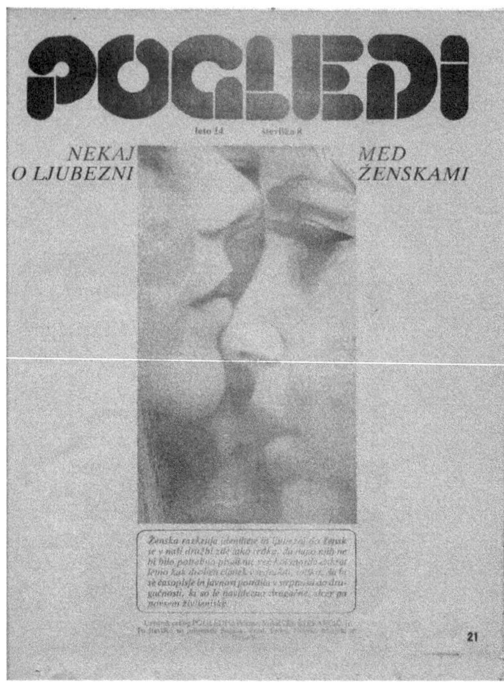

3.14   *Pogledi*, supplemental cover in *Mladina* 37, October 1987.

Problems with Mandatory Heterosexuality."[47] The first lesbian magazine would finally appear in 1988: *Lesbomagazine*.

While the underground scene in Ljubljana was successful in summoning a queer subculture that was simultaneously avant-garde and pop, lesbians in Yugoslavia were not readily out. Despite the fact that homosexuality had been decriminalized in 1977, being gay was hardly discussed in families, especially in rural contexts, and gay life remained mostly stigmatized and underground.[48] However, Franko Dota's research has also demonstrated that Yugoslavia had significantly fewer cases of persecution even before homosexuality was decriminalized, especially when compared to Western Europe. For example, from 1945 to 1977, Yugoslavia convicted only about 1,500 men for "unnatural fornication," charging them with fines, parole, or imprisonment, whereas the numbers in West Germany reached 70,000 and in England 50,000.[49] Yugoslavia even had one of the most progressive writers on homosexuality, sexologist Marijan Košiček, who as early as 1986 argued for gay marriage and gay adoption to be implemented in the socialist country.[50]

These numbers speak to why it is important to establish new histories of socialism that do not brush over these significant developments: advancements for gays and lesbians that did not arise despite socialism. Rather, socialism's complicated gender politics and general egalitarianism permitted their rise; it was a male-centered and heteronormative political culture that dampened this progress.[51] Feminists and queers in Yugoslavia were not anti-socialist; they fought for representation and for expanding the possibilities for women's pleasure and bodies. Reminiscing about the lesbian organizing in Yugoslavia during the 1980s, Mlađenović remembers: "I could say that the Yugoslav feminist movement gave me the light to intervene in the world that we interpreted as a *compulsory heterosexual institution*. A world where I started to feel that I do not belong any more, but come from, and must find my way."[52] Independence, sexual liberation, and political consciousness relied on a robust socialist women's movement to make strides into queer sexuality and resistance that rose from the underground art scene into music and popular magazines. Yugoslav women and artists were at the forefront of this progress and would become the target of the backlash after the end of Yugoslavia.

One such example was the set of smear campaigns waged against feminists who were published in *Start* magazine and who were accused of having dubious morals during the ascension of religious conservatism in the 1990s. In 1994, Vesna Kesić remarked:

> The naked women disappeared from *Start*'s pages following the Croatian Democratic Union, President Tuđman's populist, conservative, nationalistic party, victory in the 1990 election. Within a few issues after the election, the usual big white breasts on the cover page were replaced by the big white face of the Croatian Cardinal. The democratic changes in our society were, in fact, laced with patriarchal nationalism and religious conservatism. Under Tuđman's regime today, the situation for women is rapidly deteriorating.[53]

Jugoslovenkas were systematically erased from positions of visibility and power under the new nationalist discourse because they represented socialism and the old system that had prioritized gender and class equality above religious and ethnic superiority. The bodies of Yugoslav women were the battleground upon which this new, religious, patriarchal order of separate nations would rise.

Fucking is sad: feminist sexuality as antidote to masculine violence

Yugoslav sexuality and attitudes toward gender relations were deeply shaped by Tito's embodiment of partisan leadership as heroic, just, and charming— perhaps the Yugoslav equivalent of the Marlboro Man. Decades before *Start* magazine's naked breasts, or portraits of Croatian Cardinals replacing the covers, Tito's body was already an erotically charged spectacle, with his fierce history of liberation, support for women partisans, and renowned charm that made him a favorite among women as well as men. In his 1953 book *Tito Speaks*, Vladimir Dedijer narrates detailed memories of Tito with descriptions that magnify the eroticized body of the leader in the midst of war: "We should begin our talk about my journey when Tito lit a cigarette and sticking it, as is his habit, into his silver-studded, pipe-shaped holder, inhaled and crossed his legs."[54] At times, this close attention to Tito's body and his movement takes on homoerotic overtones, for example, when Dedijer notes: "Crossing his legs again nervously, Tito took a long pull at his cigarette …"[55]

This tension of venerating both the body and ideas of the socialist leader was in part what made him so effective and admired, but it was also deeply embedded in a masculine logic of domination and strength. Dedijer was a partisan, human rights activist, and a great supporter of Tito, characterizing him as a socialist leader who in 1948 had freed Yugoslavia from the grips of Stalin: "It did not only mean the right for Yugoslavia *to be independent*, it meant also the right of every people *to go forward in its own way*."[56] Tito's heroics stood in for the Yugoslav people's own independence, a highly gendered analysis of the partisan leader whose greatness was measured in comparison to the most violent male communist leader at the time. Dedijer concluded: "It meant a red rag before Stalin's eyes. The heart of his fury, of his rage against Yugoslavia, is a simple fact. Tito is the conscience of Stalin, the conscience Stalin had lost."[57] For Dedijer, moral virtues and the right to lead played themselves out within male spheres of power, which as history shows time and again, inevitably turn against each other in one way or another. In 1954, Dedijer fell out of favor with Tito for siding with Milovan Đilas, who became the most infamous critic of Tito's party and leadership and who in turn served a prison sentence.

Zagreb-based performance artist Vlasta Delimar did not care about war heroes in the 1980s, and was not interested in revering militarist machismo (see section "Absorbing the power of the Yugoslav socialist flag and its leader" in Chapter 1, specifically Delimar's collage *Woman is Not a Warrior*). Delimar did not shy away from taboo subjects and readily explored her sexual desires along with the sexual violence endured by women. But unlike the women I have described in this chapter thus far, Delimar was staunchly heterosexual and was also known to make homophobic and anti-feminist statements. In an interview published in *Dik Fagazine* in 2016, curator and art historian Leonida Kovač commented on Delimar's overt homophobia during the 1990s and quoted the artist as saying: "I despise feminists because all of them are lesbians."[58] And yet, this same magazine, which was centered on "queering" the Zagreb museum and highlighting figures in its contemporary art history relevant to queer, gay, and lesbian history, prioritized Delimar as a pivotal figure in this queered history of Yugoslav art. Why and how is Delimar's work relevant in this queer history of Yugoslavia?

Responding to critiques of Delimar, Darko Šimičić recalled that "Vlasta was in a way very provocative," because she focused on men's sexuality as her objects of artistic exploration.[59] He remembered what he called one of her "porno works" in 1980 that he participated in: "We were at the seaside, lying on the beach nude … and then she said to her husband—may I paint your balls? And he said yes, and then she said—who else wants to be painted? And all of us started to laugh and agreed to participate."[60] Šimičić would add that even though he laughed at the time, and does so to this day, her work was anything but a joke: it was an important and serious intervention, because it was extraordinary for a woman to use men's bodies for art.[61] One must only think of the female nude surrounded by fully clothed men in Édouard Manet's 1863 *The Luncheon on the Grass*, or countless other examples discussed in Berger's celebrated 1972 BBC series and book *Ways of Seeing*, where he famously critiqued sexism in art: "Men act and women appear. Men look at women. Women watch themselves being looked at."[62] Instead of being looked at and "appearing," Delimar took balls and dicks into her own hands and transformed men's bodies at a site of leisure activity at the beach into her own art environment.

Although Šimičić grouped this work under the genre "porno," it is unclear what part of this work is deemed pornographic. Is it her touching the penises? Is it the sheer act of depicting male penises? Is there an implied gang bang because of the lineup of five men with one woman? Did anybody have sexual intercourse? Or even an erotic encounter? These questions illustrate how difficult it is to categorize such work as pornography and make palpable that few would think about this action as a "porno work" if the males depicted were women. Otherwise, one might have to categorize the majority of Western art as pornographic. However, one photograph of Delimar's *Ball Painting* (Figure 3.15) does capture the gender discrepancy at the heart of the Yugoslav avant-garde art scene: a tiny naked Delimar as the sole woman standing in line with five men. The humor is not lost here when one thinks about the history of "action" painting rife with male bravado. Naked like her male peers, she is the one holding the watercolor palette in her hand, and she is the author in this lineup; the men's balls have been visibly marked by her, as if to imply that she holds the power over all those "dicks." The nervous smile of her then-husband, Željko Jerman, who was standing beside her, along with the awkward poses of the other men standing in line and holding their penises up to show Delimar's art on their bodies, amplify the shifting gender relations as we see the female artist at work. While most likely an unintended and

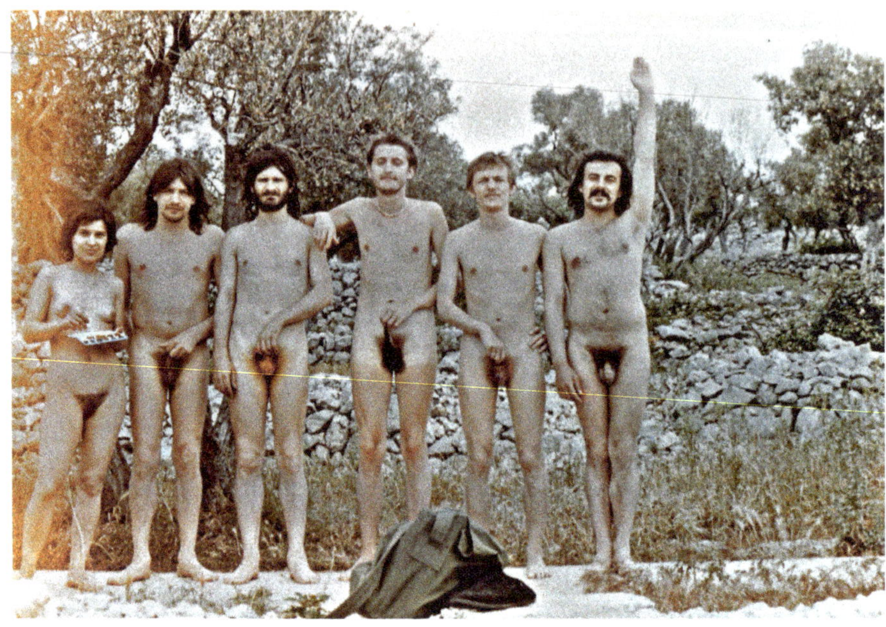

3.15   Vlasta Delimar, *Ball Painting*, 1980. Performance.

insignificant detail of the photograph capturing Delimar's action, the red color visible on Ivan Mršić's testicles remind us that Yugoslavia's socialism defied stereotypes of a bleak and sexless communist society. Ultimately, the men appear in the submissive position, paraded as the handiwork of the female artist, who looks at the camera with a confident smile. As such, one could argue that Delimar's "porno work" transformed the coordinates of socialism by overturning gender expectations and making the woman, Jugoslovenka, the main author of this more libidinal, joyous, and body-centric socialist society. Most importantly, pointing the gaze at men's genitalia marked her method of art making: she does not just look at and depict men, her process of touching and transforming their most private body parts becomes a central focus of her work throughout her entire career. Her female gaze—through which male nudity and sexualities were transformed—was equally her action. Delimar may have kept her focus on men, and may not have had much interest in other women or other women's same-sex desires, but it was her method of embracing her own and men's bodies that marked her emancipatory feminist and transgressive approach, regardless of whether or not she herself welcomed those characterizations or their implications for a feminist or queer history of Yugoslavia.

Despite Delimar's joyous embrace of her own sexuality and her transformation of male bodies into art objects for her performance works, she also explored the darker and more difficult aspects of sex and love. In her thirty-minute performance at the Expanded Media gallery in Zagreb titled *Jebanje Je Tužno* (*Fucking is Sad*) (1986), Delimar lay on her back on top of a white cross with her body painted black, her face veiled, her nipples and nails painted red, and wearing black high heel shoes (Figure 3.16).[63] On the wall above her head, we can see what appears to be another cross, in black, and featuring the repeated phrase "Jebanje Je Tužno" ("Fucking is Sad") in cursive and white paint. An androgynous male performer wearing lipstick sat against a large black cross before walking slowly up to Delimar, placing a white rose on her body, and exiting the room (Figure 3.17). Delimar lay in place for another twenty-eight minutes like a corpse, with her genitals exposed, as if she was put to rest with the parting gift of a rose. The symbolic clout of this action connotes just how sad and lonely "fucking" might become. The androgyny of the male performer also destabilized a purely heterosexual reading of the scene, and while the title indicates fucking and as such possibly yet another "porno work," there was no fucking in the performance at all. Instead, the audience was facing a woman, with her face veiled and her crucified body painted black and lying on the white cross, who would become a dark intermediary between the whiteness of the cross and the single white rose signifying virginity. But the white rose is also used at funerals, thus indicating both innocence and its destruction, which Delimar accepted in silent stillness. The recurring image of the cross, prominent in the flyer for her action, also indicated the foundational presence of religion and her critique of it in her work. Considering the intersecting political dimensions of Christian conservatism, especially when it comes to women's sexual freedoms, Delimar's emancipatory power also lied in pronouncing—over and over again here—that fucking *is* sad for women, especially for those who otherwise celebrate and embrace it. Her red fingernails also harken us back to the femme power of Yugoslav socialism manifest at the 1978 "Drug-ca Žena" conference in Belgrade (Chapter 1), complicating and expanding questions of feminist resistance within the local context of Yugoslavia.

In 1985, a year prior, she had her first solo show at ŠKUC in Ljubljana, which was vandalized. All her works that included crosses were destroyed by what some suspected were "young militant Christians."[64] In 1981, she had already scandalized the Christian cross in *Jebite Me* (*Fuck Me*), a collage that showed the artist sitting up with spread legs, covered eyes, and a large golden crucifix around her neck, along with "a miniature roundel of a church, emerging as a red phallic architectural object on top of her vagina."[65] That same year, Delimar performed an action in Zagreb in a public square tied to a tree with

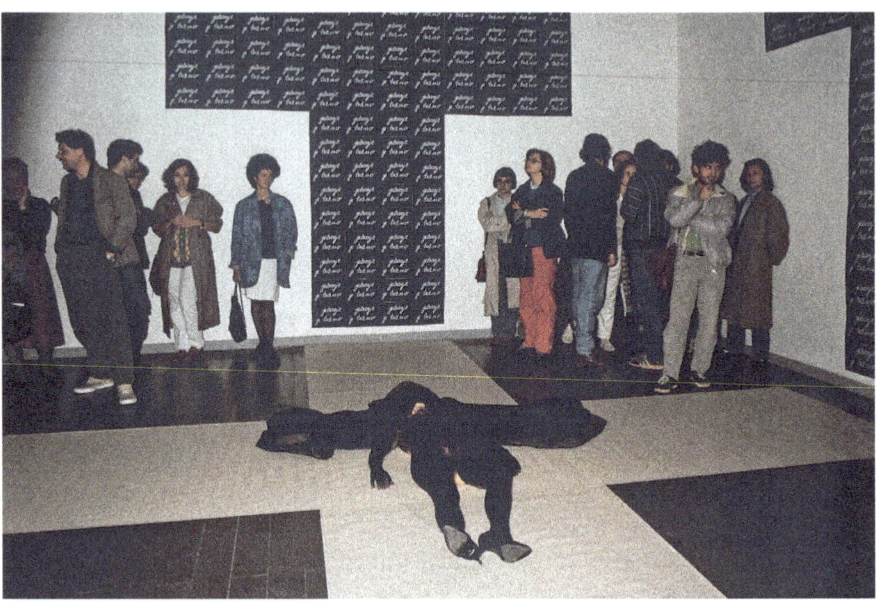

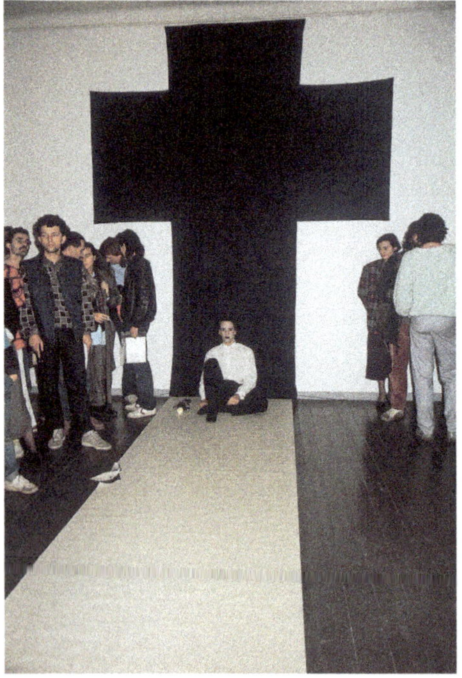

3.16–3.17   Vlasta Delimar, *Fucking Is Sad*, 1986. Performance at the Expanded Media Gallery, Zagreb.

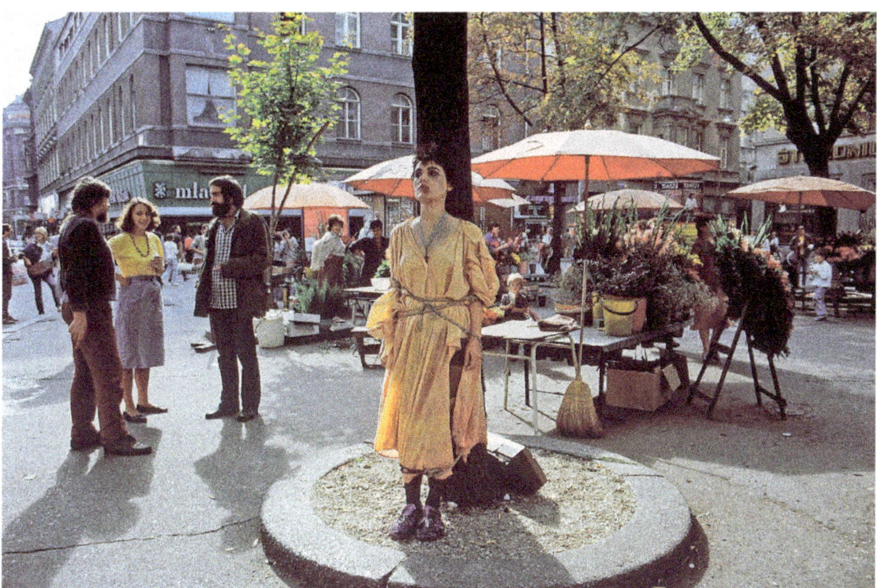

Vlasta Delimar, *Tied to a Tree*, 1985. Performance.   **3.18**

bruises on her face, reminiscent of images of battered women and witch burnings (Figure 3.18).

In photographic documentation commissioned by her for *Vezana Za Drvo* (*Tied to a Tree*), we see a man filming her from the side and young children playing while their parents shop at the market. Her public display of violence against women juxtaposed against banalities that seemed to ignore her suffering—reminiscent of the image of Joan of Arc in golden armor—made potently clear what outspoken women were up against in Yugoslavia and elsewhere: demonization and violence. Much like the Slovenian collective Neue Slowenische Kunst's theater faction, the Scipion Nasice Sisters Theater, which embraced ideas around religion and the sacred as a spectacular critique of Yugoslav authoritarianism and nationalism (see Chapter 4), Delimar played with the spectacular by contrasting the assumed sacred purity of the cross with the desiring and punished female body. Delimar's work transformed the iconography of resurrection into the explicit emancipatory performance of her body.

Delimar's evocation of religious suffering would anticipate the heightened role religion took in Yugoslavia in the 1990s, as ethnic and religious divides tore the nation asunder. During this tumultuous change of power, a cult Yugoslav film director Želimir Žilnik released his film *Marble Ass* (1995), starring Merlinka, a well-known transgender woman sex worker in her mid-thirties, who worked the streets of Belgrade, Serbia. Merlinka was the nickname for Vjeran Mladenović Merlinka, who also went by "Merlin" and "Marilyn Monroe," and who had starred in Žilnik's 1986 film *Lijepe žene prolaze kroz grad* (*Beautiful Women Walking Through the City*). Less than ten years after their first collaboration, Žilnik serendipitously ran into Merlinka at a train station in the summer of 1994, an accidental meeting that prompted the director to rewrite the script for a film he was making at the time.[66] This chance meeting changed the history of film in Yugoslavia and stands as one of the earliest and most important films to visualize transgender life in the Balkans. In addition, *Marble Ass* exhibited a political commitment to peace and unity emblematic of a socialist Yugoslavia that was already disintegrating by then.

In the decades prior, Žilnik had already established a record of films that centered on working-class struggles and women's emancipatory positions within Yugoslavia's socialist system. In his 1969 *Early Works*, Žilnik introduced the fictional young, working-class heroine, Jugoslava, who, following the revolution of 1968, toured Yugoslavia with three men and introduced revolutionary ideas centered on critiques of existing gender hierarchies in Yugoslavia. "Jugoslava brings forth a very pointed critique of real existing socialism," film and gender historian and theorist Dijana Jelača has argued. "While the proletariat is nominally put in charge and on equal footing in socialist systems, women continue to be oppressed subjects under the autocratic rule of men due to ongoing patriarchal gender dynamics. As a result, a true revolution cannot happen without disposing of this gender hierarchy—a disposal that, importantly, includes the monogamous family."[67] Jugoslava's revolutionary spirit would come at the cost of her life, as the men who accompany her feel humiliated by her strength and their own inability to bring the revolution to fruition and end up murdering her and burning her body.[68]

Poignantly, the Yugoslav woman in 1995—trans woman Merlinka—survives the murderous aggression of her male companions in *Marble Ass*. Tragically, the actual living person, Merlinka, would be murdered almost a decade later in a transphobic attack by a young man. But Merlinka as a character and person in the film in 1995 stood as a symbol of peace, embodying Delimar's 1982 proclamation that "woman is not a warrior" by playing the antithetical heroine to traumatized male chauvinism and violence. This is particularly significant, as Merlinka represents women's emancipatory positions in sex work at the exact same time that Yugoslavia is disintegrating into more conservative and religion-oriented nations.

Marble Ass is centered around blonde-haired Merlinka and her closest friend Sanela (Nenad Milenković Sanela), a brunette trans woman sex worker, who encounter traumatized Serbian men returning from the Yugoslav wars and engage in clandestine business operations. Merlinka and Sanela serve as healing forces against what Jelača theorizes as the "ethno-national collectivity engaged in a violent war." Jelača explains: "Marilyn claims that she does a kind of humanitarian work: counteracting the violence of the nation-state with the physical love and affection that she offers her customers."[69] For Jelača, Sanela and Merlinka are "too queer" and "too far removed from convention to be hailed into a collective ethno-national subjectivity constituted as 'healthy' through the violence it performs."[70] In one photograph from the set of the film, we see Sanela in a white wedding gown, smiling, and Merlinka in a pinkish-red dress, looking seriously back at us (Figure 3.19). The unlikely pair here embody a merging of colliding and multiple forms of femininity, an affirmative embrace of life palpable in Sanela's radiant facial expression, and an inquisitive, cautioning mind expressed in Merlinka. As Kevin Moss argued, Merlinka serves as a "destabilizing figure … [who] proves more resilient" than all other cis-het characters.[71]

But, Merlinka could also be read as the embodied feminine and feminist investment in emancipatory freedom for women, a political project tied to Yugoslav feminism and its emphasis on peace and transnationalism

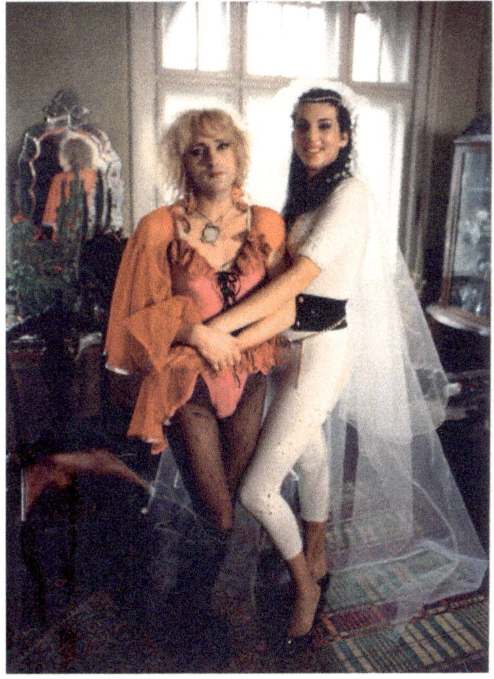

Merlinka and Sanela in Želimir Žilnik's *Marble Ass*, 1995. Film still.   **3.19**

(see Chapter 5). This reading is amplified in the end, when Merlinka's lover Johnny is murdered by one of his male mafia rivals. Just before his throat is slit, Johnny gets jealous and accuses Merlinka of being a "whore," to which she responds: "Me a whore? Are you nuts? I am a nurse. I am a (female) saint. I saved lots of girls from being raped. I spared so many girls and their parents from trauma and tears."[72] As Jugoslovenka, Merlinka champions compassion, imagination, and solidarity with her trans and non-trans women companions in the film, as well as being protective of animals.

Marble Ass puts toxic masculinity on display in various forms, including misogyny and animal cruelty. Luna Lu (Suzana Zlatanović) appears as a butch paramilitary officer (passing as a man) who had fought with Johnny (Johnny Racković) at the front and who dominates him sexually and in life. In one excruciating scene, Johnny is shooting through walls at a goat Merlinka loves dearly and keeps as a pet. For his amusement, or perhaps because he is jealous of Merlinka's affection for the animal, he ties up the animal in a bathroom, terrifying the goat with bullets flying by while he is lying on a couch in another room. Luna Lu walks in and decides to put an end to Johnny's "fun," butchering the goat by cutting its throat. This masculine female soldier is able to "finish" what Jonny could not, underlining once again what Jelača calls Johnny's "defeated masculinity,"[73] one in which the protagonist's feeling of "emasculation" is overcome by "enact[ing] masculinity to such an exaggerated, caricaturist extent."[74] Strikingly, the scene ends with Merlinka and Sanela finding Luna Lu, and the dead goat being skinned by Johnny, in the bathroom, Merlinka realizing that "she [Luna Lu] is not an officer! She is a woman!," and that she must be one of Johnny's lovers. Sanela, appalled upon hearing this, swiftly kicks through the already slightly broken wall. Merlinka and Sanela both go after Johnny calling him a traitor, while the butch officer Luna Lu remains untouched. Luna Lu then shoots the gun and also yells at Johnny, whose masculinity once again is diminished and defeated. The scene ends with another trans woman (Likana) entering the bathroom through the wall, asking: "Women, do you need any help?"

The skinning of the goat in the bathroom, the clandestine wartime shootings, and numerous other absurdities place *Marble Ass* squarely within stereotypical visions of the Balkans, while the title of the film also plays with emancipatory socialism and its forgotten heroes, as it refers to Andrzej Wajda's 1977 Polish film *Man of Marble*.[75] By rooting the story within the experiences of Merlinka—perceived as "a gay man" in Tito's Yugoslavia, but by the 1990s, living through its disintegration as a trans woman sex worker—Žilnik collapsed otherwise seemingly irreconcilable realities and modes of being into one story where "there are virtually no characters whose lives exist outside of the queer time and place," an "unapologetic relentlessness of queer vision" in which "queer subjects are imbued with a rationality and practical thinking missing from other, more normative, 'healthier' members of the society."[76] This collapsing and revealing of coexisting queer realities during the period of the disintegration of Yugoslavia was no small task, and Žilnik had to film 90 percent of *Marble Ass* in Novi Sad because Belgrade was "too dangerous" at the time.[77]

The story of how the film came to be screened adds to its significance. In my conversation with Žilnik, he recalled that he had again serendipitously seen in the news that the Ministry of Culture had announced it did not have enough films from Serbia to screen that year, and they asked that directors who had any Serbian films go to the Sava Center in Belgrade to add their films to the venue's program. This venue could seat up to four thousand viewers, so Žilnik promptly submitted *Marble Ass*. He had to fill out various forms, but the most important questions included the following (condensed):

"Is this a Serbian film?" Yes.

"Does it have Serbian actors?" Yes.

"Does it have any outside funding?" No.

As these parameters of national film dominated the ministry's interest in celebrating Serbian—not Yugoslavian—film, Žilnik's radically trans, queer, feminist, and pro-peace film passed under their radar and was screened in front of an audience of four thousand. Žilnik remembered that about half of the audience members decried the film as a lie, while the other half screamed in support and joy: "Bravo, this is us!" After the screening, Žilnik went on stage and invited the entire trans cast and their trans friends and viewers, all gay and lesbian participants and attendees, along with all sex workers, to come up on stage with him. In an act of courage and solidarity, six hundred people ended up on stage. For about two months after the screening, the Serbian media zealously interviewed many of the participants in the film in lieu of reporting about Slobodan Milošević, who had otherwise dominated the media. In this regard, it is important to note that Merlinka's and Sanela's 1997 interview with Tatjana Vojtehovski remains one of the most critical documents of trans and sex work history in the Balkans and beyond.[78]

Belgrade-based queer theorist and historian Saša Kesić has noted that *Marble Ass* "has the most revolutionary potential because that idea of 'queer' is completely in line with anti-war heroes and our queer heroes."[79] Merlinka transcended the fictional narrative of the film and brought to the foreground the beauty, but also the struggle, of a trans woman sex worker. Kesić adds:

Her task was to fight for her right, and I think she felt really humiliated working in the street and having so much money, but not a bit of dignity. That's why she appeared on television. She wanted to say that most of the important

> people, like politicians, they were coming to her for those sexual things. That is why she wanted to say that [on TV] to show that she can say those things. I think that's the reason why she was killed in the end.[80]

Merlinka's courage and life have become a source of inspiration for contemporary generations of LGBTQ people from and living in the former Yugoslavia. The region's most important queer film festival was named after her: Merlinka Festival. To this day, Merlinka remains the only film festival that is organized by different countries that comprised the former Yugoslavia, with screenings in Belgrade (Serbia), Sarajevo (Bosnia), and Podgorica (Montenegro).[81] Merlinka's sexuality and emancipatory courage as an outspoken transgender woman sex worker is the connective tissue that symbolically unites the different republics: a transgender Jugoslovenka, whose feminist performance politics—steeped in the queer and feminist underground practices of the 1980s—stood, by the early 1990s, as one of the last vestiges of Yugoslav sisterhood and unity.

Gay Jugoslovenkas in the countryside

The presence of the goat in *Marble Ass* hinted at the Balkan countryside that was usually missing as a site of gay love from LGBTQ histories. I want to end this chapter on one of the most famous "out" dykes in the post-Yugoslav art world with a rural background, Helena Janečić. Coming of age in Osijek, a small town in Croatia, Janečić sought a gay language that could address the "folk stories about lesbians" she never heard or had access to growing up.[82] "Visually, I didn't have any proof of that sort of thing. So I staged everyday life scenes for these two women."[83] In her "Snaše" ("Country Girls") series of paintings from 2008, we see rural scenes of two young women in love, often doing everyday activities like baking, preparing a meal, or picking tomatoes, all of which are painted with overt displays of lesbian desire, love, and sociality. Passionate kisses in a haystack and under a plum tree, women in folk dresses frolicking around the kitchen table, feeding each other and drinking wine and spirits together, offer up images of traditional rural life that complement the absence of a happy gay life or gay love in art (Figures 3.20–3.22). Food is just as luscious as the lesbian erotics in Janečić's series, with the signature purple plums of the Yugoslav region—familiar to many as the sweetest and most delightful fruit, reserved for plum jams, various baked goods, and rakija—featured prominently in many of the paintings. For her graduate work at the Art Academy in Zagreb, Janečić made around 30 kilograms of plum and apple jam, and she began giving viewers a jar of plum jam as a souvenir at openings, including those that featured the Snaše paintings.[84] The familiar comfort of homemade jam, often made by one's grandma or mother, is paired with

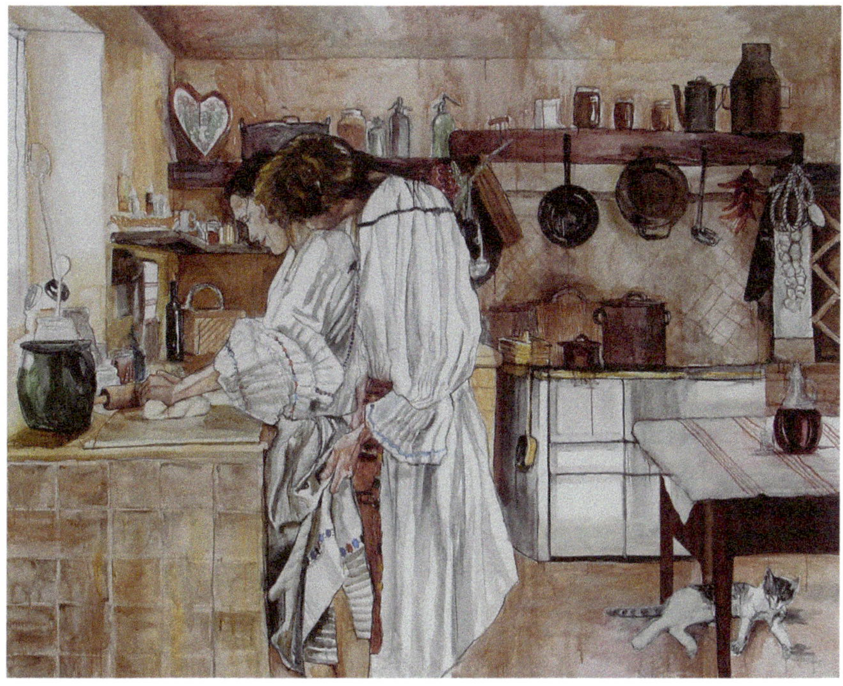

Helena Janečić, *In the Kitchen*, 2008. Painting.   **3.20**

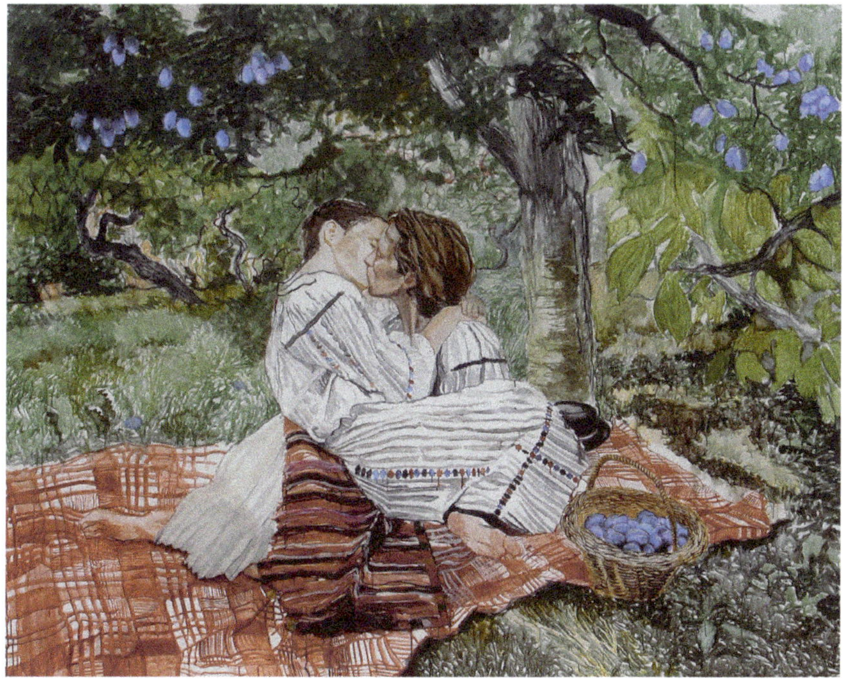

Helena Janečić, *In the Orchard*, 2008. Painting.   **3.21**

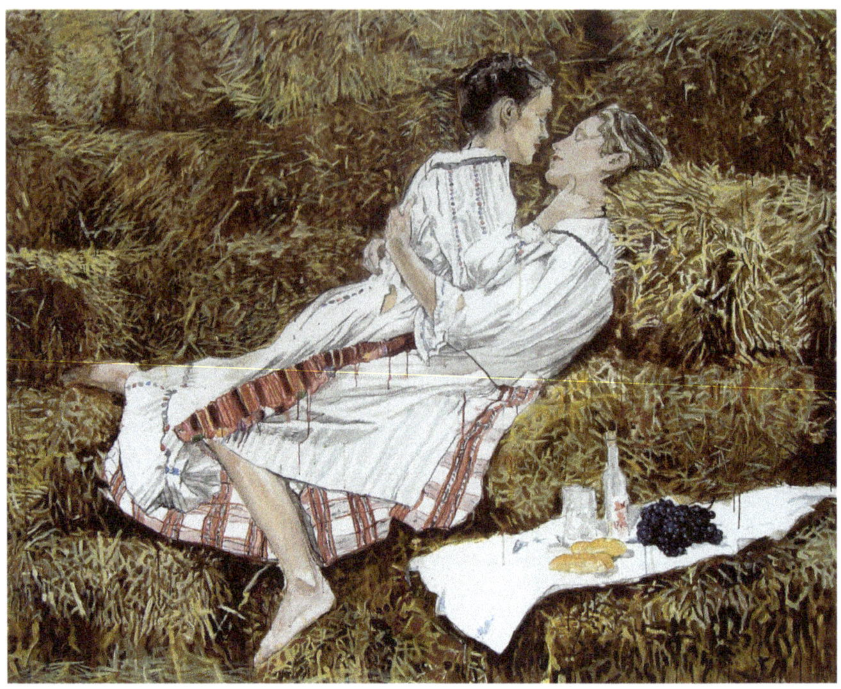

3.22   Helena Janečić, *In the Hay*, 2008. Painting.

marginalized and tabooed lesbian desire entangled within the sweet taste of the "simple" life.

The background history of how these paintings came to be is also key to understanding the queer legacy of Yugoslav women here, both imagined and real: Janečić had gone to the USA in 2004 to study art in college, where she officially "came out as gay" because she felt encouraged by her foreign environment and the more explicit gay content of the USA's pop culture compared with that of Croatia. Upon her return to Osijek, she decided to come out in her hometown too. During that time, she also discovered two older lesbians living in Bilje, an even smaller town, next to Osijek, who were renting their apartment through Airbnb on a website dedicated to "gay Croatia."[85] She contacted the women, who had grown up in that town together and who now lived openly as a gay couple there. "These women were as old as my parents," Janečić remembers, "so they were kind of [lesbian] mother figures for me."[86] They ended up gifting Janečić the folk dresses depicted in her paintings.[87] Her parents were also supportive, as she staged her painted works in her father's vineyard, with her and her friends enacting the different scenes in the Snaše series. As such, the Snaše series embodied Janečić's emancipation from the abysmal lack and erasure of gay life in contemporary Croatia in the form of fictional visual narratives of a lesbian idyllic life that had—at least in part—a basis in reality as well.

Janečić's series also defies fiction as much as it depends on it: the act of creating fictional stories is part of many people's coming of age as gay, imagining intimacy and a life for which there are no given templates, but which nevertheless exists. As such, these idyllic scenes, especially when we see women's hands running up skirts, intertwined bodies, or gentle moments of erotic pleasure between two women, seem far from fictional to the knowing— desiring—lesbian viewer. For we know that there is always a lesbian history that has never been recorded. Reimagining it is one powerful way to enliven the deadened and silenced realities that were never known to publics and histories, and that have to be imagined by the young generation of LGBTQ individuals, especially in rural areas that often lack the plurality and diversity more accessible in a big city. However, one might wonder if this idyllic lesbian life is just as out of reach as Lepa Brena's fantasy of Jugoslovenka in the countryside, free and emancipated, allowed to be herself, to enjoy her land. Just as white, thin, and nostalgic as Brena's national iconography of the Yugoslav woman, the folkloric lesbian life in Janečić's vision echoes the same whiteness that has always haunted Yugoslav nationalism beneath the surface.

And yet, the question of gay life in rural areas is also relevant considering the site of contemporary Catholic Croatia, which is arguably more conservative than it was before Yugoslavia disintegrated. In fact, Janečić's first exposure to lesbian sex was thanks to the Yugoslav *Start* magazine, which she discovered at her grandmother's house when she was thirteen years old. She noted: "I owe a lot of things to *Start* magazine. … At 13 years old, I picked up a copy of it because my grandma had it. There, I saw an article about two women who are a couple. And this was the first time I ever read anything [about lesbianism] in print."[88] As discussed in Chapter 1, *Start* featured many feminist essays and was avidly read by women and lesbians. By the early 1990s, when Janečić's home was at war, there were very few places to see or experience gay life. Janečić remembers reading *Gloria* magazine, where she saw an article about the 4 Non Blondes' Linda Perry, "who came out as a lesbian and then her career was ruined … So it was kind of a negative connotation." She added: "I also remember reading about homosexuality in one of our school books in sociology class in high school and that homosexuality was discussed under [the category of] deviant behavior."[89] With an educational system that had become more conservative due to the rise of Catholicism and nationalism in Croatia during and after the wars, *Start* magazine ended up being one of the gifts of the previous generation of Yugoslav feminists whose push for feminist and lesbian representation in Yugoslavia would end up reaching a young lesbian woman in the small town of Osijek in 1992. The fact that it was at her grandmother's house only solidifies the notion of Jugoslav women's kinship: Jugoslovenka's reach across generations.

Sexuality would feature even more prominently in Janečić's *Horny Dyke* project, which the artist began after she came out in the early 2000s. This project introduced a horny dyke in the likeness of Janečić into a primarily male-dominated visual sphere, marking a break with patriarchal and heterosexual supremacy in the comic scene. She also expanded the idea of the comic book to include performative elements, such as photographic enactments with friends, or a paper doll series of Horny Dyke that could assume different clothing. But the main focus was Horny Dyke's comedic struggle with her desire for women, which would often distract her from the heroic tasks at hand and "interfere with her superhero duties."[90] The artist explains: "I wanted to create a sexually active super heroine that uses her powers to help women with everyday tasks, like washing windows, moving heavy furniture, and laying kitchen tiles. These are the jobs that I would use my superpowers for, if I had any."[91] Again, fiction and reality merged, with everyday life as the main subject of lesbian desire and intervention.

Given these erotically charged works and their kinship with pornography, it is not surprising that Janečić would eventually be paired with Delimar for a group exhibition in 2009 in Slavonski Brod, as both artists' works are invested in the theme of desire transcending tabooed issues concerning women's sexuality in art and society. One of the erotic scenes in *Horny Dyke* is akin to a soft porn narrative, showing a woman asking Horny Dyke to wash the outside of her windows, as that is too difficult a job for her. Horny Dyke delivers and is rewarded with sex. The butch/femme theme here wittily replicates heteronormative modern chivalry by positing masculine handiwork in exchange for sex. But *Horny Dyke* also took on more overtly political topics, similarly cloaked in humor and often paired with eroticism. In the episode on "Discrimination," Horny Dyke is described as "A super heroine who uses her mystically gained powers in service of the good, protecting her 10% of the population, and girls in trouble regardless of their nationality, religion, race, politics, age, sexual orientation, even their looks" (Figure 3.23). In the episode "Catwoman," Horny Dyke ends up making out with Catwoman, while both agree about "the inefficiency of law enforcement in fighting the criminal syndicates clutching the city in its claws" (Figure 3.24). Both of these seem to suggest that lesbian life is rife with political pressures, and while Horny Dyke is ready to serve the greater good, she never forgets her sexual pleasure, which reigns supreme. In this way, *Horny Dyke* beautifully speaks to many of the works in this chapter centered on the Yugoslav legacy of female desire paired with political consciousness. The emphasis on serving all women, regardless of national and racial background, also echoes the work of feminist activists fighting for their Yugoslav sisters trapped in the divisive and nationalist wars

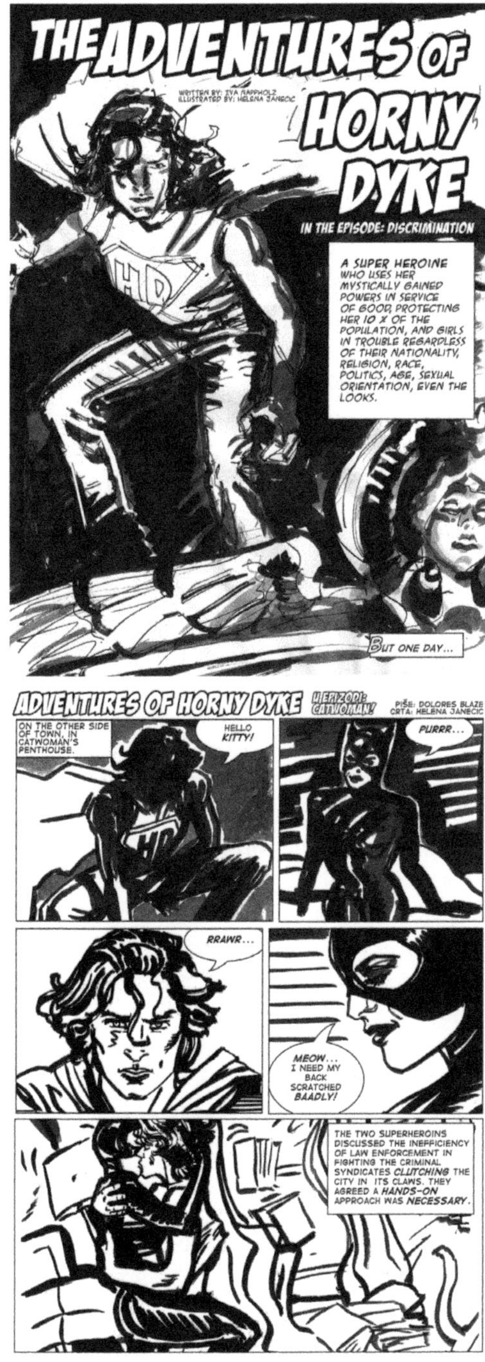

Helena Janečić, *The Adventures of Horny Dyke*, 2010–ongoing.   **3.23–3.24**

of the 1990s (see Chapter 5) and burdened by male-dominated corruption within the political sphere and the police. Through this lens, one might read Horny Dyke as one of the last generations of Jugoslovenkas to carry forth residues of the queer and antifascist legacy of Yugoslav socialism.

Pičkas and *peders* fight back: Jugoslovenka's queer resistance

Tatjana Pavlović has noted that the word "pička" ("cunt") has long been used to vilify women and also to denigrate a man's masculinity in Yugoslavia by feminizing him: a common insult is "He was quiet as a cunt" ("Šutio je kao pička").[92] This phrase is used "synonymously" with another common insult: "He is such a faggot" ("Baš je peder").[93] Pavlović goes on to explain how "peder" is also used casually to remark on the failure of men to be tough: "Don't be such a faggot" ("Ne budi peder") can be understood as "Don't be like that," while the epithet "faggot permeates all of the spaces of popular culture" to this day.[94]

The 1980s in Yugoslavia were an extraordinary time for alternative subcultures that intersected feminist and queer politics, manifested in multiple and varied types of "peders" and "pičkas" resisting state-mandated patriarchal socialism. Like the previous generation in the 1970s, artists and curators sought to challenge the status quo by establishing transnational connections and radical spaces for feminist and queer resistance. While the alternative art scene in Ljubljana created radical performance works, the gay and lesbian scenes equally expanded the territory and possibilities for queer and feminist liberation. Delimar's open embrace of her heterosexual libidinal drive, lust for sex with men, love of her own body, and her scorn for the patriarchal authority of political leaders marked her as one of the most controversial figures of feminist resistance. All this happened in a state that was paradoxically less violent toward women and homosexuals than the ethno-religious nationalist movements that followed, while remaining staunchly patriarchal and conservative as a socialist country.

The end of socialism and the arrival of "democracy" brought a religious fervor and conservatism that stood in opposition to gay rights. In the case of Croatia, for example, Andrea Spehar has noted: "Croatia can only be heterosexual."[95] By this she means that the new nation states, much more so than the Yugoslav socialist state, relied heavily on repressing the lesbian and gay movement in order to push for traditionalist societies. She provocatively deduced that "If homosexuals are free in Croatia, Croatia will cease to exist as a nation-state."[96] Socialist Yugoslavia had never relied on such a level of repression of queers to assert its nationhood. By the 1990s, however, the surge of nationalism within the independent countries amplified misogyny, homophobia, and transphobia, and men who rejected the war were considered "homos," not real men. These "failed" men, many of whom were also traumatized during the war, as Johnny in *Marble Ass* was, were in need of women to support and accept them. In this regard, Merlinka also harkens back to the figure of the epic maiden, another example of Jugoslovenka in the genealogy of the partisan Yugoslav woman who "is best described as an ideal combination of the cross-dressing warrior" and "the female Partisan nurse" "tending the wounded."[97] But instead of being a quasi-housewife who stays at home and cooks for her traumatized and violent husband or clients, Merlinka lives her life in the war zone of clandestine sexuality. She does so with autonomy and an open embrace of sexuality, protected by her political commitment to compassion and female friendships. Janečić's emphasis on the rural lives of lesbian lovers transgressed the conservative Croatian cultural erasure of queer desire and reimagined a past and future where lesbians are so mainstream that they are happy and loved even in rural areas. And if not, Horny Dyke will come to the rescue! The libidinal force of the decade of the 1980s began with queer resistance and feminist organizing and ended with the prelude to war; the power of emancipatory defiance was transformed into the healing power of sisterhood and systematic resistance by the Yugoslav "cunts" and "faggots" ("pičkas" and "peders") who sought unity and recognition in opposition to the ethnocentric wars, and who continue to resist their marginalized and tabooed conditions to this day.

Notes

1 Marina Gržinić, "A Time that Lives On, But in a Different Way: 1977–1984," in Sandro Droschl and Christiane Egger, eds., *What is Art? Resuming Fragmented Histories* (Nürnberg: Verlag für Moderne Kunst, 2015), 199–200, 205.

2 Ibid., 205.

3 See Kristen R. Ghodsee, *Why Women Have Better Sex under Socialism: And other Arguments for Economic Independence* (New York: Nation Books, 2018) and *Second World, Second Sex: Socialist Women's Activism and Global Solidarity during the Cold War* (Durham, NC: Duke University Press, 2019).

4 Marcuse was in Korčula during the invasion of Czechoslovakia by the Warsaw Pact countries, on August 20, 1968. He, along with Ernst Bloch (who was also at the school that summer), wrote a letter of protest that was signed by some fifty philosophers. Marcuse "sent a telegram to the Yugoslav leader Josip Broz Tito asking him to use his international reputation to protect the interests of the Czechoslovak socialist state and its independence," but Tito never responded. Filip Kovačević has implied, however, that just five years later "the journal was banned and the Korčula Summer School disbanded." See Kovačević, "Marcuse in Yugoslavia," *Radical Philosophy Review* 16, no. 1 (2013), 216.

5 Herbert Marcuse, *An Essay on Liberation* (Boston: Beacon Press, 1969), 25–26.

6 Ibid., 26.

7 Gržinić in conversation with the author, August 10, 2019.

8 "Barbara Borčić: Artistic Director of Škuc Gallery from 1982–1985," Škuc Gallery: www.galerijaskuc.si/barbara-borcic/ (accessed 3/09/2020).

9 Lilijana Stepančič and Breda Škrjanec, "Introduction," in Breda Škrjanec, ed., *FV Alternativa osemdesetih/Alternative Scene of the Eighties* (Ljubljana: Mednarodni Grafični Likovni Center/International Center of Graphic Arts, 2008), 278.

10 Alajbegović's performance in 1984 is the most frequently cited, but I have also found the song released by Borghesia in 1989 on their album *Resistance* (Croatia: Jugoton).

11 Quoted in Ljubica Spaskovska, *The Last Yugoslav Generation: The Rethinking of Youth Politics and Cultures in Late Socialism* (Manchester: Manchester University Press, 2017), 96, 110.

12 Gržinić and Aina Šmid had connections to the staff working for TV Slovenia, who shared the footage with them. Gržinić in conversation with the author, August 10, 2019.

13 Marina Gržinić and Aina Šmid, "Bilokacija (Bilocation)" (1990): http://grzinic-smid.si/?p=271 (accessed 5/11/2019).

14 Walter Seidl, "Video as a Matrix of Mental Consciousness: The Works of Marina Gržinić and Aina Šmid," in Marina Gržinić and Tanja Velagić, eds., *New-Media Technology, Science, and Politics: The Video Art of Marina Gržinić and Aina Šmid* (Vienna: Locker, 2008), 267.

15 A definition used by Jelena Batinić in her book *Women and Yugoslav Partisans: A History of World War II Resistance* (Cambridge: Cambridge University Press, 2015), 65.

16 Gržinić explains that they focused on Barthes because structuralism and post-structuralism took hold in Yugoslavia in the 1980s and she was especially influenced by his 1977 book, *A Lover's Discourse: Fragments*. Gržinić had bought the book during one of her trips to Italy (in Italian) and already used it in their works before 1984. "This book was never translated in Yugoslav language. It is a very special book. … The translation in English came out in 1990. When we did *Bilocation* in 1989, we translated the text directly." Gržinić in e-mail correspondence with the author, September 22, 2019.

17 Gržinić in e-mail correspondence with the author, September 21, 2019.

18 Marina Gržinić, "The Video, Film, and Interactive Multimedia Art of Marina Gržinić and Aina Šmid, 1982–2008," in Gržinić and Velagić, eds., *New-Media Technology*, 86.

19 Ibid.

20 Gržinić in conversation with the author, August 10, 2019.

21 Ibid.

22 Zsófia Lóránd, "'A Politically Non-Dangerous Revolution is Not a Revolution': Critical Readings of the Concept of Sexual Revolution by Yugoslav Feminists in the 1970s," *European Review of History: Revue européenne d'histoire* 22, no. 1 (2015), 128.

23 Gržinić, "The Video, Film, and Interactive Multimedia Art," 48.

24 Ibid.

25 Borghesia's *Cindy* video and album cover can be viewed at Dark Entries Records: www.darkentriesrecords.com/store/vinyl/lp/borghesia-clones-lp/ (accessed 5/11/2019).

26 "'We Want Censorship': A Brief Introduction to Yugoslav Queer Culture," *The Balkanist* (September 16, 2017): https://balkanist.net/we-want-censorship-a-brief-introduction-to-yugoslav-queer-culture/ (accessed 5/11/2019).

27 Marina Gržinić, Aina Šmid, and Zvonka T. Simčič, dir., *Relations: 25 Years of the Lesbian Group ŠKUC-LL* [Documentary film, 1:24:2] (Zavod CCC, Ljubljana, 2012).

28 Barbara Borčić in e-mail correspondence with the author, February 17, 2021.

29 Slađana Marković, "Zemlja bez jezika [A Land without a Language]," *Potkulture* 3 (1987), 58–60. See Zsófia Lóránd, *The Feminist Challenge to the Socialist State in Yugoslavia* (London: Palgrave Macmillan, 2018), for a detailed discussion of the topics in the issue, esp. 179.

30 Nataša Sukić speaking in *Relations: 25 Years of the Lesbian Group ŠKUC-LL*.

31 Lepa Mlađenović, "Foreword: Searching for Our Lesbian Nests in Yugoslavia and After," in Bojan Bilić and Sanja Kajinić, eds., *Intersectionality and LGBT Activist Politics: Multiple Others in Croatia and Serbia* (London: Palgrave Macmillan, 2016), viii–ix.

32 Xenia, "Moja Prijateljica," (single) EP. Jugoton, 1982. Translation by the author.

33 Videosex, "Ana," *Videosex 84* LP. Založba kaset in plošč RTV Ljubljana (ZKP RTVL), 1984. Translation by the author.

34 [keyword: Videosex]. The image was later featured on a special album, *Masters Collection*, and is widely available online on music sites. The photograph is also reproduced on the website Once Upon a Time in Yugoslavia, Graphic Journey through Pop Culture of Ex Yugoslavia: https://igoyugo.tumblr.com/post/6320235717/videosex (accessed 3/20/2019).

35 Videosex, "Stakleno Nebo," *Lacrimae Christi* LP. Založba kaset in plošč RTV Ljubljana (ZKP RTVL), 1985. Translation by the author.

36 An image of the album cover for *Videosex 84* is widely available on the web and can be found here on the Rock and Roll Archives website: www.rockandrollarchives.net/2020/10/videosex-videosex-1984-yugoslavia-new.html (accessed 8/13/2020).

37 Karlowy Vary was formerly called Korowa Bar (1981–1983). They performed as Karlowy Vary from 1983 to 1986. Their first album, *Haotika*, was rejected by Zagreb's record label Jugoton in 1984. *La Femme* was released by Belgrade's PGP RTB (Produkcija gramofonskih ploča Radio televizije Beograd) label in 1985.

38 See Boris Perić and Denis M. Peričić, "Varja Orlić, kultna grupa Karlowy Vary: Gdje je danas nekadašnja prva dama undergrounda?" *Yugopapir*, 1988: www.yugopapir.com/2017/08/varija-orlic-kultna-grupa-karlowy-vary.html (accessed 5/20/2019); and "Mistična princeza jugoslovenskog andergraunda koja je PRERANO umrla: Ko je bila Varja Orlić, žena POTPUNO DRUGAČIJA

od svake druge," *Blic* (January 8, 2018): www.blic.rs/zabava/vesti/misticna-princeza-jugoslovenskog-andergraunda-koja-je-prerano-umrla-ko-je-bila-varja/tnqw9rn (accessed 5/11/2019).

39 Anne Koedt, "Lezbično gibanje in feminizem [The Lesbian Movement and Feminism]," *Mladina, Pogledi* 12 no. 2 (Summer 1985), 10–11. See Lóránd's in-depth discussion of the first gay and lesbian texts in Yugoslavia in *The Feminist Challenge*, 178–180.

40 Author's translation. This cover of *Pogledi* is reproduced in Vlasta Jalušič's *Kako smo hodile v feministično gimnazijo* (Ljubljana: Založba/*cf., Lila zbirka, 2002), 8.

41 *Woman's Bath* disappeared in 1945 when it was taken by the Red Army from a castle in north Berlin, later allegedly sold by the KGB, and then resurfaced when it was exhibited in Azerbaijan in 1993.

42 See Lóránd, *The Feminist Challenge*, 155. Original source: Slavenka Drakulić-Ilić, "Muški su nešto drugo [Men are Something Different]," *Start* 293 (1980), 66–67.

43 Quote translated in Lóránd, *The Feminist Challenge*, 156.

44 Mojca Dobnikar in e-mail correspondence with the author, October 15, 2019.

45 Rada Iveković and Slavenka Drakulić-Ilić, "YUGOSLAVIA: Neofeminism and its 'Six Mortal Sins,'" in Robin Morgan, ed., *Sisterhood is Global* (1984; New York: Feminist Press, 1996), 735. This co-authored entry on Yugoslavia was divided: the first part, "Yugoslav Neofeminism" by Iveković, and the second part, "'Six Mortal Sins' of Yugoslav feminism" by Drakulić-Ilić, 734–738.

46 "Nekaj o ljubezni med ženskami [A Few Things about Women Loving Women]," eds. Suzana, Roni, Erika, Nataša, Marjeta, and Davorka. *Pogledi* 14, no. 8, in *Mladina* 37 (October 1987), 21–28. Translations provided by Lóránd, *The Feminist Challenge*, 211n17.

47 "Ženske, ki se identificirajo kot ženske" [Women Who Identify as Women], in *Mladina*, No. 37 (October 1987): 24–25. Translation provided in Lóránd, *The Feminist* Challenge, 258; "Deset vprašanj lezbičnosti" [Ten Questions About Lesbianism], *Mladina*, No. 37 (October 1987): 26–27. Translation provided in Lóránd, *The Feminist* Challenge, 211n17. "Problemi vsiljene heteroseksualnosti [The Problems with Mandatory Heterosexuality]," *Mladina* 37 (October 1987), 18. Translation provided in Lóránd, *The Feminist* Challenge, 211n18. For more information on the issue, see Lóránd's discussion on 180.

48 The decriminalization of homosexuality did not happen in all the republics and autonomous regions, only in Montenegro, Croatia, Slovenia, Vojvodina, and Macedonia. See Bojan Bilić and Sanja Kajinić, "LGBT Activist Politics and Intersectionality in Croatia and Serbia: An Introduction," in Bilić and Kajinić, eds., *Intersectionality and LGBT Activist Politics*, 2.

49 Interview with Franko Dota: "Kako je bilo biti gej u Jugoslaviji? Pričali smo s čovjekom koji je upravo doktorirao na tu temu," *Gayten LGBT* (October 16, 2017): www.transserbia.org/seksulanost/1301-kako-je-bilo-biti-gej-u-jugoslaviji-pricali-smo-s-covjekom-koji-je-upravo-doktorirao-na-tu-temu (accessed 06/20/2020). According to queer scholar Ana Grujić, the

general response of older gay men today is that the Yugoslav state was not very interested in bothering them. According to their recollections (discussed in private conversations), one of the few times the police would clear cruising areas was during the 1961 Non-Aligned Movement (NAM) Conference in Belgrade, or during official visits of NAM leaders. Ana Grujić in conversation with the author, March 5, 2021.

50 Marijan Košiček published *U okviru vlastitog spola* in 1986. See Franko Dota's dissertation for a close analysis, "Public and Political History of Male Homosexuality in Socialist Croatia, 1945–1989" (PhD thesis, Zagreb University, 2017).

51 Unfortunately, research on the region still privileges male homosexuality over women's lesbian histories, so the numbers listed here represent research focused on men's homosexual experiences, not those of women.

52 Mlađenović, "Foreword: Searching for Our Lesbian Nests," ix.

53 Vesna Kesić, "A Response to Catharine MacKinnon's Article 'Turning Rape into Pornography: Postmodern Genocide,'" *Hastings Women's L. R.* 5 (1994), 273.

54 Vladimir Dedijer, "Prologue," in Vladimir Dedijer, *Tito Speaks: His Self-Portrait and Struggle with Stalin* (Norwich: Weidenfeld & Nicolson, 1953), xiii. To contemporary readers, this description might evoke the highly eroticized leg-crossing scene of Sharon Stone revealing her genitalia in the 1992 Hollywood film *Basic Instinct*.

55 Ibid., xiv.

56 Ibid., xv.

57 Ibid.

58 Karol Radziszewski, "Interview with Leonida Kovač," in Karol Radziszewski, ed., "Zagreb: Queering the Museum," special issue *Dik Fagazine* 10 (2016), 60.

59 Radziszewski, "Interview with Darko Šimičić," in "Zagreb: Queering the Museum," 130.

60 Ibid.

61 Ibid.

62 John Berger, *Ways of Seeing* (London: BBC and Penguin Books, 1972), 47.

63 The phrase *jebanje je tuzno* (fucking is sad) is a quote from Vlado Martek.

64 See Delimar's chronology in Martina Munivrana, ed., *Vlasta Delimar: This is I. Retrospective Exhibition 1979–2014* (Zagreb: Museum of Contemporary Art, 2014), 16.

65 Jasmina Tumbas, "Decision as Art: Performance in the Balkans," in Katalin Cseh-Varga and Adam Czirak, eds., *Performance Art in the Second Public Sphere: Event-Based Art in Late Socialist Europe* (London: Routledge, 2018), 193.

66 Želimir Žilnik in conversation with the author, August 13, 2019. He added that she asked him then and there to leave the station and go with her to see her life and friends and explained to him the process by which she and some twenty trans women had taken over a street in Belgrade to do their sex work. Their clients included politicians and celebrities, some of whom Žilnik also met, but who remain anonymous to this day.

67 Dijana Jelača, "Double Binds: The Politics of Gender and Sexuality in the Films of Želimir Žilnik," unpublished draft, 7; Jelača in e-mail correspondence with the author, August 16, 2019.

68 As is well known, Žilnik's *Early Works* came under intense scrutiny and was banned in Yugoslavia. Žilnik remembers that he had to go to court to discuss the film, but he did not consider the country totalitarian because he was invited to have a discussion about it. Indeed, the charges were dropped afterward. While Žilnik is often theorized as a "dissident" against Yugoslavia, he has been outspoken about how during his "exile" in West Germany he encountered much harsher censorship than in Yugoslavia. Žilnik in conversation with the author, August 13, 2019.

69 Dijana Jelača, *Dislocated Screen Memory: Narrating Trauma in Post-Yugoslav Cinema* (Basingstoke: Palgrave, 2016), 117.

70 Ibid., 116.

71 Kevin Moss, "Yugoslav Transgendered Heroes: 'Virgina' and 'Marble Ass,'" *Reč* 67, no. 13 (September 2002), 363.

72 In an earlier scene, when Johnny tries to shame her about working at the train station, Merlinka quickly responds: "So what? What's wrong with that? I am not killing or robbing anyone. People pay me because they want to. I don't have a mafia around me like you, to make steal or hurt people and make others cry. People happily give me their money."

73 Jelača, *Dislocated Screen Memory*, 117.

74 Ibid., 118.

75 The female protagonist in Wajda's film, Agnieszka (Krystyna Janda) fights to celebrate the fictional character Mateusz Birkut (Jerzy Radziwiłowicz), a bricklayer whose heroic life as a worker had been forgotten.

76 Jelača, *Dislocated Screen Memory*, 118.

77 The original title of the film was *One Kilometer of Prick*, but Žilnik changed the name before the film was first screened in Belgrade to pass more easily under the censor's nose. Žilnik in conversation with the author, August 13, 2019.

78 The entire interview is available on YouTube, see www.youtube.com/watch?v=WkbmGzQV7Qg (accessed 06/10/2018).

79 Saša Kesić in conversation with the author, August 11, 2018.

80 Ibid.

81 In 2014, Stevan Bodroža directed a play about Merlinka for the festival, *Merlinka's Confession*.

82 Helena Janečić in conversation with the author, July 30, 2020.

83 Ibid.

84 Ibid.

85 Janečić cited www.gay.hr as her platform for learning about gay issues at the time, but the website has since then gone through changes and legal disputes.

86 Helena Janečić in conversation with the author, July 30, 2020.

87 Ibid.

88 Ibid.

89 Ibid.

90 Ibid.
91 Helena Janečić, *Horny Dyke Na Rubu Konvencije/Horny Dyke on the Edge of Convention* (Zagreb: Domino, November, 2011), n.p.
92 Tatjana Pavlović, "Women in Croatia: Feminists, Nationalists, and Homosexuals," in Sabrina Ramet, ed., *Gender Politics in the Western Balkans: Women and Society in Yugoslavia and the Yugoslav Successor States* (University Park: Pennsylvania State University Press, 1999), 145.
93 Ibid.
94 Ibid.
95 Andrea Spehar, "The Lesbian Question," in Tanya Renne, ed., *Ana's Land: Sisterhood in Eastern Europe* (Boulder, CO: Westview Press, 1997), 208.
96 Ibid.
97 Batinić, *Women and Yugoslav Partisans*, 67.

4 Jugoslovenka in a sea of avant-garde machismo: a feminist reading of NSK

The Slovenian collective Neue Slowenische Kunst (New Slovenian Art, NSK) created some of the most politically provocative, transgressive, innovative, and influential art of the 1980s in Yugoslavia and the larger East European region, followed by an even more fertile international career in the post-Yugoslav context even today. Based in Ljubljana, NSK was founded in 1984 by three previously existing groups: Laibach (music), IRWIN (visual art), and Gledališče Sester Scipion Nasice (Scipion Nasice Sisters Theater, SNST) (theater). Laibach and IRWIN are still active to this day, while SNST disbanded in 1987, as it intended to do from its inception. Copious publications, exhibitions, and projects have grown out of the NSK collective, due in part to the diligence of its many members and the group's ability to stay relevant to contemporary politics, but there is a significant oversight in the historicizing of, and commentary on, NSK: the role of gender in their work. NSK prioritized militarism and macho culture in its iconography, creating work with a starkly masculine-gendered visual language. The extreme masculinity of their work can be linked to an aggressive, albeit tongue-in-cheek, critique of fascism and socialism in art and culture. In line with the traditions the collective critiqued, NSK often venerated male avant-garde heroes and male voices in the discourse on art and politics. Dušan Mandič's interest in working with feminist and queer content as early as the 1980s was exceptional for the group, as was the leadership role of Eda Čufer, the sole female founding member and a dramaturge/writer for NSK.[1]

In the comprehensive 2015 catalogue on NSK, *From Kapital to Capital Neue Slowenische Kunst: An Event of the Final Decade of Yugoslavia,* Dejan Kršić summarizes NSK's political project within the history of art:

> If you want to get to the bottom of it, the basic message of NSK represents a clear critique of the ideological propositions of high modernism and a comment on the crisis of the ideology of modernism in its final phase. We cannot over-emphasize the significance of the retrogarde as a project which aims at deconstructing the entire paradigm of Western European art in the modern

epoch. What is at stake is the truly alternative project of abandoning the entire system that has defined artistic practice since the Renaissance: The notion of the genius author is confronted with the idea of anonymous collective labor; instead of insisting on style one insists on method; instead of autonomy and the purposelessness of art its ideological function is emphasized ...[2]

How do we reconcile the omission of gender in this extensive list of "deconstructing the entire paradigm of Western European art in the modern epoch"? If NSK's notion of retrogarde meant a "free borrowing of the motives, images, [and] concepts from the history of art," then why did NSK not consider the foundational totalitarianism of gender within the political ideologies of art from which they so freely borrowed?[3] Why do contemporary art critics and historians still omit this prejudiced dimension of modernism and postmodernism? The stark male bravado of the NSK collective, with its members regularly showing up in business suits (IRWIN) or military uniforms (Laibach) at openings and at their concerts, often exclusively male and sometimes with one woman appearing as part of the collective or in an artwork—repeatedly unidentified, reduced to the background, and sometimes not even dressed—make for a bleak story about the lack of gender diversity within this otherwise politically subversive group from the 1980s to the present. As what many would consider the most important political art collective of the 1980s, the lack of gender equality or even gender awareness in the group speaks to the paradoxical foundation of Yugoslav socialism, which embraced women's emancipation while simultaneously remaining staunchly male-centered.

Never a self-proclaimed feminist, Eda Čufer, in her status as the only woman member of NSK, remains enigmatic and understudied. In a 1990 photograph by Jože Suhadolnik (Figure 4.1), Čufer appears as the sole woman in a group of fourteen men, an image (and gender dynamic) characteristic of those documenting the activities of NSK, Laibach, and IRWIN in the 1980s. This photo also situates the group within the religious sphere, as it was taken in a small church on top of a hill above Trbovlje on the occasion of the tenth anniversary of Laibach.[4] We must remember here that from its origin in 1980, Laibach emphasized the location of its founding in Trbovlje, a city with a history of violent encounters between fascists and communists, including the miners' strike in 1924 against the Organization of Yugoslav Nationalists.[5] Forestry and mining were major industries in Slovenia, each tending to have a male workforce and, by implication, skewing masculine in their social implications. Laibach embraced the image of the male miner as a theme in its work, and later IRWIN would hold a large exhibition in the mines of Trbovlje.[6] This politically loaded image of the male miner as a working-class antifascist hero propagated a masculine history of Slovenia and was the foundation of NSK's critical vision. As such, Čufer's singularity as a woman in this image of male

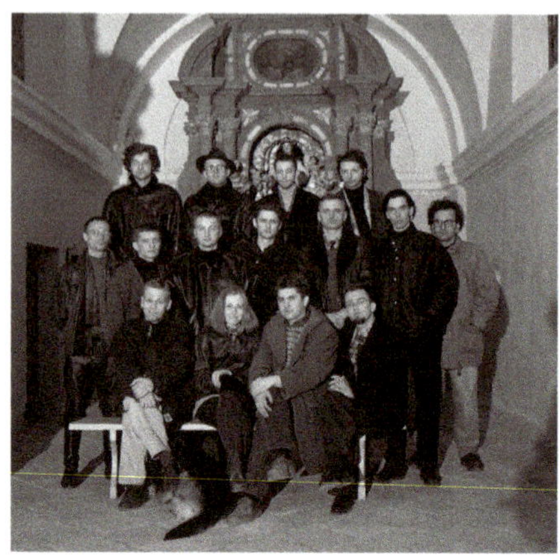

4.1 Eda Čufer with other NSK members, 1990. Kum Church, near Trbovlje, Slovenia. Photograph by Jože Suhadolnik.

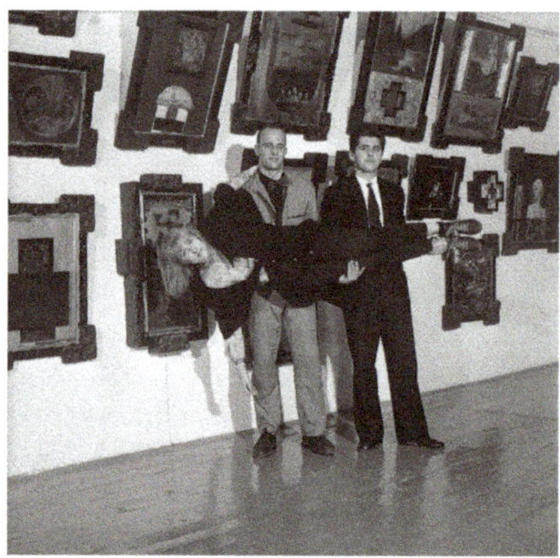

4.2 Eda Čufer, Dragan Živadinov, and Miran Mohar. *Was ist Kunst* at Equrna Gallery, Ljubljana, 1988. Photograph by Franci Virant.

artists is striking and dire at the same time, a perfectly palpable illustration of what it meant to be a female voice in the arts: alone, surrounded by men. One other photograph in the archive of NSK most forcefully drives home her embodiment of the gendered inequalities at the heart of NSK: Čufer being held horizontally by her male colleagues at the group's *Was ist Kunst* exhibition at Equrna Gallery in Ljubljana (Figure 4.2). Čufer's body signifies and also perpetuates the matrix of male hegemony, while her horizontality simultaneously embodies a different politic: that of equality and socialism.

While we must take into consideration NSK's commitment to male-centered art and its histories, this chapter injects gender into the collective's work, articulating the unspoken specter of masculinity in NSK's 1980s oeuvre while also situating femininity and women's political work as an occluded but decisive player in the history of NSK, especially the NSK collective's subgroup SNST, for which Čufer worked as a dramaturge and writer. Contrary to prevalent readings of their works, I center on this neglected perspective by first considering gender and the scarcity of feminist content in the collective's work, and then moving on to question what kind of emancipatory performance politics we can deduce from the gendered political content of SNST and NSK more broadly. This chapter asks: what role might Jugoslovenka have played in the history of SNST and NSK? Where can we situate her in the long shadow that this collective casts over art practice in former Yugoslavia?

Macho socialist art collective? Women and NSK

NSK and its subgroups, with the exception of SNST, were exclusively male-centered in the 1980s, not only with regard to their members but also in their visual programs. One of the most well-known examples of their work is the Youth Day Poster (1987) which involved NSK's design subgroup, New Collectivism, and which created a scandal.[7] While the question of gender was not prioritized as a political aspect of their intervention into Yugoslav propaganda at the time, the Youth Day poster scandal sheds light on the gendered visual paradigms of the group and wider Yugoslav society (Figure 4.3). New Collectivism participated in a call for poster designs for the annual Youth Day in 1987, which celebrated Yugoslavia and its idolized, albeit by then seven years deceased, leader Tito (see Introduction). The absurdity of such a massive youth celebration was exacerbated by the palpable tensions that had been persistently rising among the individual republics since Tito's death in 1980. In addition, the Communist Party was rife with corrupt politicians who upheld the veneer of a just and equitable socialist system while striving for individual power and aggravating divisions among the republics. When New Collectivism's poster was selected by the federal jury as the most politically appropriate design, it struck a nerve within this deteriorating system of socialist patriarchy.[8]

The scandal occurred when a letter to the Serbian daily newspaper *Politika*—the newspaper that had published the design—revealed the Youth Day poster to be identical to one by Nazi artist Richard Klein in 1936.[9] The only difference was an exchange in the symbols used: Klein's poster showed the swastika on the flag and neoclassical Third Reich architecture; New Collectivism replaced the Nazi flag with the national flag of socialist Yugoslavia and positioned the boy in a mountain landscape: Triglav in Slovenia.[10] This swapping of symbols was an offence to the ruling elite of Yugoslavia, who

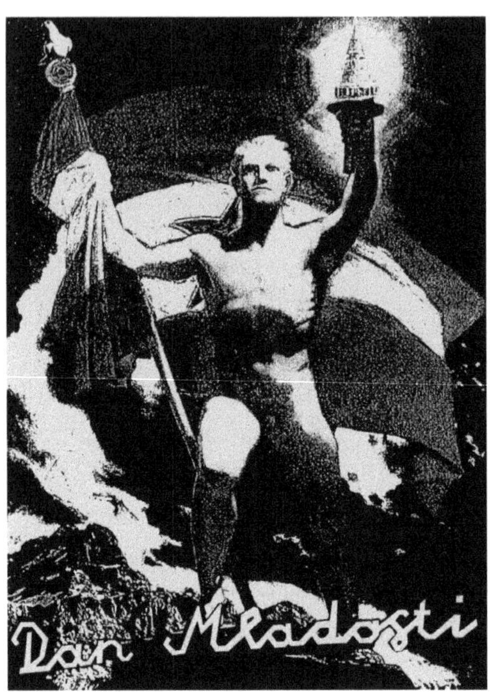

4.3   New Collectivism, *Dan Mladosti/Youth Day*, 1987. Silkscreen 100 x 70 cm, published by New Collectivism.

rejected the assumption that their aesthetic and political circumstances would have anything to do with Nazism or any other form of fascism. The federal jury of Yugoslavia was furious and tried unsuccessfully to put the members of New Collectivism in jail.[11] This was but one indication of how NSK used retrogarde aesthetics to intentionally corrode the categorizations of visual signifiers that support one ideology over another.

This corrosion and reimagination of historically established visual signifiers was already practiced by the music group Laibach in the early 1980s, another subgroup of NSK, when they used Malevich's suprematist "Black Cross" as armbands on the military uniforms they wore in public, as well as on poster designs, album covers, and performance backdrops. Laibach's appropriation of the black cross has been interpreted as a provocative way of addressing totalitarianism, conjuring the swastika worn on German Nazi uniforms while also parading the idea that fascist tendencies can be found in all political and artistic ideologies and manifestos, especially in their own local context. This reading of their work is founded on Slavoj Žižek's well-known argument that Laibach and NSK aggravated "the ruling ideology

NOT [through] ironic imitation, but [through] over-identification with it—and thereby suspending its efficiency."[12] In this line of thinking, New Collectivism's Youth Day poster and Laibach's retrograde artistic tactics showed a keen awareness of the ideological problems in socialist Yugoslavia, in which "National Socialism, German cultural identity, and political repression" were banned from public discourses, but lurked in the public's subconscious and in the political paradigms of socialism.[13]

While it is true that patriarchal nationalism was fundamentally tied to the totalitarianism NSK and Laibach critiqued in their works, these group's embodied overidentification with masculinity and sexism (both explicitly and through systems in which these ideologies were perpetuated) did not suspend patriarchy's efficiency or power. In New Collectivism's appropriation of totalitarian visual culture, for example, there is a very recognizable masculinist and heroic political-aesthetic tradition at play here: while in the post-World War II era, usually a male and female youth would appear on propaganda—for example, carrying the relay baton for Tito on his birthday—New Collectivism's Youth Day poster featured only a boy. Vital landmarks in Yugoslav feminist and lesbian activism were also happening at the time, such as the organization of the first feminist Yugoslav meeting in Ljubljana in 1987. The meeting was focused on two topics, "violence against women and lesbian love," which, according to Lepa Mlađenović, "were completely new on the socialist 'women's question'" agenda.[14] New Collectivism's poster had no interest in the woman question, or in intervening in that aspect of socialism.

Poignantly, that disinterest in NSK's work speaks powerfully to this gendered blind spot in Yugoslav art and is indicative of the patriarchy at the root of the socialist system. Borut Vogelnik from IRWIN (NSK) remembers: "at that time, [feminism was] already very relevant in the west, especially in … the art community, but [it was] not yet introduced in the everyday discourse in our country [Yugoslavia]." He added: "we were not part of the same cultural landscape. We were simply not aware that we excluded women."[15] Vogelnik's statement shows that, despite Yugoslavia's history of women's accomplishments in art, culture, or even the military, especially during the antifascist struggle in World War II, the necessity for gender equality had not reached the public and was still considered an import from the West. As such, the Youth Day poster was not only prophetic in parading the fascism and nationalism underlying the socialist system that would fully ignite in the 1990s, but it equally displayed the male-centered fantasy and workings of the socialist system. Considering that it was powerful men in politics who ended up fragmenting the country through civil war, the poster's omission of women also reveals that the deteriorating socialist system of Yugoslavia, including its cultural avant-garde, were constricted in their political vision: the past and future of Yugoslavia appear through the prism of male youth.

While NSK as a group was not interested in feminism in the 1980s, the collective did intersect with feminist organizing and knowledge making in spaces that could be called the "alternative" or "underground" cultural milieus of Yugoslav socialism, especially in Ljubljana, where the underground gay and lesbian movement flourished in the 1980s (see Chapter 3). But to be part of that underground also meant to be against state-sanctioned cultural production, especially since the underground culture in Ljubljana was resisting the conservative rise of nationalism and Slovenia's Germanic roots, a focal point of NSK's practice. NSK's covert art and actions aimed at exposing modes of distribution and circulation in culture, and especially at the lurking fascism in avant-garde and state-sanctioned art. Their artistic interventions were elite in intellectual content and deliberately shut out certain publics who were not "in the know." In part, these modes of art making were so effective because their works mimicked familiar visual artistic paradigms, such as social realism and Nazi art, but were often presented to publics who did not know the history or political background of those artistic paradigms. Frequently situated in public or working-class spaces, such as city squares or even inside an active mine in Trbovlje, NSK's artworks were "public" in appearance, but "underground" in content. That is to say, NSK deliberately activated tensions between aesthetics and politics in vigilantly manufactured music and theater performances, art exhibitions, and artistic interventions in political spectacles like the Youth Day celebration in public, but their artistic power came from the friction between the "underground" Yugoslav alternative and a repeatedly confused public.

NSK operated in the underground sphere of Yugoslavia, which ran counter to the socialist establishment, and which was propelled by the labor of many women curators, performers, and artists (see Chapter 3). NSK's lack of engagement with, or lack of interest in, the "woman question" in socialism became most obvious when women made appearances in their works. In 1982, Laibach made its first, and to my knowledge, only work overtly centered on the political position of women in socialist Yugoslavia and socialism in general. In a black-and-white poster titled *Politizacija Žena* (*The Politicizing of Women*), the concept of women and their politicization remains abstract and is at best conceptual, at worst completely disinterested in the question of women (Figure 4.4). "We didn't do it for any particular reason," Laibach member Ivan Novak remembers, adding: "[but] people did not expect something like that from Laibach."[16] If the politicization of women—let alone the discussion of gender—was outside the realm of Laibach's work, the collective did deliver in other regards, such as incorporating its signature black cross, a recurring nod to Malevich. Returning to *The Politicizing of Women*, the question of womanhood is decidedly flattened to fit Laibach's play on political ambiguity. In other words, they are overly masculine but do not, as Žižek otherwise claims, disturb or suspend its oppressiveness.

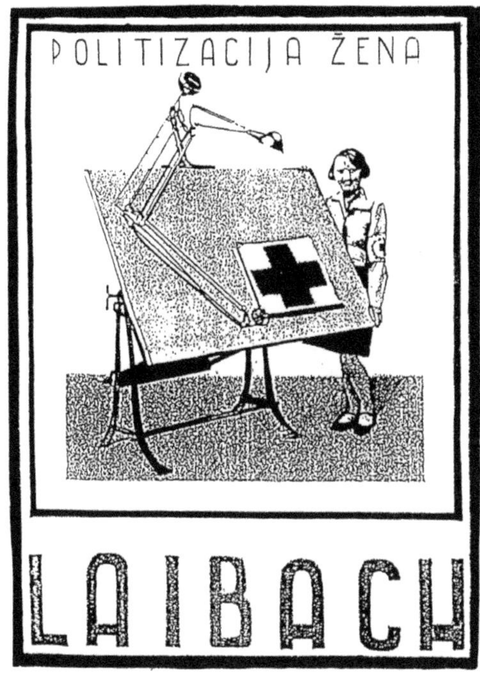

Laibach, *The Politicizing of Women*, 1982.   **4.4**

Looking at the work visually, this becomes clear: adjacent to the desk with the black cross stands a woman in uniform with short hair. On her left arm, she wears a sleeve with the same black cross, typical of Laibach's own uniforms during this time; this is also replicated on the table in a sheet of white paper featuring the cross. Her demeanor is similar to that of a young schoolgirl who is showing her creation to the teacher or class, or a young teacher who is presenting art to her class. The geometric and elegant modernist light clipped onto the drawing board accentuates the sense of a design or architectural studio. Her slender body is partly concealed behind the drawing board, her legs set together in a modest contrapposto, and her facial expression cannot be discerned, obscured by a lack of detail in this high-contrast print. Like the stark aesthetic choices of modernist angularity common in styles of abstraction such as the Bauhaus, the politicizing of woman in Laibach's vision renders her appearance stiff and abstract. This woman is emptied of any gendered experience. She blends in with the background and is diminished by the desk and even its clip-on lamp, connoting that she is part of the infrastructure here, not the protagonist. Even her legs blend in with the floor's shading, and her crotch is hidden beneath the table, intensifying the impression that she is merely an empty vessel representing male ideology, marked by the very black cross on her arm she serves. The main visual protagonists of *The Politicizing of Women* are Malevich's black cross and Laibach, whose name is written in large and bold letters at the bottom. It doesn't take much to realize that this image is not about women at all.

The Politicizing of Women is a creation of an image of woman by men, but even within that presentation, this image ignores her humanity altogether, unless we read her position as a docile, compliant yes-[wo]man, serving up the visual regime of Laibach. The uniform she wears reminds us that she is attached to an authority, subsumed in the collective and her individuality eclipsed by ideology. One might surmise that woman becomes a background concept, and her politicization is instrumentalized for men's art, perhaps mirroring the Yugoslav socialist system's complicated history of women's emancipation; a visual testimony to how women's issues were pushed more and more to the background by the ruling establishment from the onset, leading many women to abandon progress for women in order to aid the universal aims of socialism (see Introduction).

Although Laibach did not conceptualize their political art around gender, they did collaborate with numerous women, one of whom was Anja Rupel from Videosex (see Chapter 3). Laibach designed covers for Videosex's musical albums and produced two songs with Rupel relevant for this chapter: the predominantly instrumental song "Slovenska Žena" ("Slovenian Woman") in 1984, and the song and music video "Across the Universe" (1989), a cover of the famous Beatles' song.[17] While contemporary feminist researchers might wish to find a connection to the 1926 book *Slovenska Žena*, edited by Minka Govekar, such a reading is tenuous and optimistic at best.[18] Confirmed by Novak as highly unlikely, he instead stressed that Laibach produced this song to provoke the authorities, because "during the [unified] time of Yugoslavia, republics were avoiding using national[istic] adjectives like Slovenian, Croatian, Serbian, etc."[19] Novak further noted about Laibach's relationship to women:

> Laibach was very much projecting an image of an all-male group and I know that we tried to include women in the picture quite early on, but it took some time before they became [a] relevant part of the group and also on stage. Meanwhile, creatively they were always part of it, either as designers, painters, writers or theoreticians.[20]

Laibach's political critique of the arts and the state in the 1980s did not prioritize a critique of gender or an awareness of the exploitation of women's work, as the group itself seems to have upheld this gender inequality, even if unintentionally. The political critique of Yugoslavia was a more pressing priority, notwithstanding the fact that feminist and lesbian circles emerged in Yugoslavia in the 1980s, such as the founding of the feminist group Lilit in 1985 at K4 in Ljubljana (see Chapter 3). Feminists often were part of the NSK circles, one example being the group's frequent work with queer-feminist artist and curator Marina Gržinić. However, when I asked Novak why they collaborated with Rupel to sing the cover of "Across the Universe," he replied: "Anja was a good singer and had all the sex appeal we were looking for in this song."[21] This honest answer about Rupel's other key quality besides her competence as a vocalist—"all the sex appeal" Laibach needed for their song—reminds us that women in socialist countries just as in the West could often only gain recognition and ascend if deemed attractive enough, and then, only if supported by their much better-established male colleagues. While Rupel's contribution is relegated in no small part to her "sexy" appearance in Laibach's video, my book illustrates that women in Yugoslavia were crucial to social and aesthetic progress, especially when critical of norms; yet, they have remained perpetually on the outside due to gender-biased histories, which often unwittingly reproduce the systemically and culturally reinforced inequalities keeping women's contributions in the shadows of men's achievements.

Sometimes, women would not ascend at all, but instead became placeholders for male bodies. As Novak recalls, Laibach occasionally included women in their formation, such as in a set of images taken by Peter Anderson in 1984 at Karl Marx's grave in Highgate Cemetery in London (Figure 4.5). In the photographs, a woman appears in men's clothing, with a military haircut, a button-up shirt and tie, taking on the identical pose of the Laibach members. Laibach had asked her to stand in for the photograph when one of their members could not join them. Newspapers and art historians seldom observed any difference. When pressed on the issue of gender today, Novak has some contradictory thoughts: "We were not interested in masculinity, we just happen to be a male group. But we introduced women as soon as we could. But audiences saw [us] as a male group even when there was a woman [there]."[22] Perhaps audiences only saw Laibach as a male group because it, as well as its male protagonists, overwhelmingly prioritized a masculinist aesthetic? It took weeks of searching for me to learn the woman's name, and even then, I only discovered her first name: Nicolle, said to be from an "art collective" in Amsterdam.[23] The identity and gender of Nicolle at Karl Marx's grave thus remained concealed by normative notions of militarist masculinity so pervasive that audiences would likely not question a female body carrying that visual signifier of masculinity because they assume male to be the default position. While such play with gender can be wonderfully subversive, it also

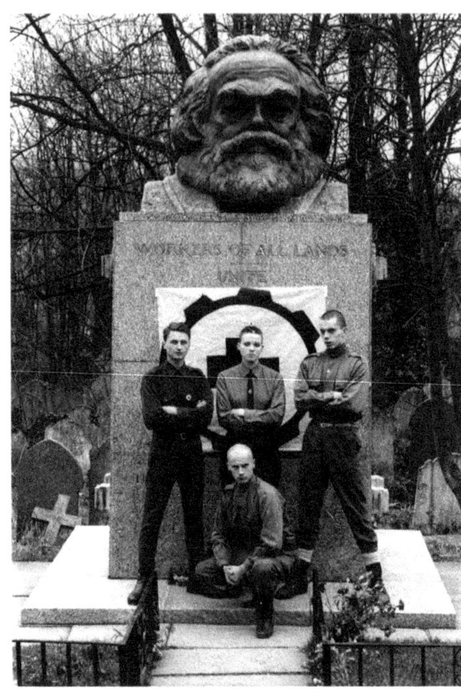

4.5   Peter Anderson, Laibach, 1984, at Karl Marx's grave in Highgate Cemetery, London.

points to Yugoslav socialism's paradoxical relationship to gender equality: gender norms could be broken on surface level, but patriarchal power staunchly remained the operative visual regime. As Marx's huge head looms above the four obedient bodies in one of the photographs (Figure 4.5), the woman is compliant to an even greater sacrificial extent: she is not working with Laibach, but for them, entirely irrelevant as a gendered person. Objectified as a stand-in for a male body—or maybe even just a body in service of a male agenda—Nicolle served as a vessel for male identity in Laibach's art.

In the case of IRWIN, the situation was similar. One of the most obvious and provocative examples of Yugoslav masculinity in IRWIN's art included a two-sided work, *L'Etat* (*The State*) (1988). Looking at only one side, which is an homage to Yves Klein, it shows members of IRWIN dressed in suits accompanied by an unidentified naked woman wearing International Klein Blue pumps, all staged in front of a backdrop of an unfinished wall painting in International Klein Blue. The naked woman holds a blue shirt disguising her pubis, and looks, not at the camera, but to the side (Figure 4.6).

By then, Yves Klein had already been widely critiqued by feminist art historians for his instrumentalist use of women's bodies as "living brushes."

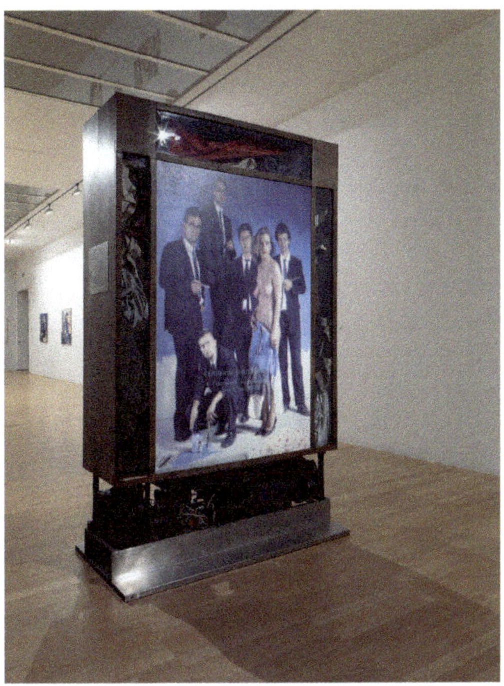

IRWIN, in collaboration with Bogoslav Kalaš, *L'Etat (The State)*, 1988.   **4.6**
Mixed media, 260 x 170 x 50 cm.
Collaborators: Brane Kovič, Jure Dobrila.

These criticisms would likely have been known to IRWIN's members if their facetious decision to demonstratively hold brushes in their hands is any indication. However, much of what Irwin's *The State* connotes is not far from the objectification of women's bodies in Klein's work. While the woman's naked body was central, her identity here too seems to have been irrelevant to the concept and execution of the piece. According to Miran Mohar, the unidentified woman in the photograph was Slovenian theater actress Damjana Černe, who also participated in SNST performances, to which I will return later in the chapter.[24] If we are to read this image of the state generously, and understand her body as a platform for IRWIN's politics, this builds on the trope of countries as female-gendered in art, such as *Liberty Leading the People* in France or the Statue of Liberty in the USA. Here, we could say she signified the gender discrepancy at the basis of the Yugoslav state and of culture. A generous reading would also give the male artists credit for embodying such a critique by reproducing sexist themes in modern art and culture. Unfortunately, such a reading does not account for the subtext of this work: gender inequality was deeply ingrained in the patriarchal apparatus of Yugoslav socialism and its artists, so much so that it went completely unquestioned. What stands out here is that they identified the side with the naked woman as "East," while the other side—"West"—has a black background with floating male heads.

The starkest distinction between the two sides is palpable in Klein's bright blue color and the naked female body. The side vitrines on the East side of *The State* hold male dress pants, ties, and on top, presumably the Yugoslav flag, folded in a manner that shows only its red and white colors, while the International Klein Blue color, used as the backdrop, completes it. What we might take away from this construction of "the State" in the East is that masculinity is auratic—and as mythical and erotically charged as its leader Tito—and that it is men in business suits who get to intervene in histories of art and culture in Yugoslavia, while women remain tied to long established methods of representation: the nude, unidentified, and allegorical at best.

In one work from the late 1990s, however, a Yugoslav woman whose identity was so well established it could not be reduced to anonymity became the center of IRWIN's artistic inquiry. In the notorious image of IRWIN with Marina Abramović, shot by Bojan Brecelj, the five by then middle-aged members of IRWIN appear in a state of partial undress, gathered around Abramović on a hotel bed, in what looks to be a moment just prior to an orgy (Figure 4.7). She is the center of the image this time, the favored protagonist, as the men are all turned toward her and touching her. Wearing a black negligee corset with black tights and lying with her legs spread, Abramović looks straight at the camera with a serious expression, ignoring the men around her. Although she is marked by the signature black cross armband we saw in *The Politicizing of Women*, she is a far more recognizable entity than those men or their tiny black cross replicas of Malevich could be: a powerful female name in the arts globally, Abramović outshines them all as an instantly recognized artist, more famous than IRWIN, and perhaps even more famous than Malevich at the time. Abramović, IRWIN, and the photographer Brecelj conceptualized the work as a critique of authorship and celebrity culture in the visual arts, reproducing the exact same photograph, three times, each signed by one of the participating artists (Abramović, Brecelj, IRWIN), and each image priced according to each artist's market rate."[25] As such, the idea of aura as a sellable product re-emerges in another homage to Klein's selling of "immaterial pictorial sensibility zones" (1959–1962), where each value is determined by the signature of the artist. The three registers of authorship and hierarchy play out in the image: Abramović, a single author and celebrated artist; IRWIN, a collective that depends on its members' quasi-anonymity; and Brecelj, a relatively unknown photographer. The image captures something

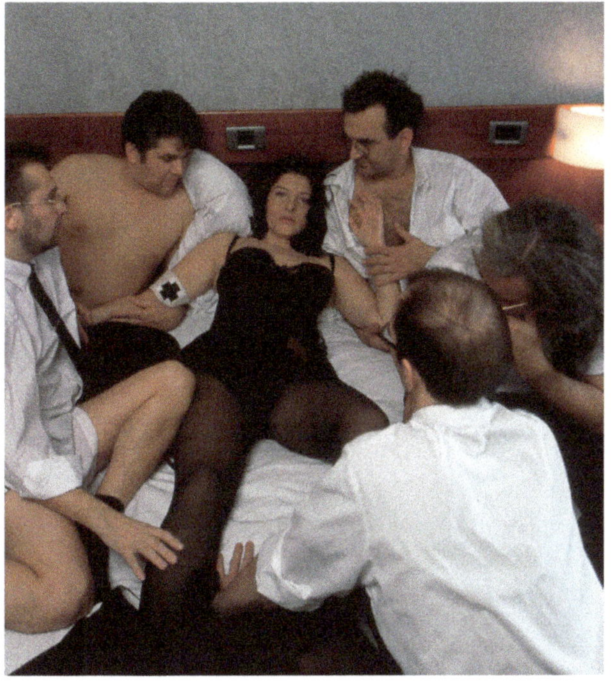

IRWIN and Marina Abramović, *Namepickers*, 1999. Photo: Bojan Brecelj.   **4.7**

greater than this conceptual play on signature and market value, exhibiting the crude cringe-worthiness of art and its commodification through the bodies of artists.

As noted, IRWIN (as part of NSK) had a long and established history of engaging with totalitarian aesthetics and politics in this manner. What I want to single out here is how Abramović troubles stigmas surrounding prostitution and the great artistic taboo of selling out. This work provoked moralized accusations against her willingness to sell herself for her art and for fame. These were common charges leveled at people who left "the Balkans," "the East," or other cultural "peripheries" in the global art market. Her embrace of these charges, and the sexism at their base, are the most striking elements of this photograph. The discomfort of looking at it, however, lies in the fact that whereas she, and her IRWIN colleagues, all debase themselves similarly for the sake of art, for men such debasement rarely carries the same negative connotations as it does for women. Abramović willingly puts her body at the center of their objectification. It might leave a bad taste in feminists' mouths, but it also challenges us to contend with the fact that people in the arts, as in every other sector of society, are deeply enmeshed in the order of patriarchy, and that women are players in that game, willingly and unwillingly.

Sisters in the underground: the feminine and the spiritual as resistance

While a feminist critique of NSK is easy to make by pointing to what the collective did not address or include in the 1970s and 1980s, particularly in the examples given, understanding what generative role women and femininity might have played under such conditions is more challenging. In this section, I turn exclusively to Eda Čufer and her work with SNST. Čufer remained underacknowledged and undercelebrated throughout her career and work with NSK, while also deliberately staying relatively underground in her activities. Neither devalued as an instrument representing sexual desire in art, nor placed in the position of the muse, Čufer, and her work with SNST, produces a crack in the masculinist foundation of the group, a point of access to explore the gender politics of NSK, the alternative art scene, and Yugoslavia.

SNST held the monumental mission of transmuting the dysfunctional Yugoslav state by expanding ideas about performance, theater, and participation. Strikingly, the group gendered itself female: Scipion Nasice *Sisters* Theater. Despite its notoriously aggressive founding leader, Dragan Živadinov, the performances and conceptualizations of SNST signaled a discord with dominant male visibility in the arts, while staying committed to NSK's political critique of authoritarianist nationalism.[26] Following his departure from the academy because one of his performances was rejected, Živadinov invited Čufer and Mohar to create the SNST in 1983.[27] By the early 1980s, the impulse for violence in experimental performance art and theater was common in the East and West, and SNST shared a common figure of inspiration, Antonin Artaud. The Italian name SNST evoked Antonin Artaud's *Theatre and its Double* (1938), which discusses the Roman republican politician Publius Cornelius Scipio Nasica Corculum, who in 151 BC destroyed the Roman stone theater because it "represented the site where old pagan rituals tend to survive although in modified forms."[28] Inspired by Artaud's conceptualization of the Roman politician as a Christian ruler, SNST explicitly introduced the religious dimension and transformed the historical destruction of theater into an experimental rejection of theater as a state-dependent institution altogether.

Monroe has characterized Živadinov's style as "brutal" and "violent," "combined with an explicit sense of mysticism and utopianism, and an attempt to insist on drama as a heroic form."[29] While this element of SNST's work resonates with masculinist strategies of domination by Laibach, here I want to draw on other aspects that intimated a different emphasis, namely that of its position as "sisters." The founding document from 1983 offers no insight into why this theater group was gendered female, as "sisters" of the notorious

Roman politician, nor why the SNST might be, metaphorically, an "order" of nuns attached to the Roman leader despite only having one female founding member, the dramaturge Čufer. She had studied dramaturgy, a field that was conservative and dominated by men in Yugoslavia at the time. It is vital to underscore here that the theater faction of the NSK collective was the only group that explicitly identified as female, even if simply in their name. Yet in no literature to my knowledge is this fact acknowledged or discussed. Perhaps this was due in part to the group's behavior; it preserved an air of mystery, remaining militantly silent about members' names, its political motives, or the actual meaning of its work from early on. In his review of SNST's first play, *Retrogarde Event Hinkemann* (1984), Slovene writer and theater director Tone Peršak stressed this radical resistance to legibility and individualism within the group: "It must also be pointed out that respecting the wishes of those I spoke to, no names will be mentioned, including the names of actors performing in the show."[30] This anonymity reinforced the commitment to activating ideals of socialist collectivism in lieu of individual fame at the heart of bourgeois aesthetics.

When, more than three decades after their founding, I asked Čufer about her position as a woman in NSK, she diverted attention away from herself and foregrounded the gendering of SNST as female instead: "'Sisters' in the name plays with the moral authority and authoritarianism of the Church. Similar to Laibach, who appropriated the [male] authoritative voice of the state, SNST appropriated the voice of religious authority in its feminine expression (Sisters)."[31] Čufer's statement begs the question that if we are not to focus on Čufer alone, how do we interpret the complexity of this "religious authority in its feminine expression"? It is generally understood that nuns in the Christian Orthodox and Catholic traditions, are expected to live a life of chastity and obedience, subordinating themselves to patriarchal institutional religious authority and imposing this authority on generations of children as well. But later historical analyses have begun to reconsider this narrow description of nuns. According to historian of religion Ulrike Strasser, nuns have a long history of agency, which they exercised by "[invoking] obedience to a higher authority, be it the abbess or God, to defy the dictates of another [institutional] authority, family, Church, or state."[32] Sometimes these forms of defiance would be public, but mostly they were secret. Moreover, nuns' contributions to what Strasser calls the "history of the modernizing state" have been systematically erased, limiting their roles to "merely" religious matters, ignoring the larger reach of their actions and the entanglements of religion and the state. As she notes: "Religion became privatized and feminized as the state became secular, modern, and masculine."[33] The religious feminine of SNST that Čufer evokes can be, under Yugoslav socialism, understood as a transmuted, alternative feminist sphere of experimental theater that construed a simulated religious space as an experiential moment of defiance for a select audience within the alternative underground of Yugoslav culture.

For the young generation coming together in SNST as members, official state theater was instrumentalized by the government as "headquarters of nationalist ideology."[34] In the context of Tito's Yugoslavia, which united the six republics and their respective local theaters under the umbrella of the unified socialist state, the group charged Yugoslavia with relying on nineteenth-century bourgeois models of nationalism in theater at its very foundation, calling it, "the hegemonic cultural institutional base of the late socialist state."[35] To distance themselves from such hegemonic institutions, SNST's founding came with a self-ascribed expiration date: "Its activities are limited to a period of four years. The self-abolition of the Scipion Nasice Sisters Theatre is scheduled for 1987."[36] This was built into the concept of the group in order to help members resist falling into the trap of monumentalizing themselves, as the Yugoslav state had done. The group planned only three performances, conceptualized in the following way:

1) Underground (*Retrogarde Event Hinkemann*, January 1984) (performed at an apartment)
2) Resurrection (*Retrogarde Event Marija Nablocka*, May 1985) (performed in a private residence)
3) Retro-Classics (*Retrogarde Event Baptism Under Triglav*, September 1985 to October 1986) (performed in public, at Cankarjev Dom, the largest convention, congress and culture center in Slovenia.)

These three plays were to be followed by *Act of Self-Destruction* from September 1986 to May 1987, which was achieved in an unexpected, dramatic way through a poster design competition. Working with New Collectivism and IRWIN, SNST had been invited by the League of Socialist Youth of Slovenia to perform for Yugoslavia's Youth Day celebration. But this performance never transpired, as the above-mentioned poster scandal for them was the conceptual endgame. The poster's aesthetic and political methods, like those of NSK, had "touched the vortex of real history, and inscribed itself into the irreversible process through which Yugoslavia, in just a few years, dissolved in front of its petrified citizenry."[37]

For SNST, the fact that the Yugoslav state clung to bourgeois, nationalist theater was a great betrayal of the socialist ideal that had first motivated the internationalism of the Yugoslav project during World War II: namely, that socialist Yugoslavia was to be anti-nationalist, antifascist, and anti-authoritarian. By adhering to the insidious pull of nationalism, Tito's Yugoslavia was replicating the very systems of power that the antifascist partisans fought against in World War II, despite its pan-ethnic and multinational structure and *de jure* advocacy of gender equality. SNST wanted to resist the nationalist institution of theater and intervene in a conservative tradition of passive viewers that helps to enable nationalism. Drawing on Bertolt Brecht's concept and techniques of distantiation (*Entfremdung*) in his epic theater, the group pushed it even further by introducing "retrogardism." Retrogardism was understood as "a revitalization of the avant-garde," a return to radical socialist ideas of equality, anti-capitalism, and antifascism, especially in historical and (failed) utopian avant-garde movements of Russian constructivism and suprematism. SNST critiqued the use of nationalist rhetoric and policies to uphold state power; many in the alternative art scene thought that the Yugoslav state had hijacked the utopian possibilities of socialism and corrupted them with authoritarian control. Resisting the official cultural program of the state, SNST returned to the promises of socialism as enacted through retrogardism: "The group's ultimate task was thus to adjust the existing dysfunctional state apparatuses with the true (aesthetic) ideology of the (impossible) state."[38] Retrogardism conveyed an ironic play on avant-gardism—especially potent because of its military metaphor and history of political instrumentalization—while still a serious mode scrutinizing and untangling the authoritarian politics of art.

SNST's first performance in 1984, *Retrogarde Event Hinkemann*, makes clear how significant it was that members chose to embody their status as retrogarde artists in a religious sphere that had been overtly transvalued as feminized and privatized in the Yugoslav context, though ultimately also more complexly positioned in the larger Yugoslav political psyche. As announced in their manifesto, the group did not use a theater stage; instead, they used a transformed apartment at Titova cesta 56 in Ljubljana as their venue. Relying on word of mouth and postal mail, they invited twenty-nine people who, upon arrival, "were directed to the scene of the event by a PRIEST, an ARMY OFFICER, and a SISTER."[39] Čufer recalled, "We always carefully choreographed the transition from the secular space of the street, town, urban sphere to the 'holy' space of theatre."[40] This induction into the holy space by a priest (Christian authority), an army officer (state authority), and a *sister* (moral authority) might be read as a prophetic indication of how the subordination of religion to the secular socialist state would, just some five years later, explode into ethno-religious genocides and war.

In the 1980s, when SNST began their performance works, religious uprisings gradually became major co-agents of nationalism in Serbia and Croatia in the underground, most famously in the politicized grievances by Serbian Orthodox nuns in Kosovo about Kosovo-Albanian Muslim men attacking them. By 1989, as we have seen with Gržinić and Šmid's *Bilocations* (see Chapter 3), the Yugoslav State Army would intervene against Kosovo Albanians on behalf of Milošević's political Serb Orthodox following, making it palpable that religion would be at the forefront of the wars and genocides to come (see also Chapter 5). It is within this complicated context of Yugoslav socialism that we must consider the question of religious politics and its feminine expression within SNST. In refusing to repress religion and instead making it a conduit for a feminist socialist politics through a renovated theater practice, these performances commented presciently on the possibility of incipient religious violence and how it might be counteracted.

It is also constructive to draw a distinction between Laibach and SNST here: while Laibach was aggressively public with their works, SNST retreated from publicity, catering to smaller audiences and remaining more underground until its final performance at Cankarjev Dom in Ljubljana, Slovenia's largest cultural center, which was opened in the early 1980s and which was an apparatus of political power.[41] Their decision to stay more underground in the beginning is significant in relation to Laibach. As discussed, Laibach was known for its use of Malevich's suprematist *Black Cross*, playing with it as a symbol of totalitarianism. Members often wore the black cross on white armbands on uniforms, not just in performances but in public when shopping, frequenting cafés, and visiting art openings. Additionally, Laibach often referred to Malevich on cassette and vinyl covers, paintings, and in its general logo. Members were also known for provoking the authorities with their use of swastikas, such as when their 1983 exhibition, *Ausstellung Laibach Kunst—The Regime Trans-Avant-Garde* at the Expanded Media Gallery in Zagreb, was shut down for displaying a coffee cup with a swastika, or when in the same year the police interfered with their concert at the Zagreb Music Biennale for screening films of Tito side by side with erotic films.[42] Contrary to such overt public provocations, SNST's ritualism and feminized space of religious authority were deliberately subtle, with the group remaining covert in its inception period; one might even argue that such underground work touched something in the Yugoslav society's unconscious, seeking the desire for authoritarianism within hidden, traumatized, and repressed parts of society.

This is especially pertinent given the topic of *Retrogarde Event Hinkemann*, an homage to the antifascist play written by left-wing expressionist Ernst Toller during the nationalist surge in Germany, centered on an emasculated and traumatized soldier called Eugene Hinkemann (Figure 4.9). Toller wrote *Hinkemann* during his 1921–1922 imprisonment in Niederschönenfeld, Germany. Toller's life experience of fighting in World War I, along with the surge of nationalism and socialism in the immediate postwar era, found expression in the wounded masculinity of the main protagonist, Eugene Hinkemann:

> Ernst Toller, who had been studying law in Grenoble, rushed home to enlist in the Kaiser's army. After witnessing the horrors of war firsthand, getting seriously wounded, and suffering a complete physical and psychological

collapse, he was disabused of his youthful nationalist political leanings and embraced revolutionary change. In 1919, he joined the leadership of the short-lived Bavarian Soviet Republic in Munich, serving six days as its president, before being captured, tried for treason, and sentenced to five years in prison. … The play recounts the unthinkable, the fate of a man returned home from the War with his genitals blown off … the desperate unemployed protagonist, Eugene Hinkemann, accepts a job as a carnival strongman biting off the heads of live mice and rats.[43]

SNST adopted this story in a set of "one-minute dramas," which were categorized as theater, ideology, religion, or art, and which were performed by three actors: Damjana Grašič, Jonas Žnidarršič, and Brane Završan. Čufer remembers: "Grašič was the main actress in all three performances and represented SNST as an actress, iconically. We invited her to become a member of the group, but she refused. She had a knack for Brechtian technique, which was not taught in school."[44] As the play was designed to take place in an apartment, the "actors could hardly move [and were] situated in a specially built iron stage structure."[45] As such, the experience of the play itself—in a domestic setting with a small audience gathered through clandestine advertising—was intimate and close and included the sacrificial use of a dead fish, which at one point in the play "symbolise[d] a child and was then symbolically slaughtered, submerged in water and sacrificed all over again when an anonymous hand pierced a plastic bag filled with water suspended from the ceiling."[46] These visual and thematic elements operate as a feminine object that is conjured through evocations of birth, placing the performance squarely within the realm of the wet, dark, and emotional underground marked female.

While in his review Peršak merely addressed Hinkemann's injury as "physical and … moral decrepitude" due to war,[47] he likened SNST's anonymity and the group's decision to remain "underground" as a way to avoid surrendering to "self-castration."[48] In other words, SNST's decision to go underground allowed their work to rise to the level of revolutionary art and not be auto-mutilated by participation in any of the conventions of bourgeois, nationalist culture. He explains:

Since the group does not wish to constitute itself in an ordinary, well-established and socially recognized way, it clearly maintains that conceding to such ways is a form of self-castration. The reason for the underground and conspiracy, following the example of underground political parties and anarchist terrorist groups, can be found in and justified by the concept of art as ideology (a revolutionary one, of course). The formulation is understood as an attempt at replacing political ideologies with art as a new integrative and revolutionary force or consciousness that creates a vision of the new world with equal efficiency in the manner of political ideologies. The formulation therefore contains the idea of the insufficiency of all contemporary political ideologies and their destructive practices.[49]

While the conclusions Peršak drew about the underground status of SNST have been widely accepted, especially members' resistance to becoming subsumed in the violence of state-sanctioned political theater ideology, I want to push against his gendered theorization of that very underground artistic resistance, which he classifies as an intact (non-castrated) masculinity, for the group he describes was, after all, the Scipion Nasice *Sisters* Theater. If the Sisters succeeded in avoiding subsumption into the nineteenth-century nationalist bourgeois state theater, and instead "replaced political ideologies with art as a new integrative and revolutionary force," one might argue that the group did so *because* it refused the masculinist, phallocentric "rise" within the patriarchal nationalist Yugoslav state theater. To read against his characterization of castration as a negative lack is also to remember that it was Toller's war wounds that have been credited with changing "his youthful nationalist political leanings" to an "embrace [of] revolutionary change." Can we then read the wound, the castration, as a complex metaphor for a positive lack?

Despite being theorized ten years after SNST's *Hinkemann*, Judith Butler's notion of the lesbian phallus offers a theoretical framework to understand this positive lack. Butler's theory destabilizes Lacanian assumptions about an intact phallus within the anatomy of a man, or the objectification of a woman who stands in for that phallus.[50] We see Toller's protagonist Hinkemann, castrated by a nationalist war, fittingly finding a new life in the circus. He lives in a nightmarish fantasy world that requires him to enact an abject performance of masculinity as a "homunculus." But what if this mockery of mutilated masculinity can also open onto an economy that doesn't revolve around a positivized, individuated phallus? This may be in keeping with Jordana Rosenberg's reading of the lesbian phallus, which she argues is also always imaginary yet nonetheless forceful and real: "The lesbian phallus becomes a joke at the expense of the visual field."[51] Hinkemann's desperate attempts to cling to his masculinity only serve to degrade him and his nation. As stated ironically in Teller's play once more:

> Homunculus, the German Bearman! Devours living rats and mice before your very eyes! The German hero! The pinnacle of German culture! The peak of German manhood! German strength! The darling of fashionable ladies the world over. … You can't say you've seen Europe, if you haven't seen The Homunculus![52]

SNST's decision to remain underground in the beginning, not to "rise," can indeed be interpreted as its most feminine, underground activity: the lesbian phallus that remains invisible and undetected, part of a recessed, collective scene of desire and agency, rather than wielded in the register of spectacle by privileged individuals. Here, the feminist emancipatory potential lies in conspiracy, in the ability to abdicate the seductive power of fame and self-glorification and instead remain within the underground. That conspiracy ended when SNST began to perform for the larger public, which is also when the group disbanded.

This reading also summons Luce Irigaray, who, in *Marine Lover of Friedrich Nietzsche* (1980), made a chief distinction between men's propensity to seek land and bridges as expressions of their power, and women's manifestation in the earth-bound substance of water, uncontrollable and undeniably life-giving. In Chapter 1, I have commented on the significance of this gendered distinction in Raša Todosijević's work *Drinking Water* (1974), in which the artist drinks and vomits water while trying to adjust his breathing to a dying fish on the ground, witnessed by his wife Marinela Koželj, who sits compliantly and silently on a chair, watching him.[53] Todosijević was a decisive figure for NSK and inspired IRWIN's series *Was ist Kunst*, based on Todosijević's performances of screaming "Was ist Kunst?" at his wife (or sometimes other women) repeatedly, while the woman would endure and remain soundless and expressionless. Once again, Irigaray's words convey a commanding response to Todosijević's patriarchal violence:

> Are you waiting for me to scream out so loudly in distress that the wall of your deafness is broken down? … Endlessly, you turn back to that enigmatic question, but you never go on, you leave it still in the dark: Who is she? Who am I? How is that difference marked?[54]

Todosijević acting out as a misogynist artist, sometimes even smearing his wife's face with black paint while screaming at her, is not so far from the pathetic homunculus performances by Hinkemann, biting off the heads of doves and rats in abusive re-enactments of his (broken) masculinity. But their brokenness comes from different places: Hinkemann was wounded and humiliated by patriarchal nationalism, while Todosijević humiliated himself by screaming barbarically in the name of art. Perhaps not so coincidently, the question of gender and the betrayal of Hinkemann's masculinity was thematized in SNST's "Art" segment of *Retrogarde Event Hinkemann*:

> With a great effort SISTER lifts HINKEMANN's body and carries it into the eros of retro-Art.
>
> SISTER: Why are you silent?
>
> HINKEMANN: The sound of words betrays me. I am betrayal itself.
>
> SISTER: The birth of your child unites the masses in expectation.

> HINKEMANN: There is no child in me. I am sexless. What I am giving birth
> to is always the same spawning fish of History for the masses.

> Hinkemann falls asleep in the numb lap of SCIPION'S SISTER[55]

The "sexless" man seeks solace in the lap of a nun, symbolically remaining in the underground, the unconscious sphere of sleep.

In 1983 SNST announced in a series of letters called the "Sisters Letters" that the "creation of Style" in their theater "cannot originate in the Actor, Space or Staging, but only in Culture and Civilization, renewed and recurrently traumatized in the retro-production of the Scipion Nasice Sisters Theatre."[56] The traumatizing retro-production of Teller's antifascist play opened up new levels of engagement, many of which remain obscure to this day, especially for those of us who could not witness this exclusive performance. The Sisters, though composed of more men than women, overidentified with the religious feminine to trouble and reflect the pending religious authoritarianism buried within the private sphere in Yugoslavia and its basis in wounded masculinity.

The repression of religion, under a socialist state at the time, had done very little to address the conservative and authoritarian underbelly of socialist Yugoslavia, which with the rise of privatization and an emphasis on capitalism and individualism after 1989, would fully flourish and devastatingly hurt women. This might also give insight into why the first play, categorized as underground, deals with the castration by German nationalism, and why it was followed by *Retrogarde Event Marija Nablocka* (1985), categorized as resurrection (through exorcism). *Marija Nablocka* was centered on the historical figure Maria Nablocka, an actress who had immigrated to Slovenia after the Russian Revolution and who was known for her experimental approach to theater. After World War II and Tito's break with Stalin in 1948, she had fallen out of favor because of her Russian background. *Retrogarde Event Marija Nablocka* resurrected the importance of Russian avant-garde and constructivist theater. Retrogarde here reached back to the roots of early Russian avant-garde art, which as an artistic method was instantly inimical to the ideology of progression through violent negation. The resurrection of Russian constructivism lay in the homage to a visionary but ignored Russian woman forgotten in Yugoslavia. This also gave the Sisters an opportunity to fully embrace the idea of being more socialist than Yugoslavia itself, which peaked in their *Retrogarde Event Baptism under Triglav* (1985–1986), when the entire production echoed the constructivist language of the Russian avant-garde, such as Tatlin's unrealized *Tower*, the *Monument to the Third International* (1919–1920) (Figure 4.8).

One important difference characterizes the entire concept and production of *Krst pod Triglavom* (*Retrogarde Event Baptism under Triglav*): it was not performed in the underground but at the venerated congress and cultural center of Ljubljana, the Cankarjev Dom. The other change was that Goran Schmidt, who had invited them, also suggested the theme and occasion for the performance: France Prešeren's 1936 poem "Baptism on the Savica" ("Krst pri Savici") to be staged on Slovenian Culture Day.[57] As Monroe notes, this was NSK's "most monumental" act yet, and arguably its most costly, encompassing seventy actors, with Laibach managing sound, and IRWIN handling scenography.[58] Čufer remembered that "it was the first time we had actually been approached by an institution, and the first time we had encountered a situation in which we were not choosing the theme."[59] For her, this topic carried political resonance, especially because of Dominik Smole's contemporary adaptation of Prešeren's poem, which radically departed from traditional interpretations. While the violent Christianization of Slovenia is at the center of both the play and poem, in Prešeren's vision the love between two protagonists (anti-Christian pagan leader Črtomir and Christian convert Bogomila) is romantic and eternal, a theme Smole inverts by making the characters' love despondent, alienated, and ego-driven.[60] The central struggle is the question of self-sacrifice in the act of baptism; Črtomir's love for Bogomila drives him to submit to a new religion, and in turn Bogomila's embrace of Christianity through baptism implies a pressure to conform. One can deduce how the romantic struggle maps onto the national struggle with its own religious history, and how religious conflict was already brewing in the Slovene and other regions of Yugoslavia. Čufer summed up the themes underlying SNST's interpretation of the story in *Retrogarde Event Baptism under Triglav*:

> What happens when a certain social, religious, moral, and emotional state transforms dramatically and, of course, also violently into a different state? Like the transformation from a pagan into a Christian society as voiced by Prešeren, or the tectonics of the ideological tensions during the communist period as articulated by Smole …

> Then there is the problem of *Baptism* as a constitutive myth of Slovenian national identity, marked by—as we know—our historical fate of persistence in the tectonic field of endless cultural and ideological re-baptisms dictated by external currents of progress. We need not look further than our most recent past. In the twentieth century, the Slovenians have been under four social systems. First, we were part of the Austro-Hungarian Empire, then part of the Kingdom of Yugoslavia, and then one of the republics in Tito's communist Yugoslavia. Well, during our production of *Baptism*, one could clearly sense a certain social and political dynamic that was going to result in a new tectonic shift, which in the 1990s led to the inauguration of the independent state of Slovenia in 1991.[61]

Staged half a decade before Slovenia's formation as an independent republic, *Retrogarde Event Baptism under Triglav* was conceived as a play that would bring to the foreground these struggles of national identity within Slovenia, and would do so in an open manner. The change to a public venue here is relevant, as it also was the last time the group performed together. Visually, SNST was "plainly flirting" with the *Gesamtkunstwerk* (total work of art), which they signaled in their visual homages to Wassily Kandinsky's paintings and Adolphe Appia's sketches for Wagner's *Parsifal*.[62] The total work of art, of course, is also what connects SNST's method to German totalitarianism, essential to NSK's artistic paradigm as a whole. Two frames stand out: (1) "the Cardinal," submerged in red color and donning a "Hugo Ball at Cabaret Voltaire" Dadaist costume and (2) the reproduction of a Kandinsky painting in glaring pink and red (Figures 4.8–4.9). Miran Mohar's set design drawings for the play look almost identical to the finished work, with the important distinction of the choice of red and pink, which were not part of the original design.[63]

To reference two hugely venerated male modernists, Tatlin and Kandinsky, in glaring reds and pink homages deserves a short note here. One might read Tatlin's *Tower*, his failed (read: castrated) tower (modernism) submerged in red, again through the lens of the feminine, here symbolizing both menstrual blood and socialism. The phallic figure of the Cardinal looms threateningly within this religious underground feminine realm, almost as if avenging Tatlin's failure through a different masculine violence. According to Čufer, the absurdity of the Cardinal embodied in the Dadaist dress was not meant to be threatening;[64] yet, it is hard not to see him as threatening now. Once fully assimilated back into political life during the Yugoslav wars in the 1990s, religious misogyny would ascend to a new level: cardinals would replace naked women on the cover of *Start* magazine and women were steered towards the home to serve as loyal mothers for their new nations (see Chapter 5).

The bright pink shades of the Kandinsky frame, on the other hand, point to a more playful and less pragmatic approach in modernism. The Sisters summon the spiritual cosmology of Kandinsky's color schemes, dragging the artwork into the realm of obviously gendered associations in a bright pink playground. One could argue that the SNST's pink stage rebuked what then stood as the most important color theory in the twentieth century to come out of Germany, as the collective transformed Kandinsky's masculinist vision in *Concerning the Spiritual in Art* (1911) into a feminine embodiment immersed in pink.

Although *Retrogarde Event Baptism under Triglav* was the most public work SNST staged, it was also accompanied by another action that signified SNST's underground and obscure femininity: *Suitcase for Spiritual Use,*

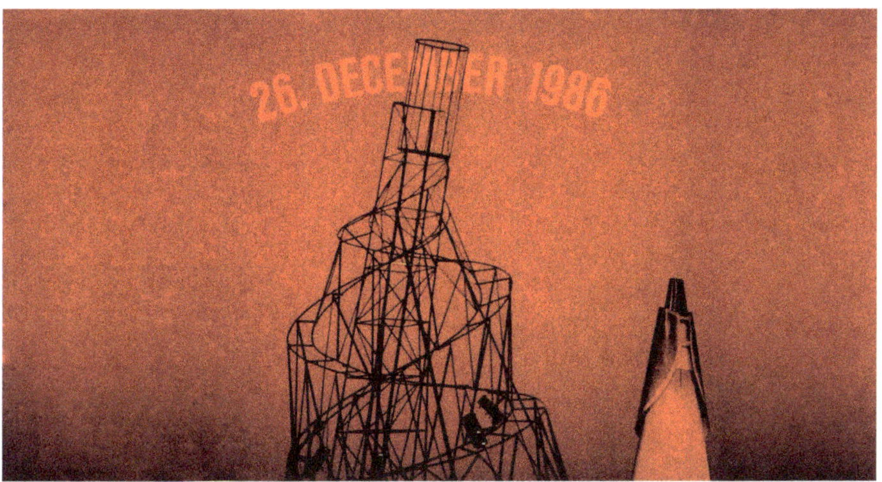

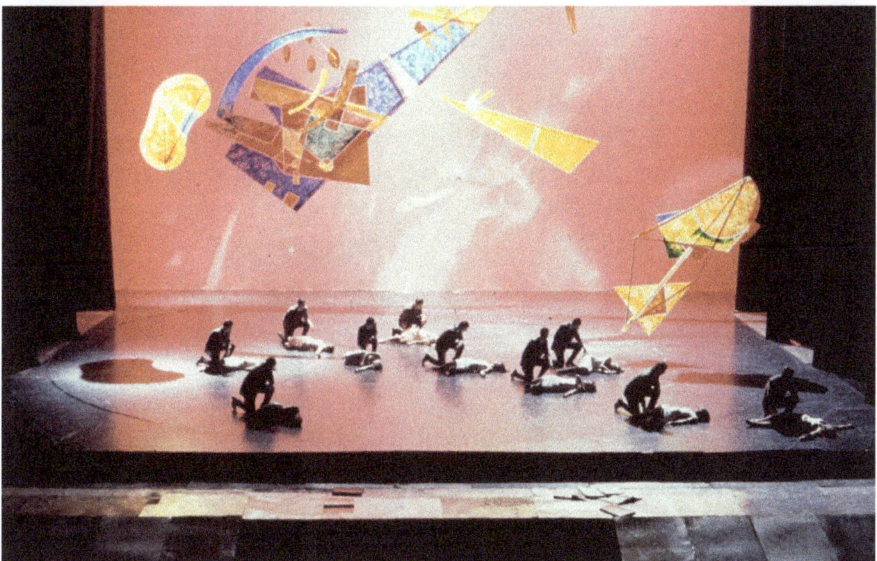

Scipion Nasice Sisters Theater, *Retrogarde Event Baptism under Triglav*, 1986. Photos: **4.8–4.9**
Marko Modic.

which consisted of a suitcase entirely wrapped in fur in homage to Meret
Oppenheim's *Object* (1936) (Figure 4.10). Like Oppenheim's, this object further
magnified the feminine element of the artwork by making it a sensual experience and politically progressive through its collapsing of art and life. As SNST
explained: "During the preparations for the exhibition, a *Suitcase for Spiritual
Use* containing symbols and documents of all NSK groups was circulated

among the inhabitants of Ljubljana. It was sent to selected citizens as a personal delivery through a special messenger, and it was at their disposal for one day. Every day the name of the current holder of the suitcase was published in the newspaper."[65] Once the current holders opened the suitcase—painted entirely red inside—they found five framed works stacked on top of each other, which folded out into the shape of a cross (Figure 4.11). At the bottom of the suitcase, viewers would encounter their own reflection in a mirror printed with NSK's black logo. In the context of SNST, the use of red inside the suitcase symbolically places the moment of discovery of art and the self (or one's mirror image) within the feminine and spiritual realm, charged erotically by the fur outside and the bloody red inside. Instead of encountering Christ's body on the cross, viewers encounter themselves in a mirror image bathed in socialism's signature red. Thus, the transformation of religious followers into political subjects is enacted in this intimate and hidden play with a suitcase. SNST decided to publish each holder's name in the newspaper as one way to solidify the spectacle of transformation by offering it as evidence for posterity. This political and spiritual transformation might take place in private, but it is made public and given to the historical record. It suggests that the reach of socialism is into the home, and that the subject will always be made public. Just as women are erased to serve patriarchy, the viewers of this work end up serving the state; for to view oneself through the socialist state is to trump even one's own sense of self. First and last, the participant viewer is a socialist.

NSK's work took another dramatic turn after Slovenian Independence in 1991. NSK had always been concerned with creating "new networks and autonomous institutions" that would pose a threat to the existing institutional powers.[66] They wanted "to create alternative imagery spaces in which existing social and artistic conditions might be viewed differently."[67] This aim found its fullest realization in NSK's *State in Time* project, which was launched in the early 1990s and has continued for three decades.[68] In the context of post-communist globalization, NSK created satellite embassies in different countries that belonged to the virtual state of NSK. As a paradoxically anti-nationalist or anti-state state, NSK declared "Anybody can become an NSK Passport holder and acquire NSK citizenship. The NSK state denies in its fundamental acts the categories of (limited) territory, the principle of national borders, and advocates the law of transnationality."[69] NSK reproduced signifiers of power, such as passports, stamps, and actual places for diplomacy, while undermining the juridical implications of such fiat forms. Among other places, NSK embassies were established in Moscow (1992), Florence (1993), Berlin (1993), Umag (1994), and Sarajevo (1995).[70] The *State in Time* project, therefore, offered an alternative to the ethnically charged territorial conflicts in Yugoslavia and all over Europe. Čufer and IRWIN wrote: "NSK confers the status of a state not

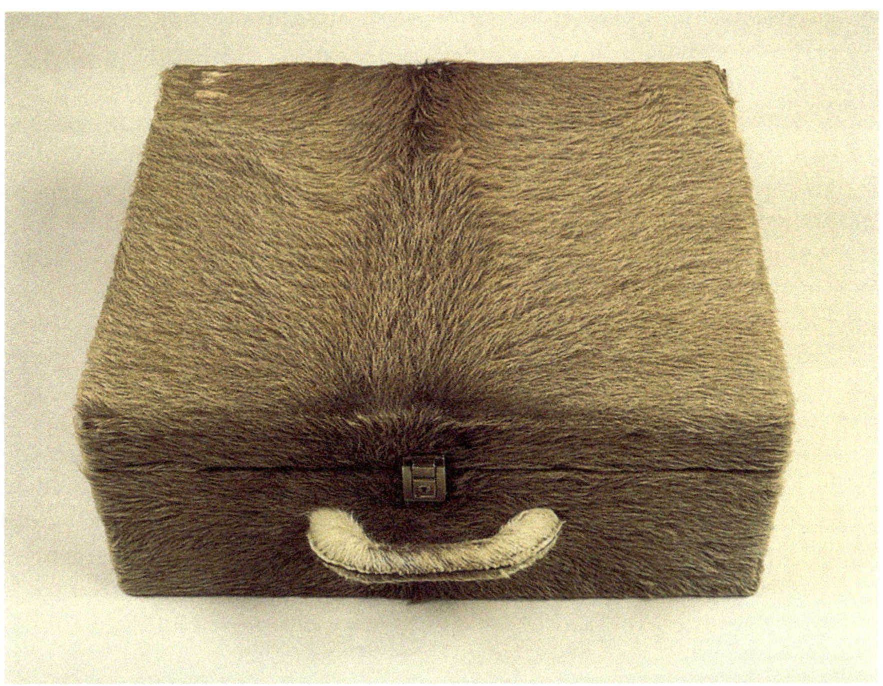

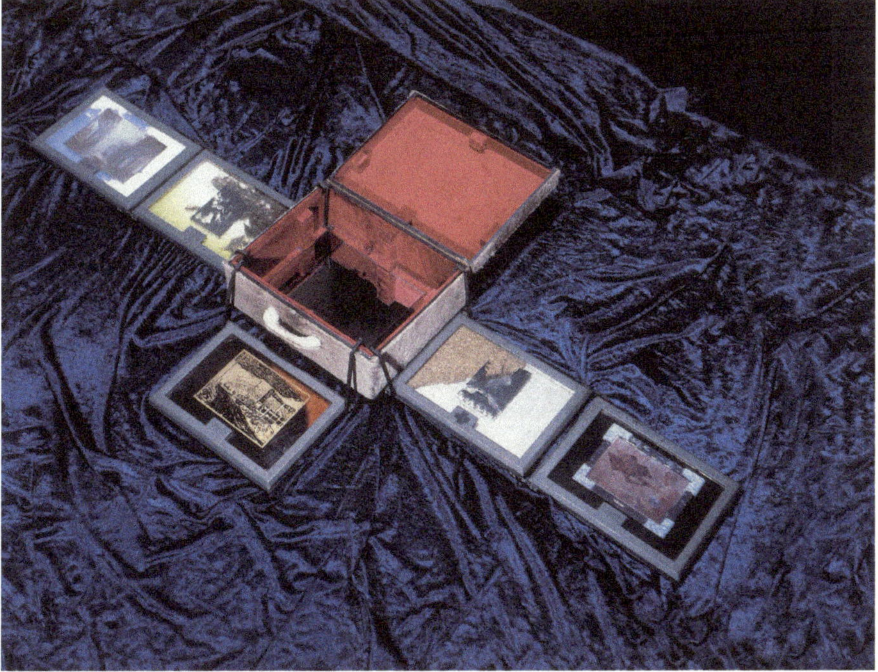

New Collectivism and Scipion Nasice Sisters Theater, *Suitcase for Spiritual Use*, 1986.   **4.10–4.11**
Mixed media, 21 x 240 x 80 cm.

upon territory but upon the mind, whose borders are in a state of flux, in accordance with the movements and changes of its symbolic and physical collective body."[71] As opposed to political states, NSK recreated the basis of sovereignty in the imaginative, political participation of the mind, rather than in a defensive enclosure of territory. The NSK state's emphasis on immigration has become an important point of reference within the European Union's changing borders since the 1990s, and was featured in art exhibitions on questions of immigration and nationalism, most recently in the 2017 Venice Biennale as the *NSK STATE Pavilion.*

From the project's inception in 1992, Čufer again became a pivotal figure. She remained loyal to the idea of collectivity and anonymity within the collective. In this regard, it is important to note that Čufer has identified Yugoslavia's socialist system as a pivotal foundation for her sense of self and ambition as a woman: "I never felt like girls or boys were treated any differently in the socialist system." She added: "There was no doubt that my family would send me to university if I did well in school, which was very different from the position my mother had to face. She grew up in a poor family and there was only enough money for a boy to be sent to a school." She concluded: "I thought girls were always stronger and smarter and we were doing better in terms of grades in our classes. I had no restrictions from my family or anybody else on how to shape my future."[72] She felt no need to push herself into the foreground of the collective and has thus remained a mysterious figure to scholars of NSK. She only publicly commented once, in Gržinić and Šmid's 1993 documentary *Transcentrala* (1993), on what it meant for her to be part of NSK. She read from a prepared statement:

> What made me decide to subject my individuality to the manifesto? … *My decision was also conditioned by emotional dislike of the fact that being a member of NSK, I embody and anesthetize the most brutal and dark picture of the world, which is the object of permanent suppression in the civil relation between individual and society.* Within the tension of this relation, between conscious acceptance of the postulates of the Laibach manifesto and permanent emotional dislike of its consequences, I discovered a satisfying aesthetical and ethic attitude. My adherence to the aesthetic image of NSK is, to me, a state of permanent experimental position that calls for an active attitude towards the dangerous relations in social life that are suppressed by subjectivistic society.[73]

This is simultaneously a devastating and again evasive statement about her position. As she describes herself as the embodiment of "the most brutal and dark picture of the world," who is "the object of permanent suppression," it is difficult to understand how Čufer could find solace in her own "state of permanent experimental position." In her dissertation on NSK, Inke Arns comments on this ambivalence in Čufer's statement and asks provocatively: "the reading is one of a prepared statement which could have been authored by the collective. But who is speaking when Eda Čufer speaks?"[74] Arns's provocation points to what is unimaginable to the capitalist model of art making and its related economy of fame: the idea that an artist would work without venerating her own position. Čufer forces us to question whether feminist resistance and artistic resistance are only legible when members of a collective prioritize their prominence over others.

Perhaps this is not the only path for feminist resistance. In my conversation with Čufer in August 2019, she summed up her position as a woman in the collective:

> People would read me as [a] completely unimportant female subject who is just serving these obnoxious militant guys. But once I became more present through my name and through my writing, suddenly there was a quick shift in opinion. Then people would argue that "she was behind the entire scene, maybe she is the real thinker." But for me, the truth is that it was a relational and dialogical project. These men are all very talented and smart and [I] enjoyed working with them. But I did not necessarily enjoy how our lives unfolded. Some things were easier for them than for me. Mostly also because you can sell a painting, but if you are a dramaturge for NSK State, who will pay the taxes for the superstructure of that kind of state? So these issues were never completely figured out.[75]

Čufer's position within NSK offers us a very different role, one which ties her to the antifascist, collectivist legacy of Yugoslav socialism: she put the needs and integrity of the collective above her own. Her work was primarily geared toward anti-institutional and antifascist revolution. She—as the dramaturge of NSK—became a thinker, scribe, and editor for the new, transnational (anti-national) state in the 1990s, which could arguably be one of the most profound extensions of the Yugoslav socialist state. In this way, she represents a very different and often overlooked Jugoslovenka: her obscurity and anonymity are the inverse of Lepa Brena and Marina Abramović's individual ascensions to fame; her lack of explicit sexual or emancipatory politics of the body stand in stark contrast to the gay and lesbian scenes in Ljubljana; and she has done almost nothing to historicize herself as an artist or secure her legacy. As a result, she has largely been subsumed as just another member of NSK. But her contribution as a woman, herself marginalized in a male-dominated context, and her conceptual contribution as a visionary of NSK, opened up the possibility for a feminine and anti-nationalist underground spectacle that was manifestly an anti-authoritarian and anti-heroic experience of Yugoslav socialism.

Across the universe: the dark fate of Jugoslovenka

To conclude, I want to return once more to Laibach and to my question at the beginning of the chapter: what role might Jugoslovenka have played in this history of NSK? Just a year after the dissolution of SNST, Laibach produced the song and music video "Across the Universe" from their Beatles cover album, *Let it Be*. The song was released by Mute Records for Christmas 1988 and was, according to cultural theorist Monroe, an "unusually romantic" work for Laibach. Monroe adds: "the line 'nothing's gonna change my world' also had a totalitarian implication that was particularly ironic as the socialist systems of the East began to collapse."[76] Its impact also derived from Anja Rupel, whose lovely voice and haunting presentation as a medieval princess—wearing a red velvet dress flanked by young Hitler Youth-like boys—amplified the desperate and devastating irony of the song, knowing what would happen shortly thereafter to women in Yugoslavia (Figures 4.12–4.13).

While the Sanskrit in the chorus suggests that the connotation leans toward peace, meditation and togetherness, reviewers of "Across the Universe" and *Let it Be* repeatedly inject a bellicose masculinity for both the album and the song.

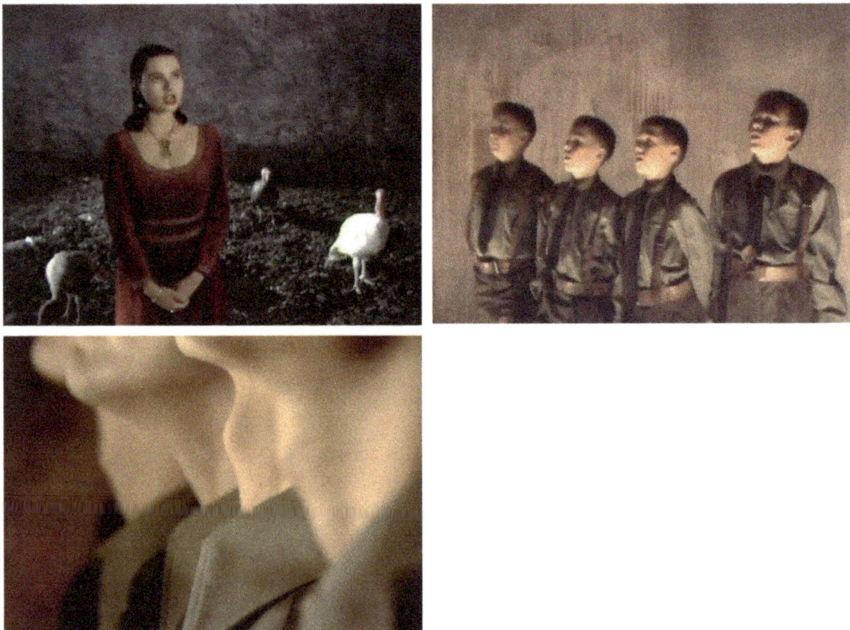

4.12–4.14   Laibach, *Across the Universe* (film stills), 1988. Music video directed by Bucko i Tucko (Boris Miljković and Branimir Dimitrijević).

"Laibach brought a new vision that subverted the melody," a reviewer noted, "transforming it into a military march, giving it an epic sound remitting to militarism, war, and fascism."[77] In a 1989 *Phoenix New Times* article, "The Rolling Slaves," Judge I-Rankin' called Laibach's cover a "strategic penetration by way of cover versions" and a "perverse refitting of fundamental pop into a framework some might consider heretical nihilism."[78] The perversity is indeed apparent, as is the penetrative visual language marked overwhelmingly as masculine. In the music video of "Across the Universe," we potently see what is to happen to Jugoslovenka, and in extension, to women of the Yugoslav region: immature male machismo takes over like a competitive sport, with frequent shots of boys on mountain tops skiing, while women end up being pushed back to traditionally static roles, such as being mothers and wives serving the nation.

Directed by Bucko i Tucko (Boris Miljković and Branimir Dimitrijević), the video to "Across the Universe" ended up winning an MTV Award. With complete freedom in the concept and design of the video, Bucko i Tucko alluded to Slovenian nationalism when using the metaphor of the dragon, a symbol of Ljubljana's coat of arms,[79] as well as in their use of medieval visual language, which chimed well with the goth genre following of Laibach while also easily reinforcing conservative fantasies about the pride of the Slovene land. The video mimics silent films from the early twentieth century and begins with boys' hands adding eyes onto a cave painting of a horse and leaving a handprint in the sand, reminding viewers of the primordial act of art making and standing in as an homage to Plato's cave. The boys then make a female face out of clay, which seems almost biblical as Rupel sings her lines angelically. Considering the emphasis on masculine creativity, it summons art historical references such as German émigré Hans Hofmann, who after leaving Germany during the rise of fascism in 1932, had been credited with teaching generations of early twentieth-century American action painters. That style of painting also commands associations that are deeply macho, in addition to calling on US propaganda of individual liberty and freedom, an ideology of liberalism that was a potential choice for the deteriorating socialist state of Yugoslavia in 1989, especially its northern republics like Slovenia, which swiftly gave up socialism in favor of neoliberal capitalism and European democracy.

According to Miljković, Laibach had instructed Bucko i Tucko to make Rupel into a prototypical Germania.[80] The subtext of this video is transformation and impending change, change that is deeply fascist, gendered, and haunting, which plays out on the body of the Yugoslav—soon to be reimagined as Slovenian—woman here becoming Germania, Slovenia's nationalistic kin. Her position stands in sardonic opposition to the chorus, "nothing's gonna change my world," and is met at the end with a gravelly masculine Nazi growl by Laibach singer Milan Fras. The most potent gendered moment of the video occurs when the camera focuses in on a close-up of the Hitler Youth boys' throats, their individual Adam's apples moving in sync with the change of vocalized melodies (Figure 4.14).

Around the same time that Lepa Brena would sing about being Jugoslovenka, with "Across the Universe," the male-dominated Laibach group seemed to herald the end of Jugoslovenka and the beginning of Germania. Among the Hitler boys, Rupel is static and somber; the only remnants of her socialist past are her red (read: socialist) velvet dress and singing while standing among geese and grey puddles on an uneven, gravely ground, perhaps foreshadowing the scarcity and embrace of traditionalism in the region to come. But, as this chapter argues, Laibach and NSK never really acknowledged Jugoslovenka's critical position in Yugoslav culture: with all the militarism and interest in war imagery, NSK mostly omitted women from that vision. There was no Yugoslav woman warrior, or allegory of peace, such as in Antun Augustinčić's *Peace* monument (1952–1954) at the UN Headquarters in New York (see Introduction); the Yugoslav woman was not envisioned as someone with her own agency in NSK, including SNST, or Laibach's work. And yet, her feminine power surfaced in the spiritual realm of theater, palpable in SNST and Čufer's work, as well as in the angelic atmosphere of Laibach's "Across the Universe." Jugoslovenka remained obscure, even though she was the driving force and voice of the collective's song.

Notes

1 For example, while he was serving in the military, Dušan Mandič regularly sent postcards to feminist artist and theorist Marina Gržinić, his partner at the time. These mail artworks frequently displayed violated and defaced bodies of women and drew a political correlation between religion, fascism, sexuality, and gendered violence, including explicit homoerotic subject matter. See Mateja Podlesnik, ed., *Vojak D. M. (Private D. M.) Die Welt ist Schön—Svet je lep—The World is Beautiful* (Ljubljana: Muzej in Galerije Mesta Ljubljana, 2013).
2 Dejan Kršić, "Fragments on the Matter of New Collectivism," in Zdenka Badovinac, Eda Čufer, and Anthony Gardner, eds., *From* Kapital *to Capital: Neue Slowenische Kunst: An Event of the Final Decade of Yugoslavia* (Cambridge, MA: MIT Press, 2015), 381.
3 Borut Vogelnik in e-mail correspondence with the author, August 9, 2020.
4 Eda Čufer in e-mail correspondence with the author, November 4, 2019.
5 NSK, *Neue Slowenische Kunst* (Los Angeles: Amok, 1991), 43.
6 Michael Benson, dir., *Predictions of Fire* [Documentary film, 1:30] (Kinetikon Pictures, Ljubljana, 1996).
7 This was an additional group that joined NSK in 1984, and which focused on graphic design. Its members included Darko Pokorn, Roman Uranjek, Miran Mohar, and Dejan Knez.

8 Youth Day was a special holiday that commemorated Tito's birthday (May 7, 1892) (see Introduction for more details). In 2007 the National Museum of Contemporary History, Ljubljana, held an exhibition named *Poster Scandal 20 Years Later* that showed several versions of the poster and other works.

9 Marina Gržinić, "Neue Slowenische Kunst," in Dubravka Đurić and Miško Šuvaković, eds., *Impossible Histories: Historical Avant-Gardes, Neo-Avant-Gardes, and Post-Avant-Gardes in Yugoslavia, 1818–1991* (Cambridge, MA: MIT Press, 2003), 254.

10 Ibid.

11 Ibid.

12 Slavoj Žižek, "Why are Laibach and NSK Not Fascists?" in Laura Hoptman and Tomas Pospiszyl, eds., *Primary Documents: A Sourcebook for Eastern and Central European Art since the 1950s* (Cambridge, MA: MIT Press, 2002), 287.

13 Miško Šuvaković, "Art as a Political Machine: Fragments on the Late Socialist and Postsocialist Art of Mitteleuropa and the Balkans," in Aleš Erjavec, ed., *Postmodernism and the Postsocialist Condition: Politicized Art under Late Socialism* (Berkeley, Los Angeles, and London: University of California Press, 2003), 110.

14 Lepa Mlađenović, "Foreword: Searching for Our Lesbian Nests in Yugoslavia and After," in Bojan Bilić and Sanja Kajinić, eds., *Intersectionality and LGBT Activist Politics: Multiple Others in Croatia and Serbia* (London: Palgrave Macmillan, 2016), vi.

15 Borut Vogelnik in e-mail correspondence with the author, August 9, 2020.

16 Ivan Novak in e-mail correspondence with the author, July 3, 2020.

17 Ivan Novak in e-mail correspondence with the author, July 7, 2020.

18 For a discussion of *Slovenska Žena* by Minka Govekar, see Jelena Petrović, *Women's Authorship in Interwar Yugoslavia: The Politics of Love and Struggle* (Cham, Switzerland: Palgrave Macmillan, 2018), 115–120. Also, Vlasta Jalušič has noted that the women's movement, including that surrounding the publication of *Slovenska Žena*, ended up aligning with ideologies of "national emancipation" during the early twentieth century, abandoning the formulation of their own political needs for larger national goals of liberation which ultimately hurt the movement. As Jalušič states: "The result of the amalgamation of national and women's goals was, however, paradoxical: it seems that the national issue gained more and more benefits from it than women themselves." See Vlasta Jalušič, "Women in Interwar Yugoslavia," in Sabrina Ramet, ed., *Gender Politics in the Western Balkans: Women and Society in Yugoslavia and the Yugoslav Successor States* (University Park, PA: Pennsylvania State University Press, 1999), 54.

19 Ivan Novak in e-mail correspondence with the author, July 7, 2020.

20 Ibid.

21 Ibid.

22 Ivan Novak in e-mail correspondence with the author, July 10, 2020.

23 Ivan Novak could not remember her name, but she is identified by Peter Blase on the Laibach Facebook forum as "Nicolle from Amsterdam."

24 Miran Mohar in e-mail correspondence with the author, July 20, 2020.

25 "Namepickers," IRWIN, Works and Projects: http://irwin-nsk.org/works-and-projects/namepickers/ (accessed 06/17/2019).

26 Monroe has noted that Živadinov's aesthetics were deliberately aggressive and violent: "As with Laibach, the audience is the target of this violence." See Alexei Monroe, *Interrogation Machine* (Cambridge, MA: MIT Press, 2005), 89.

27 Eda Čufer, "The Athletics of the Eye: Baptism and the Problem of Writing and Reading Contemporary Performance," in Badovinac, Čufer, and Gardner, eds., *From* Kapital *to Capital*, 235.

28 Eda Čufer in e-mail correspondence with the author, August 21, 2019.

29 Monroe, *Interrogation Machine*, 89–90.

30 Tone Peršak, "The Retrogarde as Alternative Avant-Garde?" in Badovinac, Čufer, and Gardner, eds., *From* Kapital *to Capital*, 87. Peršak's essay was originally published in 1984.

31 Čufer in e-mail correspondence with the author, August 21, 2019.

32 Ulrike Strasser, "Early Modern Nuns and the Feminist Politics of Religion," *Journal of Religion* 84, no. 4 (October 2004), 553–554.

33 Ibid., 554.

34 Zdenka Badovinac, Eda Čufer, and Anthony Gardner, "Introduction: Neue Slowenische Kunst from *Kapital* to Capital," in Badovinac, Čufer, and Gardner, eds., *From* Kapital *to Capital*, 14.

35 Ibid., 15.

36 Scipion Nasice Sisters Theater, "The Founding Act," in Badovinac, Čufer, and Gardner, eds., *From* Kapital *to Capital*, 474.

37 Badovinac, Čufer, and Gardner, "Introduction," 17.

38 Ibid., 15.

39 The exact number of invited guests differs depending on sources. In NSK, *Neue Slowenische Kunst*, thirty-seven spectators are listed (164). Twenty-nine spectators are listed in Badovinac, Čufer, and Gardner, "Introduction," 16. Alexei Monroe lists thirty-seven audience members, see Monroe, *Interrogation Machine*, 89.

40 Eda Čufer in e-mail correspondence with the author, August 21, 2019.

41 As the director of the theater program at Cankarjev Dom, dramaturge Goran Schmidt invited SNST to stage their last performance in that space. See Čufer, "The Athletics of the Eye," 235.

42 See fn. 18 in Barbara Borčić, "The ŠKUC Gallery, Alternative Culture, and Neue Slowenische Kunst in the 1980s," in Badovinac, Čufer, and Gardner, eds., *From* Kapital *to Capital*, 302.

43 Peter Wortsman, "The Imagination Unmanned: Reviving Ernst Toller's Tragedy *Hinkemann* in English," *The Mercurian* 6, no. 4 (Fall 2017): https://the-mercurian.com/2017/11/16/hinkemann/ (accessed 06/08/2019).

44 Eda Čufer in e-mail correspondence with the author, August 21, 2019.

45 Gržinić, "Neue Slowenische Kunst," 267.

46 Peršak, "The Retrogarde as Alternative Avant-Garde?" 91.

47 Ibid.

48 Ibid., 88.

49 Ibid.

50 See Judith Butler, *Bodies That Matter: On the Discursive Limits of Sex* (New York: Routledge, 1993).

51 Jordana Rosenberg, "'Lesbian Phallus,'" or, What Can Deconstruction Feel?" *GLQ* 9, no. 3 (2003), 393.

52 Wortsman, "The Imagination Unmanned."

53 See also Jasmina Tumbas, "Decision as Art: Performance in the Balkans," in Katalin Cseh-Varga and Adam Czirak, eds., *Performance Art in the Second Public Sphere: Event-Based Art in Late Socialist Europe* (London: Routledge, 2018), 187–190.

54 Ibid., 190.

55 NSK, *Neue Slowenische Kunst*, 167.

56 Scipion Nasice Sisters Theater, "The First Sisters Letter," in Badovinac, Čufer, and Gardner, eds., *From* Kapital *to Capital*, 475. The letter was first published in 1983.

57 Čufer, "The Athletics of the Eye," 235.

58 Monroe, *Interrogation Machine*, 90.

59 Čufer, "The Athletics of the Eye," 235 and 238.

60 For a comparison of these two versions, see Irena Avsenik Nabergoj, "Poetics of Love and Devotion in Prešeren's Poem The Baptism on the Savica," *Religious and Sacred Poetry: An International Quarterly of Religion, Culture and Education* 2 (2013), 67–84.

61 Čufer, "The Athletics of the Eye," 238.

62 Ibid., 242.

63 See a comparison of his sketches with photos of the performance in ibid., 236–237.

64 Ibid., 247.

65 Stane Bernik, ed., *Oblikovanje: Novi kolektivizem/Design: New Collectivism* (Ljubljana: NSK Info Center, 1999), 46–47. The book was published on the occasion of the exhibition, *Oblikovanje: Novi kolektivizem/Design: New Collectivism* at Moderna Galerija (Museum of Modern Art), Ljubljana, 1999.

66 Monroe, *Interrogation Machine*, 39.

67 Ibid.

68 Ibid., 28.

69 NSK state passports: www.savanne.ch/balkania/papers/nskpassports.html (accessed 5/13/2017).

70 Discussed in detail in Inke Arns, *Irwin: Retroprincip 1983–2003* (Frankfurt am Main: Revolver, 2003).

71 Eda Čufer and IRWIN, "NSK State in Time," in Laura Hoptman, ed., *Primary Documents: A Sourcebook for Eastern and Central European Art since 1950s* (Cambridge, MA: MIT Press, 2002), 301.

72 Čufer in conversation with the author, August 7, 2019. Her mother worked as a chef in a hotel and her father was chief of the police in a small town.

73 Marina Gržinić and Aina Šmid, *Transcentrala (Neue Slowenische Kunst State in Time)* (Ljubljana: TV Slovenia/ Artistic Programme, 1993), emphasis added.

74 Inke Arns, "Objects in the Mirror May Be Closer Than They Appear! Die Avantgarde im Rückspiegel. Zum Paradigmenwechsel der künstlerischen Avantgarderezeption in (Ex-)Jugoslawien und Russland von den 1980er Jahren bis in die Gegenwart" (PhD dissertation, Humboldt-Universität, Berlin, 2003), 229. Translation by the author.

75 Čufer in conversation with the author, August 7, 2019.

76 Alexei Monroe, "Laibach, Let it Be, Mute Records, 1988, London," in Zdenka Badovinac, cur., *From* Kapital *to Capital: Neue Slowenische Kunst: An Event of the Final Decade of Yugoslavia: Exhibition Guide*, May 11–August 16 (Ljubljana: Moderna Galerija, 2015), 61: https://d2tv32fgp01xal.cloudfront.net/files/mg-msum_nsk_vodic_eng.pdf (accessed 6/12/2019).

77 Lidia Zuin de Moura, *Kunst ist Krieg: Música industrial e discurso belicista* (São Paulo: Casper Libero College, 2011), 13. Translation by Charla Fisher.

78 Judge I-Rankin', "The Rolling Slavs," *Phoenix New Times* (February 15, 1989): www.phoenixnewtimes.com/music/the-rolling-slavs-6412866 (accessed 6/15/2019).

79 Boris Miljković in e-mail correspondence with the author, July 14, 2020.

80 Ibid.

The last generation of Jugoslovenkas: diverse forms of emancipatory resistance and performance strategies {.chapter-number}

5

Rapidly disenfranchised by the ideological influence of patriarchal nationalism, women, children, and ethnic Roma paid the highest price for the destruction of socialist Yugoslavia. The Yugoslav wars were not only waged between different religious factions but against all minorities that defied the newly sanctified identity categories imposed on them. These new impositions included ethnic purity, the role of women as mothers serving the nation, a willingness to sacrifice for the national good, belief in the exceptional status, victimhood, and righteousness of re-established or newly formed nations, and the condoning of violence to protect and advance said nations and their leaders. Women's bodies were instrumentalized to serve as physical and symbolic battlegrounds upon which military and paramilitary men sadistically sought revenge or humiliated their enemies; they also kidnapped and raped women to "satisfy the officers' needs."[1] If Yugoslav women were seen as freedom fighters in their roles as *partizanke* (female antifascist partisans) during World War II, and hard-working *drugarice* (female comrades) who experienced a sexual revolution and enjoyed reproductive rights, paid maternity leave, and equal access to education during socialism, then the end of Yugoslavia reversed expectations. It limited their status to mothers and moral supporters of the new regimes, or feminist "witches," traitors, and "whores" who could be used—no matter their age—to embolden genocidal power plays. Nonetheless, while Yugoslavia came to an end, Jugoslovenkas prevailed in these new countries and fought for the dignity and rights of women, children, and ethnic minorities in every sector, including the arts. This last chapter of *"I am Jugoslovenka!" Feminist Performance Politics during and after Yugoslav Socialism* begins with a discussion of various modes of women's emancipatory resistance strategies and their visual manifestations during the struggles of the early 1990s, and ends with case studies of contemporary women artists whose practices most intriguingly and profoundly speak to the legacy of feminism in Yugoslavia and its multiethnic politics of respect and unity.

I concluded Chapter 1 with Biljana Regodić's words, and I want to return to them once more, but from a different point of view: Jugoslovenka's body under siege during war:

> My body is my biggest trap. … When I think about my country, when I search for it, I find it in the boundaries of my body. My country spreads along my body, reaches the boundaries of my senses, searching for colors, for sights, for smells and sounds. Inside my body I carry the coast of Istria, with the grass rushing into the sea, the politeness of the local people; the walls of the ancient town of Motovun woven into the rocky hills behind the coast; the trees of Slovenia on the road to Porec; the sounds of Bascarsija on a sunny morning; the face of an Albanian who, in Sarajevo, talks lovingly about Belgrade the very moment that the war begins; the heated cobblestones of Stradun; the sounds of different languages in a summer camp in Makarska; Slavonian villages like swans in blue-green waters; the vineyards on the slopes of Macedonia; the silence in Ravanica; the liveliness of impoverished Kosovo, swarming with children; huge snowflakes about the fir trees of Zlatibor and the closeness of starlit waterfalls in the night; the sand of Sutumore; skies, skies across Vojvodina, the endless rich soil, crows, rains, frosts, and wheat. … Peace is the possibility to realize one's country. To make it grow. To discover new colors. To find out that countless forms of existence are within it. War kills with its lack of imagination. It imposes life in limited forms. Whatever happens in a war has happened thousands of times already.[2]

Regodić's description is potent with longing and portrays an image of a Yugoslavia that in its expansiveness resonates with Lepa Brena's "Jugoslovenka" (Chapter 2): a country that is multicultural, pan-ethnic, and vast in its geographical diversity and scope. As she describes in mesmerizing detail her search for her lost country, Regodić traces the contours of her own body. The memory of her country is one of harmony between the different ethnicities under the specter of war, "the face of an Albanian who, in Sarajevo, talks lovingly about Belgrade the very moment that the war begins." The beauty of this diversity, with all its stunning sounds and smells, marks an extreme contrast to the devastation of war and pushes the boundaries of her senses. Her love for her body/country hurts; it carries the mark of her betrayal. Regodić's essay is titled "Homeland as a Form of Women's Disloyalty," but she is careful to explain that the disloyalty is not contingent on religious or ethnic hatred alone. A much worse force has ravaged her body and nation: "I do not need Croats, Serbs, or Muslims to blame for grabbing my homeland," she states in the last paragraph of her essay. "Mere men are quite enough. The closer they get to me, the more dangerous they become."[3] For Regodić, ethnic hatred was one of many masks for the toxic root cause of the nationalist war: patriarchal supremacy. While it disguises itself with a mask of a new, young freedom, patriarchal supremacy merely imposes centuries-old violence: "Whatever happens in a war has happened thousands of times already." In this history, women's bodies are repeatedly reduced to their citizenship or their religious or ethnic background.

In its simplest terms, the survival of the ideals of Yugoslav socialism in the 1990s found two opposing manifestations, both of which were played out over women's bodies. First, corrupt communist elites who aligned themselves with the patriarchal and authoritarian elements of socialism and called themselves Yugoslav, Marxist, and socialist. Second, feminists who, despite often rejecting the term Yugoslav, nevertheless carried the legacy of Yugoslavia into the 1990s by fighting for the political ideals that marked the most egalitarian aspects of Yugoslav socialism: anti-patriarchy, peace, and the pan-ethnic state. These feminists were acutely aware that those old communist elites were now capitalizing on ethnic tensions to gain political power.[4] Many feminists who had fought for socialist ideals and against patriarchal domination in the 1970s were subsequently framed as dissidents against socialist Yugoslavia. By the mid-1980s and early 1990s, feminists would often be called traitors for being "Yugonostalgics" and betraying their ethnic backgrounds in favor of defending the multicultural, anti-militarist unity of Yugoslavia. It is the work of these "traitor" feminists that the first section of this chapter explores. These women organized, published, and spoke out against gender violence, carrying the generative elements of socialist Yugoslavia into the 1990s with one important goal: to banish toxic masculinity and replace it with transnational sisterhood. This first section is followed by a discussion of the perception of Yugoslav women during the war, such as the famous case of "Miss Besieged Sarajevo" in 1993.[5] The chapter ends with analyses of feminist performance works that critically engage with the positionality of Yugoslav women and their agency within the ex-Yugoslav republics as well as in the diaspora. These analyses of visual and embodied elements of feminist resistance will clarify that Jugoslovenka is a term that describes feminists who were not uncritical proponents for a better but squandered state (Yugoslavia), but whose tirelessly critical and socially engaged positionality, along with a commitment toward equality and women's rights, set them apart and against state and institutional ideologies founded upon simplistic narratives of nationhood.

Yugonostalgic witches and other feminist crimes: Jugoslovenkas resist ethnocentrism

As discussed in the preceding chapters, socialist Yugoslavia had its own history of misogyny, which did not mysteriously materialize in 1990. Because feminists were continuously critical of the Communist Party and socialist system repressing women's rights, they were marked as dissidents in the 1960s and 1970s, whether they were part of the student movement in 1968 or not. However, in the 1980s, the political meaning of a dissident changed dramatically, especially just before Slobodan Milošević took power by pushing a nationalist and divisive narrative that charged Yugoslavia with undermining the position of ethnic Serbs. During the rise of nationalism and ethnic conflict in the 1980s, being a dissident meant being against socialist Yugoslavia and its legacy of "brotherhood and unity," which allegedly oppressed and erased ethnicities. Narratives of unjust suffering became the bedrock of the political propaganda, employed largely for the benefit of men such as Franjo Tuđman (Croatia), as well as Vojislav Šešelj and Vuk Drašković (Serbia).

Feminists who rejected nationalist opposition and identified as Yugoslav were marginalized in all the new dissident and oppositional networks and struggled to find employment in places such as Belgrade and Zagreb.[6] Let's remember Kesić's discussion of the music newspaper *Polet* stating that "'[f]eminists should be kicked in *pička*'"[7]—kicked in their "cunts" for *being* "cunts" (Introduction).[8] The position of feminism in the new ethnic states of the 1990s, formed as a result of the disintegration, became even more complex and contested than in socialist Yugoslavia. Not only did the feminists fight against the nationalist dissolution of Yugoslavia, they also energetically rejected the new sexual and gender conservatism that rapidly sprouted through new ethnocentric institutions and cultural politics. As such, it is all the more vital to consider the seminal role of Jugoslovenkas not only in socialist Yugoslavia, but after its demise, when these women became the most important defenders of the legacy of leftist progressivism, a position ferociously contested and demonized over the next several decades.

By the early 1990s, the old misogynist desire to kick women in their cunts, to punish them, transformed into even more violent realities for women. But this time, feminists were to be punished for being too Yugoslavian. Tito had always publicly supported women and spoken about them as equal comrades at the root of the socialist project. "We are Tito's" would become an important phrase that connoted the political idea of unity in which everyone belonged to Yugoslavia, no matter their ethnic background or religious beliefs. Feminist women's sin during the 1990s—which earned them the label "traitors"—was that they identified with a transnational Yugoslavia and that they resisted nationalist politics, even if they didn't identify with the patriarchal slogan "We are Tito's." Moreover, impending and actual war, coupled with a state of emergency, legitimized all types of cruelties. As American women's studies scholar Beverly Allen concluded, it brought "murderous misogyny coupled with rabid nationalism, all released by the specter of limitless power of one human over another, where the one with the power bears absolutely no responsibility, no accountability, for his actions."[9]

In his famous speech given during his visit to Kosovo Polje on April 27, 1987, Milošević addressed the Serb minority's grievances by fueling their hatred of Kosovo Albanians instead of seeking reconciliation.[10] The conflict between the Serb minority and Kosovo Albanian majority had already intensified with the notorious 1985 "Memorandum," written by Serbian academics who claimed that Serbian citizens were "subjected to nothing less than 'genocide'" in Kosovo.[11] And even prior to the "Memorandum," after the student uprisings in 1981, Serbian priests and nuns began to voice their fears of Kosovo Albanian domination and the destruction of their churches. Most famously, Mother Superior Paraskeva of the Dević monastery published her complaints about young Albanians tyrannizing the monastery: "I was beaten, had broken ribs, my head was bloodied ten times …"[12] These narratives of hostilities between Orthodox Serbs and Kosovo Albanians, along with what the Serb minority in Kosovo perceived as the threat of the Albanian agenda for expansion, haunted the entire decade following Tito's death in 1980 and undermined the unity of the late president's pan-ethnic state. As the leader of the Serbian League of Communists at the time, Milošević, on the same occasion at Kosovo Polje, proclaimed, "Nobody will ever beat you [Serbs] again," at the same time as Albanians in the crowd, still pleading for brotherhood and unity, chanted "murderers," and "We are Tito's, Tito is ours."[13]

In March 1989, Milošević, now president of the Serbian republic, seized power over Kosovo and Vojvodina, which, under Tito, had been autonomous provinces within the republic of Serbia. This power grab from the president of Serbia sparked the unofficial beginning of the disintegration of Tito's Yugoslavia. It also resulted in Milošević implementing dramatic changes that signaled the marginalization of Albanians in that part of the Serbian republic: in a province whose population was 90 percent Albanian, Milošević prohibited the use of the Albanian language, threatening "people speaking Albanian in public" with prison. He also made it mandatory for all state workers to "sign a loyalty oath to Serbia."[14] In short, by 1990 Milošević's Serb-dominated ideology replaced that of the formerly multiethnic republic, which had honored the autonomous status of Kosovo Albanians within the Yugoslav project, with a new "system of apartheid against the ethnic Albanians."[15] This apartheid hit ethnic Albanian women of Kosovo the hardest as they lost their jobs and livelihoods. In such a toxic and paranoid environment, reinforced by powerful narratives of the respective nations under attack, the status of women, especially those who dared to espouse feminism, was increasingly precarious and contested by both the ruling elite and the opposition in former Yugoslavia, including Kosovo. Any vision that attempted to offer a paradigm that questioned or exceeded the narrow narrative of ethnic victimization (such as that by Žene u Crnom/Women in Black) was quickly shunned and shamed as a conspiracy jeopardizing the nation's struggle against extinction.

For the feminist movement, this unhinged patriarchal power was as detrimental as it was fodder for more resistance. While the wars threatened and destroyed many transnational and pan-ethnic collaborations and networks during the era of socialist Yugoslavia, and war made travel and partnership very difficult and often impossible, Yugoslav feminists managed to organize for peace and for the protection of women. In 1990 a Yugoslav-wide coalition of feminists met in Dubrovnik to make a public declaration against war and to demand peace.[16] That same year, Lepa Mladenović designed a poster for the Third Yugoslav Feminist Meeting at the Student Cultural Center (SKC) in Belgrade (March 30–April 1), which featured an image of older women protesting, smiling, and holding signs proclaiming "women's solidarity now" ("ženska solidarnost sada") and "women against violence against women" ("žene protiv nasilja nad ženama").[17] In 1990, Women's Lobby (Ženski Lobi) was founded in Zagreb and Belgrade, as was the lesbian and gay group, Arkadija.[18] Slovenia hosted its eighth Gay and Lesbian Film Festival in Ljubljana that year,[19] and the Institute of Ethnology and Folklore Research in Zagreb founded one of the most important feminist archives in Eastern Europe, Lydia Sklevicky's Feminist Collection.[20] These are just a few of the important feminist initiatives at the height of nationalist divisionism in 1990 and 1991, after which everything changed. Mladenović remembers:

> [In] 1991, the war broke out. Nationalism swept our streets, entered families and institutions like a typhoon, and conflicts over "What's your nationality?" and "Which side of the war are you on?" divided people, including the activists of women's groups. We had to stop Yugoslav feminist encounters. Soon there were no trains or buses between Zagreb and Belgrade or Sarajevo; the borders closed down, telephone lines too. The news announced the first men were killed on the front. And my life changed completely …[21]

Mladenović's words pierce through the veneer of political ambition by pointing to the very toxicity of civil war: such war divides families, friends, and coalitions among people who otherwise have the same moral and ethical convictions and who to that point had shared the land and its cultural foundations. The resulting emotional confusion and devastation is only the tip of the iceberg of the underlying concrete fractures created by war, such as cutting communications, closing down borders, shutting down telephone lines, and worst of all, murdering people who were once fellow citizens. Nonetheless, Yugoslav feminists carried the political foundation of ethnic unity into the 1990s under these divisive circumstances that characterized the death of Yugoslavia: Jugoslovenkas as agents for peace, unity, and women's rights.

To create a united women's movement against patriarchal nationalism was no small task, as the rise of anti-feminist women's movements was concomitant with a renewed celebration of the heterosexual family, religion, and the woman's position in the home. For example, the first public protests in Serbia against the impending war were led by mothers of young sons in the Federal Yugoslav Army, which was under Serbian leadership at the time. These mothers were not explicitly feminist in their orientation, but they relied on the "patriarchal belief that mothers are supposed to save men."[22] Counter-intuitively, this motivated their "stand against authority" and their attempt to save their sons from a war they saw as imperialist in its motivations.[23] Despite their non-feminist position, they understood the gender dynamics of their actions, as they declared their protest to be "a feminine spontaneous reaction to the disgrace of civil war."[24]

In 1989, Milošević began to mobilize the ideal of the "mother," when on the 600th anniversary of the Battle of Kosovo, he collaborated with the Serbian Orthodox Church to produce the "Mother Jugović" medal for mothers who had lost their Serbian sons in Kosovo.[25] By mobilizing the idea of the Jugović, Milošević also harkened back to the antifascist Yugoslav partisan era, when such women "served as a model for the Partisan notion of motherhood."[26] But the women in Yugoslavia were not so easily manipulated. Feminist activist Staša Zajović, who became one of the most important voices for peace and women's rights in the 1990s, knew that this emphasis on "Mother Jugović" reignited the idea of motherhood "as an obligation … not as a free option for women" based on the "symbolic figure of the long-suffering, brave, stoic mother of nine, offering her children up for death in defense of the father-land."[27] She added: "As nationalism replaced class struggle as the basis of political discourse in Serbia, the obsession with reproduction was transferred to the nation."[28]

In 1991, Zajović founded Women in Black Against War, known as Women in Black (Žene u Crnom Protiv Rata, Žene u Crnom), a women's peace organi-zation that organized protests—the women all dressed in black—proclaiming solidarity with women across Yugoslavia, especially their Muslim sisters in Bosnia, and vehemently critiquing "the Serbian criminal regime."[29] The group Lesbian and Gay Men Action (LIGMA), formed in 1992 in Croatia, published the first Croatian gay magazine, *Speak Out*, as a supplement to *Arkzin*. This issue featured two gay men with bandages over their eyes and one of them wearing a T-shirt with the words "I'm not gay but my boyfriend is."[30] The com-bination of the eye bandages, along with the ironic denial of homosexuality, was a "metaphor of 'silenced homosexuality' in Croatia," according to Tatjana Pavlović, a way to "render visible what is rendered unspeakable."[31] A year later, in 1993, the Autonomous Women's Center (Autonomni Ženski Centar) was set up in Belgrade, followed by the founding of the lesbian group Labris, also in Belgrade, in 1995.[32] In 1996, Lydia Sklevicky's Feminist Collection published a collection of the late feminist writer's texts in *Horses, Women, and Wars* (*Konji, Žene, Ratovi*), edited by Dunja Rihtman-Auguštin, which remains one of the most important documents on women's roles in Yugoslavia.

Such feminist, lesbian, and gay organizing met consistent pushback, erasure, and even violence. For example, feminists in Slovenia were not taken seriously when they founded the Commission for Women's Politics after the Declaration of the Republic of Slovenia that July (1990). Despite Yugoslavia's foundational history of women's involvement in party politics, Metka Mencin remembers that when the new Slovene country was founded, "the great majority of government institutions behaved as though this were the first time they had heard of the juxtaposition of the words women and politics."[33] In Croatia, too, pushback against women's progress was swift. When Franjo Tuđman rose to power in 1990, the lesbian group Lila Initiative, which had been founded a year prior, ended up disbanding after losing access to "the physical space in which it was organized," in addition to receiving no financial support to build and sustain the group.[34] But the most scandalous incident happened in 1992, when the weekly magazine *Globus* published a piece titled "Croatian Feminists Rape Croatia" that targeted five feminists in Croatia and accused them of betraying their nation. *Globus* named five "witches"—Jelena Lovrić, Rada Iveković, Dubravka Ugrešić, Slavenka Drakulić, and Vesna Kesić—who were charged with lying to the Croatian nation for falsely equating recent stories of women being raped by Serbs with the larger question of gender and war, not solely Serbian aggression.[35] But these feminists worked hard to separate gender from ethnicity, because under the umbrella of nationalist hatred, ethnicity "works as a homogenizing and hegemonic practice" to which gender is "subordinated."[36]

Beyond their refusal to diminish the causes of rape and equate them with nationalism, the five "witches" were also charged with damaging the reputation of the Croatian nation by "publishing their criticism abroad."[37] But as Tatjana Pavlović notes, this was the most ironic accusation, as it was "precisely when no one dared to publish them within Croatia."[38] In an almost comical manner, the women's intellects were undermined and they were dismissed as unattractive women who suffered from a lack of men in their lives. "Since most of these ladies had serious problems in finding male partners as well as real and serious fields of intellectual interest, they chose feminism as their own 'destiny,' ideology and profession." The article singled out three of the "witches," "who, despite their physical appearance, did succeed in finding marriage partners, [whom they] chose according to the official Yugoslav standards;" three Croatian witches married ethnic Serbs.[39] What stands out here, again, is the notion that these feminists betrayed the newly formed Croatia by refusing to indulge in generalizing narratives of Serbian men as inherent aggressors. Their interethnic marriages and their feminism represented the old Yugoslav regime, which at this point was historicized as oppressive. In this way, the generation of feminists who for decades had critiqued the Yugoslavian government during socialism was now accused of being Yugoslav sympathizers. Dubravka Ugrešić, one of the five "witches," remembered in 2013:

> In the immediate wake of independence, Croatian politicians and the local media (particularly the media) introduced the lilting coinage "Yugonostalgia" as a synonym for hostility toward the newly created Croatian state. Yugonostalgics were castigated as dinosaurs in human form, people who grieved for the death of Yugoslavia. Yugoslavia, Tito, Partisans, the slogan *brotherhood and unity*, the Cyrillic alphabet, Yugoslav popular culture—all this stuff, and a lot of other stuff besides, was tossed into the "dustbin of history," into a memory zone to which admittance was strictly prohibited. Accusations of Yugonostalgia whizzed back and forth past people's heads like bullets. People erased their biographies and changed their names and places of birth, sworn atheists were baptized, restaurants scratched "Yugoslav" dishes (those believed to be Serbian) from their menus, and in school the mention of Yugoslavia in history books was reduced to a few lines.[40]

To be Yugoslav, or to identify with the transnational project as a feminist, was to betray the exceptionalism of ethnic backgrounds. Six months after the article in *Globus*, Vesna Kesić published a response to the allegations in *Nedjelja Dalmacia*, "Confessions of a Yugo-Nostalgic Witch," where she reflected on this position as witch and Yugoslav representative: "Naturally, I am scared. Of course, I'm appalled and sad about what is happening to people and the countries of my former homeland. I became a witch there, and early traumas are never forgotten. Some would call that 'Yugo-nostalgia.'"[41]

Kesić, like many of her feminist colleagues in Yugoslavia, had lost a homeland that bound them in their struggle for women's liberation. This loss was accompanied by hostilities from the newly established nations, but also from abroad. For example, Yugoslav feminists' stands on rape often clashed with perceptions from the West, and most dramatically with the conclusions drawn by US lawyer Catharine MacKinnon, who sweepingly classified Serbs as especially prone to rape. Most egregious was the fact that MacKinnon had spread inaccurate stories about the Serbian government manipulating and screening hardcore pornographic films depicting the actual rape of Bosnian women by Serbian men on TV and in public spaces in Belgrade. Feminists in former Yugoslavia debunked MacKinnon's work as soon as it was published. Kesić offered a meticulous critique of MacKinnon's claims and argued that MacKinnon's unconfirmed stories would do little to help the war-ravaged region, but instead would "become a part of the war propaganda which stirs ethnic hatred and promotes revenge, both of which often find expression in violence perpetrated by men against women."[42] Besides, these spectacularized and unsubstantiated stories supported MacKinnon's anti-pornography politics. Kesić gave one specific example of how such Western prejudices could cause monumental misinterpretations of a foreign context:

> MacKinnon alleges that these videotapes which actually depict rapes of Muslim and Croatian women by Serbian soldiers, were altered to make it appear as though the women were Serbian and the rapists were Muslim or Croatian … I am unaware of any such reports being made in Zagreb or Belgrade until after MacKinnon's article appeared. I do not claim that such actions did not happen—all sorts of horrors have been videotaped and televised—but to assert that pornography played the primary role and is responsible for the rape of women in this war, some quantity of proof and evidence is needed. To me, it all looks like television vaudeville with a *quid pro quo* plot which has been constructed by MacKinnon and her informers for the sake of supporting her anti-pornographic theories. As evidence of the Serbian identity of the rapists, MacKinnon cites the "unmistakable Serbian intonation and word choice of the soldiers, one of whom was yelling 'harder.'" Yet it is absolutely impossible to distinguish whether somebody is yelling "harder" in Serbian or Croatian: the word "jače" has the same intonation in both languages. Thus MacKinnon displays a lack of understanding of South Slavic linguistics, which raises further doubts about the credibility of reports she receives and the conclusions she draws from them.[43]

Despite the debunking of such outsider analyses of ex-Yugoslav women's fate during war, many Western scholars and news media still cited MacKinnon's findings as facts.[44]

Outsider analyses also turned against local Yugoslav feminists, holding on to ethnic divisions as markers of innate differences between the Yugoslav people, instead of thinking about questions of unity that were central for feminists in the region. As such, US-centric interventions often replicated the assumption that Yugoslavia is synonymous with the Balkans and the concomitant stereotypes of discord, and that Yugoslavia's people must be plagued by inevitable difference and propensity for violence, not cohesion and reconciliation. US-based scholar Beverly Allen offered a scathing critique of Slavenka Drakulić in her 1996 book *Rape Warfare: The Hidden Genocide in Bosnia-Herzegovina and Croatia*, arguing that Drakulić's approach erased women's suffering by reducing it to gender and patriarchy and ignoring that pregnancy was part of genocide.[45] For Allen, the rape of Bosnian women supported her diagnosis of Serbian rape as "genocidal rape," which "aimed at enforced pregnancy and eventual childbirth," with the genocidal aim of "eras[ing] the cultural identity of the victim."[46] Refusing to look at rape victims only through the lens of ethnic origin and nationalism, the local Croatian "witches" had a different political agenda: instead of classifying rape according to the perpetrators' origins, they resisted the reductive narratives so prevalent in nationalist and racist generalizations about "the Other." Let's remember Regodić's words at the beginning of this chapter: "Mere men are quite enough." These examples, which equate genocidal impulses with Serbian men's predilection to rape and violence—as prevalent then as they are now, such as in Angelina Jolie's film *In the Land of Blood and Honey* (2011) or Srđan Spasojević's *A Serbian Film* (2010)—distract from the larger issue of misogyny at the root of militarization and nationalism.[47] And while there is no doubt that Serbian forces were egregious aggressors against women during this war, Yugoslav feminists wanted to remain in solidarity with all female victims of the senseless war. As Women in Black explained in 1992:

> The feminists of Belgrade and Serbia do not support the position about symmetrical suffering. They are conscious that the more powerful and better-armed military-political forces of Karadžić in Bosnia (the army of the Serb's Republic) have the largest number of rapes on their consciences. How many exactly, it will be difficult to know, even after the war. The high percentage of Muslim women raped in the war in Bosnia is not a reason to forget the suffering of women of other nationalities and religions, atheists, or those claiming no particular nationality.[48]

Following the example of the Israeli feminist group Women in Black, which had publicly condemned their government's discrimination against Palestinians, Women in Black in Belgrade decried militarism and charged socialist Yugoslavia with having produced obedient and docile men who were willing to follow orders. The feminist curator at the SKC in Belgrade, Bojana Pejić, similarly argued that in socialist Yugoslavia, the military "was central to the context because the 'struggle for world peace' proclaimed as the highest ideal in all of the communist states was simply a justification of their steady militarization."[49] Women in Black opposed all forms of nationalism, including that of former socialist Yugoslavia. Goranka Matić, another SKC feminist (see Introduction and Chapter 1), worked for the newspaper *Vreme* (*Time*) in the early 1990s and was closely associated with Women in Black. In one of her photographs (Figure 5.1), women of all ages, dressed in black, walk with somber facial expressions through the city of Belgrade.

Holding a large banner at the front with the words "Žene u Crnom Protiv Rata" ("Women in Black Against War"), as well as signs stating "Women do not ask for Rape," these women stood in solidarity with their Bosnian sisters, who at the time were being shelled and raped en masse. These women knew how dangerous it was to speak out against Serbian ethnically charged hatred and misogyny, as they themselves could become the targets of rape and violence at any moment. But they proudly walked the streets of Belgrade, because it was imperative to them to show solidarity with their brutalized Yugoslav sisters. At the Third International Conference, "Network of Women's Solidarity Against War" in Novi Sad, Women in Black did a large action in the city:

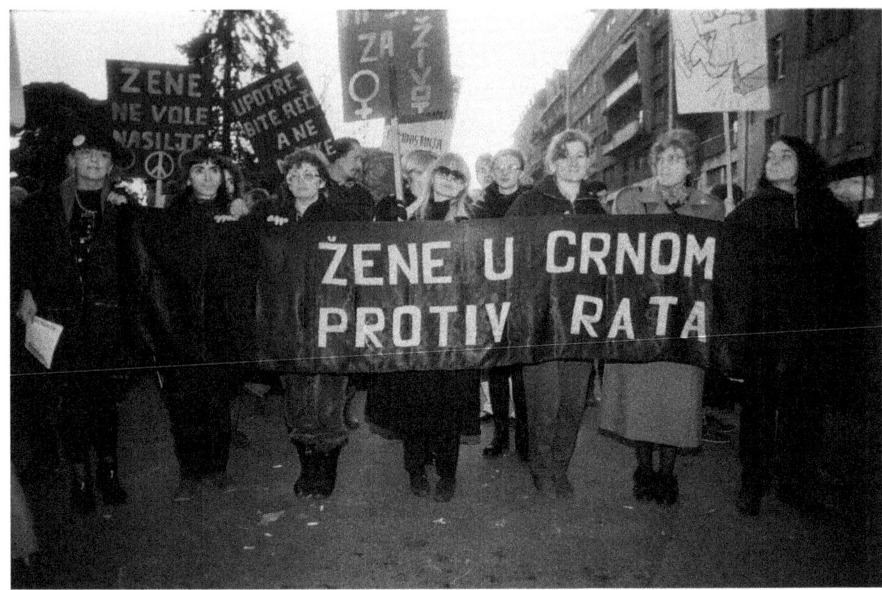

5.1   Goranka Matić, *Women in Black*, Belgrade, December 17, 1992.

women formed a circle with their bodies lying on the ground, surrounded by a ring of sunflowers. On the one hand, this action pointed to solidarity among one another, and on the other hand, it made palpably clear how vulnerable that bond is when confronted with unbridled destruction (Figure 5.2).[50] Women in Black created impactful moments of solidarity and adopted a visual language that the group, and many others that have followed since, have sustained: large black banners with white typeface, always emphasizing an anti-war and pro-women position.

In 1994, Women in Black visited refugee camps at Mala Krsna, Kovilovo, and Mikulja, where, along with artist Vesna Pavlović and the collective Škart, they took photographs and collected handwritten stories and drawings that they eventually published in a book called *Sjećam se* (*I Remember*), which was "printed with money raised by street sale campaigns by female comrades-in-arms from Italy and Spain" (see Figures 5.3–5.4).[51] One of the Women in Black activists, Radmila Žarković, remembers that

> The idea of the book was to collect their memories of times before war. It is not about reality, it is about their past, about those little big things that meant so much to them. Sometimes it was just a tree in the yard, other times, it was a memory of friendship and love, sometimes it was a cat, looking as they were going away. It is a collection of all those things they wanted and could share with us, illustrated by their own hand. It was important for us to preserve all

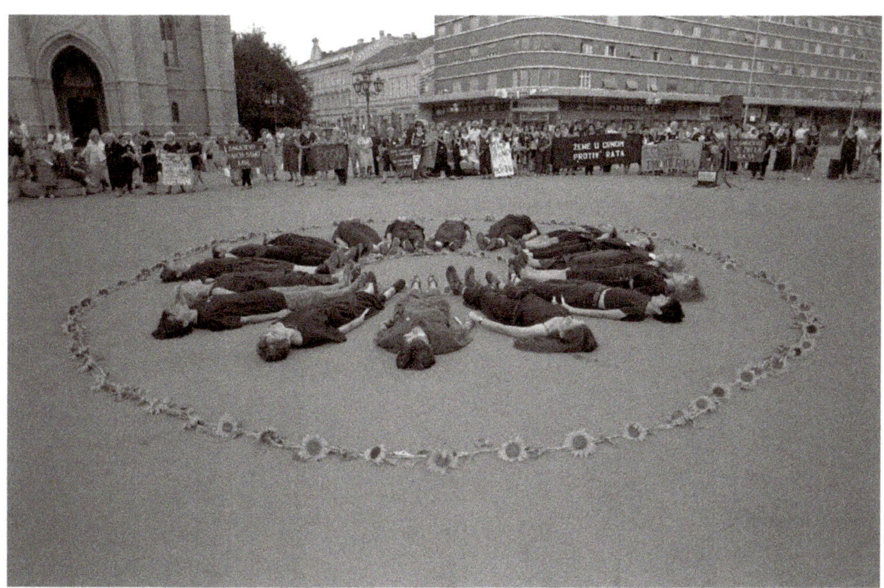

Vesna Pavlović, *The Circle*, the Third International Conference "Network of Women's
Solidarity Against War," Novi Sad, August, 1994. From Women in Black series.

5.2

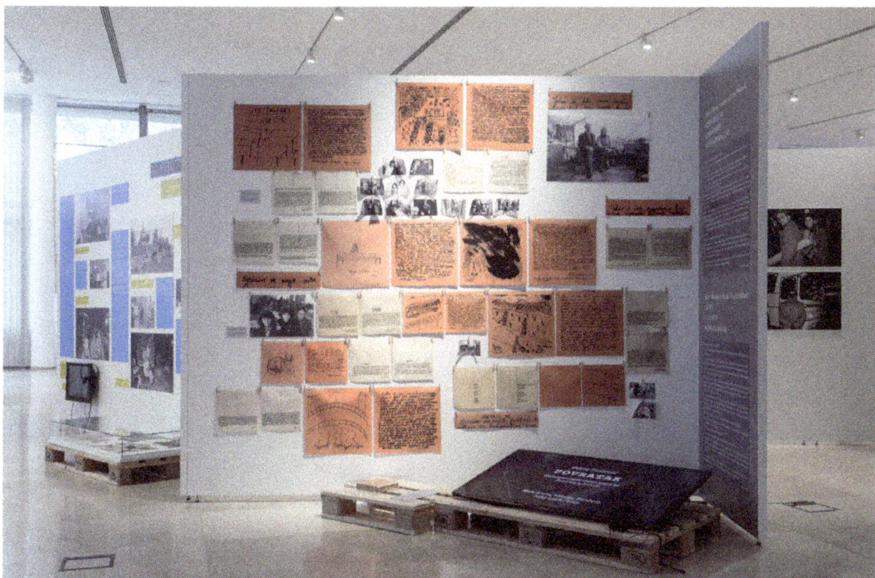

Škart + Women in Black, installation view of pages from the book *I Remember
1993–1995*. Published by Women in Black, Belgrade, 1995. Installation view of Vesna
Pavlović, *Povratak. Dokumentarni Video Zapis Sa Zenama u Crnom (Return: A
Documentary Video with Women in Black)* 1993–1996/2019.
Installation photograph from *The Nineties: A Glossary of Migrations* exhibition at the
Museum of Yugoslavia in December 2019.

5.3

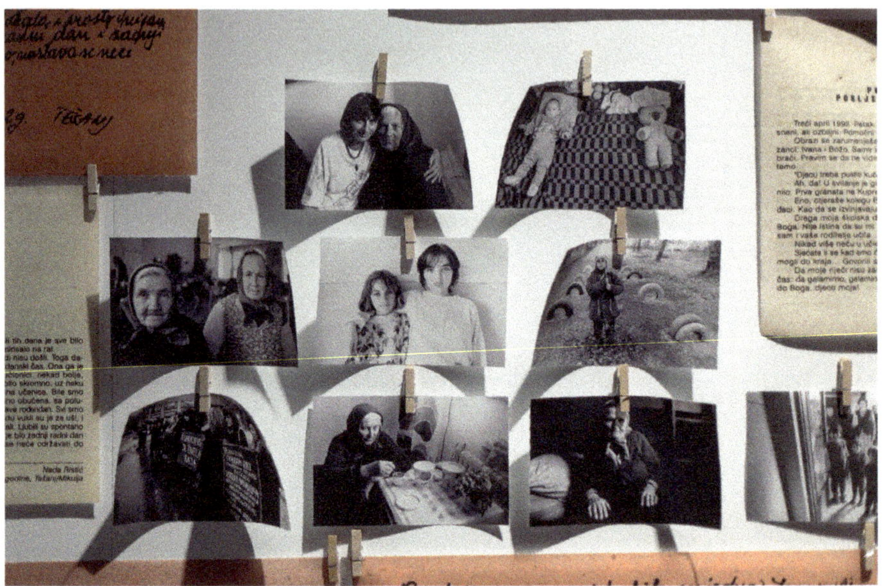

5.4   Vesna Pavlović, *Visiting the Refugee Camp Miloševac*, 1993
Installation photograph from *The Nineties: A Glossary of Migrations* exhibition at the
Museum of Yugoslavia in December 2019.

this, not only in the book, but in themselves, too. We wanted to preserve the memory of different times, so far away from hatred. And that they would manage to keep a small piece of that inside, making it a basis for a new start.[52]

In 2019, Pavlović made a film with four of the Women in Black protagonists from the 1990s era, Radmila Žarković, Jadranka Miličević, Staša Zajović, and Violeta Đikanović; they sat down together to reflect on those early times and read from the pink-colored *I Remember* book. One story involved a woman mourning the pot of violets she used to have in her apartment, wondering if she will ever be able to touch them again and care for them. Each entry included the city or town the women were from, sometimes even a complete address. Another story had me in tears when I first saw Pavlović's video during the exhibition *The Nineties: A Glossary of Migrations* at the Museum of Yugoslavia in December 2019. Violeta Đikanović reads Sanja Ristić's memories and would-be letter to her best friend, Aida:

We were together all the time. You can't talk about me and not talk about Aida, you can't be with Aida and not be with me. That is simply not possible. We were the symbol of friendship and sincerity. With whom else would I talk about my sorrows, laugh out loud, who else's secrets would I keep, listen to your troubles, if it wasn't for you? You, my bestie. Tonight, if you're awake, don't be sad. We will get together again. We will complain to each other about professors' and lack of parents' understanding. We will go again and take presents to Eid, eggs on Easter. We will go together downtown for a walk on hot summer nights. We will not fear anyone, then. No one will be able to break us apart, just because you're a Muslim and I am a Serb. Don't be sad tonight and don't you ever cry for me. I will be back, that's for sure. I'll come to hug you, to talk and laugh with you, like no one else. Remember all the good things we've experienced together, and this will turn into our future. Don't cry tonight. I will come for your smile and give you the most beautiful song.[53]

These tender stories of friendship and love—the longing to be together again and not to live in fear—are ubiquitous among survivors of war and trauma, especially those stuck in refugee camps with uncertain futures. Songs can do much to soothe that pain and connect people across time and place. In the documentary, Zajović notes how she had learned about the significance of the local musical genre of Sevdalinka (or Sevdah) in Bosnia, which is comprised of folk songs by mostly unknown creators but, which are well known by people and often covered by pop singers. Women in Black begin to reminisce over how they often ended up singing Sevdalinka songs in the car, after a hard day's work, to let out their pain, to have a moment of mourning and solidarity that would allow them to keep doing their hard work the next day. They start singing a song called "Žute Dunje" ("Yellow Quinces"), an emotional moment for them and us viewers, and the film ends with a version by Damir Imamović playing during the credits.[54] Pavlović's 2019 film about these four women is as important as her work in the 1990s, allowing us to see the continuity of Yugoslav feminist solidarity among the main organizers then and their continued dedication to the recognition and healing of their fellow sisters who have been torn apart by war.

In this way, the root of Women in Black's militant anti-war position was tied to women's suffering, a feminist commitment that was in conflict with the official patriarchal and nationalist military decisions that further fragmented the people of the once united country throughout the decade of war in the 1990s and its aftermath. What's more, the feminist position of Women in Black was also influenced by the dedicated work of lesbian activists such as Lepa Mlađenović, who worked hand in hand with feminist activists to resist nationalist violence within their own context as well as globally. In one representative photograph by Pavlović from that time, we see a close-up of Mlađenović and Zajović holding a banner at a protest in Belgrade in 1994 (Figure 5.5). Pavlović's camera angle here captures the determined and serious expressions on their faces, along with a fragment from their banner, "ŽENSK" (women's), visually solidifying their historic dedication to women's rights in their writing and

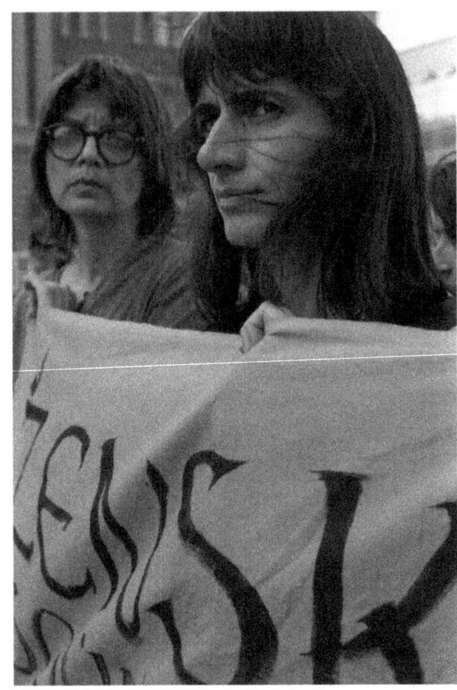

5.5   Vesna Pavlovic, *Lepa Mlađenovic and Staša Zajović*, Republic Square Belgrade, 1994
From Women in Black series.

activism. Finally, Mlađenović and Zajović, coupled with the "ŽENSK" sign, evince the centrality of femininity to deconstructing the ideologies, rhetoric, and methods of waging war.

In "No Ending," the last part of an essay on "Feminist Resistance to War and Violence in Serbia," originally published in 1994 and revised and reprinted in 1997, feminist authors Mlađenović and Donna M. Hughes refused to give "an ending" for their paper with the following heart-wrenching explanation:

> In 1994, as the paper was sent to the publisher, the city of Bihac in Bosnia was being destroyed by Serbian artillery. It is now April 1999 as we write an update for this paper, and still an ending cannot be written. As this update of the paper is sent to the publisher, Serbian police, military, and paramilitary units are emptying all of Kosovo of ethnic Albanians. NATO is dropping bombs on Belgrade, Novi Sad, Karljevo, and on Pristina and other cities in Kosovo and Montenegro.[55]

Women in Black continued to fight against war violence and the mass rapes of women, including Serbian aggression against Albanian women in Kosovo,

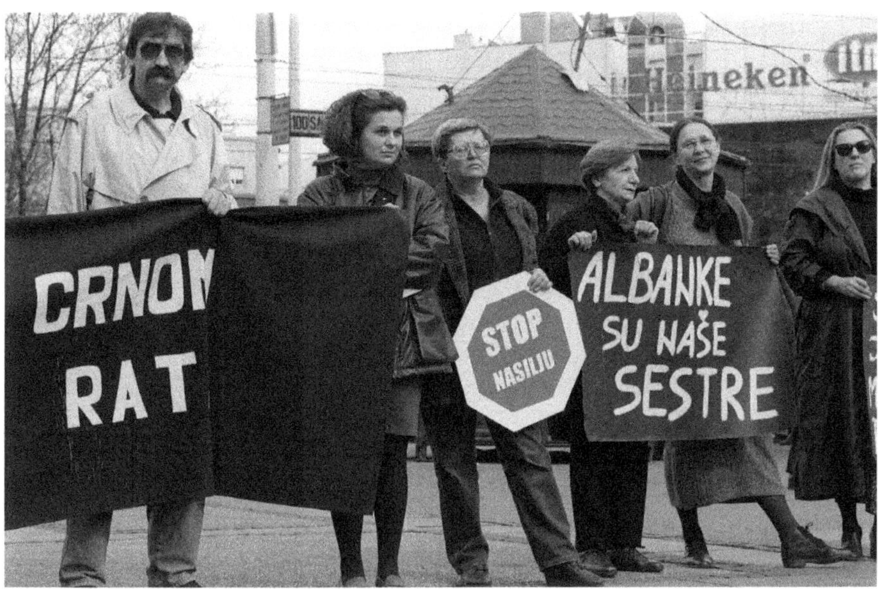

Vesna Pavlović, Women in Black, Republic Square Belgrade, March 1998.   **5.6**
From Women in Black series.

which resulted in rape of an estimated 20,000 women.[56] Women in Black organized protests in Belgrade to raise awareness about the political situation in Kosovo as early as the mid-1990s. In a photo taken during a Women in Black protest in 1998, women are holding banners proclaiming "Albanke Su Naše Sestre" ("Albanian Women Are Our Sisters") and "Stop Nasilju" ("Stop Violence") (Figure 5.6). Other banners featured at such protests were often multilingual—in English, Serbian, and Albanian—deliberately avoiding the Serbian Cyrillic mobilized by local right-wing nationalists.[57] Zajović commented:

> We were in a different position from the women in Kosovo at that time, meaning that while we in Serbia were hostages to an aggressive, fascist regime, the women in Kosovo and in Bosnia and Herzegovina were victims of the expansionist imperialist policy of Serbia. It's a big difference between us; we were the aggressor state, and Kosovo was living through the highest type of institutional apartheid.[58]

Zajović's characterization of being held hostage by the Serbian aggressor state offers a remarkably accurate description of the authoritarian suppression of the Yugoslav project of unity in Serbia. Showing such solidarity with Kosovo was dangerous in Belgrade, but as Zajović points out, the stakes were even higher in Kosovo, where Albanian women organized to resist Serbian violence.

Igballe and Safete Rogova, better known as the "Rogova Sisters," became the most well-known organizers for feminist causes in Kosovo, including founding the Motrat Qiriazi organization aimed at helping young girls and women attend school in rural and urban areas.[59] The name Motrat Qiriazi also honored another pair of sisters, Sevasti and Parashqevi Qiriazi, who made feminist history in 1891 when they opened the first school for girls in Albania.[60] Beyond advancing educational opportunities for girls and women in the 1990s, the Rogova Sisters also worked with women in more remote villages to overcome "patriarchal mindsets" attached to tradition and local customs, and helped them maintain and expand traditional values. Offering classes and other educational opportunities, the Rogova Sisters emphasized the worth and dignity of sewing, dancing, and other forms of female solidarity. As Safete Rogova noted: "The harmony of the sewing that exists in the traditional clothing of Has women is an art in itself," adding, "the beautiful parts of the traditions don't have to be erased—they need to be preserved."[61]

Motrat Qiriazi was part of a larger movement of women's resistance in Kosovo, which blossomed under horrific political conditions, most poignantly visible to the public in multiple street marches and demonstrations in 1998. By then, the Center for Protection of Women and Children had been established and was run by two other prominent feminist figures, Vjosa Dobruna and Sevdie Ahmeti, who would soon become fugitives hunted by the Serbian police for their subversive feminist activism, including participation in, and organizing of the March 8 and March 16 protests in Kosovo. The latter, the Drenica march, remains one of the most important women's protests of the twentieth century. Thousands of women marched toward the besieged area of Drenica, waving large loaves of bread in the air, to highlight the murders and atrocities committed by the Serbs against women and children, in addition to mass starvation in the region due to the Kosovo War, which began in February 1998. On March 8, the mass protest on International Women's Day in Pristina, the capital of Kosovo, was deemed "the largest" International Women's Day protest in the world that day (by BBC), and included thousands of women holding up white pieces of paper to raise awareness of the human rights violations against Kosovo Albanians. According to Dobruna, the women had initially planned to hold up "sanitary towels" to prioritize women's struggles under Serbian rule, but the Albanian Democratic League of Kosovo (Lidhja Demokratike e Kosovës, LDK) pushed against such a feminist symbolic gesture.[62] As we have seen during the rise of socialist rule in Yugoslavia, here again women's advances for gender equality were sacrificed or ignored by a male-dominated ruling party, in this case the LDK, in favor of more universal goals of national liberation.

Astonishingly, women in Kosovo remained subversive voices against the Serbian regime, but their dissent did not circulate as dramatically in the Western media or in the former states of Yugoslavia. Racial and gender biases inform the visual politics of how images become icons, revealing a great deal about the complicated emancipatory position of ethnic Albanian and Muslim women and how they are marked in the context of former Yugoslavia. One image from the Drenica march elucidates the patriarchal and racial biases in the media: a photograph of a middle-aged or perhaps elderly woman with a headscarf holding up a large loaf of bread in front of an intimidating row of armed Serbian police (Figure 5.7).[63] Like Dragana Milojević during the March 1991 protests in Belgrade against Milošević (see Introduction), this anonymous woman has a similar hand gesture symbolizing victory and perseverance. But her courage has received far less attention than that of the younger and more glamorous Milojević in Belgrade. At first glance, one might suggest that viewers favor black-and-white images, as they seem more historically distant and less revealing about the details of a moment, allowing projections of identification and longing. Colored images signal something less ambiguous, harkening back to a more proliferated set of visuals from video footage in color showing various war conflicts on TV in the 1990s. But here, something else might be at play. Hito Steyerl's theorization of visibility and invisibility in her 2013 *How Not to Be Seen: A Fucking Didactic Educational .MOV File* is useful in

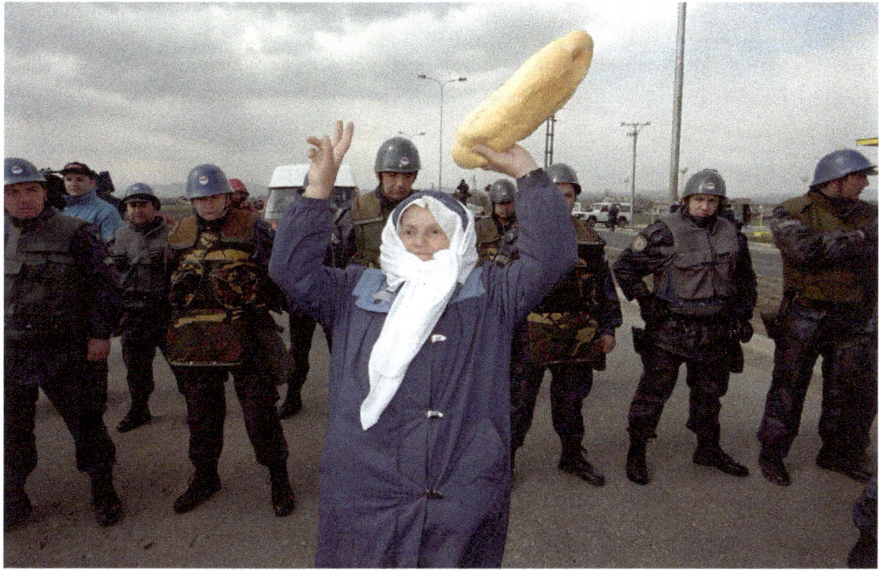

Mladen Antonov, Yugoslavia-Kosovo-Woman, March 16, 1998.   **5.7**

ascertaining some of the multiple intersecting factors contributing to the lack of circulation and glamorization of this woman at the Drenica march. Steyerl facetiously outlines how some people don't even need to try to be invisible as they are already disappeared subjects in dominant visual culture, where one becomes invisible by "being female and over fifty [years old]," "undocumented or poor," "a disappeared person as an enemy of the state," and by "living in a military zone."[64] Milojević was not only younger, she was also technically not acting in a military zone at the time, as Belgrade wasn't bombed until 1999 by NATO. She was, however, facing police water cannons and Belgrade was a zone in which demonstrators were repeatedly met with Milošević's military tanks. Steyerl's video also visually integrates political dichotomies leveled at women globally who wear burqas and hijabs, in the West laden with prejudices of oppressing women and making them invisible, which Steyerl deconstructs and complicates. The non-Muslim religious, as well as secular atheist population of the multicultural and multiethnic state of Yugoslavia harbored similar prejudices, which came to the forefront most starkly in the treatment of women in and from Kosovo and Bosnia and Herzegovina in the 1990s. As such, the lack of interest in an older woman's emancipatory gesture, especially a woman wearing a headscarf or a hijab (*hidžab*), must therefore also be understood within this complicated matrix of patriarchy, Islamophobia, and ageism in the media. That type of prejudiced framework makes it almost impossible to identify and thus honor her emancipatory position.

Belgrade's Women in Black activists resisted such erasure of Muslim women's voices and exhibited solidarity within and beyond the borders of their states. Women in Black also turned to the plight of Roma women and their families in the former Yugoslav region. In 2001, for example, they held a "Stop razismu protiv Roma" ("Stop Racism against the Roma Population") rally in Novi Bečej. The photographs from the march show familiar banners emphasizing the strength of solidarity, stating "United against Discrimination" and "Stop Racism against Roma and Roma Women." But one photograph by Srđan Veljović reveals an added reality: Women in Black not only thought about transnational solidarity, but the group was also invested in supporting women living outside large urban areas (Figure 5.8). The camera angle, coupled with the high contrast of the black-and-white photograph, exacerbates the urgency of this small group of women marching in the middle of a narrow and otherwise empty street in Novi Bečej. Only one woman is seen standing on the left side, at the gate to her house, separated from the group by the grassy shoulder of the street lined with brick houses characteristic of Yugoslav villages. This image is antithetical to the bravado of activist images documenting interventions at imposing architectural cites in urban areas. As such, Women in Black took on the challenge of exposing and addressing racial and gender violence not only within members' respective nations and cities,

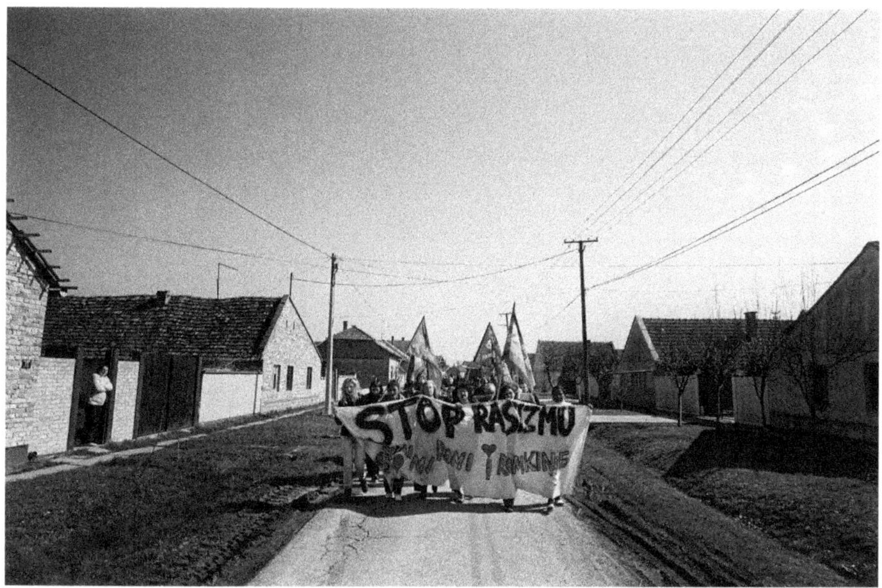

Women in Black, "Stop Racism against the Roma Population" march, Novi Bečej,   **5.8**
March 23, 2011. Photograph by Srđan Veljović.

but also in smaller towns, often ignored by other liberal and leftist activists at
the time.

Zajović's leadership shows an enduring commitment to eradicating racism
and ethnic divisions that has not ceased to this day. "The idea of Yugoslavia
was kidnapped by the JNA (Yugoslav People's Army)," Zajović noted, stressing
that Serbian nationalism had appropriated socialism for its own political
agenda without adhering to Yugoslavia's antifascist, pro-unity legacy.[65] Serbian
nationalists have also frequently accused Women in Black of having neglected
Serbian women by only focusing on "foreigners" and "Muslims," a feeble
accusation that has no basis in reality.[66] Women in Black has worked in refugee
camps and with women all over Serbia and other republics, including Roma
women, who, to this day, remain third-class persons, often not even citizens,
in the region. In this way, Women in Black uphold and continue to espouse
the Yugoslav idea of unity. At yet another protest in Belgrade in 2011, their
banners read: "Anti-fazisam je moj izbor!" ("Antifascism is my choice"),[67] one
of the most important characteristics harkening back to Yugoslavia's partisan
slogan during World War II against the Third Reich: "Smrt fašizmu, sloboda
narodu!" ("Death to fascism, freedom to the people!"). Like the generations
of feminists opposing patriarchal militarism in Yugoslavia during the 1970s
and 1980s, Women in Black carried on the legacy of antifascist feminism in

Yugoslavia. Today (in 2021), the default message of their website says, "Always disobedient to patriarchy, war, nationalism, and militarism."[68]

The Yugoslav women's struggle for peace in the 1990s is of global significance. And while Mlađenović and Hughes refused to "end" their essay, they gave Women in Black the last word:

> Women will remember, women are telling each other stories of the reality we live in, and we are witnesses of many crimes for which this regime is responsible. Women, our friends from all parts and states of the former Yugoslavia, are still telling us about the suffering they went through and what is happening to them now. Nationalism didn't separate all of us; a stream of trust still exists between women of all names.[69]

Women in Black carried the performance politics of such resistance and healing into the heart of the streets and continue to do so to this day. This passage most profoundly illustrates what lies at the heart of this book and my wish to re-establish Jugoslovenka as a feminist figure that transcended the man-made, misogynist, nationalist wars of the 1990s: the fight for transnational solidarity among women, regardless of their class, race, ethnicity, religion, or national background, and a commitment to serving as witnesses to other women's pain and suffering.

Strike a pose! Jugoslovenkas under siege

Yugoslav women became a focus of Western media in the early 1990s, which often emphasized their beauty despite war and hardship. In these stories, these women's beauty was also often indirectly equated with nonviolence, victimhood, and a need to be rescued. But knowing the hard work of Women in Black and considering the harsh treatment they endured, as well as the scorn the "beautiful" feminist witches in Croatia received, beauty, or rather, what people deem beautiful, often has little to do with a peaceful predisposition or passivity, least of all with the need to be rescued. This section considers the complicated implications for Yugoslav women's emancipatory performance politics within such a heightened state of personal and political stress, in addition to the international fascination with their youth and beauty. This section begins with an analysis of the intersection of fashion photography and war upon the bodies of Yugoslav women, and ends with images of Yugoslav women snipers that defy the misogynistic logic of "peaceful, docile, pretty girls" who need to be saved. Instead, I argue, they visually echo the Yugoslav legacy of antifascist resistance by partisan women soldiers during World War II. In that way, these Jugoslovenkas embodied what drag queen and gay icon RuPaul has theorized as a specific type of beauty in survival: "I love stories of people who, against all odds, triumph in an unjust world while looking fabulous and kicking serious ass."[70] Through my feminist reading of these images of Yugoslav beauty queens and snipers and soldiers, this section drives home the point that Yugoslav feminist performance politics manifested in divergent and often opposing ways: emancipation in the Women in Black group took form through protesting war, while emancipation for other women under siege meant weaponizing their beauty or taking up arms to defend their families and children from military aggression.

An image of a "Sarajevo woman and a UN peacekeeper" from 1994 is an iconic war scene expunged from the patriotic iconography in the service of militaristic patriotism and yet firmly embedded in the violence waged on women's bodies that contrast this militarism (Figure 5.9). The glaring disparity between the beautifully dressed, unidentified woman rushing past a fully armed young man in full military gear is striking. Joshua S. Goldstein discusses this image as "embody[ing] the division between armed protector man and civilian protected woman."[71] For Goldstein, "[g]ender comes to center stage in another psychological defense used widely by male soldiers—the construction of a feminine 'normal' sphere of experience from which war is separated psychologically."[72] Following the logic of his analysis, the Sarajevo woman's appearance, beautifully dressed and running unarmed, represents the civility and "normalcy" of the female gender versus the governmentality of the male soldier. In war, according to Goldstein, "[w]omen collectively …

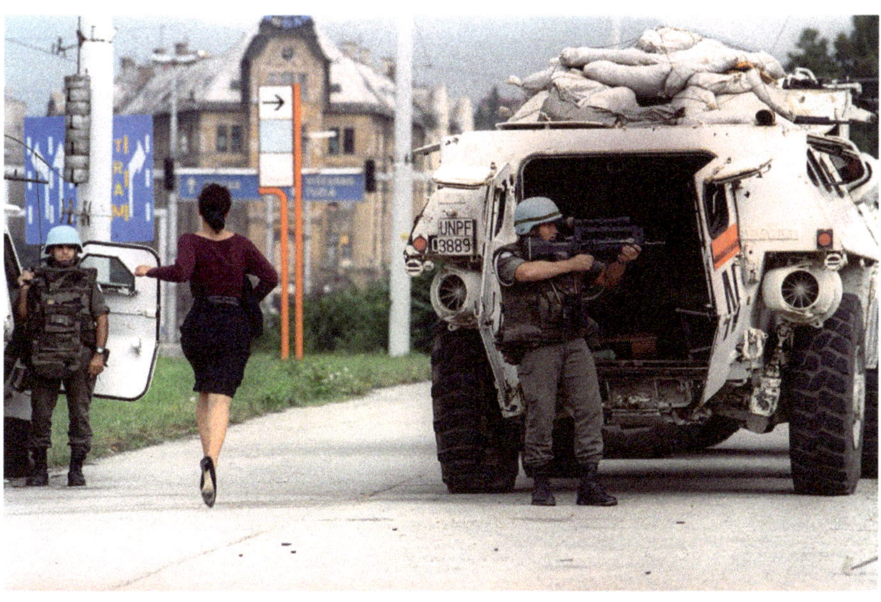

Chris Pfuhl, *Sniper Alert*, August 4, 1994.   **5.9**

serve as a kind of metaphysical sanctuary for traumatized soldiers, a counterweight to hellish war."[73] Women are peacemakers; men are warriors.

This metric between what is considered "normal/civil" and "beautiful" is embedded in a patriarchal logic that can be violent to women when deeming beautiful women pure and innocent (unless femme fatales) and others disposable and degenerate (women in refugee camps, for example). In the context of the history of Western perceptions of the Balkans, this theorization of the beautiful and peaceful Yugoslav woman in the raging Balkans reveals a deep-seated form of Orientalism for which Western scholarship on the region is notorious. Given this cultural clash, this image of the Sarajevo woman also represents something else: the alleged normality of war and violence often attributed to the Balkan region is augmented by the woman's awe-inspiring dignity of dressing to perfection despite imminent danger. Even during war, the Sarajevo woman looks impeccable, an image all too familiar for those of us who grew up with Yugoslav mothers, and an image equally familiar to those who followed the Bosnian conflict from abroad. To an exoticizing eye, this image may signal that the woman needs to be protected, flanked as she is by a military Humvee and a young United Nations Protective Force (UNPRO-FOR) soldier holding a large assault weapon aimed at an unknown target.

I propose a reading that is more situated in the lived experiences of Yugoslav women negotiating gender relationships and political crises in the Western Balkans, as I seek to excavate the narratives that remain buried to an imperialist savior's eye and suppressed by the banal rhetoric of domestic patriotic militarism. While her face remains hidden, we can make out this Sarajevo woman's dark hair, carefully arranged in a bun, a tightly fitting knee-length black pencil skirt with a black leather belt and a fitted, long-sleeved, maroon top. Her right leg is midair as she runs, revealing a black high heeled shoe. She is carrying something in her right arm—it could be a bag or a jacket. She could be of any ethnic or religious background, as Bosnia, and particularly Sarajevo, was remarkably multiethnic at the time. She could be a working woman coming home from her job, or a woman who met a friend for coffee. She could have been on the way to retrieve important documents for someone, to hear the orchestra play in Sarajevo's ruins, or just simply to see a relative—the image does not disclose any of these narratives. What we do know is that she has been identified as a "Sarajevo woman," beautiful, well dressed, and clearly in a hurry.[74] Widely circulated around the world, such an image quenched Westerners' thirst for asserting ethical and cultural superiority undergirded with pity. However, to those with familial and personal ties to this part of the world, this scene signifies Balkan women's bodily and cultural integrity—in the face of both domestic patriarchal carnage and the international rescue campaign, which proved to be catastrophically ineffectual and may have been based on imperialist and Orientalist assumptions.

Thus, while the fetish of young women remaining gorgeous during war often provokes fantasies of the Orient—fantasies in which women are held captive in uncivilized carnage and in need of rescuing by the West—this familiar trope doesn't account for the important work women of all classes, ages, and shapes do during war. As Lejla Somun has observed:

> So many women living in shelled and bombarded cities are heard of only in the traditional role they have: as mothers, as pretty women, good looking and well-dressed … but then there were all those women working as doctors, nurses, as interpreters and politicians, trying to work in impossible conditions under bombardment and shelling who never made the news, and whose images never became the icon of a woman defying shelling in a besieged city.[75]

As they remain invisible and ignored, their unacknowledged perseverance should be recognized in the strength of this unidentified Sarajevo woman, because she may also be one of them. Her anonymity allows for such an optimistic projection from a viewer like me, whose own mother's strength and illegal labor as a refugee within the Yugoslav diaspora in Germany was what kept our family alive and my father—who had deserted Milošević's army—out of harm's way. Situated perspective is important in unsettling a common perception of such an image. I want to provide my own projection on the image here because it illustrates just how subjective and multivalent its interpretation can be, depending on the vantage point.

With her hourglass figure, high heels, and air of civility, this Sarajevo woman's appearance also contrasts with the countless images of sickly, poor, starved, begging children, crying mothers, and devastated elderly women wearing headscarves from the region. Such images, while eliciting sympathy, often diminish the dignity of their subjects and contribute to an image of "the East" as "lesser than" and in need. We will see that it is precisely this association with the Balkans as "in need" that would haunt and demean even the "prettiest" Yugoslav women who sought refuge in Western Europe and North America in the 1990s. Images of strong and prevailing Sarajevo women inverted these narratives of endless helplessness, suffering, and submission, not just for the Western audience, but even more importantly for Yugoslav women living in the region or the diaspora.

Instead of focusing on how images of prevailing women have been instrumentalized by the West and its imperial gaze, it is pertinent to focus this analysis on what the same images might have meant to the women they resonated with in or from the region and in its diaspora, and when known, to the women that are actually in the photos. What role models can young women in the Balkans have if all they see is images of older generations of women as beggars, victims of trafficking, or worse? I argue that the images of powerful Bosnian women become iconic in their representation of Jugoslovenka's unapologetic investment in self-love and self-care regardless of life circumstances, a radical manifestation of the difficult feminist requirement for self-respect during militarized conflict.

In 1994, a year after she had directed *Waiting for Godot* in Sarajevo, Susan Sontag published an article in the *Performing Arts Journal* reflecting on her experience in Sarajevo and charging her readers to ask themselves why so little international attention was paid to such political carnage and injustice. She observed that Sarajevo residents didn't identify with nationalism, but instead held on to the transnational Yugoslav project that for them paralleled the democratic possibilities of a united Europe: "We are part of Europe. We're the people in former Yugoslavia who stand for European values: secularism, religious tolerance, and multiethnicity."[76] One of the most urgent questions included: "How can the rest of Europe let this happen to us?" Sontag was disgusted by the lack of international care for the fate of Sarajevo residents and linked that lack of interest to Islamophobia and racism. She noted: "When I replied that Europe is and always has been as much a place of barbarism as a place of civilization, they didn't want to hear. Now, a few months later, no one would dispute such a statement."[77]

The binary construction of civility versus barbarism has haunted the European continent for centuries, including Yugoslavia, where the more northern parts often espouse closeness to civilized European politics while southern Yugoslav countries are deemed more barbaric. Despite the shifting parameters of this colonial and imperial logic due to different political moments, the strictures of gender usually play out negatively for women, be it in "civilized" or "barbaric" parts of the land. Somun has pointed out that the onset of the war in Sarajevo was gendered, as the first victims of the siege in April 1992 were two women, Suada Dilberović and Olga Sučić, who had demonstrated against the war.[78] Somun adds: "Women living in bombarded cities end up being heroes of peace, while men are esteemed for the battles they win."[79] Ultimately, Sarajevo heroines would become most well known for their beauty. The year 1993 was when legendary photos of the Miss Sarajevo contest circulated, showing the winner, Inela Nogić, and other contestants holding up a banner stating in bold capital letters: "DON'T LET THEM KILL US" (Figure 5.10).[80] This plea for international help and support happened during the siege of Sarajevo and the celebration took place in a cellar due to constant sniper attacks. It became a sensation when the song "Miss Sarajevo," co-written by Brian Eno and U2 singer Bono and featuring Luciano Pavarotti's vocals, was released on the album *Original Soundtracks 1* (Bono and Eno used the pseudonym "Passengers"). Two years prior, Bono had met aid worker Bill Carter, who filmed the Miss Sarajevo contest during his work in Sarajevo. Bono produced Carter's documentary, which ended up with the same name as the music video, *Miss Sarajevo* (1993–1995). For the "Miss Sarajevo" music video,

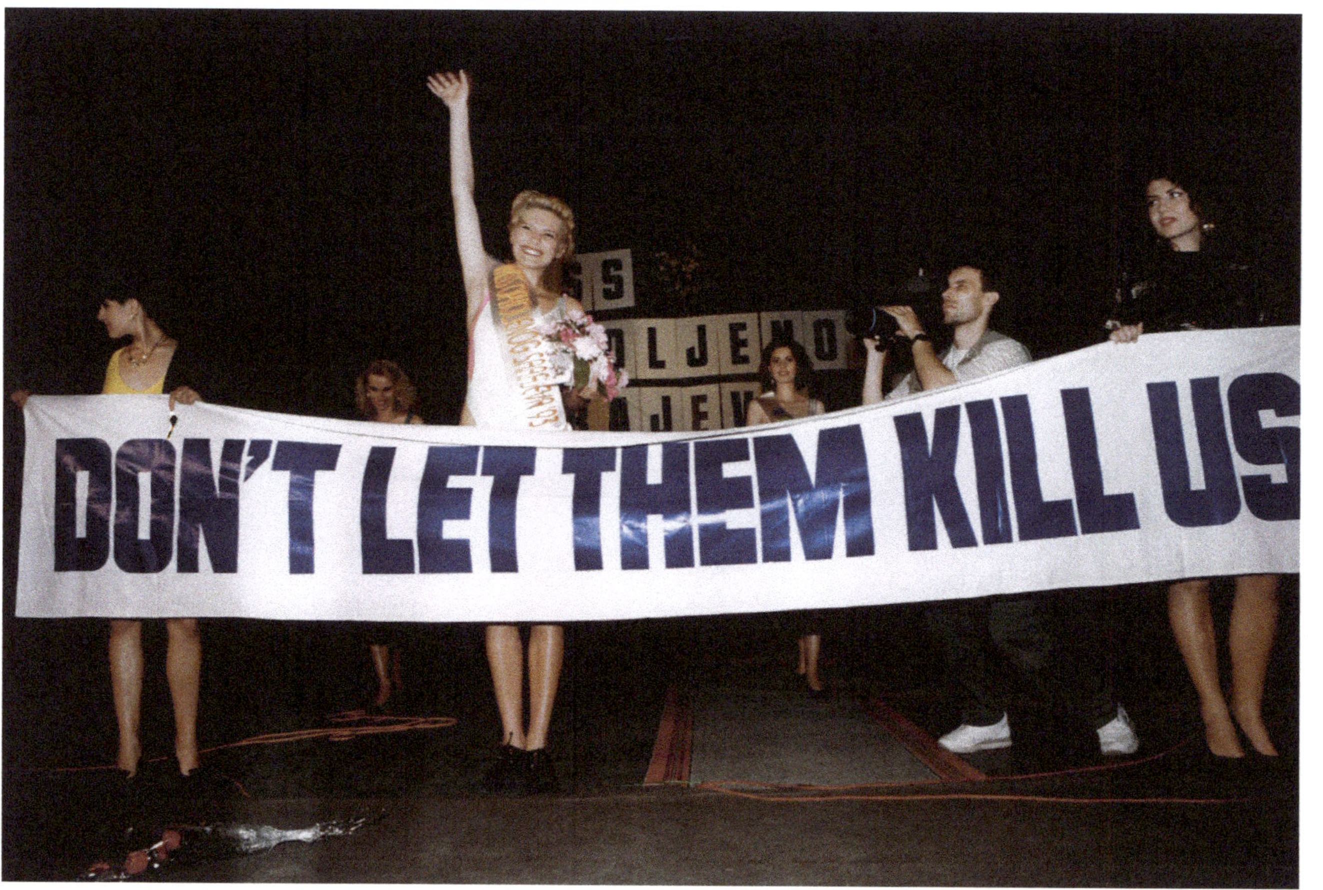

5.10 Patrick Robert, *Miss Sarajevo Pageant during the Yugoslavian Civil War*, 1993.

Bono asked Maurice Linnane to serve as director, but still featured footage from Carter's documentary along with concert shots of U2 and Pavarotti performing the song at a 1995 War Child charity benefit concert in Modena, Italy. Using Carter's footage, the barren city, shootings, burning buildings, and women walking through ruins and smiling at the camera were interlaced with clips from the Miss Sarajevo contest. In addition, the video showed more burning buildings whose flames would fade into the beautiful face of the Miss Sarajevo winner. Bono noted that he wrote this song to show how, despite war, Sarajevo women still embraced the joy of everyday life as a resistance to war.[81] This narrative was the most prevalent in approaching this legendary Miss Sarajevo contest in the 1990s and remains active decades later.

Although Carter's documentary was named after the Miss Sarajevo contest, *SPIN* magazine reported in 1996 that those beautiful women were an incidental focus of the film and that the main protagonist was the then thirteen-year-old Alma Catal, who becomes a principal narrator in the film.[82] Bill Carter noted: "Miss Sarajevo is Alma … it's her irrepressible spirit that represents the hope of Sarajevo," "a bright, animated fairy, surrounded by her friends rendered mute by the language barrier while she explains, in a blended tone of innocence and detachment, the inexpressible horror of the world."[83] In one gut-wrenching scene of the film, we see Catal with her even younger friends running to an abandoned bombed-out car, yelling "Let's go to the seaside (Idemo na more)!" Other kids echo, "I am going too (Idem I ja)!" Hearing those words, even writing them in this book, is difficult, because the essence of this moment feels so familiar to many of us who grew up in Yugoslavia: families going to the seaside in the summer was very common during Yugoslav times. War had destroyed that way of life and being, sealing it off in the past. The tenderness of the moment is augmented when the kids begin to pretend that the car radio works and start singing Swedish pop act Ace of Base's then widely popular song, "All That She Wants." The fact that the kids still dream of going on vacation, amid all the carnage, sniper alleys, shelling, and bombed-out homes, is tragic and symbolic. Not only does it bring home the reality that their childhoods were taken from them by war, it also signals the end of an era: no more Yugoslav peace where seaside vacations in the summer were the norm. Those luxuries would be out of reach for many citizens of the former Yugoslavia in the 1990s.

We must not forget, however, that it is precisely this type of "tear-jerking" footage that means different things in different contexts: while for Bosnian residents it was an opportunity to reach out to the world, this footage of their lives was instrumentalized by Western capitalist nations with corporate interests in those regions to raise funds, support anti-war causes, and demonize enemies. And much too quickly, those very videos and songs would help the people living in luxury forget about such troubling circumstances elsewhere.

Carter's description of Alma as the ultimate Miss Sarajevo, an "animated fairy," perfectly sums up what Ana Kothe has argued fulfills Western Orientalist fantasies of saving these otherworldly, beautiful, and innocent creatures from their savage Balkan context.[84]

Decades after the Bosnian war, U2 would adapt "Miss Sarajevo" and change it to "Miss Syria" in 2017, screening video footage of young Syrian children, bombed-out cities, markets, and close-ups of Syrian girls during their concerts.[85] One such fifteen-year-old girl became the focus of the video, holding a cell phone, standing in the sun with her eyes closed. At one point, she is also shown looking straight into the camera filming her, while Bono tells the crowd her name. The video ends with a close-up of her closed eyes, slowly opening. Bono had said of Sarajevo that he loved "this idea of the heroic resistance to oppression being the everyday dignity of a sense of humor, or refusing to become like the animals that are attacking you."[86] Despite the momentous contribution of honoring and recording women's resistance during war, Miss Sarajevo became the Balkan's "noble savage," reduced to her beauty that stood in contrast to the masculine savages of the primitive Balkans (or now, Syria).

While this Western male savior complex endorsed by U2, Pavarotti, Eno, and Carter haunts Miss Sarajevo, it was the women of the Miss Sarajevo contest who had dared to make such a potent and profound political statement about their lives. Their emancipatory performance politics became acutely tied to their dignity. This dignity was equally tied to the celebration of their beauty, which they presented deliberately in stark and bizarre contrast to the realities of war. Signifying their impossible position in the modest request— "DON'T LET THEM KILL US"—was their power. That in itself is a feminist plea if ever I've heard one: women asking not to be killed. Most have interpreted this action as a sign that normality can prevail during war, as noted, and argued that these pretty women served the Western gaze. Kothe offers one of the most insightful analyses of the music video and its reception by the U2 fan base.[87] But Kothe, too, mainly considers the reception of the video(s), not the action of the women themselves. Kothe's distanced look at the actual women in the videos becomes jarring when she casually remarks that they looked "a bit too thin?"[88]

Under such scrutiny, and carrying such intense cultural weight, the starving Miss Sarajevo contestants, and Sarajevan women in general, became some of the most visible Jugoslovenkas in the 1990s. These Yugoslav women represented dignity and a longing for peace, aware that at any moment they might be killed. In that regard, the young girls in Carter's documentary singing the hit "All That She Wants" by Ace of Base heightened the absurd and almost invasive presence of frivolous international pop music in war-era Bosnia from places in the world that had the privilege of peace and stability and failed to help: "All that she wants is another baby, she's gone tomorrow, boy." Carter was a lucky bystander, watching; the girls' and women's embodiment of resistance is of significance here. Their yearning for peace and dignity haunts every scene of Carter's film—and every life that might indeed be gone tomorrow—as does every interviewee's wish to be seen, understood, and heard. In one moment, a woman interviewee notes that "Every single person is surprised how women here take care of themselves, they are trying to look nice, to be beautiful, to dress nice." Another woman adds: "It was one of the ways to show that to the world, and to the enemies maybe. And to us."[89]

Why might Western viewers be surprised that Bosnian women "take care of themselves"? That answer was obvious to me as soon as the woman in *Miss Sarajevo* posed it. As a woman who came of age as a foreigner in Germany and whose racial otherness was often confused with numerous non-Northern European nationalities, most frequently Turkish and Bosnian, my body and clothing choices were continually scrutinized and rationalized as a source of diminishment, violence, and exclusion. Such social exclusion was prompted not only by difference in the quality of clothes, but by a racist prejudice that people from the Balkans are unclean, beggars, thieves, and illegal workers in the service sector. Western European nationalism has long labeled people from the Southeast European and Balkan region as uncivilized, with a propensity to continually wage war on one another. As such, for those in the Yugoslav diaspora and at home during the 1990s, dressing nicely and looking your best was not just a source of self-realization and vanity, but a form of survival and dignity.

Bosnian artist Šejla Kamerić's *Bosnian Girl* (2003), one of the most well-known works in the history of feminist art in the region, offers a powerful commentary on this very prejudice from "Western saviors" (Figure 5.11). In a black-and-white self-portrait, Kamerić's body is debased with graffiti from around 1994 or 1995 she replicated from army barracks in Potočari, Srebrenica: "No Teeth …? A Mustache …? Smel Like Shit …? Bosnian Girl! [sic]." It is speculated that a Dutch soldier of the Royal Netherlands Army Troops, while stationed with UNPROFOR in Bosnia and Herzegovina to protect civilians (1992–1995), wrote this on the army barracks in Srebrenica. This suspected perpetrator was stationed in Bosnia to protect its citizens, but instead he exhibited his own racism and misogyny toward these women. It is no secret how lucrative the war was for international soldiers, too, who apart from sex trafficking, had easy access to women in precarious positions during the war. As such, this soldier's words exhibited a disregard for women's bodies, easily used and discarded, and also demonstrated what the idea of the Jugoslovenka had become in the European male imagination just five years after Lepa Brena's 1989 song: not a blonde Southeast European beauty as in Brena's video, but a besmirched, toothless woman whose racial otherness is augmented by her excessive hair growth and whose femininity is ridiculed by her mustache,

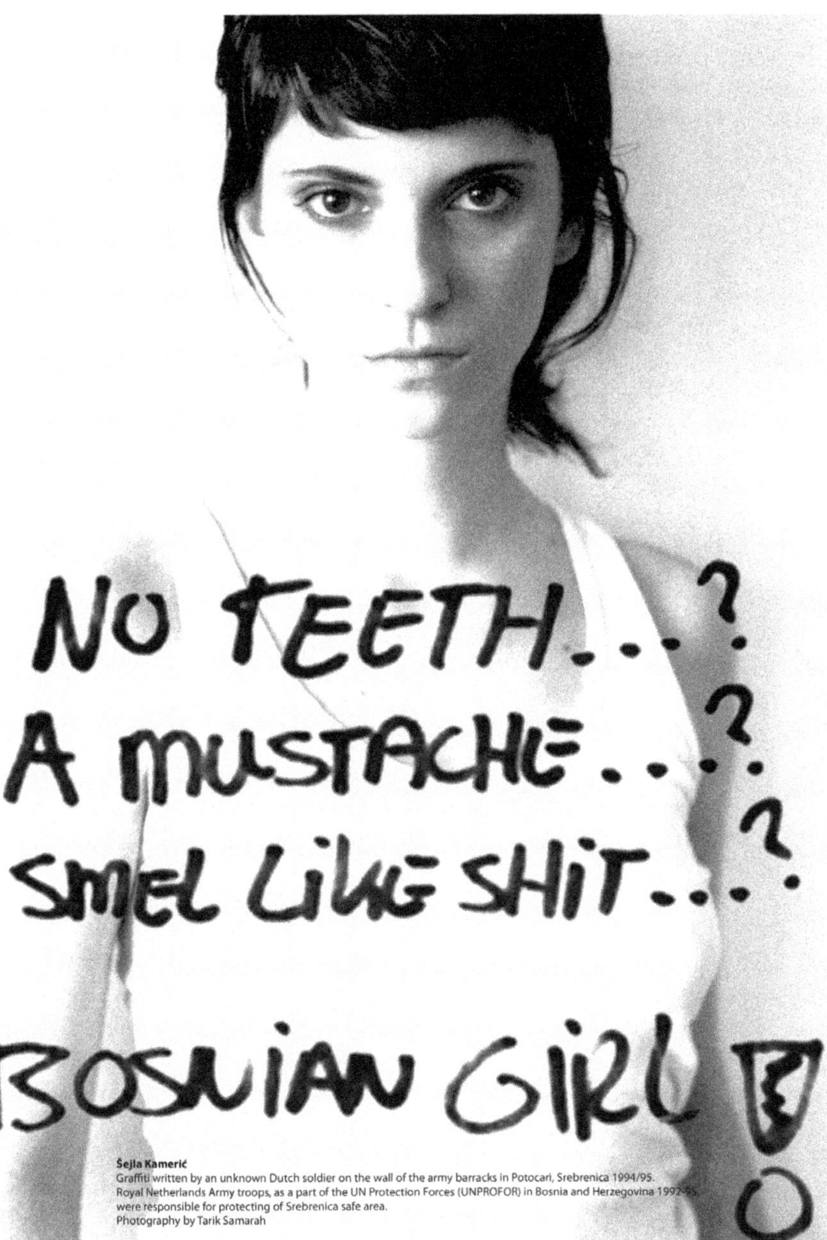

Šejla Kamerić
Graffiti written by an unknown Dutch soldier on the wall of the army barracks in Potocari, Srebrenica 1994/95.
Royal Netherlands Army troops, as a part of the UN Protection Forces (UNPROFOR) in Bosnia and Herzegovina 1992–95,
were responsible for protecting of Srebrenica safe area.
Photography by Tarik Samarah

Šejla Kamerić, *Bosnian Girl*, 2003.   **5.11**

and above all, smelling like shit. The gorgeous photograph of Kamerić beneath the graffiti, however, unravels the strength of that prejudice. Her beauty is central to heralding her as a confident woman who survived the siege of Sarajevo and whose marked body is a surviving and living monument to Yugoslavia.

In the 1990s, Sarajevo under siege became a topic of interest in the international world of fashion. *Vogue* magazine covered the Miss Sarajevo contest in an article written by Janine di Giovanni in 1997 called "*Vogue*'s View: Armed and Glamorous" with the subtitle "Janine di Giovanni Discovers How Women Find Strength in Stilettos, Designer Dresses, and Midnight-Blue Nail Polish."[90]

The article featured stories and images of women from diverse war-torn regions, including an insight into Miss Sarajevo winner Inela Nogić's life, whose "pathetic array of beauty supplies—two-year-old lipstick, broken nail files, tweezers lovingly polished, a blusher compact so worn it had a hole in the center" stood out to di Giovanni.[91] She described in detail how Nogić put on make-up and dressed beautifully despite the walls shaking from bombings in the city:

> It was midsummer of 1993, and the siege had gone on for more than a year. This city still had no running water, no electricity, no phones, no contact with the outside world … I had not bathed or washed my hair in a week. And yet Inela Nogić, seventeen years old and newly crowned as Miss Sarajevo, had awakened and, despite the shaking from incoming shells, had carefully applied make up and dressed in skintight faded Levi's, a low-cut red blouse, earrings, bracelets, and necklaces—as though she were going to an opening instead of out for a walk down Sniper's Alley.[92]

Snipers were notorious in Sarajevo, causing people to go about their lives with systems of protection in place and routes that were never truly safe. Because mountains surrounded the city, its citizens had no place to go. In a documentary film by Jennifer Rawlings, *Forgotten Voices, Women in Bosnia* (2008), women who survived the siege of Sarajevo described their circumstances.[93] They had to find a way to live in the war conditions to which they were subjected. One woman recalled that the electricity was cut off in the cities for most of the day, so a lot of families had to cook by burning whatever they could find. This too would pose a huge risk, as snipers would shoot at apartments that showed signs of life, so many women ended up cooking in the dark, with the drapes shut, and with one candle burning. The entire situation was unimaginably difficult. Many lost friends and loved ones every week. Nobody was safe. Somun described how "Women always changed their underwear and clothes before going out to the streets of Sarajevo, because the constant bombing and shelling meant that there was such a high probability of getting bombed, injured or killed." Women recalled the many times they made sure to be "neat and tidy in case we ended up in the hospital emergency room."[94]

The *Vogue* article did not pick up on the subtleties of this situation for women. In large red letters, the magazine highlights one additional observation: "In Sarajevo, a woman soldier applied lipstick in the trenches and wore high-heeled boots with her fatigues 'because you never knew when you might get lucky.'" It is hard to imagine that the woman quoted was saying this without deep cynicism or sarcasm, perhaps even ironically. Given the massive violence against women during this particular war, we must consider that for most women soldiers, feeling beautiful might have had little to do with sexiness or appealing to a man, or woman for that matter. It most likely had everything to do with retaining their dignity, the last thing they might be able to control when patriarchal nationalist violence is all-pervasive and deadly. But the fact that a woman from Yugoslavia would say that, nonchalantly, also attests to the comfort with which women were used to expressing their own sexuality and desires under the socialist system.

The *Vogue* article featured a photo of the Miss Sarajevo contestants smiling and overjoyed at the moment of the three women's win for the night. They all embrace in their joy, and the second runner-up is shown kissing Nogić on the cheek. In Rawlings's interview for *Forgotten Voices*, the brunette silver medal winner (not named) recalled: "I was second runner-up—that was the happiest time in my life ... there was a [newspaper] story about the pageant. And on one page, we were carrying this big sign, 'Don't Let Them Kill Us,' and on the other page of the newspaper it showed eighteen people were killed, and fifty-eight were injured (she guesses). That was a comparison to what was going on during the same day. We were trying to be beautiful, and during the exact time, people would be killed."[95] She ended that thought with one word: "Amazing." While to outsiders it might have been sadder and more perverse than amazing, those in the zone of survival rarely have the luxury to be cynical about the beauty they get to experience or embody. Indeed, Merriam-Webster defines the adjective amazing as "causing astonishment, a great wonder, or surprise." For this second runner-up to win Miss Sarajevo during the siege, being alive and beautiful while others were massacred was astonishing and the "happiest time" of her life.

The now-celebrated photo of Meliha Varešanović, wearing a dress, high heels, and pearls, and holding a purse, walking past a soldier was featured on the cover of the article (Figure 5.12).[96] This image of a dignified, fashionable, working Sarajevo woman circulated through the fashion world. Some twenty years later, Varešanović would recall this moment as both a source of pride and of sadness. She noted that if one "looked a bit deeper," beyond the pride in her face and posture, one could detect that her pride was masking her grief. She had just lost her mother that spring. "For me that was a tremendous loss,

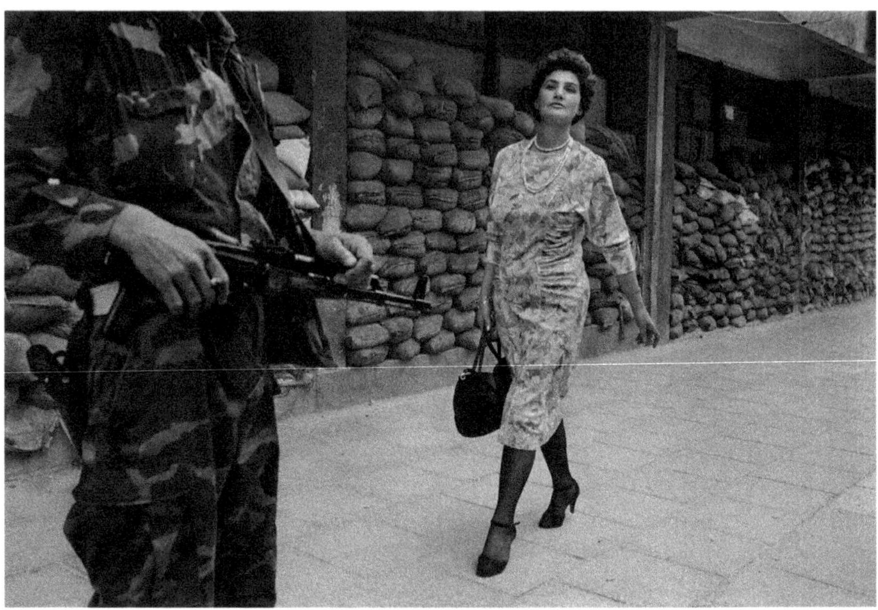

5.12   Tom Stoddart, Meliha Varešanović, 1995.

an enormous hurt and heaviness."[97] She remembered that she was on the verge of falling apart, but then her mother's words came to her: "In life, you have to stand up, fight for your dignity, and keep going."[98]

This multigenerational emancipatory strength is made manifest in a photo that renders the male soldier anonymous and transforms the ordinary everyday steps of a Yugoslav woman walking through her war-ridden city into a momentous event that politicized her body, beauty, and movement into a symbol of dignity within a region that is habitually denigrated. In the *Vogue* piece, di Giovanni recalled other sad stories, such as that of a woman who had already died, but who came to her in the story of a coat she found "in the black market on Marsala Tito Street." She elaborates: "The jacket—black wool with a white piqué collar and gold buttons—was hanging alongside a row of used sleeping bags. An elegant Sarajevo woman had bought it just as the war was breaking out but never got a chance to wear it; the price tags from a smart German store were still attached."[99] The two sentences devastate in their banality: the loss of a life summarized in an item of clothing that hangs like a sleeping bag among other found objects, no less from Germany, reminding us just how deeply the West was implicated in allowing the conflict to reach such depths and tally so many victims. But here too, the story takes a turn toward hope. According to di Giovanni, the woman's neighbor had salvaged the coat and sold it to give her son funds for firewood. Here is how she ends her discussion of the Sarajevo women survivors:

> They wanted 50 Deutsche Marks; I paid double that. I could never bring myself to wear it, but for a time it hung in my wardrobe like a talisman of hope and endurance. And I never stop thinking of that woman, who knew that a civil war was breaking out but still bought something glamorous and frivolous, waiting for the moment when it would take her out of her war-torn world and into someplace beautiful.[100]

The attachment to fashion, along with the lingering sexiness of these Yugoslav women—and the absurdity of both in the frame of war—marks Yugoslav feminist performance politics. Sanja Iveković brilliantly intersected beauty and violence in her famous *GEN XX* series (1997–2001) when the artist paired contemporary advertisement photos of supermodels with names and captions that honored World War II-era antifascist women fighters from Yugoslavia. Ljubica Gerovac, "charged with anti-fascist activities," who "to avoid capture … committed suicide" at the age of 22, or Nada Dimić, "charged with anti-fascist activities" and "tortured and executed" at age 19 in Nova Gradiska in 1943, are just two examples Iveković introduced to a younger generation far removed from socialist Yugoslavia which honored those women as national heroines.[101] As such, we must understand that the politicization of beauty by feminist artists from the region is often strategic and potent with resistance, as when Kamerić engaged conceptually with photos taken of her in 1994 by Hannes M. Schlick for *Magazine MODA Italy*, during the siege of Sarajevo (Figure 5.13). Women performance artists are often charged with narcissism, with being too beautiful, and when they are non-white and/or non-Western, with self-exoticization.

Wearing a short see-through camouflage shirt revealing her breasts, with matching pants, and standing with one foot resting on a large assault weapon, Kamerić poses like a model, showcasing her slender figure and donning a typical melancholic and mysterious facial expression. "This photo was taken during the hardest and most brutal part of my life," Kamerić noted, adding, "But the image shows something else."[102] At the time, Kamerić did not claim to be performing as an artist or engaging in what is categorized as performance art proper. But her performance politics of resistance were clear nevertheless as early as 1994: her sexy body is hers; the gun is at her feet; she is dangerous; and she possesses dignity and courage. Many examples in the history of art and visual culture mark women's emancipatory politics within the embrace of guns, such as Valie Export's *Action Pants: Genital Panic* (1969), re-enacted by Marina Abramović in her *7 Easy Pieces* at the Guggenheim

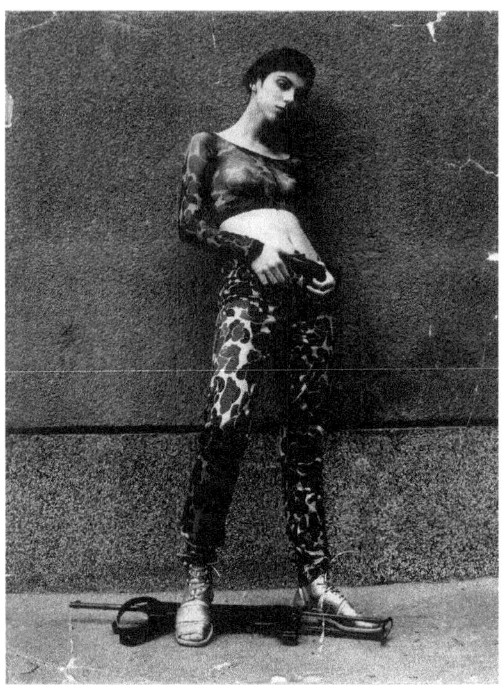

5.13   Šejla Kamerić, *Behind the Scenes I*, 2019 (original photo by Hannes M. Schlick, 1994).

Museum in 2005 (Figure 5.14). Considering the history of the Yugoslav wars, and Abramović's parents' participation in WWII, her re-enactment of Export's radical feminist action paired with an actual photograph of Kamerić during the war heightens the context of both artists' Yugoslav war backgrounds, a burden not present in Export's action in 1969, but one which many women confronting violent patriarchy have to face every day.

Another burden, which neither Export nor Abramović had to face, lies hidden beneath the surface, but is equally relevant for women's struggles against patriarchy, especially in Bosnia during the early 1990s: trying to find work in an environment where being taken advantage of was normalized and death was imminent. The photograph shows Kamerić in a phase of her life when she worked as a model, a job made most difficult under the circumstances. At this point of the war, Kamerić remembers, a kilo of sugar was worth 100 Deutsche Marks in the underground market.[103] The photographer, Hannes M. Schlick, who had come to Bosnia from Italy to do the shoot, offered to pay Kamerić and the other models with sugar, for which he undoubtedly had paid a negligible amount of Deutsche Marks in Italy. While one might be shocked by his behavior, calculating the profits he might make by taking advantage of

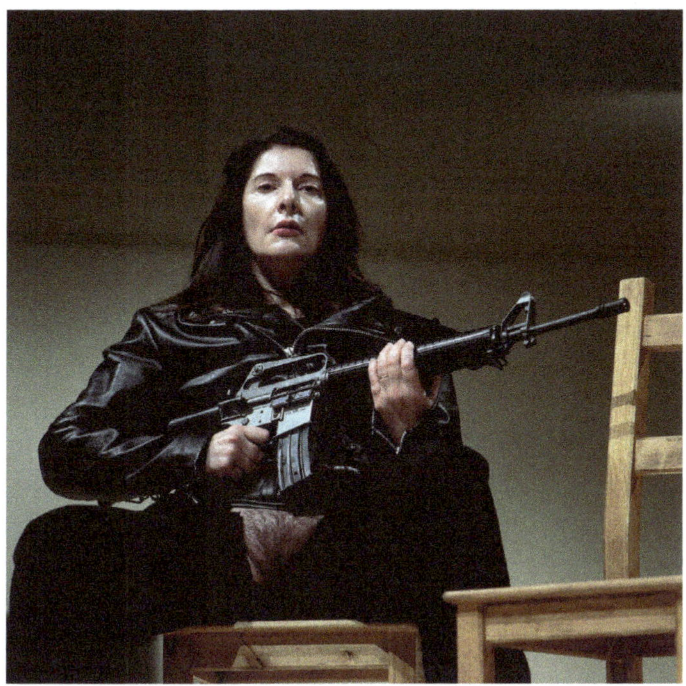

Marina Abramović, *7 Easy Pieces*, performing Valie Export, *Action Pants: Genital Panic*   **5.14**
(1969), Solomon R. Guggenheim Museum, New York, 2005.

struggling young women, war-profiteering on the backs of women was hardly
a new trade. The models knew very well what he was trying to do, cursed him
out, and demanded fair pay.[104] This story gives but a glimpse into the innumer-
able ways that Yugoslav emancipatory resistance was entangled with racialized
identities in Europe, exacerbated by UNPROFOR's presence, NATO's surveil-
lance, and Western profiteering, all explicitly thematized in Kamerić's *Bosnian
Girl* and latently readable in Yugoslav women's war experiences.

Kamerić's body paired with an assault weapon for the fashion shoot also
signals another reality: the Yugoslav women who became snipers during the
1990s wars, often captured by Western journalist photographers. I became
fascinated with the circulation of these images some years ago, but soon real-
ized throughout my research that cryptic stories about female Bosnian snipers
had become a fetishized currency in American gun-owner chatrooms and the
blogosphere, especially prevalent on sites that auction or discuss guns.[105] One
gun owner even dedicates a whole hour to teaching viewers how to use the
same rifle that the most mysterious of all the Yugoslav female snipers, code-
name "Arrow," had used.[106] Identified as Slobodanka Šakotić, "Arrow" was an

ethnic Serb sniper who competed professionally during the Yugoslav era. She is said to have changed political sides to protect the children and innocent victims in Bosnia.[107] A black-and-white photograph of "Arrow" sitting with her hair covering her face and holding a gun can be found on Google with a simple search for "Female Bosnian Sniper" or "Arrow Sniper," with headlines crowning the image that read, "Serbian Sniper Woman Killing Serbs," or "Woman is a Top Sniper in the War of Sarajevo." She is often quoted saying that she was walking and singing at a march with a group of demonstrators and that all of a sudden "from behind a building this man jumped out, fully armed, and began to shoot." She adds: "I couldn't believe a man could jump out and shoot at people just walking and singing."[108] While considered one of the deadliest snipers, she continues to be framed in heroic terms, again quoted saying, "if I do not pull the trigger, the target will pull his trigger, and maybe he'll kill a child or somebody standing in line for bread. … Every time I see a target and hit it, I don't have the feeling I killed a man. I have the feeling I saved somebody."[109] The veracity of these reports remains unclear, but their circulation speaks to the continued fascination with Yugoslav women and the collision of feminine beauty with violence. Yugoslav women in the early 1990s were not only subject to being circulated in music videos and fashion magazines as beauty queens, they also reached the curious minds of war fanatics.

Beyond being fetishized by male gun enthusiasts in the USA, it is important to note that these women were indeed heroines in their own right when they were active in the 1990s. For example, the "Bluebird Brigade" ("Plave ptice"), a unit of women soldiers formed in August 1992 in Pofalici just outside Sarajevo, became an important front against the advancing Serbs (Figure 5.15). In this black-and-white photo from 1992, we see three women holding assault weapons, two sitting down and one standing in front of a broken wall. Wearing camouflage and with long hair, two of these women are caught mid-chat, while the closest to the frame looks down at the floor. The women closest to the foreground reveal carefully manicured hands, with painted nails. The official caption for the photograph identifies them as "Members of the Bosnian government Army's female unit, the 'Bluebird Brigade' at their bombed-out base near Sarajevo on October 10, 1992. Many of the women in the unit are widows of soldiers who have died in the war." Two of them appear to be wearing wedding rings. Given their motives, one might surmise that these women's sense of dignity and self-care had little to do with attracting new sexual partners, but everything to do with remaining themselves and protecting their lives, including their own standards of beauty, from further annihilation.

But there is also an overtly political dimension. The woman in the front is wearing a headband with the signature Bosnian fleur-de-lis symbol, the golden lily, which became an important symbol of resistance against Serb aggression in the 1990s, harkening back to the golden lilies on blue background featured

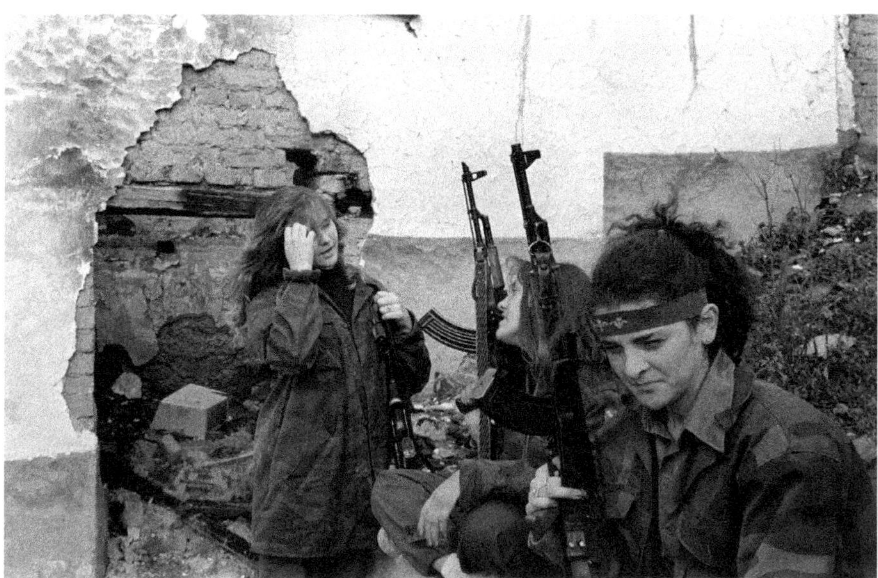

Morten Hvaal, "Bluebird Brigade" ("Plave ptice") photographed in 1992, Pofalici   **5.15**
(Sarajevo), Bosnia and Herzegovina.

on the coat of arms of Bosnian kings in medieval times. The golden lilies on blue background became the emblem for the new Bosnian and Herzegovina flag designed in the early 1990s and adopted in 1998. Tragically, the image of the female partisan once fighting on the Yugoslav front is now replaced by women who are forced to defend their families and loved ones from the ethno-religious violence dividing a nation. Wearing the golden lily became a signifier of being pro-Bosnia, pro-diversity, and pro-Sarajevo, as Bosnia was the most ethnically diverse republic of former Yugoslavia, making ethnic divisions all the more painful and devastating for the people living there.

The golden lily also appears in a photograph of a female Bosnian sniper, Nadia Jeriagić, who is not in camouflage but in "civil" clothing and filmed inside her apartment (Figure 5.16). The Getty description of the photograph states: "Bosnian sniper Nadia Jeriagić aims a rifle at Serbian snipers in the mountains from her position on the 20th floor of a Sarajevo building. Jeriagić, who works a regular shift sniping at Serbs, was an artist before the war."[110] Looking at the image, one might assume it is staged, especially given her attention to her make-up and overall appearance: she has on bright-red lipstick, her nails are done, and golden lily earrings dangle from her ears as she is focusing on a target. Her husband sits on the couch smoking a cigarette, watching her attentively. This striking image of the New Yugoslav woman in 1992, in a condition of survival—again marked by impeccable outer appearance—is

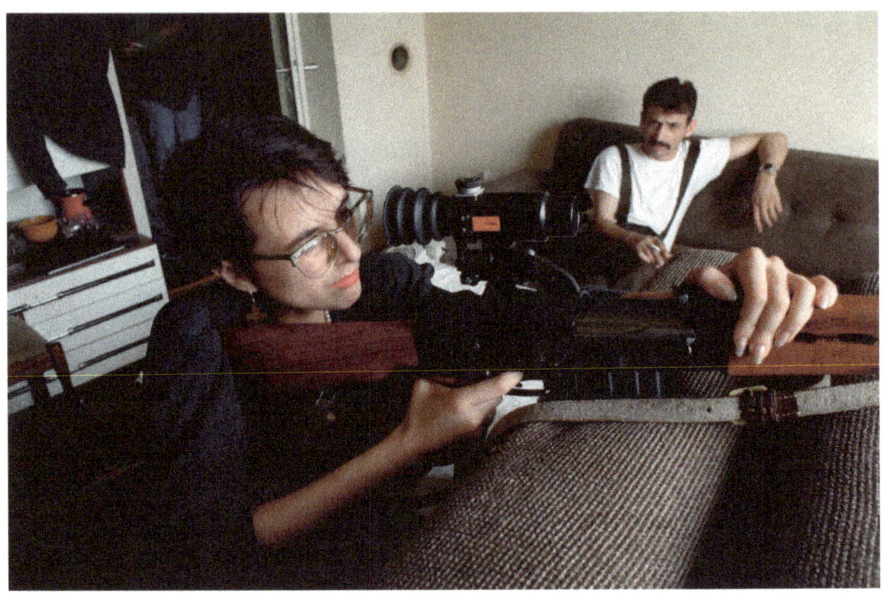

5.16   David Turnley, Nadia Jeriagić (Bosnian snipers), 1992.

deeply tied to violence and echoes the Yugoslav legacy of militarized socialism. In addition, just as beauty is often synonymous with allegories of peace
and stability, the notion of the artist is often associated with concern for the
beauty of the world, or if not beauty, then at least the creation of something
new, even if through destruction. One must only think of Niki de Saint Phalle's
Shoot Paintings. Interestingly, she modeled for *Vogue* before making a name
for herself as a painter, and her shoot paintings were often linked to her
"mental" state (disturbed), rather than creative genius. But of course, de Saint
Phalle's destruction resulted in the creation of art that would be exhibited,
while actual snipers like Jeriagić had no such edifying goals in mind. What
kind of "artist" Jeriagić was remains unknown, but what does operate in the
image is a feminist performance politics embodied in this female warrior
outshining her husband in courage, skill, and distinction, and standing for
women's power to defend themselves and their families.

Embodiment of a fractured land and culture: feminist resistance in contemporary performance, Jugoslovenkas today

Feminist performance artists from the region have integrated the Yugoslav
female body—now living in a post-Yugoslav world—as centerpieces of emancipatory strength in their works. Living between New Orleans and Sarajevo,

Bosnian artist Lala Raščić takes up the idea of the warrior woman by re-mythologizing famous Greek figures like Medusa and bringing them to life with her own body. A survivor of the Yugoslav wars, and part of a new genera-tion of ex-Yugoslav feminist performance artists, Raščić's practice is deeply committed to research, especially around stories in which folktales of the Balkan region intersect with reality and history. These intersections form a point of departure for performative inventions and explorations, such as in her work *The Damned Dam* (2010), where she foretells a flood in Bosnia in 2027, based on an actual Orson Welles-like radio event in Bosnia in 2000, where the radio played "Catastrophe" on Radio Lukavac. This radio broadcast falsely announced that the dam in the town was breaking, which lead to mass hysteria. In her fictional narration of yet another dam break set in 2027, based on the very same fake dam break from 2010, Raščić portrays two lovers, Merima and Tarik, who grew up in the new Bosnia under the neoliberal control of the European Union (EU), undergoing difficulties of survival and love using a dramatic storytelling style accompanied by Sevdalinka music. At the 54th October Salon in Belgrade, Raščić performed *The Damned Dam* in English for the first time and prominently featured Bosnian musician Jusuf Brkić. Just as in Pavlović's Women in Black documentary footage, the Sev-dalinka music in *The Damned Dam* is very familiar and moving to the knowing listeners from the region, whether from Bosnia, Croatia, Macedonia, or Serbia. These now-fractured Yugoslav identities were united in their understanding and knowledge of this music as well as the difficult conditions of the protago-nists. The struggles of two lovers who constantly have to adjust based on the irresponsible and reckless decisions made by people "above" them, such as bosses and city mayors, resonate deeply with people who grew up in the war-torn region, or whose lives were uprooted by political, economic, and climate catastrophes. As someone working in New Orleans and Bosnia, Raščić's own body is tied to such catastrophes, traumas, and movements across the globe. The artist puts survival, in the form of creative resistance, at the center of her practice.

In *Gorgo* (2019), her body is transformed into a modern archetypal warrior: she wears heavy copper armor and is equipped with small microphones that create a soundscape of her movements in that metal surface, which is central to the recorded performance (Figure 5.17). For Raščić, "Medusa's decapitation was a violent act of colonial patriarchy, as is the appropriation of her head as decoration for shields, armor, gables, plates, cups, and buttons."[111] For the warrior woman in *Gorgo*, the artist wanted to make "Medusa's dismembered body [...] whole again" by "using formulas from folktale and myth such as resurrection after initiation and the arming of the hero."[112] For her armor, the artist collaborated with Nermina Beba Alić, the only known female copper-smith in Bosnia, "breaking with the patrilineal tradition of this craft."[113] In the

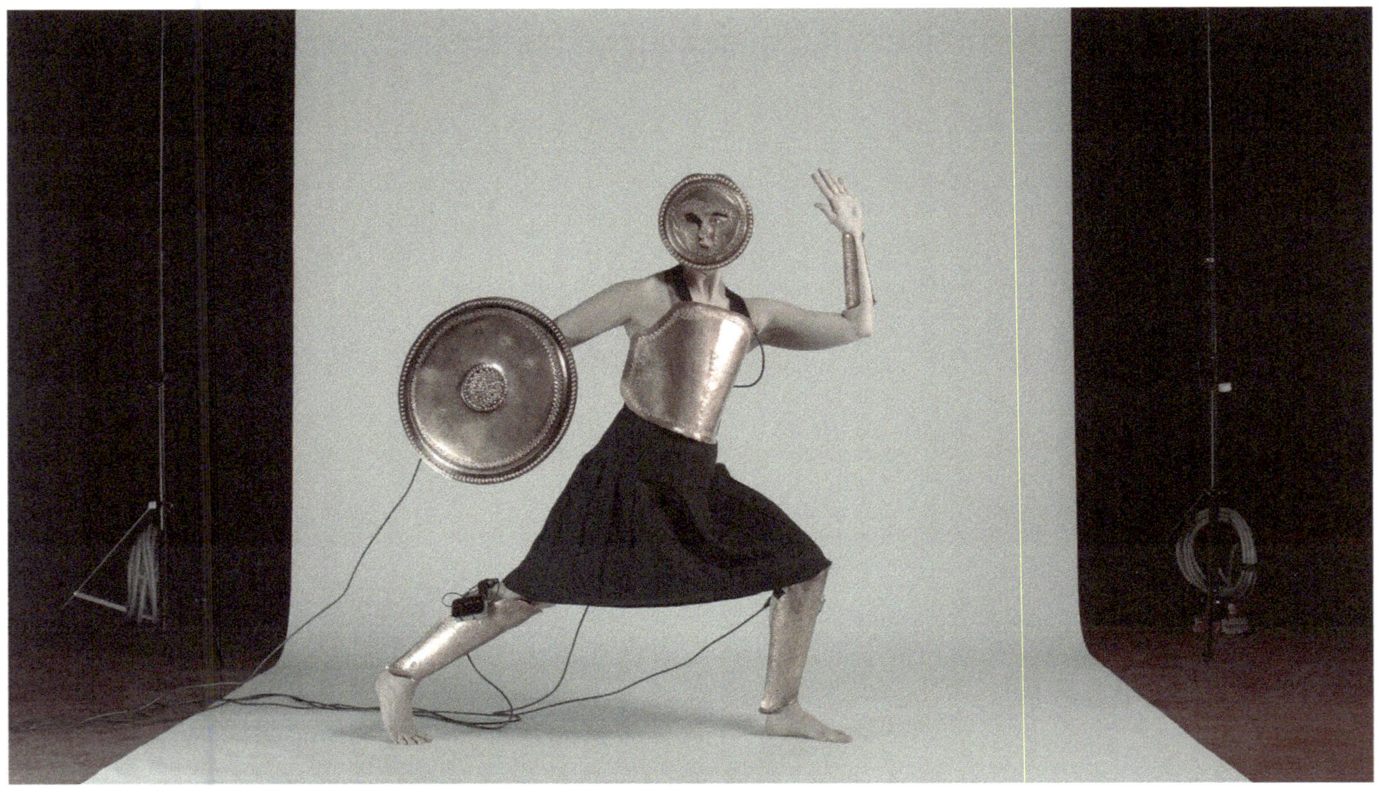

5.17   Lala Raščić, *Gorgo*, 2019. Video still.

performance, Raščić's body is magnificent in its ability to carry the burden of both the armor and the silence, which is just as piercing as the loud sounds emanating from the armor. Raščić, as warrior, carries a mask of Medusa but is the antithesis of the femme fatale. Raščić has said that she wanted to liberate Medusa from this burden of the femme fatale, and that she wanted "bodily integration" for Medusa.[114] Given this emphasis on fighting the patriarchal appropriation of Medusa and her disintegration, I couldn't help but wonder if the subtext of this performance could also be read as the appropriation of Yugoslavia by patriarchal nationalism, as well as its fragmentation. For me, watching Raščić in her armor, stiff behind the cold metal and silent, yet ready to fight, signifies the female Yugoslav warriors of the 1990s struggling for dignity, emancipation, and most of all, the unity of a people torn apart by violent civil war. A fictional, illegitimate performer who links together the histories of women's oppression in her own region through local oral epic traditions and Greek mythology, Raščić's emancipatory strength lies in embracing these oral and emotional histories, appropriating them, and forming new possibilities for women.

There is an urgent need to think about the illegitimate position of Yugoslav women's bodies in the 1990s and 2000s, plagued by changes in political power at home in addition to contending with the EU's superiority over immigrants relying on opportunities to live and work there. Tanja Ostojić's work most profoundly thematizes this diasporic position through her performance practice and her actual life. When I asked her what it felt like to be from Yugoslavia in the 1990s, she recounted all the visa problems she encountered because of the shifting borders and new nations when she had artist residencies. But one memory from an encounter she had in France stood out to me. There, she had been asked where she was from, to which she instinctively responded, "I am from Yugoslavia." This sentence, so familiar to many of us who lived through the disintegration, was swiftly and harshly countered with "That country no longer exists."[115] While someone from France or Germany could so easily sum up the fracture of Yugoslavia with the total negation of a country's existence, the painful fracture within the self of those who came from this "non-"country was not so quickly understood. The violence from the ongoing civil war at home and the racism and stereotypes projected onto ex-Yugoslav immigrants made the 1990s the most brutal time for Jugoslovenkas.

Ostojić's five-year project *Looking for a Husband with an EU Passport* (2000–2005) spoke to this brutality when she conceptually debased herself by asking to marry a man in order to enter the EU (Figure 5.18). In this way, her work spoke directly to the precariousness of Yugoslav women's lives and stereotypes of mail-order brides. In the poster advertising her performance, Ostojić's body doesn't show any of the "excessive" hair associated with *Bosnian Girl* in Kamerić's work. Instead, Ostojić does away with her hair by shaving it

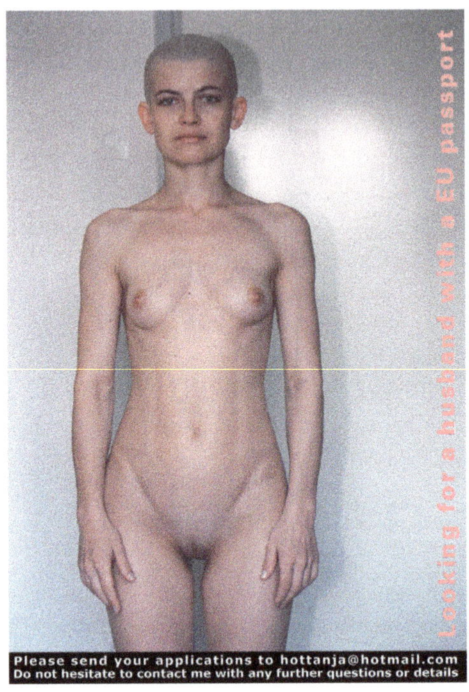

5.18   Tanja Ostojić, The "Ad" from Looking for a Husband with EU Passport, 2000–2005. Participatory web project/combined media installation.

and thereby removing the markers of her racial otherness. Her skinny body, however, echoes images of concentration camp survivors familiar to anyone coming of age in Europe at that point and tragically also very much part of the Yugoslav geographic space during the early 1990s in Bosnia. The fact that she ended up marrying a German man at the Museum of Contemporary Art in Belgrade and then ritually divorcing him a few years later exposed her embodied struggles of going through the EU's discriminatory immigration processes, which stigmatize single women and make them dependent on men's sexuality for mobility and legal status.

In her 2001 conceptual and performance work *I'LL BE YOUR ANGEL*, Ostojić pushed her outsider and Yugoslav immigrant status in the arts to the foreground by accompanying renowned curator and director of the Biennale that year, Harald Szeemann, as his unofficial escort at the opening of the 49th Venice Biennale (Figure 5.19). Visibly discomfited by Ostojić, who never left his side and insistently smiled at him, Ostojić picked Szeemann as the person to officially "open" her exhibition at the Venice Biennale (see Chapter 1). Her exhibition was her own body, specifically her pubis, on which she shaved

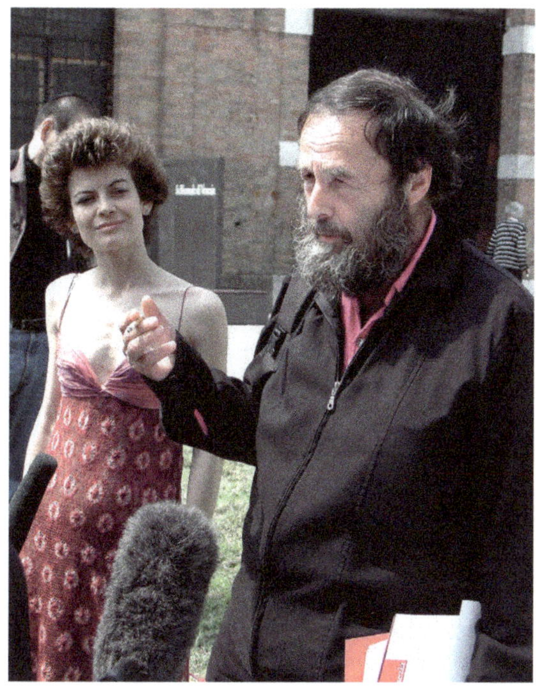

Tanja Ostojić, *I'LL BE YOUR ANGEL*, 2001, four-day performance with Harald Szeemann   **5.19**
during his exhibition *Plateau Humankind* at the 49th Venice Biennale.

her hair into the shape of a black square resembling Malevich's painting. Appropriating Malevich on her own body can be read as a potent feminist intervention in the arts on two levels: (a) Malevich has frequently been used by the male artists of the Neue Slowenische Kunst collective, who evacuated any reference to women, and when they did, they overwhelmingly objectified them (Chapter 4); and (b) Malevich's suprematism, deeply masculinist in the discursive sphere of modernism, is replaced with raw female sexuality, which inevitably is rendered a threat. Szeemann never officially "opened" her exhibition, but Ostojić circulated postcards with the image of her shaved Venus hill, *Black Square on White* (2001), among art goers in Venice. According to Ostojić, this unofficial and unsanctioned action had negative consequences: her text was subsequently censored in the Biennale catalogue.[116] Ostojić provocatively made visible what so many women already knew and what since the #MeToo movement has become poignantly evident: a woman's rise or fall in the arts often lies in the hands of men whose gatekeeping powers are habitually sexually charged. Choosing to act as the obnoxious, overfriendly, and uninvited guest Szeemann could not easily get rid of, Ostojić also brilliantly exhibited the powers of immigrant Jugoslovenkas' survival in Europe: smiling and persisting while enduring the humiliating position of constantly being "lesser than."[117]

Jugoslovenkas to this day remain uninvited yet tolerated guests. Their position is only worsened when they carry an additional ethnic marker: that of being Roma. Questions of citizenship and legal status are relevant for Selma Selman, the youngest artist in this book, born in 1991, long after Tito's death and at the time of the burgeoning wars. Selman has lived in the United States for several years, but the artist was born and grew up in a Roma settlement called Ružica in Bosnia. Her works often thematize the position of being Roma in the post-Yugoslav context. The legal rights for Roma worsened significantly after socialism and with the rise of neoliberal capitalism, especially for Selman's community in Ružica, where Tito's era of socialism is remembered as a time "when everything was perfect."[118] Her grandmother in Bihac, for example, was the first woman to sell gold at the local market; in fact, Selman recalls she was the only woman working at the market at the time, and that Tito loved her and she allegedly danced for him once. Selman's father also had good economic and social standing and was close friends with Alan Islamović from Bijelo Dugme, who sang in Lepa Brena's "Jugoslovenka" (1989) (see the Introduction). Right before the war, Islamović had offered to take Selman's father with him out of the country on a private jet, but her father did not want to leave behind his brother because of the impending war. Selman remembers her father saying, "Once war starts, it never ends."[119] And indeed, the consequences of war have been immense in her community. Selman has used her art and her international connections to help her village and to raise funds for girls to go to school, a philanthropic engagement that has inspired young children to scream "Tito! Tito!" when they see her; she now drives a van with the words "Selma Je Tito" ("Selma is Tito") painted on them. She explained, "everybody here looks at me as Tito, because I bring them happiness" (Figure 5.20).[120]

But Selman's performances also take on embodied violence. In *Composition: Bori, Nevjesta, Bride*, performed at Dreamland Buffalo in 2016, the artist pushed a rusty barbed wire into the skin of her hips for approximately fifty minutes (Figure 5.21). Standing in the corner with her back to the audience and her face concealed by her hair and the walls surrounding her, Selman's screams and her pain, amplified by a microphone, became a soundscape of terror in the room. For many visitors, this profound moment of witnessing another human's pain was too much; for others, it activated their own experiences of suffering. And for many of us, this work spoke to the tragedy of borders that cost so many people their lives and that continue to scar and violate those who do not fit within the hegemonic powers of nations and those

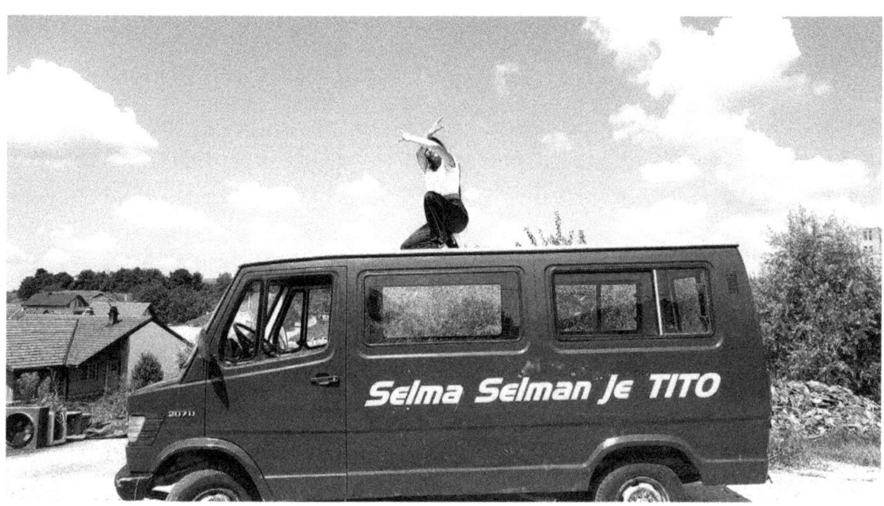

Selma Selman, *Selma Je Tito (Selma Is Tito)*, 2018.   **5.20**

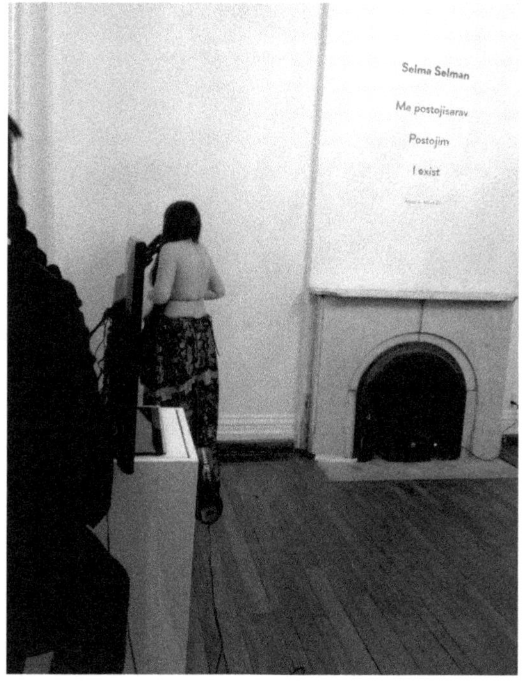

Selma Selman, *Composition: Bori, Nevjesta, Bride*, 2016, performance, Dreamland Arts   **5.21**
Gallery, Buffalo, NY.

who are criminalized because of their lack of citizenship, their ethnic or religious backgrounds, or their gender.[121]

For Selman, this work took on an additional and very personal dimension: the artist's relationship to her mother's past. Selman's mother was married off at an early age and remained segregated in the small Roma community of Ružica. Selman's decision to hide her face in the corner while inflicting such gruesome pain on her own body metaphorically and metonymically connected her to her mother's existence, which was, according to Selman, "made insignificant and invisible to the outside world." The barbed wire, therefore, not only connotes the borders imposed by nations and states, but also gendered hierarchies and traditions, which reduce women's bodies to landscapes of power struggles and violence.

Her mother's fate was also deeply linked to the cruel divisions that arise when citizenship and nationhood determine one's ability or inability to move in this world. Selman's mother was trapped without a proper passport in Bosnia for a long time during the disintegration of Yugoslavia. Citizenship here meant limits to mobility and action for her body. In *SALTWATER AFTER 47*, Selman represents her mother's first contact with the sea (Figure 5.22):

> Her big wish was always to see for herself if it is really salty like she heard that it was. In this video, I captured that first moment and her reaction. "AFTER

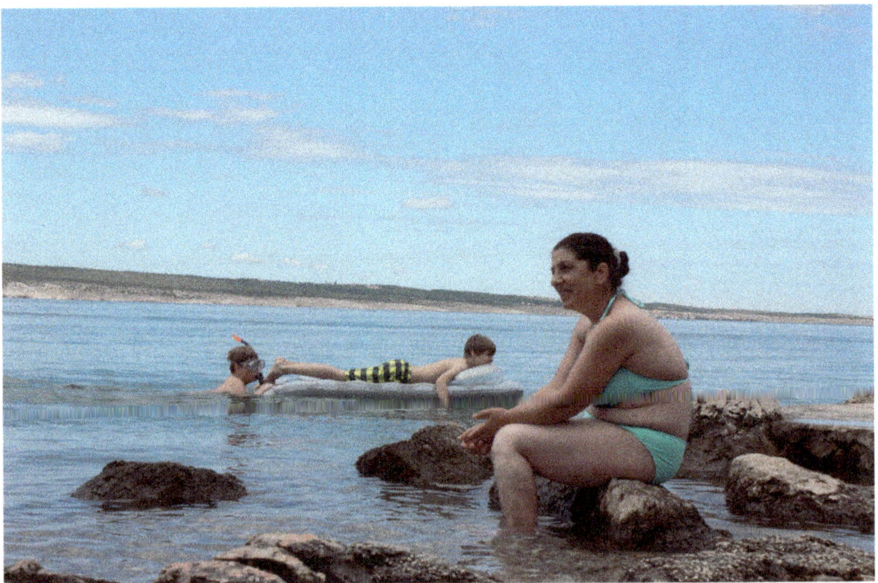

47" refers to her lack of documents when she came from Kosovo to Bosnia. Culturally, the act of a woman leaving her paternal home to live with her "husband" is perceived as a marriage, whether or not it is officially recognized by the state or religious authorities. At that time in particular, there was no concept of simply "living together." Hence, at thirteen, she was unofficially married to my then seventeen-year-old father, but the marriage was not state-certified. After the dissolution of Yugoslavia, she was left stateless. In 2014, after many discussions with authorities in Bosnia and Herzegovina, she managed to obtain Bosnian citizenship. After 47 years, she received her first passport. I decided to make her wish come true. I took her on a vacation to the sea.[122]

Selman's mother's fate is intertwined with her daughter's life; the latter's performance work fluctuates between continents, cultures, and temporalities marked by political instability, racism, sexism, war, and survival. I want to return to Selman once more, who reminds us that the era of Yugoslavia, and the era of Jugoslovenka, is far from over, even if fictional and counter to the nationalist narratives emerging stronger and stronger every day. In a random moment when Selman was on the border between Trieste (Italy) and Slovenia, she felt relaxed, let her hair flow in the wind, and had her picture taken (Figure 5.23). She then decided to call it *Ja Sam Jugoslovenka* (*I am Jugoslovenka*),

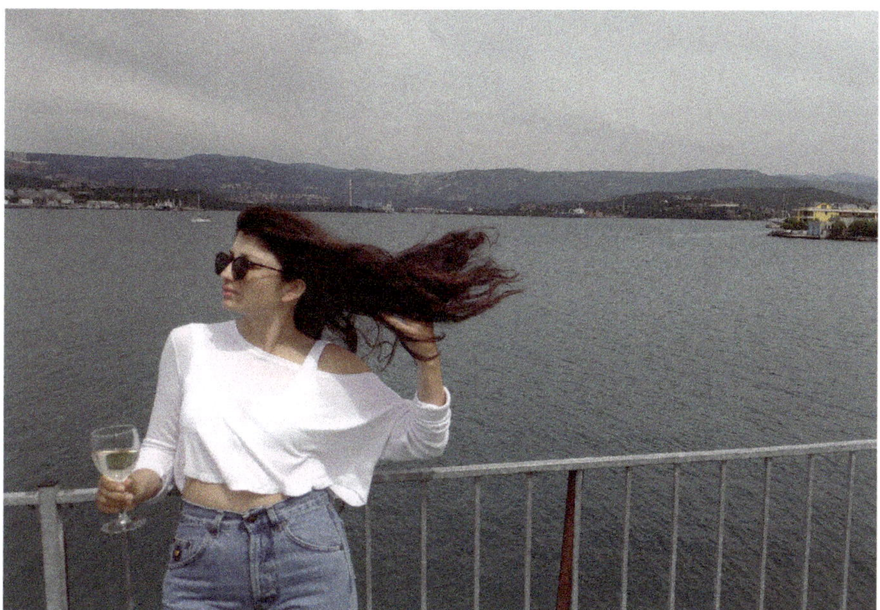

Selma Selman, *Ja Sam Jugoslovenka (I am Jugoslovenka)*, 2018.   **5.23**

because, as she recalled, she felt "really great" and "connected across borders." She added: "I felt like Lepa Brena."[123] If a young ethnic Roma woman originally from Bosnia, living in the USA, and working as a performance artist internationally lives and breathes the life of Yugoslavia and Jugoslovenka, then we might indeed deduce that while the Yugoslav political project was destroyed by nationalism and neoliberal capitalism in the early 1990s, its feminist and multiethnic legacies live on in the bodies of new generations of Yugoslav women.

Conclusion

In her 1999 book, *Café Europa*, Drakulić described the humiliating experiences of what it meant to be "Eastern European" while traveling to Oslo, Norway, with a Croatian passport in the 1990s. Accompanied by her Swedish husband, who had no problem whatsoever at the border, Drakulić was inspected and interrogated, despite an official invitation to Oslo. "By now, I feel poor, smeared, and embarrassed," she noted. Adding: "and that is the mood in which I take my first steps in a Western country."[124] Humiliation within the West was one definitive marker of Jugoslovenka's experience, but at home too, the rise of conservativism and heteropatriarchal pressures tightened the rope around feminists' work. Many feminists felt freer in the united Yugoslav context than they did once the country had disintegrated. Kesić summed up the adverse conditions for women, and feminists, in the 1990s the following way: "On one hand, to be a woman in a war zone meant one stood a good chance of being raped. On the other, to be a feminist within the nation provoked political, and sometimes even bodily, threat."[125] While being a feminist was dangerous, being invested in helping women was plagued by another specter: the rise of homophobia and religious conservatism. Mladenović stated:

> Working with victims of war meant that the patriarchal order of ethics had to cut through me again: I had to understand that the phenomenon of victims of war was imprinted with moral purity, innocence, and righteousness … in front of which I had to hide my lesbian life that was still seen as "an immoral outlaw against nature." I did not know how to fuse these two phenomena together … neither in my body nor in the language.[126]

The end of Yugoslavia in the 1990s also meant the end of certain emancipatory embodiments feminists had fought for, and achieved, in the 1980s, such as LGBTQ activism and solidarity. Morally charged, sexually harassed, and under the gaze of international Orientalist projections, the changed signification of Jugoslovenka's body during and after the Yugoslav wars is one of the most complicated and understudied subjects in the history of art and visual culture of the region. It has been the aim of this chapter to reveal some of the difficulties Yugoslav women encountered entering into the 1990s and to high-light their varied feminist resistance strategies until today. While peaceful activism was at the heart of an older generation of feminists upholding their transnational ties in the early 1990s, other Yugoslav women turned toward preserving their dignity in caring for their outer appearances, or taking up arms against patriarchal military aggression. Performance artists in contemporary art thematized these diverse forms of resistances in their embodied actions and performances, which to this day are tied politically to the unresolved and traumatic experiences of war, the fragmentation of the country, and the pervasive power of patriarchal, racist nationalism that Yugoslav women's feminist performance politics continually contest.

Notes

1 Beverly Allen, *Rape Warfare: The Hidden Genocide in Bosnia-Herzegovina and Croatia* (Minneapolis: University of Minnesota Press, 1996), 61.
2 Biljana Regodić, "Homeland as a Form of Women's Disloyalty," in Tanya Renne, ed., *Ana's Land: Sisterhood in Eastern Europe* (Boulder, CO: Westview Press, 1997), 176.
3 Ibid., 178.
4 Lepa Mlađenović and Donna M. Hughes, "Feminist Resistance to War and Violence in Serbia," in Marguerite R. Waller and Jennifer Rycenga, eds., *Frontline Feminisms: Women, War, and Resistance* (London: Routledge, 2001), 249.
5 Bill Carter, *Miss Sarajevo* (1995). Produced by Bill Carter and Liam Cabot; executive producers: Bono and Ned O'Hanlon.
6 Svetlana Slapšak, "Mein Feminismus ist eine logische Konsequenz von 1968," in Boris Kanzleiter and Krunoslav Stojaković, eds., *1968 in Yugoslawien: Studentendproteste und kutlturelle Avantgarde zwischen 1960 und 1975* (Bonn: Dietz, 2008), 95. Translation by the author.
7 Vesna Kesić, "Confessions of a Yugo-Nostalgic Witch," in Renne, ed., *Ana's Land*, 197.
8 Ibid. Kesić gives an explanation of how "pička" could be translated: "a vulgar popular term for women's genitalia." "Pička" is also a term often used like "bitch" in English, but because of the aggressive charge behind kicking in the "pička", "cunt" seems like the most fitting translation here.
9 Allen, *Rape Warfare*, xii.
10 "Yugoslavia FR," in Bojana Pejić, ed., *After the Wall: Art and Culture in Post-Communist Europe* (Stockholm: Moderna Museet, 1999), 204.
11 Tim Judah, *Kosovo: War and Revenge* (New Haven, CT: Yale University Press, 2000), 49. Judah also notes here that although Milošević openly denounced the *Memorandum* in 1987, he was already pushing his campaign against Kosovo. Judah rightly comments that Milošević "proved past master at telling people what they want to hear and, in this way, enlisting their support," 50.

12 Ibid., 42–43.

13 "Yugoslavia FR," 204.

14 Mlađenović and Hughes, "Feminist Resistance to War," 249.

15 Ibid.

16 Slapšak, "Mein Feminismus," 102.

17 Lepa Mlađenović's poster is featured on the cover of Zsófia Lóránd's book, *The Feminist Challenge to the Socialist State in Yugoslavia* (Cham, Switzerland: Palgrave Macmillan, 2018).

18 Lepa Mlađenović, "Foreword: Searching for Our Lesbian Nests in Yugoslavia and After," in Bojan Bilić and Sanja Kajinić, eds., *Intersectionality and LGBT Activist Politics: Multiple Others in Croatia and Serbia* (Cham, Switzerland: Palgrave Macmillan, 2016), x.

19 Mlađenović, "Foreword: Searching for Our Lesbian Nests," x.

20 The archive was founded after Sklevicky died in a car accident in January 1990. Sklevicky had begun the collection of feminist material decades earlier, in 1976. The research project *COURAGE Cultural Opposition: Understanding the Cultural Heritage of Dissent in the Former Socialist Countries* describes the current state of the archive: "The collection consists of a newspaper and periodicals collection, a documentation section and a library, which testify to Sklevicky's professional work and interests, and are primarily related to feminism and issues of women's rights in Yugoslavia and the world, while a smaller part of the collection is related to research into folkloric customs and new holidays in Croatia. The Collection was originally located at the Institute in Zvonimirova Street in Zagreb, in Sklevicky's room on the fourth floor, which was left untouched after her death. In 2006, the Institute of Ethnology and Folklore Research moved to Šubićeva 42, and with it the Sklevicky Collection. After the move, the collection was no longer physically consolidated; the newspaper and periodicals collection was separated and stored in the Library's archives, while the library from the Sklevicky collection was attached to the library fund under the separate LS signature. The documentation section remains a part of the documentation of the Institute of Ethnology and Folklore Research. The documentation and library parts of the collection are filed and processed, and are visible in the library catalogue and in the documentation database, while the newspaper and periodicals collection remains unlisted but is available to the public in the library's premises." See: http://cultural-opposition.eu/registry/?uri=http://courage.btk.mta.hu/courage/individual/n95916 (12/18/2018).

21 Mlađenović, "Foreword: Searching for Our Lesbian Nests," x–xi.

22 Mlađenović and Hughes, "Feminist Resistance to War," 261.

23 Ibid.

24 Quoted in ibid. Original source: in Women in Black, ed., *Women for Peace Anthology* (Belgrade: Women in Black, 1993), 8.

25 Suzanne Evans, *Mothers of Heroes, Mothers of Martyrs: World War I and the Politics of Grief* (Montreal: McGill-Queen's University Press, 2007), 139. Milošević delivered his famous "Gazimestan speech" on June 28, 1989 in

Kosovo, at the site where Serbs fought against Ottoman forces in 1389, which Milošević claimed meant that the Serbs had defended all of Christian Europe from the Muslim Ottomans.

26 Jelena Batinić, W*omen and Yugoslav Partisans: A History of World War II Resistance* (Cambridge: Cambridge University Press, 2015), 51.

27 Staša Zajović, "Nationalism and Serb Women," in Renne, *Ana's Land*, 169.

28 Ibid.

29 Mlađenović, "Foreword: Searching for Our Lesbian Nests," x.

30 Tatjana Pavlović, "Women in Croatia: Feminists, Nationalists, and Homosexuals," in Sabrina Ramet, ed., *Gender Politics in the Western Balkans: Women and Society in Yugoslavia and the Yugoslav Successor States* (University Park: Pennsylvania State University Press, 1999), 146.

31 Ibid.

32 Mlađenović, "Foreword: Searching for Our Lesbian Nests," x.

33 Metka Mencin, "Women and Politics: A Note of Introduction," in Renne, *Ana's Land*, 218.

34 Andrea Spehar, "The Lesbian Question," in Renne, ed., *Ana's Land*, 207.

35 Pavlović, "Women in Croatia," 136.

36 Vesna Kesić, "Muslim Women, Croatian Women, Serbian Women, Albanian Women …," in Dušan I. Bjelić and Obrad Savić, eds., *Balkan as Metaphor: Between Globalization and Fragmentation* (Cambridge, MA, and London: MIT Press, 2005), 314.

37 Pavlović, "Women in Croatia," 136.

38 Ibid.

39 Translated and quoted in ibid., 137. Original quote is from "Hrvatske feministice siluju Hrvatsku," *Globus* (December 11, 1992), 33.

40 Dubravka Ugrešić, "Nostalgia," in Dubravka Ugrešić, *Europe in Sepia*, trans. David Williams (Rochester: Open Letter, 2014), 9–10.

41 Kesić, "Confessions of a Yugo-Nostalgic Witch," 200.

42 Vesna Kesić, "A Response to Catharine MacKinnon's Article 'Turning Rape into Pornography: Postmodern Genocide,'" *Hastings Women's L. R.* 5 (1994), 267–268.

43 Ibid., 269.

44 For example, Joshua S. Goldstein's 2001 book, *War and Gender: How Gender Shapes the War System and Vice Versa* (Cambridge: Cambridge University Press, 2001), 354, includes MacKinnon's claims: "Abundant pornography in Serbia primed soldiers for rapes of non-Serbian women, which in turn produced more pornography as films of the actual rapes were sold on Serbian and foreign markets. Completing the cycle, these rape films were aired on Bosnian-Serb TV news with a dubbed soundtrack to make it appear that the victims were Serbian women being raped by Croatian or Bosniak men— priming xenophobia that served as the regime's bedrock of power." Goldstein also added MacKinnon's diagnosis that "'genocide…[became] explicitly sexually obsessed."

45 Allen, *Rape Warfare*, 88–96.

46 Ibid., 101.

47 Kesić, "A Response to Catharine MacKinnon's Article," 275.

48 Women in Black Against War quoted in Mlađenović and Hughes, "Feminist Resistance to War," 263.

49 Bojana Pejić, "Proletarians of All Countries, Who Washes Your Socks? Equality, Dominance and Difference in Eastern European Art," in Bojana Pejić, ed., *Gender Check: Femininity and Masculinity in the Art of Eastern Europe* (Cologne: Walter König, 2009), 22.

50 Vesna Pavlović, who at the age of twenty-one became one of the most important documentarians of this feminist movement, had previously used the metaphor of the sunflower circle in her *Sadness* (*Tuge*) project when she was part of the group Škart. For *Sadness*, Škart circulated small pieces of cardboard with short poems printed on them to random people in everyday spaces such as train stations, children's playgrounds, food markets, and city squares.

51 Neda Knežević, ed., *Devedesete: Rečnik migracija/The Nineties: A Glossary of Migrations* (Belgrade: Museum of Yugoslavia, 2019), n.p.

52 See Vesna Pavlović's film *Povratak Dokumentarni video zapis sa Zenama u Crnom* (*Return: A Documentary Video with Women in Black*), 1993–1996/2019.

53 Translation in form of subtitles in Pavlović's film *Povratak Dokumentarni*.

54 The song had a revival in 1989 when, sung by Davorin Popović, it featured in Ademir Kenović's film *Kuduz*.

55 Mlađenović and Hughes, "Feminist Resistance to War," 270.

56 Dafina Halili, "Fighting for the Doubly Oppressed," *Kosovo 2.0: '90s* 10 (Spring/Summer 2016), 121.

57 Valerie Hopkins, "The Color of Resistance," *Kosovo 2.0: '90s* 10 (Spring/Summer 2016), 122–127. A 2017 documentary film on women's solidarity during the Kosovo conflict in the 1990s, *Albanke su naše sestre/Lëvizja kundër luftës në Serbi/Albanian Women are Our Sisters*, by Milena Popović, Sanja Kljajić, Taulant Osmani, Darko Šper, and Vanja Đurić, is available online: https://vimeo.com/220794317 (accessed 5/06/2019).

58 Hopkins, "The Color of Resistance," 124.

59 Halili, "Fighting for the Doubly Oppressed," 117.

60 Ibid.

61 Safete Rogova quoted in ibid., 118.

62 Ibid., 120.

63 The Getty Images caption notes the following: "An ethnic Albanian woman holds a loaf of bread during a protest 16 March as riot police block the street and stop the march outside Pristina, the capital of Kosovo. Hundreds of Albanian women started a march toward the Drenica region, where Serbian police launched a bloody crackdown against ethnic Albanians earlier this month." See: www.gettyimages.com/detail/news-photo/an-ethnic-albanian-woman-holds-a-loaf-of-bread-during-a-news-photo/860910220 (accessed 1/13/2021).

64 Hito Steyerl, *How Not to be Seen: A Fucking Didactic Educational .MOV File*, 2013. The video can be found on Artforum: www.artforum.com/video/

hito-steyerl-how-not-to-be-seen-a-fucking-didactic-educational-mov-file-2013–51651 (accessed 05/06/2019).

65 Staša Zajović in conversation with the author, December 25, 2019.

66 Ibid.

67 For images of these protests, see Srđan Veljović, *Fotografije, Žene u crnom u kotekstu grada* (Serbia: Simbol Petrovaradin, 2012), 6–7.

68 Original: "Uvek neposlušne patrijarhatu, ratu, nacionalizmu, militarizmu …" Translation by the author. See *Žene u Crnom* official website: http://zeneucrnom.org/sr/.

69 Mlađenović and Hughes, "Feminist Resistance to War," 270.

70 RuPaul, *Guru* (New York: HarperCollins, 2018), 137.

71 Goldstein, *War and Gender*, 305.

72 Ibid., 304.

73 Ibid.

74 Goldstein featured this photograph by Chris Pfuhl in his book, *War and Gender*, 305, and titled it: "Sarajevo Woman and UN Peacekeeper." The European Press Agency, which currently holds rights for this photograph (along with Chris Pfuhl), titles the image as "Sniper Alert" with an added caption: "A young woman runs for cover as sniper fire is heard in the capital centre while UN UNPROFOR soldiers [sic] points his automatic weapon in the direction of fire in Sarajevo, Bosnia and Herzegovina, 04 August, 1994." See EPA online database, https://www.epa.eu (accessed 02/20/2021). The original photograph shows two UNPROFOR soldiers. In Goldstein's black-and-white reproduction, the photograph is cropped to only include one of the soldiers. I want to thank Goldstein for helping me identify the photographer and rights holders for this image. Goldstein in e-mail correspondence with the author, February 16–19, 2021.

75 Lejla Somun, "Dressed (Not) to Kill," *Peace in Progress* 26 (2015): www.icip-perlapau.cat/numero26/articles_centrals/article_central_5/ (accessed 03/27/2019).

76 Susan Sontag, "Waiting for Godot in Sarajevo," *Performing Arts Journal* 16, no. 2 (May 1994), 90.

77 Ibid.

78 Somun, "Dressed (Not) to Kill."

79 Ibid.

80 Getty Images provides the following caption for this image: "Pageant winner Inela Nogic (C), 17, stands behind a banner as she waves to the audience during the 1993 Miss Sarajevo Pageant. The banner reads 'DON'T LET THEM KILL US.' The beauty pageant was held in a movie theater in the midst of the Yugoslavian Civil War, with the sound of gunfire just outside." See www.gettyimages.com/detail/news-photo/pageant-winner-inela-nogic-stands-behind-a-banner-as-she-news-photo/542383402 (accessed 1/13/2021).

81 Carter, *Miss Sarajevo*.

82 Bob Guccione Jr., "Life after Death," *SPIN* (August 1996), 76.

83 Ibid.

84 Ana Kothe, "Saving the Maidens: Reading 'Miss Sarajevo,'" *Modern Language Studies* 29, no. 2 (Autumn 1999), 137–152.

85 Kevin Boger, *U2: Miss Sarajevo (Miss Syria)* (January 23, 2018): www.youtube.com/watch?v=u0Lt4arcoy8 (accessed 2/18/2019).

86 Bill Carter Productions, *U2, Miss Sarajevo and 20 Year Anniversary of U2 Sarajevo Concert* (September 23, 2017): www.youtube.com/watch?v=qRo2v UpnWmk (accessed 06/07/2019).

87 Kothe, "Saving the Maidens," 137–152.

88 Ibid., 144.

89 Carter, *Miss Sarajevo*.

90 Janine di Giovanni, "*Vogue*'s View: Armed and Glamorous: Janine di Giovanni Discovers How Women Find Strength in Stilettos, Designer Dresses, and Midnight-Blue Nail Polish," *Vogue* 187, no. 9 (September 1, 1997), 376.

91 Ibid.

92 Ibid.

93 Jennifer Rawlings, *Forgotten Voices, Women in Bosnia* (Squeaky Tula Productions, 2008).

94 Somun, "Dressed (Not) to Kill."

95 Rawlings, *Forgotten Voices*.

96 Getty Images provides the following caption for this image: "Sarajevo, Bosnia—1995: In the dangerous suburb of Dobrinja, Meliha Varesanovic walks proudly and defiantly to work during the Siege of Sarajevo, 1995. Her message to the watching Serb gunmen who surround her city is simple, 'you will never defeat us.' After the war Meliha revisited the street with Getty Images photographer Tom Stoddart who captured her striking appearance and attitude." See: www.gettyimages.com/detail/news-photo/in-the-dangerous-suburb-of-dobrinja-meliha-varesanovic-news-photo/555360455 (accessed 03/14/2019).

97 Translation by the author. "Manekenka usred rata: Meliha Varešanović o prkosu i ponosu na fotografiji koja je obišla svijet," klix (December 27, 2015): www.klix.ba/lifestyle/manekenka-usred-rata-meliha-varesanovic-o-prkosu-i-ponosu-na-fotografiji-koja-je-obisla-svijet/151227023 (accessed 03/14/2019).

98 Ibid.

99 di Giovanni, "*Vogue*'s View," 376.

100 Ibid.

101 Nataša Ilić and Kathrin Rhomberg, eds., *Sanja Iveković: Selected Works* (Barcelona: Fundacio Antoni Tapies, 2008), 162–169.

102 Šejla Kamerić, "Behind the Scene," Instagram (April 24, 2019): www.instagram.com/p/BwopRZTBRJx/ (accessed 4/24/2019).

103 Šejla Kamerić in conversation with the artist, January 28, 2021.

104 Ibid.

105 Examples are: www.theliberalgunclub.com, Rec.guns, and www.texastrading post.com (accessed 3/25/2020).

106 Riflechair, *Code Name ARROW: Bosnian Sniper* (August 29, 2018): www.youtube.com/watch?v=gO9phEodW9Y (accessed 3/25/2020).

107 The Liberal Gun club: www.theliberalgunclub.com/phpBB3/viewtopic.php?t=6748&start=30 (accessed 3/25/2020). Texas Trading Post: www.texastradingpost.com/yugosniper/Bosniansnipers.html (accessed 3/25/2020).

108 Texas Trading Post: www.texastradingpost.com/yugosniper/Bosniansnipers.html (accessed 3/25/2020).

109 Ibid.

110 Getty Images: www.gettyimages.dk/detail/news-photo/bosnian-sniper-nadia-jeriagic-aims-a-rifle-at-serbian-news-photo/635931755?adppopup=true (accessed 7/19/2019).

111 Lala Raščić, "Gorgo," Portfolio (August 16, 2019): https://lalarascic.com/portfolio/gorgo/ (accessed 5/20/2020).

112 Ibid.

113 Ibid.

114 Lala Raščić in conversation with the author, September 5, 2019.

115 Tanja Ostojić in conversation with the author, November 13, 2019.

116 Tanja Ostojić in conversation with the author, November 9, 2018.

117 I first developed this analysis of Ostojić's work when I published a short essay on the figure of Jugoslovenka in contemporary art for *Art Monthly* in 2019. See "Yugonostalgia," *Art Monthly* 425 (April 2019), 6–10.

118 Selma Selman in conversation with the author, August 5, 2019.

119 Ibid.

120 Ibid.

121 For a more in-depth analysis of Selman's works in her solo exhibition, please see my monographic essay in Selman's artist book and catalogue: "Selma Selman," in Štefan Simončič, ed., *Selma Selman: Visual Artist* (Slovenia: EPEKA Scientific and Research Association, 2016), 6–24.

122 Selman, "*SALT WATER AFTER 47*," artist statement shared with the author in e-mail correspondence, February 29, 2016.

123 Selman in conversation with the author, August 5, 2019.

124 Slavenka Drakulić, "Invisible Walls between Us," in Slavenka Drakulić, *Café Europa* (London: Penguin, 1999), 21.

125 Kesić, "Muslim Women, Croatian Women, Serbian Women, Albanian Women …," 312.

126 Mlađenović, "Foreword: Searching for Our Lesbian Nests," x–xi.

Conclusion
Jugoslovenka: a wide-ranging model for feminist performance politics in art and culture

In a 1908 colored etching by Nasta Rojc, titled *Žena Spaja Kontinente* (*Woman Brings Together Continents*), a naked woman's body is shown hovering elegantly above a gap between two landmasses (Figure 6.1). Behind her, we can partially see the Sphinx of Giza, whose powerful static gaze has captivated the attention of historians and tourists for centuries. While her stiff body, made of limestone, contrasts with the fragility of a woman's living body, they are linked in subject matter: both act as connective tissues between East and West, the Sphinx with her gaze, and the naked woman with her body. The mesmerizing strength of her arms and legs, as she displays her physique, magnifies the tenuousness of the actual act of hovering in place like that, a pose unsustainable for long and extremely arduous for her body. In other places, the work has the title *Spajam Kontinente* (*I Bring Together Continents*) *and Žena Svjetionik* (*Woman Lighthouse*).[1] With *I Bring Together Continents*, Rojc claims this struggle for herself, when she declares that *she* brings together continents, delivering an iconic image of a woman's creative Herculean strength in connecting disparate lands and cultures.

I begin this book with a self-portrait of the lesbian painter Rojc holding a rifle, and I end with a quasi-self-portrait that implies an even greater signification for the argument throughout the entire book: Jugoslovenka as the bridging force of a multiethnic, transnational, and united socialist Yugoslavia; the embodiment of the interwoven cultural connections between the Habsburg (West) and Ottoman (East) empires in a newly formed, antifascist state; and as a challenge to the patriarchal foundations of socialism, war, and nationalism. In the post-Yugoslav context, Jugoslovenka's diasporic condition—in newly formed nations of a destroyed Yugoslavia and beyond—sustains the legacy of feminist resistance and antifascism. As such, Jugoslovenka's body not only bridges continents, but various political and geographic temporalities, and offers up new possibilities for feminist resistance today.

It was the aim of this book to unpack the layers and states of being a woman in one of the most progressive—if also deeply patriarchal—political experiments that followed World War II: socialist Yugoslavia. In focusing on the

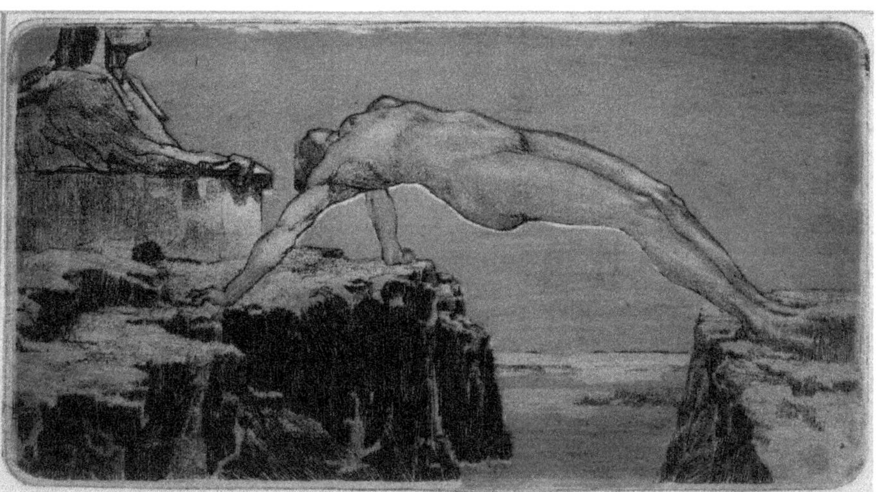

Nasta Rojc, *Žena Spaja Kontinente* (*Woman Brings Together Continents*), 1908.   **6.1**
Colored etching.

figure of Jugoslovenka, this book pays homage to those women whose visual
and performative politics can change how we understand the gendered history
of twentieth-century socialism and its relevance today. Jugoslovenka, as an
iconic figure, takes many divergent and sometimes incompatible incarnations.
The most famous figure in this history remains Marina Abramović, who in
her 2016 memoir, described life under Yugoslav socialism as "a dark place"
with "drabness everywhere." She concluded her reflections with this insight:
"There is something about Communism and socialism—it's a kind of aesthetic
based on pure ugliness."[2] *"I am Jugoslovenka!" Feminist Performance Politics
during and after Yugoslav Socialism* positions itself against such bleak narratives of socialism by complicating and expanding how we might understand
feminist emancipation, resistance, and performance within this unique Yugoslav context and its aftermath. The book seeks to demonstrate that Yugoslav
women's embrace of emancipatory performance strategies is deeply rooted in
socialist Yugoslavia's feminist and antifascist legacies, and that these legacies
remain critical influences on the latest generations of Yugoslav women today.

To conclude, I turn to one more Jugoslovenka in the arts, whose visual
compositions magnify the importance of viewing Yugoslav socialism, its past
and its possibilities for the future through a female lens. Jasmina Cibic, who
lives and works between London and Ljubljana, and who represented (the
former Yugoslav republic of) Slovenia at the Venice Biennale in 2013, both
celebrates and critiques Yugoslav socialism in epic filmic installations that
reimagine Yugoslavia's past and its possible future as feminist. Cibic's work is

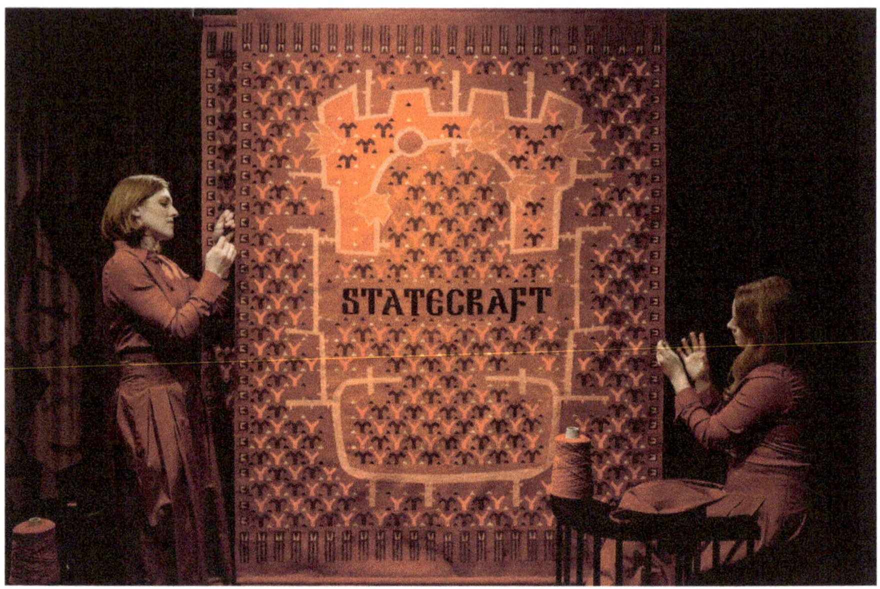

6.2 Jasmina Cibic, *An Atmosphere of Joyful Contemplation*, seating, performance with song, tapestries, 2018.

primarily performative, and cunningly sparks ideas about women and their role in Yugoslav and post-Yugoslav politics. The performance, *An Atmosphere of Joyful Contemplation*, which I saw at DHC/Art Montreal in 2019, brings together young, living women, who sing while crafting a beautiful, red tapestry with their hands (Figure 6.2). In addition to their soothing voices, which bridged the gap between the coolness of architecture and sculptural surfaces in the gallery, the bright-red colors of their clothing and the tapestry summoned Jugoslovenka's spirit. Cibic's work allows protagonists in her videos and installations to revisit politically charged architectural spaces, reviving questions of Yugoslav solidarity and possibility.

In contrast to Abramović's diagnosis of socialism as an aesthetic of "pure ugliness," Cibic's visual economies of citational narratives, always haunted by political tensions, emphasize the beauty of the architecture, art, and women of Yugoslavia, creatively interweaving actual historical moments with fictional innovations by the artist. It is my hope that *"I am Jugoslovenka!"* offers a study that sheds light on these disparate and paradoxical positions of Jugoslovenka, and that honing in on the feminist history of Yugoslav women and their emancipatory performance politics will allow us to intervene in established histories of socialism and feminism that have ignored, erased, or depreciated Yugoslav women's voices in art and culture.

Notes

1 Leonida Kovač, *Anonimalia: normativni diskurzi i samoreprezentacija umjetnica 20. Stoljeća* (Zagreb: Izdanja Antibarbarus, 2010), 84.
2 Marina Abramović, *Walk through Walls: A Memoir* (New York: Three Rivers Press, 2016), 2.

List of interviews and correspondence

Borčič, Barbara. E-mail correspondence with the author, February 17, 2021.

Cibic, Jasmina. Conversation with the author, March 3, 2019.

Čufer, Eda. Conversation with the author, August 7, 2019; e-mail correspondence with the author, August 21 and November 4, 2019.

Čupić, Rada. E-mail correspondence with the author, February 14–18, 2021.

Delimar, Vlasta. Conversation with the author, June 12, 2019.

Dimitrijević, Olga. Conversation with the author, December 25, 2019.

Dobnikar, Mojca. E-mail correspondence with the author, October 15, 2019.

Đurić, Dubravka and Miško Šuvaković. E-mail correspondence with the author, January 27, 2021.

Galántai, György. Conversation with the author, December 21, 2011.

Goldstein, Joshua S. E-mail correspondence with the author, February 16–19, 2021.

Gržinić, Marina. Conversation with the author, August 10, 2019; e-mail correspondence with the author, September 21 and 22, 2019.

Iveković, Sanja. Conversation with the author, June 13, 2019.

Jakšić, Jasna. Conversation with the author, June 11, 2019.

Janečić, Helena. Conversation with the author, July 30, 2020.

Jelača, Dijana. E-mail correspondence with the author, August 16, 2019.

Kamerić, Šejla. Conversation with the author, January 29, 2021.

Kesić, Saša. Conversation with the author, August 11, 2018.

Ladik, Katalin. Conversation with the author, January 8, 2012.

Miljković, Boris. E-mail correspondence with the author, July 14, 2020.

Mlađenović, Lepa. Conversation with the author, December 25, 2019.

Molnar, Miran. E-mail correspondence with the author, July 20, 2020.

Murkus, Amal. Conversation with the author, February 23, 2021.

Novak, Ivan. E-mail correspondence with the author, July 3 and 7, 2020.

Ostojić, Tanja. Conversation with the author, November 13, 2019.

Pavlović, Vesna. E-mail correspondence with the author, August 22, 2020.

Raščić, Lala. Conversation with the author, September 5, 2019.

Selman, Selma. Conversation with the author, August 5, 2019.

Tijardović, Jasna. Conversation with the author, October 13, 2019.
Tomić, Biljana. Conversation with the author, August 4, 2011.
Tratnik, Suzana. Online chat correspondence with the author, August 9, 2019.
Tumbas, Eržebet. Conversation with the author, June 15, 2018.
Videkanić, Bojana. E-mail correspondence with the author, March 8, 2020.
Vogelnik, Borut. E-mail correspondence with the author, August 9, 2020.
Vukadinović, Dragica. E-mail correspondence with the author, July 12, 2019.
Zajović, Staša. Conversation with the author, December 25, 2019.
Žilnik, Želimir. Conversation with the author, August 13, 2019.

Bibliography

Abramović, Marina. *Walk through Walls: A Memoir*. New York: Three Rivers Press, 2016.

Allen, Beverly. *Rape Warfare: The Hidden Genocide in Bosnia-Herzegovina and Croatia*. Minneapolis: University of Minnesota Press, 1996.

Alujević, Darija and Dunja Nekić. "Women's Art Club and Women's Group Exhibitions in Zagreb from 1928 until 1940." *Artl@s Bulletin* 8, no. 1 (2019): Article 11.

Anđelković, Branislava and Branislav Dimitrijević. "The Body, Ideology, Masculinity and Some Blind Spots in Post-Communism." In *After the Wall: Art and Culture in Post-Communist Europe*, edited by Bojana Pejić, 67–73. Stockholm: Moderna Museet, 1999.

—. "The Final Decade: Art, Society, Trauma and Normality." In *On Normality: Art in Serbia 1989–2001*, 9–129. Belgrade: Museum of Contemporary Art, 2005.

András, Edit. "Gender Minefields." *n.paradoxa* 11 (1999): 4–9. www.ktpress.co.uk/nparadoxa-issue-details.asp?issueid=11 (accessed May 6, 2019).

Archer, Rory and Goran Musić. "Approaching the Socialist Factory and its Workforce: Considerations from Fieldwork in (Former) Yugoslavia." *Labor History* 58, no. 1 (2017): 44–66.

Archer, Rory and Krisztina Rácz. "Šverc and the Šinobus: Small-Scale Smuggling in Vojvodina." In *Subverting Borders: Doing Research on Smuggling and Small-Scale Trade*, edited by Bettina Bruns and Judith Maggelbrink, 59–83. Wiesbaden: VS Verlag für Sozialwissenschaften, 2011.

Arns, Inke. *Irwin: Retroprincip 1983–2003*. Frankfurt am Main: Revolver, 2003.

—. "Objects in the Mirror May Be Closer Than They Appear! Die Avantgarde im Rückspiegel. Zum Paradigmenwechsel der künstlerischen Avantgarderezeption in (Ex-) Jugoslawien und Russland von den 1980er Jahren bis in die Gegenwart." PhD dissertation, Humboldt-Universität, Berlin, 2003.

Badiou, Alain. *Handbook of Inaesthetics*. Translation by Alberto Toscato. Stanford, CA: Stanford University Press, 2005.

Badovinac, Zdenka, Eda Čufer, and Anthony Gardner. "Introduction: Neue Slowenische Kunst: From *Kapital* to Capital." In *From* Kapital *to Capital: Neue Slowenische Kunst: An Event of the Final Decade of Yugoslavia*, edited by Zdenka Badovinac, Eda Čufer, and Anthony Gardner, 8–25. Cambridge, MA: MIT Press, 2015.

Bago, Ivana. "A Window and a Basement: Negotiating Hospitality at La Galerie des Locataires and Podroom—The Working Community of Artists." *ARTMargins* 1, nos. 2–3 (June–October, 2012): 116–146.

—. "The Question of Female Guilt in Sanja Iveković's Art: From Yugoslav Beauty Pageants to Wartime Witch-Hunts." In *Unknown Heroine: A Reader*, edited by Helena Reckitt, 62–87. London: Calvert 22, 2013.

—. "Sanja Iveković. Becoming Woman Artist." In *Sanja Iveković. Unknown Heroine*, edited by Lina Džuverović, 49–64. London: Calvert 22, 2012.

Bakić-Hayden, Milica. "What's so Byzantine about the Balkans?" In *Balkan as Metaphor: Between Globalization and Fragmentation*, edited by Dušan I. Bjelić and Obrad Savić, 61–78. Cambridge, MA, and London: MIT Press, 2005.

Balkanist. "'We Want Censorship': A Brief Introduction to Yugoslav Queer Culture." September 16, 2017. https://balkanist.net/we-want-censorship-a-brief-introduction-to-yugoslav-queer-culture/ (accessed May 11, 2019).

Batinić, Jelena. *Women and Yugoslav Partisans: A History of World War II Resistance.* Cambridge: Cambridge University Press, 2015.

Benson, Michael, dir. *Predictions of Fire* [Documentary film, 1:30]. Kinetikon Pictures, Ljubljana, 1996.

Berger, John. *Ways of Seeing.* London: BBC and Penguin Books, 1972.

Bertellini, Giorgio. "Making Spaces: At War." In *New-Media Technology, Science, and Politics: The Video Art of Marina Gržinić and Aina Šmid*, edited by Marina Gržinić and Tanja Velagić, 193–214. Prag: Löcker, 2008.

Biesenbach, Klaus. *Marina Abramović: The Artist Is Present.* New York: Museum of Modern Art, 2010.

Bijelić, Biljana. "Nationalism, Motherhood, and the Reordering of Women's Power." In *Serbia since 1989: Politics and Society under Milosevic and After*, edited by Sabrina P. Ramet and Vjeran Pavlaković, 286–305. Seattle: University of Washington Press, 2006.

Bilić, Bojan and Sanja Kajinić, eds. *Intersectionality and LGBT Activist Politics: Multiple Others in Croatia and Serbia.* London: Palgrave Macmillan, 2016.

Bill Carter Productions. "U2, Miss Sarajevo and 20 Year Anniversary of U2 Sarajevo Concert" [Video, 9:07]. September 23, 2017. www.youtube.com/watch?v=qRo2vUpnWmk (accessed June 7, 2019).

Blic. "Umesto Tita stigla Lepa Brena." February 13, 2014. www.blic.rs/zabava/vesti/umesto-tita-stigla-lepa-brena/wjx1lmh (accessed June 7, 2019).

—. "Mistična princeza jugoslovenskog andergraunda koja je PRERANO umrla: Ko je bila Varja Orlić, žena POTPUNO DRUGAČIJA od svake druge." January 8, 2018. www.blic.rs/zabava/vesti/misticna-princeza-jugoslovenskog-andergraunda-koja-je-prerano-umrla-ko-je-bila-varja/tnqw9rn (accessed May 11, 2019).

Boger, Kevin. *U2: Miss Sarajevo (Miss Syria)* [Video, 5:12]. June 3, 2017. www.youtube.com/watch?v=uoLt4arcoy8 (accessed May 3, 2018).

Bonfiglioli, Chiara. "Remembering the Conference 'Drugarica Zena. Zensko Pitanje—Novi Pristup?' 'Comrade Woman: The Women's Question: A New Approach?' Thirty Years After." MA thesis, Utrecht University, 2007–2008.

—. "Revolutionary Networks: Women's Political and Social Activism in Cold War Italy and Yugoslavia (1945–1957)." PhD dissertation, Utrecht University, 2012.

—. "Feminist Translations in a Socialist Context: The Case of Yugoslavia." *Gender & History* 30, no. 1 (March 2018): 240–254.

Borčić, Barbara. Interview by Alenka Pirman. ŠKUC Gallery. www.galerijaskuc.si/barbara-borcic/ (accessed May 30, 2019).

—. "The ŠKUC Gallery, Alternative Culture, and Neue Slowenische Kunst in the 1980s." In *From* Kapital *to Capital: Neue Slowenische Kunst: An Event of the Final Decade of Yugoslavia*, edited by Zdenka Badovinac, Eda Čufer, and Anthony Gardner, 299–318. Cambridge, MA: MIT Press, 2015.

Boym, Svetlana. "Nostalgia." *Atlas of Transformation.* 2011. http://monumenttotransformation.org/atlas-of-transformation/html/n/nostalgia/nostalgia-svetlana-boym.html (accessed November 10, 2018).

Brena, Lepa. *Interview* [Video, 1:28:55]. Iz Profila TV Grand. May 13, 2014. www.youtube.com/watch?v=uRVEk9RItOc (accessed June 3, 2019).

—. *Lepa Brena se rasplakala zbog susreta sa Slatkim Grehom* [Video, 5:36]. Happy TV (Nacionalna Televizija Happy). March 12, 2017. www.youtube.com/watch?v=5ymB-NAj3sLc. (accessed June 3, 2019).

Bringa, Tone. "The Peaceful Death of Tito and Violent End of Yugoslavia." In *Death of the Father: An Anthropology of the End in Political Authority*, edited by John Borneman, 148–200. New York: Berghahn Books, 2004.

Bulc, Gregor. "Hard Bosom: Top Pro-Gay Tracks from ex-Yugoslavia (Part One)." *Bturn.* May 21, 2012. http://bturn.com/8384/hard-bosom-top-pro-gay-tracks-from-ex-yugoslavia-part-one (accessed May 23, 2019).

Butler, Judith. *Bodies that Matter: On the Discursive Limits of Sex.* New York: Routledge, 1993.

Carter, Bill, dir. *Miss Sarajevo* [Music video]. Dreamchaser Productions, 1995.

Carl, Katherine Ann. "Aoristic Avant-Garde: Experimental Art in 1960s and 1970s Yugoslavia." PhD dissertation, State University of New York, Stony Brook, 2009.

Cartwright, Garth. "Among the Gypsies." *World Literature Today* 80, no. 3 (May–June 2006): 51–55.

Crowley, David and Susan E. Reid. "Introduction: Pleasures in Socialism?" In *Pleasures in Socialism: Leisure and Luxury in the Eastern Bloc*, edited by David Crowley and Susan E. Reid, 3–51. Evanston, IL: Northwestern University Press, 2010.

Čufer, Eda. "The Athletics of the Eye: Baptism and the Problem of Writing and Reading Contemporary Performance." In *From* Kapital *to Capital: Neue Slowenische Kunst: An Event of the Final Decade of Yugoslavia*, edited by Zdenka Badovinac, Eda Čufer, and Anthony Gardner, 47. Cambridge, MA: MIT Press, 2015.

Čufer, Eda and IRWIN. "NSK State in Time." In *Primary Documents: A Sourcebook for Eastern and Central European Art since the 1950s*, edited by Laura J. Hoptman and Tomáš Pospiszyl, 301. Cambridge, MA, and London: MIT Press, 2002.

Cvetkovich, Ann. *An Archive of Feelings Trauma, Sexuality, and Lesbian Public Cultures.* Durham, NC: Duke University Press, 2003.

Čvoro, Uroš. *Turbo-Folk Music and Cultural Representations of National Identity in Former Yugoslavia.* Farnham: Ashgate, 2014.

—. *Transitional Aesthetics: Contemporary Art at the Edge of Europe.* London: Bloomsbury Academic, 2018.

Dark Entries Records. "Borghesia—Clones LP." www.darkentriesrecords.com/store/vinyl/lp/borghesia-clones-lp/ (accessed May 11, 2019).

Dedijer, Vladimir. "Prologue." In Vladimir Dedijer, *Tito Speaks: His Self-Portrait and Struggle with Stalin*. Norwich: Weidenfeld & Nicolson, 1953.

Delić, Zatan. "Fantasy, Sexuality, and Yugoslavism in Lepa Brena's Music." In *Made in Yugoslavia: Studies in Popular Music*, edited by Danijela Š. Beard and Ljerka V. Rasmussen, 152–161. Abingdon: Routledge, 2020.

de Moura, Lidia Zuin. *Kunst ist Krieg: Música industrial e discurso belicista*. Translation by Charla Fisher. São Paulo: Casper Libero College, 2011.

Denegri, Ješa. "Inside or Outside 'Socialist Modernism'? Radical Views on the Yugoslav Art Scene, 1950–1970." In *Impossible Histories: Historical Avant-Gardes, Neo-Avant-Gardes, and Post-Avant-Gardes in Yugoslavia, 1818–1991*, edited by Dubravka Đurić and Miško Šuvaković, 170–208. Cambridge, MA: MIT Press, 2003.

Dević, Ana. "Theatre of Diversity and Avant-Garde in Late Socialist Yugoslavia and Beyond: Paradoxes of the Disintegration and Cultural Subversion." In *Theatre in the Context of the Yugoslav Wars*, edited by Jana Dolečki, Senad Halilbašić, and Stefan Hulfeld, 199–219. Cham: Palgrave Macmillan, 2018.

di Giovanni, Janine. "*Vogue*'s View: Armed and Glamorous: Janine di Giovanni Discovers How Women Find Strength in Stilettos, Designer Dresses, and Midnight-Blue Nail Polish." *Vogue* 187, no. 9 (September 1, 1997): 348, 358, 368, 370, 376.

Dimitrijević, Branislav. "Altered Identities: Goran Đorđević as an Artist, SKC as an Institution." *PRELOM Journal for Images and Politics* 8 (Fall 2006): 241–248.

Dota, Franko. "Public and Political History of Male Homosexuality in Socialist Croatia, 1945–1989." PhD dissertation, Zagreb University, 2017.

Drakulić, Slavenka. *How We Survived Communism and Even Laughed*. New York: HarperCollins, 1993.

—. *Café Europa: Life after Communism*. London: Penguin, 1999.

Đurić, Dubravka. "Radical Poetic Practices: Concrete and Visual Poetry in the Avant-Garde and Neo-Avant-Garde." In *Impossible Histories: Historical Avant-Gardes, Neo-Avant-Gardes, and Post-Avant-Gardes in Yugoslavia, 1818–1991*, edited by Dubravka Đurić and Miško Šuvaković, 64–95. Cambridge, MA: MIT Press, 2003.

Ekipa, Blica. "Heroj otpora koga su svi zaboravili." *Blic*. September 16, 2010. www.blic.rs/vesti/reportaza/heroj-otpora-koga-su-svi-zaboravili/q777vr4 (accessed May 23, 2019).

Erjavec, Aleš. "Neue Slowenische Kunst—New Slovenian Art: Slovenia, Yugoslavia, Self-Management, and the 1980s." In *Postmodernism and the Postsocialist Condition: Politicized Art under Late Socialism*, edited by Aleš Erjavec, 135–174. Berkeley, Los Angeles, and London: University of California Press, 2003.

Gayten LGBT. "Kako je bilo biti gej u Jugoslaviji? Pričali smo s čovjekom koji je upravo doktorirao na tu temu." October 16, 2017. www.transserbia.org/seksulanost/1301-kako-je-bilo-biti-gej-u-jugoslaviji-pricali-smo-s-covjekom-koji-je-upravo-doktorirao-na-tu-temu (accessed June 20, 2020).

Ghodsee, Kristen and Adriana Zaharijević. "Fantasies of Feminist History in Eastern Europe: A Response to Slavenka Drakulić." *Eurozine*. July 31, 2015. www.eurozine.com/fantasies-of-feminist-historyin-eastern-europe/ (accessed March 20, 2019).

Gilman, Sander L. *Disease and Representation: Images of Illness from Madness to AIDS.* Ithaca, NY: Cornell University Press, 1988.

Goldstein, Joshua S. *War and Gender: How Gender Shapes the War System and Vice Versa.* Cambridge: Cambridge University Press, 2001.

Gravenor, Natalie. "Post-Modern, Post-National, Post-Gender? Suggestions for a Consideration of Gender Identities in the Visual Artworks and Moving Images of Neue Slowenische Kunst." *Acta Universitatis Sapientiae, Film and Media Studies* 14, no. 1 (2014): 175–196.

Griffin, Gabriele and Rosi Braidotti. *ATHENA, Thinking Differently: A Reader in European Women's Studies.* London: Zed Books, 2002.

Gržinić, Marina. "Neue Slowenische Kunst." In *Impossible Histories: Historical Avant-Gardes, Neo-Avant-Gardes, and Post-Avant-Gardes in Yugoslavia, 1818–1991*, edited by Dubravka Đurić and Miško Šuvaković, 246–269. Cambridge, MA: MIT Press, 2003.

—. "Tanja Ostojić: 'Yes it's Fucking Political'—Skunk Anansie." In *Strategies of Success/ Curators Series 2001–2003*, edited by Tanja Ostojić, 11–31. Belgrade: SKC; Bourges: La Box, 2004.

—. "Feminism and Performance in the Territory of Ex-Yugoslavia." In *Casting Gender: Women and Performance in Intercultural Contexts*, edited by Laura B. Lengel and John T. Warren, 165–182, Critical Intercultural Communication Studies 7. New York: Peter Lang, 2005.

—. "A Time That Lives On, But in a Different Way: 1977–84." In *Vojak D. M. (Private D. M.) Die Welt ist Schön—Svet je lep—The World is Beautiful*, edited by Mateja Podlesnik, 39–55. Ljubljana: Muzej in Galerije Mesta Ljubljana, 2013.

—. "A Time That Lives On, But in a Different Way: 1977–1984." In *What Is Art? Resuming Fragmented Histories*, edited by Sandro Droschl and Christiane Egger, 196–220. Nürnberg: Verlag für Moderne Kunst, 2015.

Gržinić, Marina, Aina Šmid, and Zvonka T. Simčić, dir. *Relations: 25 Years of the Lesbian Group ŠKUC-LL* [Documentary film, 1:24:2]. Zavod CCC, Ljubljana, 2012.

Guccione, Bob, Jr. "Life after Death." *SPIN* (August 1996): 72–84, 114–116, 123.

Halili, Dafina. "Fighting for the Doubly Oppressed." *Kosovo 2.0: '90s* 10 (Spring/ Summer 2016): 116–121.

Held, John, Jr. "The Mail Art Exhibition: Personal Worlds to Cultural Strategies." In *At a Distance: Precursors to Art and Activism on the Internet*, edited by Annemarie Chandler and Norie Neumark, 88–115. Cambridge, MA: MIT Press, 2005.

Hock, Beáta. "Gendered Artistic Positions and Social Voices: Politics, Cinema, and the Visual Arts: In State-Socialist and Post-Socialist Hungary." PhD dissertation, Central European University, Budapest, 2009

—. *Gendered Artistic Positions and Social Voices: Politics, Cinema, and the Visual Arts: In State-Socialist and Post-Socialist Hungary.* Stuttgart: Steiner, 2013.

Hofman, Ana. "Lepa Brena: Repolitization of Musical Memories on Yugoslavia." *Glasnik Etnografskog instituta* 60, no. 1 (January 2012): 21–32.

—. "Music (as) Labour: Professional Musicianship, Affective Labour and Gender in Socialist Yugoslavia." *Ethnomusicology Forum* 24, no. 1 (April 2015): 28–50.

Hopkins, Valerie. "The Color of Resistance." *Kosovo 2.0: '90s* 10 (Spring/Summer 2016): 122–127.

Hughes, Henry Meyric. "The Reception in the West of Art from Central and East Central Europe." In *Aspects/Positions: 50 Years of Art in Central Europe 1949–1999*, edited by Achim Hochdörfer, Dieter Schrage, Hanno Millesi, Herald Krejči, Sophie Haaser, Bernhard Fellner, Uli Todoroff, Christa Mittermayr, Michaela Herreiner, Pavlina Morganová, and Andreas Wenniger, 47–58. Vienna: Museum Moderner Kunst Stiftung Ludwig Wien, 1999.

Husedžinović, Meliha. "Aspects and Positions of Art from Bosnia-Herzegovina 1949–1999." In *Aspects/Positions: 50 Years of Art in Central Europe 1949–1999*, edited by Achim Hochdörfer, Dieter Schrage, Hanno Millesi, Herald Krejči, Sophie Haaser, Bernhard Fellner, Uli Todoroff, Christa Mittermayr, Michaela Herreiner, Pavlina Morganová, and Andreas Wenniger, 109–114. Vienna: Museum Moderner Kunst Stiftung Ludwig Wien, 1999.

Ilić, Nataša and Kathrin Rhomberg, eds. *Sanja Iveković: Selected Works*. Barcelona: Fundació Antoni Tàpies, 2008.

Iordanova, Dina. *Cinema of Flames: Balkan Film, Culture and Media*. London: BFI Publishing, 2002.

Irigaray, Luce. *Marine Lover of Friedrich Nietzsche*. Translation by Gillian C. Gill. New York: Columbia University Press, 1991.

—. *In the Beginning, She Was*. London and New York: Bloomsbury Academic, 2013.

IRWIN. "Namepickers" [Photograph]. 1999. http://irwin-nsk.org/works-and-projects/namepickers/ (accessed June 17, 2019).

—. *East Art Map: Contemporary Art and Eastern Europe*. Cambridge, MA, and London: MIT Press, 2006.

Iveković, Rada and Slavenka Drakulić-Illić. "YUGOSLAVIA: Neofeminism and its 'Six Mortal Sins.'" In *Sisterhood Is Global*, edited by Robin Morgan, 734–739. New York: The Feminist Press, 1996.

Jakovljević, Branislav. "Human Resources: June 1968, Hair, and the Beginning of Yugoslavia's End." *Grey Room* 30 (Winter 2008): 38–53.

—. *Alienation Effects: Performance and Self-Management in Yugoslavia, 1945–91*. Ann Arbor: University of Michigan Press, 2016.

—. "The Howling Wilderness of the Maladaptive Struggle in Belgrade in New York." *ARTMargins* 7, no. 2 (June 2018): 17–41.

Jalušič, Vlasta. "Women in Interwar Yugoslavia." In *Gender Politics in the Western Balkans: Women and Society in Yugoslavia and the Yugoslav Successor States*, edited by Sabrina P. Ramet, 51–66. University Park: Pennsylvania State University Press, 1999.

—. *Kako smo hodile v feministično gimnazijo*. Ljubljana: Založba/Lila Zbirka, 2002.

Jancar-Webster, Barbara. *Women and Revolution in Yugoslavia, 1941–1945*. Denver, CO: Arden Press, 1990.

Janečić, Helena. *Horny Dyke Na Rubu Konvencije/Horny Dyke on the Edge of Convention*. Zagreb: Domino, November, 2011.

Jeffs, Nikolai. "'FV and the Third Scene,' 1980–1990." In *FV Alternativa osemdesetih/Alternative Scene of the Eighties*, edited by Breda Škrjanec, 345–394. Ljubljana: Mednarodni Grafični Likovni Center/International Center of Graphic Arts, 2008.

Jelača, Dijana. *Dislocated Screen Memory: Narrating Trauma in Post-Yugoslav Cinema*. New York: Palgrave Macmillan, 2016.

Jovićević, Aleksandra. "Censorship and Ingenious Dramatic Strategies in Yugoslav Theatre (1945–1991)." *Primerjalna Književnost* 31 (2008): 139–152.

Judah, Tim. *Kosovo: War and Revenge.* New Haven, CT: Yale University Press, 2000.

Judge I-Rankin'. "The Rolling Slavs." *Phoenix New Times.* February 15, 1989. www.phoenixnewtimes.com/music/the-rolling-slavs-6412866 (accessed June 15, 2019).

Kamerić, Šejla. "Behind the Scene" [Post]. Instagram. April 24, 2019. www.instagram.com/p/BwopRZTBRJx/ (accessed April 24, 2019).

Karanović, Mirjana. "Yubilej: Ja sam Jugoslovenka." *Peščanik.* December 12, 2018. https://pescanik.net/yubilej-ja-sam-jugoslovenka/ (accessed December 12, 2018).

Kesić, Vesna. "Nije li pornogra ja cinična?" *Start* 355 (August 28, 1982): 74–75.

—. "A Response to Catharine MacKinnon's Article 'Turning Rape into Pornography: Postmodern Genocide.'" *Hastings Women's Literary Review* 5 (1994): 267–280.

—. "Confessions of a Yugo-Nostalgic Witch." In *Ana's Land: Sisterhood in Eastern Europe,* edited by Tanya Renne, 195–200. Boulder, CO: Westview Press, 1997.

—. "Muslim Women, Croatian Women, Serbian Women, Albanian Women …" In *Balkan as Metaphor: Between Globalization and Fragmentation,* edited by Dušan I. Bjelić and Obrad Savić, 311–321. Cambridge, MA, and London: MIT Press, 2005.

klix. "Manekenka usred rata: Meliha Varešanović o prkosu i ponosu na fotografiji koja je obišla svijet." December 27, 2015. www.klix.ba/lifestyle/manekenka-usred-rata-meliha-varesanovic-o-prkosu-i-ponosu-na-fotografiji-koja-je-obisla-svijet/151227023 (accessed March 14, 2019).

Knežević, Neda, ed., *Devedesete: Rečnik Migracija/The Nineties: A Glossary of Migrations* [Exhibition catalogue]. Belgrade: Museum of Yugoslavia, 2019.

Kobolt, Katja. "Nailstories." *ArtLeaks Gazette* 5 (2019): 123–129.

Kolešnik, Ljiljana. "Intuitivni feminizam Vlaste Delimar." *Quorum, časopis za književnost* 13, no. 4 (1997): 197–201.

Korchnak, Peter. "Remembering 25 May, Dan Mladosti (Day of Youth)." *Remembering Yugoslavia: Journeys through the Memory of a Disappeared Country.* https://rememberingyugoslavia.com/dan-mladosti/ (accessed April 3, 2020).

Korda, Neven. "Alternative Dawns." In *FV Alternativa osemdesetih/Alternative Scene of the Eighties,* edited by Breda Škrjanec, 281–343. Ljubljana: Mednarodni Grafični Likovni Center/International Center of Graphic Arts, 2008.

Kovač, Leonida. *Anonimalia: normativni diskurzi i samoreprezentacija umjetnica 20. Stoljeća.* Zagreb: Izdanja Antibarbarus, 2010.

Kovačević, Filip. "Marcuse in Yugoslavia." *Radical Philosophy Review* 16, no. 1 (2013): 205–222.

Kothe, Ana. "Saving the Maidens: Reading 'Miss Sarajevo.'" *Modern Language Studies* 29, no. 2 (Autumn 1999): 137–152.

Kralj, Ana and Tanja Rener. "Slovenia: From 'State Feminism' to Back Vocals." In *Gender (In)equality and Gender Politics in Southeastern Europe,* edited by Sabrina P. Ramet and Christine M. Hassenstab, 41–61. New York: Palgrave Macmillan, 2014.

Kršić, Dejan. "Fragments on the Matter of New Collectivism." In *From Kapital to Capital: Neue Slowenische Kunst: An Event of the Final Decade of Yugoslavia,* edited by Zdenka Badovinac, Eda Čufer, and Anthony Gardner, 376–393. Cambridge, MA: MIT Press, 2015.

Leighten, Patricia. "Colonialism, L'art Negre, and Les Demoiselles d'Avignon." In *Picasso's Les Demoiselles d'Avignon*, edited by Christopher Green, 77–103. Cambridge: Cambridge University Press, 2001.

Leighten, Patricia and Mark Antliff. *"Primitive": Critical Terms for Art History*, edited by Robert Nelson and Richard Schiff, 217–233. Chicago: University of Chicago Press, 2003.

Levi, Pavle. *Disintegration in Frames: Aesthetics and Ideology in the Yugoslav and Post-Yugoslav Cinema*. Stanford, CA: Stanford University Press, 2007.

Lóránd, Zsófia. "'A Politically Non-Dangerous Revolution Is Not a Revolution': Critical Readings of the Concept of Sexual Revolution by Yugoslav Feminists in the 1970s." *European Review of History: Revue européenne d'histoire* 22, no. 1 (2015): 120–137.

—. *The Feminist Challenge to the Socialist State in Yugoslavia*. London: Palgrave Macmillan, 2018.

Lukić, Jasmina. "Media Representations of Men and Woman in Times of War and Crisis: The Case of Serbia." In *Reproducing Gender: Politics, Publics, and Everyday Life after Socialism*, edited by Susan Gal and Gail Kligman, 392–425. Princeton, NJ: Princeton University Press, 2000.

Manne, Kate. *Down Girl: The Logic of Misogyny*. Oxford and London: Oxford University Press, 2018.

Marcuse, Herbert. *An Essay on Liberation*. Boston, MA: Beacon Press, 1969.

Matić, Đorđe. "Lepa Brena." In *Leksikon Yu Mitologije*, edited by I. Andrić, V. Arsenijević, and D. Matić, 223–226. Zagreb and Belgrade: Rende and Postscriptum, 2005.

Matičević, Davor. "The Zagreb Circle." In *The New Art Practice in Yugoslavia 1966–1978*, edited by Marijan Susovski, 20–28. Zagreb: Gallery of Contemporary Art Zagreb, 1978.

Mencin, Metka. "Women and Politics: A Note of Introduction." In *Ana's Land: Sisterhood in Eastern Europe*, edited by Tanya Renne, 218–219. Boulder, CO: Westview Press, 1997.

Milevska, Suzana. "Art System(s) The Faulty Ready-Made Versus the Perfect One (1998)." In *After the Wall: Art and Culture in Post-Communist Europe*, edited by Bojana Pejić, 134–136. Stockholm: Moderna Museet, 1999.

—. "Gender Difference in the Balkans." PhD dissertation, Goldsmiths, University of London, 2005.

—. "Solidarity and Intersectionality: What Can Transnational Feminist Theory Learn from Regional Feminist Activism." *Feminist Review* 9, no. 1 (September 2011): e52–e61.

Mladenović, Lepa. "Foreword: Searching for Our Lesbian Nests in Yugoslavia and After." In *Intersectionality and LGBT Activist Politics: Multiple Others in Croatia and Serbia*, edited by Bojan Bilić and Sanja Kajinić, v–xiv. London: Palgrave Macmillan, 2016.

Mladenović, Lepa and Donna M. Hughes. "Feminist Resistance to War and Violence in Serbia." In *Frontline Feminisms: Women, War, and Resistance*, edited by Marguerite R. Waller and Jennifer Rycenga, 247–273. New York: Routledge, 2001.

Monroe, Alexei. *Interrogation Machine*. Cambridge, MA: MIT Press, 2005.

—. "Laibach, Let it Be, Mute Records, 1988, London." In *From Kapital to Capital: Neue Slowenische Kunst: An Event of the Final Decade of Yugoslavia* [Exhibition guide], curated by Zdenka Badovinac, 60–61. Ljubljana: Moderna Galerija, 2015. https://d2tv32fgpo1xal.cloudfront.net/files/mg-msum_nsk_vodic_eng.pdf (accessed June 12, 2019).

Moss, Kevin. "Yugoslav Transgendered Heroes: 'Virgina' and 'Marble Ass.'" *Reč* 67, no. 13 (September 2002): 347–367.

Munivrana, Martina, ed. *Vlasta Delimar, To Sam Ja/This is I* [Exhibition catalogue]. Zagreb: Museum of Contemporary Art, 2014.

Muscio, Inga. *Cunt: A Declaration of Independence*, 2nd ed. Emeryville, CA: Seal Press, 2002.

Nabergoj, Irena Avsenik. "Poetics of Love and Devotion in Prešeren' Poem The Baptism on the Savica." *Religious and Sacred Poetry: An International Quarterly of Religion, Culture and Education* 2 (2013): 67–84.

Nicolov, Alice. "The Gay 'Gypsy' who became Bulgaria's Biggest Star." *Daze*. May 12, 2016. www.dazeddigital.com/music/article/31084/1/meet-the-gay-gypsy-who-became-bulgaria-s-biggest-star (accessed May 23, 2019).

NSK. *Neue Slowenische Kunst*. Los Angeles: Amok, 1991.

Novosti. "Žena-hrabrost otišla u legend." September 14, 2010. www.novosti.rs/vesti/naslovna/aktuelno.69.html:300102-Zena-hrabrost-otisla-u-legendu (accessed May 23, 2019).

—. "Lepa Brena: Ne stidim se muslimanskog porekla." March 4, 2014. www.novosti.rs/vesti/spektakl.147.html:481139-Lepa-Brena-Ne-stidim-se-muslimanskog-porekla (accessed June 7, 2019).

Papić, Žarana. "Dvostruka prisutnost žena: snaga i slabost žena u masovnim medijima." *Gledišta* 1–2 (1990): 143–147.

—. "Women in Serbia: Post-Communism, War, and Nationalist Mutations." In *Gender Politics in the Western Balkans: Women and Society in Yugoslavia and the Yugoslav Successor States*, edited by Sabrina P. Ramet, 153–169. University Park: Pennsylvania State University Press, 1999.

—. "Europa nakon 1989: etnički ratovi, fašizacija života i politika tijela u Srbiji." *Treća* 3, nos. 1–2 (2001): 30–46.

—. "Dvostruka prisutnost žena: snaga i slabost žena u masovnim medijima." In *Žarana Papić. Tekstovi 1977–2002*, edited by Adriana Zaharijević and Daša Ivanović, 140–148. Belgrade: Centar za Studije Roda i Politike, Fakultet Političkih Nauka, 2012.

—. "Europa nakon 1989: etnički ratovi, fašizacija života i politika tijela u Srbiji." In *Žarana Papić. Tekstovi 1977–2002*, edited by Adriana Zaharijević and Daša Ivanović, 343–372. Belgrade: Centar za Studije Roda i Politike, Fakultet Političkih Nauka, 2012.

Pavlović, Tatjana. "Women in Croatia: Feminists, Nationalists, and Homosexuals." In *Gender Politics in the Western Balkans: Women and Society in Yugoslavia and the Yugoslav Successor States*, edited by Sabrina Ramet, 131–152. University Park: Pennsylvania State University Press, 1999.

Pavlović, Vesna. *Povratak Dokumentarni video zapis sa Zenama u Crnom (Return: A Documentary Video with Women in Black)*. 1993–1996/2019. [Video, 10:30].

Pejić, Bojana. "Serbia: Socialist Modernism and the Aftermath." In *Aspects/Positions: 50 Years of Art in Central Europe 1949–1999*, edited by Achim Hochdörfer, Dieter Schrage, Hanno Millesi, Herald Krejči, Sophie Haaser, Bernhard Fellner, Uli Todoroff, Christa Mittermayr, Michaela Herreiner, Pavlina Morganová, and Andreas

Wenniger, 115–125. Vienna: Museum Moderner Kunst Stiftung Ludwig Wien, 1999.

—. "Balkan Baroque Balkan Mind." In *Marina Abramović: Balkan Epic*, edited by Adelina von Furstenberg and Steven Henry Madoff, 28. Milan: Skira, 2006.

—. "Marina Abramović." In *Kontakt … Works from the Collection of Erste Bank Group*, edited by Museum Moderner Kunst Stiftung Ludwig Wien. Vienna and Cologne: Museum Moderner Kunst Stiftung Ludwig Wien, Buchhandlung Walther König, 2006.

—. "Proletarians of All Countries, Who Washes Your Socks? Equality, Dominance and Difference in Eastern European Art." In *Gender Check: Femininity and Masculinity in the Art of Eastern Europe*, edited by Bojana Pejić, 19–29. Cologne: Walter König, 2009.

—. "And Now, Let's Remember … Yugoslavia." In Marina Abramović, *The Cleaner*, 250–259. Stockholm: Moderna Museet; Berlin: Hatje Cantz Verlag, 2017.

Perić, Boris and Denis M. Peričić. "Varja Orlić, kultna grupa Karlowy Vary: Gdje je danas nekadašnja prva dama undergrounda? (1988)." *Yugopapir*. August 2017. www.yugopapir.com/2017/08/varija-orlic-kultna-grupa-karlowy-vary.html (accessed May 11, 2019).

Peršak, Tone. "The Retrogarde as Alternative Avant-Garde?" In *From Kapital to Capital: Neue Slowenische Kunst: An Event of the Final Decade of Yugoslavia*, edited by Zdenka Badovinac, Eda Čufer, and Anthony Gardner, 87–91. Cambridge, MA: MIT Press, 2015.

Petrović, Jelena. *Women's Authorship in Interwar Yugoslavia: The Politics of Love and Struggle*. London: Palgrave Macmillan, 2018.

Piotrowski, Piotr. *In the Shadow of Yalta: Art and the Avant-Garde in Eastern Europe, 1945–1989*. London: Reaktion Books, 2009.

Pomeroy, Sarah B. *Spartan Women*. Oxford: Oxford University Press, 2002.

Popivoda, Marta. *Yugoslavia: How Ideology Moved Our Collective Body*. Belgrade: TkH (Walking Theory), 2013.

Prva TV. "Lepa Brena—Exkluziv—Premijera predstave 'LEPA BRENA PROJECT'" [Video, 5:56]. December 12, 2019. www.youtube.com/watch?v=ntW4rfQ9Z20 (accessed December 25, 2019).

Pyzik, Agata. *Poor but Sexy: Culture Clashes in Europe East and West*. Croydon: Zero Books, 2014.

Radziszewski, Karol. "Interview with Darko Šimičić." *Dik Fagazine* 10 (2016): 114–133.

—. "Interview with Leonida Kovač." *Dik Fagazine* 10 (2016): 58–83.

Ramet, Sabrina P. "In Tito's Time." In *Gender Politics in the Western Balkans: Women and Society in Yugoslavia and the Yugoslav Successor States*, edited by Sabrina P. Ramet, 89–105. University Park: Pennsylvania State University Press, 1999.

—. "The Sirens and the Guslar: An Afterword." In *Serbia since 1989: Politics and Society under Milosevic and After*, edited by Sabrina P. Ramet and Vjeran Pavlaković, 395–413. Seattle: University of Washington Press, 2006.

Raščić, Lala. "Gorgo." Portfolio. August 16, 2019. https://lalarascic.com/portfolio/gorgo/ (accessed May 20, 2020).

Rawlings, Jennifer, dir. *Forgotten Voices, Women in Bosnia* [DVD]. Squeaky Tula Productions, North Hollywood, CA, 2008.

Redžepova, Esma. *Interview* [Video, 16:08]. TVKopernicus. September 5, 2016. www.youtube.com/watch?v=b_HXr4dffzY (accessed August 6, 2020).

Regodić, Biljana. "Homeland as a Form of Women's Disloyalty." In *Ana's Land: Sisterhood in Eastern Europe*, edited by Tanya Renne, 176–178. Boulder, CO: Westview Press, 1997.

Rexhepi, Piro. "The Politics of (Post) Socialist Sexuality: American Foreign Policy in Bosnia and Kosovo." In *The Cultural Life of Capitalism in Yugoslavia: (Post) Socialism and Its Other*, edited by Dijana Jelača, Maša Kolanović, and Danijela Lugarić, 243–261. London: Palgrave Macmillan, 2017.

Riflechair. "Code Name ARROW: Bosnian Sniper" [Video, 18:31]. August 29, 2018. www.youtube.com/watch?v=gO9phEodW9Y (accessed April 15, 2020).

Ridgeway, James and Jasminka, Udovički, eds. *Burn This House: The Making and Unmaking of Yugoslavia*. Durham, NC: Duke University Press, 2000.

Rock and Roll Archives. "Videosex 1984 Yugoslavia." www.rockandrollarchives.net/2020/10/videosex-videosex-1984-yugoslavia-new.html (accessed February 20, 2021).

Rosenberg, Jordana. "'Lesbian Phallus,' or, What Can Deconstruction Feel?" *GLQ* 9, no. 3 (2003): 393–414.

Rugg, Rebecca Ann. "How She Look?" In *Femme: Feminists, Lesbians and Bad Girls*, edited by Laura Harris and Elizabeth Crocker, 175–189. Abingdon: Routledge, 2013.

RuPaul. *Guru*. New York: HarperCollins, 2018.

Scipion Nasice Sisters Theater. "The First Sisters Letter (1983)." In *From* Kapital *to* Capital: Neue Slowenische Kunst: An Event of the Final Decade of Yugoslavia, edited by Zdenka Badovinac, Eda Čufer, and Anthony Gardner, 475. Cambridge, MA: MIT Press, 2015.

—. "The Founding Act." In *From* Kapital *to* Capital: Neue Slowenische Kunst: An Event of the Final Decade of Yugoslavia, edited by Zdenka Badovinac, Eda Čufer, and Anthony Gardner, 474. Cambridge, MA: MIT Press, 2015.

Selman, Selma. "*SALTWATER AFTER 47.*" *Artist Statement*. February 29, 2016.

Senjković, Reana. "Popular Hybrids the Yugoslav Way: What a Girl Would Buy for Her Pocket Money." In *The Cultural Life of Capitalism in Yugoslavia: (Post) Socialism and Its Other*, edited by Dijana Jelača, Maša Kolanović, and Danijela Lugarić, 209–222. London: Palgrave Macmillan, 2017.

Silverman, Carol. *Romani Routes: Cultural Politics and Balkan Music in Diaspora*. Oxford: Oxford University Press, 2012.

Šimičić, Darko. "From *Zenit* to *Mental Space*: Avant-Garde, Neo-Avant-Garde, and Post-Avant-Garde Magazines and Books in Yugoslavia, 1921–1987." In *Impossible Histories: Historical Avant-Gardes, Neo-Avant-Gardes, and Post-Avant-Gardes in Yugoslavia, 1818–1991*, edited by Dubravka Đurić and Miško Šuvaković, 294–331. Cambridge, MA, and London: MIT Press, 2003.

Slapšak, Svetlana. "What Are Women Made Of?" In *Gender, Nation, and Immigration in Contemporary Europe*, edited by Gisela Brinker-Gabler and Sidonie Smith, 358–373. Minneapolis: University of Minnesota Press, 1996.

—. "Mein Feminismus ist eine logische Konsequenz von 1968." In *1968 in Yugoslawien: Studentendproteste und kutlturelle Avantgarde zwischen 1960 und 1975*, edited by Boris Kanzleiter and Krunoslav Stojaković, 92–103. Bonn: Dietz, 2008.

—. "Kako smo mrzeli Tita." *Peščanik*. April 6, 2010. https://pescanik.net/kako-smo-mrzeli-tita/ (accessed June 10, 2019).

Somun, Lejla. "Dressed (Not) To Kill." *Peace in Progress* 26 (February 2016). www.icip-perlapau.cat/numero26/articles_centrals/article_central_5/ (accessed March 27, 2019).

Spaskovska, Ljubica. *The Last Yugoslav Generation: The Rethinking of Youth Politics and Cultures in Late Socialism*. Manchester: Manchester University Press, 2017.

Spehar, Andrea. "The Lesbian Question." In *Ana's Land: Sisterhood in Eastern Europe*, edited by Tanya Renne, 205–210. Boulder, CO: Westview Press, 1997.

Sretenović, Dejan. *Was ist Kunst? Art as Social Practice*. Belgrade: Geopoetika, 2001.

Stafford, Peter. *Sexual Behavior in the Communist World: An Eyewitness Report of Life, Love, and the Human Condition Behind the Iron Curtain*. New York: The Julian Press, 1967.

Stane, Bernik, ed. *Oblikovanje: Novi kolektivizem/Design: New Collectivism* [Moderna Galerija (Museum of Modern Art) Ljubljana exhibition]. Ljubljana: NSK Info Center, 1999.

Stiles, Kristine. "Synopsis of the Destruction in Art Symposium (DIAS) and Its Theoretical Significance." *The Act* [New York] 1 (Spring 1987): 22–31.

—. "Cloud with Its Shadow." In Kristine Stiles, Klaus Biesenbach and Chrissie Iles, *Marina Abramović*, 33–95. London and New York: Phaidon, 2008.

Stiles, Kristine and Peter Selz, eds. *Theories and Documents of Contemporary Art: A Sourcebook of Artists' Writings*, 2nd ed. Berkeley and Los Angeles: University of California Press, 2012.

Stipančić, Branka. "Body Language in Croatian Art." In *The Body and the East: From the 1960s to the Present*, edited by Zdenka Badovinac, 58–61. Cambridge, MA, and London: MIT Press, 1998.

—. "Some Aspects of Croatian Contemporary Art 1949–1999." In *Aspects/Positions: 50 Years of Art in Central Europe 1949–1999*, edited by Achim Hochdörfer, Dieter Schrage, Hanno Millesi, Herald Krejči, Sophie Haaser, Bernhard Fellner, Uli Todoroff, Christa Mittermayr, Michaela Herreiner, Pavlina Morganová, and Andreas Wenniger, 127–138. Vienna: Museum Moderner Kunst Stiftung Ludwig Wien, 1999.

Strasser, Ulrike. "Early Modern Nuns and the Feminist Politics of Religion." *Journal of Religion* 84, no. 4 (October 2004): 529–554.

Stryker, Susan. "My Words to Victor Frankenstein Above the Village of Chamounix: Performing Transgender Rage." *GLQ* 1, no. 3 (1994): 237–254.

Suber, Daniel and Slobodan Karamanic, eds. *Retracing Images: Visual Culture after Yugoslavia*. Leiden: Brill, 2012.

Šuvaković, Miško. "The Post-Avant-Garde: The Group of Six Artists 1975–1978 and After." In *Grupa Šestorice Autora*, edited by Janka Vukmir, 67–73. Zagreb: SCCA Zagreb, 1998.

—. "Art as a Political Machine: Fragments on the Late Socialist and Postsocialist Art of Mitteleuropa and the Balkans." In *Postmodernism and the Postsocialist Condition: Politicized Art under Late Socialism*, edited by Aleš Erjavec, 90–134. Berkeley, Los Angeles, and London: University of California Press, 2003.

—. *Konceptualna Umetnost*. Novi Sad: Muzej Savremene Umetnosti Vojvodine, 2007.

—. "The Power of a Woman: Katalin Ladik. Narratives of Interpretation, of Subjectification, Women and Art between the Cold War and Transition in Central Europe." In *The Power of a Woman: Katalin Ladik*, edited by Dragomir Ugren, 7–240. Novi Sad: Museum of Contemporary Art Vojvodina in Novi Sad, 2010.

Šuvaković, Miško, Dragomir Ugren, and Gabrijela Šuler. *Moć žene: Katalin Ladik Retrospektiva 1962–2010/The Power of a Woman: Katalin Ladik Retrospective 1962–2010*. Novi Sad: Muzej Savremene Umetnosti Vojvodine, 2010.

Tijardović-Popović, Jasna. "Performance Art in Belgrade in the 70s: On the Exhibition of Photo-Documentation and Photographs." In *Performance/1968–1978*. Belgrade: Gallery Beograd, 2006.

Toller, Ernst. "Hinkemann." Translated by Peter Wortsman. *The Mercurian* 6, no. 4 (Fall 2017). https://the-mercurian.com/2017/11/16/hinkemann/ (accessed May 8, 2019).

Tselegraf. "MARIJA ŠERIFOVIĆ OTKRIVA: Lezbijka sam, seks sa devojkom je divan!" November 27, 2013. www.telegraf.rs/jetset/888120-ispovest-marije-serifovic-oprastam-ocu-sto-nas-je-maltretirao-ali-ne-zaboravljam (accessed May 8, 2019).

Tumbas, Jasmina. "Selma Selman." In *Selma Selman: Visual Artist*, edited by Štefan Simončič, 6–24. Slovenia: EPEKA Scientific and Research Association, 2016.

—. "Decision as Art: Performance in the Balkans." In *Performance Art in the Second Public Sphere: Event-Based Art in Late Socialist Europe*, edited by Katalin Cseh-Varga and Adam Czirak, 184–201. London: Routledge: 2018.

—. "Yugonostalgia." *Art Monthly* 425 (April 2019): 6–10.

Turai, Hedwig. "Bojana Pejić on Gender and Feminism in Eastern European Art." In *Working with Feminism: Curating and Exhibitions in Eastern Europe*, edited by Katrin Kivimaa, 190–201. Tallinn: Tallinn University Press, 2012.

Ugrešić, Dubravka. *Europe in Sepia*. Translated by David Williams. Rochester, NY: Open Letter, 2014.

Vatić, Bojana. Comment on YouTube video. December 14, 2019. https://www.youtube.com/watch?v=nf56qoF_vRs (accessed December 14, 2019).

Veljović, Srđan. *Fotografije. Žene u crnom u kotekstu grada*. Serbia: Simbol Petrovaradin, 2012.

Vesić, Jelena. "Oktobar 75." In *SKC in ŠKUC: The Case of Students' Cultural Centre in 1970s: SKC and Political Practices of Art*, edited by Prelom Kolektiv, 5. Ljubljana: ŠKUC Gallery, 2008.

—. "The Conference Comrade Woman: Art Program (On Marxism and Feminism and their Mutual Political Discontents)." Parallel Chronologies: An Archive of East European Exhibitions. http://tranzit.org/exhibitionarchive/the-conference-comrade-woman-art-program/ (accessed June 18, 2019).

Videkanić, Bojana. "First and Last Emperor: Representations of the President, Bodies of the Youth." In *Remembering Utopia: The Culture of Everyday Life in Yugoslavia*, edited by Breda Luthar and Maruša Pušnik, 37–63. Washington, DC: New Academic Publishing, 2010.

—. *Nonaligned Modernism: Socialist Postcolonial Aesthetics in Yugoslavia, 1945–1985*. Montreal: McGill-Queen's University Press, 2019.

Vukmir, Janka, ed. *Grupa Šestorice Autora*. Zagreb: SCCA Zagreb, 1998.

Vuković, Vesna. "A Prospective Retrospective: About the Exhibition *Pearls of Revolution* by Sanja Iveković." In *Sanja Iveković. Pearls of Revolution*, 8–17. [Exhibition catalogue]. Pula: HDLUI, 2016: 8–17.

Westcott, James. *When Marina Abramović Dies: A Biography*. Cambridge, MA, and London: MIT Press, 2010.

Wheeler, Leigh Ann. "'Handmaiden of the Pornographer: Champion of Free Speech': The American Civil Liberties Union and Sexual Expression in the 1970s and 1980s." In *Porno Chic and the Sex Wars: American Sexual Representation in the 1970s*, edited by Bronstein Carolyn and Strub Whitney, 229–248. Amherst and Boston: University of Massachusetts Press, 2016. www.jstor.org/stable/j.ctv346vqm.13 (accessed March 26, 2020).

Women in Black, ed. *Women for Peace Anthology*. Belgrade: Women in Black, 1993.

Wortsman, Peter. "The Imagination Unmanned: Reviving Ernst Toller's Tragedy Hinkemann in English." *The Mercurian* 6, no. 4 (Fall 2017): https://the-mercurian.com/2017/11/16/hinkemann/ (accessed May 8, 2019).

XXZMagazin. "Ekskluzivno: Retro fotografije Lepe Brene, sredinom osamdesetih. Galerija: Sitnije, Cile, sitnije." March 20, 2018. www.xxzmagazin.com/fotogalerija/sitnije-cile-sitnije (accessed June 15, 2018).

Zaharijević, Adriana. "The Strange Case of Yugoslav Feminism: Feminism and Socialism in 'the East.'" In *The Cultural Life of Capitalism in Yugoslavia: (Post) Socialism and Its Other*, edited by Dijana Jelača, Maša Kolanović, and Danijela Lugarić, 263–283. London: Palgrave Macmillan, 2017.

Zajović, Staša. "Nationalism and Serb Women," in *In Ana's Land: Sisterhood in Eastern Europe*, edited by Tanya Renne, 169–171. Boulder, CO: Westview Press, 1997.

Index

Note: page numbers in *italics* refer to illustrations.

EU authorised representative for GPSR:
Easy Access System Europe, Mustamäe tee 50,
10621 Tallinn, Estonia
gpsr.requests@easproject.com

www.ingramcontent.com/pod-product-compliance
Ingram Content Group UK Ltd.
Pitfield, Milton Keynes, MK11 3LW, UK
UKHW062135150726

7214IPUK00024B/419